Roger Parkinson is a naval historian with a PhD in Naval History from the University of Exeter. He is the author of *The Late Victorian Navy*.

'An informative and readable book, it provides a useful summary of the subject, placing it in a wider context.' – Michael Duffy

For My Brother Oliver
1949–2008
Requiescat in Pace

DREADNOUGHT
THE SHIP THAT CHANGED THE WORLD

ROGER PARKINSON

Published in 2015 by I.B.Tauris & Co. Ltd
www.ibtauris.com

Distributed worldwide by I.B.Tauris & Co Ltd
Registered office: 6 Salem Road, London W2 4BU

Copyright © 2015 Roger Parkinson

The right of Roger Parkinson to be identified as the author of this work has been asserted by the author in accordance with the Copyright, Designs and Patents Act 1988.

All rights reserved. Except for brief quotations in a review, this book, or any part thereof, may not be reproduced, stored in or introduced into a retrieval system, or transmitted, in any form or by any means, electronic, mechanical, photocopying, recording or otherwise, without the prior written permission of the publisher.

Every attempt has been made to gain permission for the use of the images in this book. Any omissions will be rectified in future editions.

References to websites were correct at the time of writing

ISBN: 9781780768267
eISBN: 9780857737052

A full CIP record for this book is available from the British Library
A full CIP record is available from the Library of Congress

Library of Congress Catalog Card Number: available

Typeset in FairfieldLH by APTARA

Printed and bound by CPI Group (UK) Ltd, Croydon, CR0 4YY

Contents

List of Illustrations	vii
Preface	xi
1 The Origins of the Pre-Dreadnought Era	1
2 The Pre-Dreadnought Era in the 1890s	25
3 The New Navies of the 1890s	53
4 Fisher and the Dreadnought	79
5 The Imperial German Navy (Kaiserliche Marine)	105
6 The Politics and Diplomacy of Naval Policy	135
7 From Dreadnoughts to Super-Dreadnoughts	161
8 The Worldwide Dreadnought Arms Race	187
9 World War I to Jutland	215
10 From Jutland to Washington	239
Appendix	249
Notes	259
Bibliography	287
Index	297

List of Illustrations

Figures

1 Armour: from ironclads to pre-dreadnoughts, HMS *Alexandra*. *Brassey's Naval Annual 1895*   16
2 Battleships of the late 1880s, *Victoria* and *Sans Pareil*, *Nile* and *Trafalgar*. *Brassey's Naval Annual 1895*   20
3 The Naval Defence Act battleships, Royal Sovereign class. *Brassey's Naval Annual 1902*   21
4 Majestic class battleships. *Brassey's Naval Annual 1902*   27
5 Battleships of the late 1890s, Canopus and Formidable class. *Brassey's Naval Annual 1909*   30
6 The penultimate pre-dreadnoughts, Duncan class. *Brassey's Naval Annual 1909*   31
7 Drake and Cressy class cruisers. *Brassey's Naval Annual 1909*   37
8 The last pre-dreadnoughts or semi-dreadnoughts, King Edward class. *Brassey's Naval Annual 1909*   82
9 British semi-dreadnoughts and the *Dreadnought* herself. *Brassey's Naval Annual 1914*   90
10 The first dreadnought battlecruisers, Invincible class. *Brassey's Naval Annual 1914*   97
11 The first German battleships, Nassau class. *Brassey's Naval Annual 1914*   119
12 Kriegsmarine: From armoured cruiser to battlecruiser, *Blücher* and *Von Der Tann*. *Brassey's Naval Annual 1914*   123
13 The three German battlecruisers, Moltke class. *Brassey's Naval Annual 1914*   126

14 The super-dreadnought battlecruisers, Lion class. *Brassey's Naval Annual 1914*   165

15 British super-dreadnought of the 1912 programme, Iron Dukes and Tiger. *Brassey's Naval Annual 1914, 1919*   168

16 Oil burning super-dreadnoughts, Queen Elizabeths and Royal Sovereigns. *Brassey's Naval Annual 1919*   169

17 German super-dreadnoughts 1919–1914, Kaiser and Koenig class. *Brassey's Naval Annual 1919*   176

18 The Japanese 'very nearly' dreadnoughts, *Satsuma, Aki, Ibuki* and *Kurama. Brassey's Naval Annual 1914*   190

19 Punch cartoon. *Punch Magazine*   247

Plates

1 HMS *Dreadnought* after her completion in 1906. *IWM Q38705*

2 HMS *Dreadnought* and ship's cat. The cat was called Togo and was treated with great affection by everyone from the captain downwards. *IWM Q22887*

3 HMS *Dreadnought*, underway in 1907 as flagship of the Home Fleet. *IWM Q211837*

4 HMS *Orion*, the first of the super-dreadnoughts, armed with ten 13.5-inch guns. *IWM Q21599*

5 HMS *Inflexible*, first generation battlecruiser of the Invincible class. *IWM SPI1797*

6 HMS *Bellerophon* at sea. *IWM Q23340*

7 HMS *Neptune* at anchor. *IWM RP2112*

8 HMS *Birmingham*, 5,400 tonnes, sister of cruiser Nottingham. Both ships were completed in 1914.

9 HMS *Nottingham*, 5,440 tonnes, sunk by a U-boat on 19 August 1916.

10 The two fore turrets of HMS *Iron Duke* during rough weather in the North Sea. *IWM Q55500*

11 England's sea power, HMS *Iron Duke. IWM Q75209*

12 Battleship HMS *Iron Duke* photographed early in the war.

13 Another view of HMS *Iron Duke*, super-dreadnought armed with ten 13.5-inch guns and twelve 6-inch guns. Flagship of Sir John Jellicoe 1914–16. *IWM Q021397*

LIST OF ILLUSTRATIONS

14 HMS *Centurion*, super-dreadnought armed with ten 13.5-inch guns. *IWM Q21080*
15 The ill-fated battlecruiser HMS *Queen Mary*, which blew up at Jutland with the loss of 1,266 men. Her loss tended to condemn the battlecruiser type. *IWM Q21661*
16 The battlecruiser HMS *Tiger*, the most elegant of the British battlecruisers. *IWM SP1674*
17 Admiral Jellicoe climbs to the bridge of *Iron Duke*. *IWM Q55499*
18 Admiral Scheer, German Commander-in-Chief. *IWM Q20348*
19 Admiral Beatty. *IWM Q19572*
20 Admiral Hipper, German battlecruiser commander. *IWM Q20352*
21 HMS *Warspite* in 1917. *IWM SP395*
22 Admiral Beatty, the King and Queen of Belgium, Admirals Goodenough, de Brock and de Robeck on board *Queen Elizabeth*. *IWM 23219*
23 The German Cruiser *Emden*, 3,600 tonnes, completed in 1908.
24 The destruction of the *Emden* as seen from HMAS *Sydney*, one of the great early triumphs of the Royal Australian Navy.
25 The naval battle in Heligoland Bight, during the sinking of the *Mainz*, as seen from the deck of a British cruiser.
26 The Dardanelles: A barge full of soldiers passing a man-o-war in the Straits.

Preface

In a letter from Kaiser Wilhelm to Prince Von Bülow dated 3 April 1909 the Kaiser described British naval policy as 'Dreadnoughtschweinerei'.[1] This extraordinary word may in some sense be taken as the epitaph of the pre-World War I world. The years before World War I were characterised by intensifying Anglo-German naval competition, with an often forgotten extra-European element in the form of the rapidly developing navies of the United States and Japan. In addition the navies of France, Russia, Italy and Austria-Hungary all contributed to the extraordinary growth of navies in the 25 years before World War I. Added to this, the naval activities, if not to say the antics, of the South American republics need close examination. Exactly how and why these navies became the centrepiece of so many different national strategies needs a careful analysis that goes far beyond a mere description of the Anglo-German naval building race. Any contemporary analysis, especially one at the centenary of the outbreak of World War I requires a range and depth not often attempted before. For example the pre-dreadnought era, from the 1880s to 1906, needs most careful scrutiny and perhaps a fundamental re-evaluation in terms of exactly how it influenced the successor dreadnought era. An alternative title for this book might have been *The Navalist Era in Defence 1889–1922*, taking this 33-year period as a cohesive whole, not narrowly a history of the dreadnoughts.

From the British perspective in the annals of the Royal Navy two names will always be linked: those of Admiral Sir John 'Jacky' Fisher and the ship he created, the *Dreadnought*. In her day, the *Dreadnought* was the cynosure of the early twentieth-century battleship. So epoch making was this one ship that all subsequent battleships are usually referred to as dreadnoughts, the name becoming a generic term. The names of Fisher and the *Dreadnought* are virtually synonymous, yet Fisher was not just a product of the pre-dreadnought era but played a large part in its inception, as Captain of HMS *Excellent*, Director of Naval Ordnance, Third Sea Lord and Controller, Commander-in-Chief at Portsmouth, and again as Third Sea Lord and Controller. The late 1880s and 1890s were the years when Fisher had a decisive influence on pre-dreadnought naval policy, and this needs careful analysis.

Arthur Marder made the case that 'Jacky' Fisher was the man who not only created the *Dreadnought*, but more or less single-handedly dragged the Victorian and Edwardian Royal Navy 'kicking and screaming' into the twentieth century. Marder stated the following:

> In reality the British Navy at the end of the nineteenth century had run in a rut for nearly a century. Though numerically a very imposing force, it was in certain respects a drowsy, inefficient, moth-eaten organism.[2]

An alternative view might suggest that the Victorian Royal Navy was indeed not a war-ready navy – that was not its strategic purpose; it was the Royal Navy of the Pax Britannica, a peacekeeping deterrent force. Marder never distinguished between a war-ready navy and a peacekeeping deterrent force and in consequence muddled the two and missed the point.

The pre-dreadnought era is usually taken to end abruptly in 1906, with the launching of HMS *Dreadnought*. The *Dreadnought* herself is more often than not considered revolutionary and an enormous advance over all previous types. The truth is somewhat different; every piece of technology that made the *Dreadnought* possible came out of the pre-dreadnought era and that included steam turbines. The case will be made that the transition from pre-dreadnoughts to dreadnoughts was a much smoother and more evolutionary process than has been generally realised. It will be argued that Fisher and his wonder ship were the logical end products of the development of navies in the Victorian and Edwardian world.

The use of the term pre-dreadnought has its own problems. Those who lived through the period 1889 to 1906 did not know it would be labelled the pre-dreadnought era and that this was the prelude to the dreadnought era and World War I. Retrospective labelling can be dangerous and distorting. As a prelude it is often assumed that the pre-dreadnought era is less important than the dreadnought era that followed it and has received less consideration from historians as a result. Where historians have written about the pre-dreadnought period, they have usually taken the Naval Defence Act of 1889 as their starting point.

PREFACE

The *Dreadnought* owed a great deal to the naval war between Japan and Russia, fought in the Far East, 1903–5. In the case of the first battlecruisers, they were a direct reply to the large numbers of armoured cruisers built by France and clearly identifiable as commerce raiders in any future war. The battlecruisers were the rapid reaction force of the early twentieth century. Equipped with radio, they could go anywhere and deal with any armoured cruiser built or projected, but the ententes with France and later Russia rather invalidated the early battlecruiser concept. This was also the age of the large, fast Atlantic liner. Germany had a number of these ships and there was a fear they might be used as armed merchant cruisers in wartime.

It was only after 1905 and the first Morocco crisis that Germany became identified as the primary threat to Britain's maritime supremacy. Two classes of British dreadnoughts followed, totalling six ships but in 1909 matters came to a head. Successive attaché reports from Berlin suggested an acceleration in German building programmes. Britain reacted with eight dreadnoughts laid down in one year and seven the next. An era of intensifying naval competition became a full-blooded naval arms race. It was an arms race defined by the move from dreadnoughts to super-dreadnoughts. America and Japan participated in full and both countries overtook France and Russia as naval powers of the first rank. In the Mediterranean, Austria-Hungary and Italy built against each other in their own naval arms race. In South America, Brazil, Argentina and Chile produced their own highly idiosyncratic naval arms race. By 1914 the dreadnought fever had raged around the world. Britain won the building race with Germany, but by a narrower margin than might have been expected.

In the long drift to war, best described as the pre-1914 hubris, the part played by the Royal Navy and its dreadnoughts shows how these were the ships that changed the world and not necessarily to Britain's advantage. World War I has been described as 'Stalemate and Strain', an accurate summation of the grim reality of the war both on land and at sea.[3] During the year of 1915, the submarine came into its own and the inconclusive result at Jutland forced Germany down the road to unrestricted submarine warfare. More than any other single factor this brought the United States into the war on the winning allied side.

The war was won but left Britain economically and financially weakened; the nation was traumatised, with hardly a family in the land left unaffected by the mass slaughter in the trenches. The United States emerged from the war as the greatest creditor nation in history. At Washington in 1922, Britain ceded its long-held naval supremacy and reduced its navy to a one power standard, a navy the size of that of the United States. It was the conclusion not just of the 33-year navalist era in defence, but of the Pax Britannica itself.

1

The Origins of the Pre-Dreadnought Era

Prelude: The *Belle Époque*

The *Belle Époque* was, to the purist, the years 1900–14, but it can be argued that the period extends back to about 1890, the 25 or so years before the disastrous World War I. It was a world of the 'monde' and the 'demi-monde', of aristocratic 'salon' life. Emperors, kings and princes abounded and nowhere was this more apparent than at the court of Edward VII, where the presence of foreign princes and maharajahs reflected the wealth and strength of the British Empire.

In the *Belle Époque*, new means of travel came to the fore in the form of bicycles, motor cars and even the first primitive aeroplanes lumbered into the air. Electricity made the underground railway system possible in London and trams in provincial cities. Tennis, golf, swimming and skiing were the new-age sports of the *Belle Époque*. Steamships, by now true liners, made for easy comfortable travel between continents, at least for those with money. Impressionist painters such as Monet and Manet were vastly popular, as was the music of Ravel and Puccini. The discovery of X-rays and the electron revolutionised science.

The *Belle Époque* was also the era of navies, navalism and an industrial age arms race that signalled a European war in the making, with disastrous consequences for all who participated. It is to navies and navalism and the 'how' and 'why' of the pre-1914 hubris that this narrative must turn.

Naval Policy and Strategic Doctrine in the Victorian Age

The Victorian navy has been variously described, often in rather unflattering terms. Arthur Marder's description, mentioned earlier, may be taken as typical: 'Though numerically a very imposing force, it was in certain respects a drowsy, inefficient, moth-eaten organism.'[1] Marder was not the first to have described the Victorian navy in such terms. Others have suggested a fusty, musty, often mildly comic Victorian navy, personified by Gilbert and Sullivan's HMS *Pinafore*. Against this backdrop it may be questioned what exactly was the truth about strategy in the Victorian age. It is certainly the case that the Victorian navy was not inclined to write down its core strategic doctrine and would have regarded such an exercise as merely stating the blindingly obvious; indeed, the charge of complacency so frequently levelled against the Victorian Royal Navy is tied in to the fact that a great deal of core doctrine was not written down. As far back as 1817 Lord Castlereagh had introduced the idea of a two-power naval standard as the basis of British security and in 1818 he admitted that the two powers were France and Russia.[2] The two-power standard became the basis for British security throughout the nineteenth century and, as a well-defined policy, lasted into the first decade of the twentieth. Despite the opinions of some historians to the contrary, successive generations of politicians and naval officers ensured that the two-power standard was more or less adhered to.[3] It is often forgotten that there was a strong political dimension to the two-power standard; this was the 'big stick' with which the admirals could beat the politicians if they felt that naval strength was slipping. The 'big stick' was wielded by an entire Admiralty Board threatening to resign.

In the Victorian world there was a perfectly reasonable appreciation of the role of the navy in defence and foreign policy. The ironclad-era ships and their successors, the pre-dreadnoughts, were designed primarily for home waters and the Mediterranean, as a deterrent threat deployed against other European powers, mainly France and Russia. At any one time there were usually just three armoured warships deployed outside home waters and the Mediterranean, the flagships on the North America and West Indies station, the China station and the Pacific station. A second set of armoured ships, the coast defenders, was the core component of Particular Service Squadrons for deployment in the Baltic or Black Sea, to directly confront Russia. In 1878 and 1885 the mobilisation of these Particular Service Squadrons caused Russia to back down and revert to the status quo, but the development of mines and torpedoes ensured that by the mid-1890s the idea of littoral warfare in the Baltic and Black Sea was being abandoned.[4] Finally, the small cheap unarmoured ships, designated corvettes, sloops, gunboats and gun vessels were deployed on foreign stations for trade protection, the suppression of piracy and slavery, and that most important and usually forgotten role: hydrography.

The Naval Defence Act: A Retrospective on Its Origins

In March 1889, a highly unusual piece of legislation was passed by the House of Commons, the Naval Defence Act. This was the only time in British history that naval or military strength has been the subject of parliamentary legislation. The Naval Defence Act came at the end of a decade of fierce debate about the navy, its strength and its role in national defence.

The origins of the act can be traced back to the Great Near East crisis of 1878 and the Russian advance to Constantinople. After a great deal of hesitation, the Royal Navy's Mediterranean Squadron was ordered up the Dardanelles passage and anchored in front of the Russian army camped on the plains of San Stephano, just outside Constantinople. Back in England a Particular Service Squadron was mobilised for Baltic service. In the face of a British squadron in the Sea of Marmora and a Baltic squadron ready for deployment, the Russians backed down. The subsequent Congress of Berlin was Disraeli's big foreign policy success, achieved by naval power, without a shot fired in anger – a fact that cannot have been lost on his Foreign Secretary, Lord Salisbury, the man destined to be prime minister four times at the end of the nineteenth century and the prime minister responsible for the Naval Defence Act.

Behind the scenes a great deal had gone on that suggested that Britain had been lucky to get away with as much as it did. A squadron of Russian cruisers had left the Baltic and steamed around the north of Scotland and the first the Admiralty had known about it was when they read in the newspapers of the squadron's arrival at New York.[5] If this squadron had attacked British trade on the high seas, particularly on the route to the Cape of Good Hope, the effects could have been catastrophic for Britain.

The Russian cruisers at New York engendered real fears about the protection of trade. In 1878 Admiral Sir Alexander Milne, a former First Naval Lord and one of the few senior officers of the mid-Victorian period to give proper consideration to the vexed issue of trade protection, was appointed to head a committee of enquiry into the consequences of a maritime war with Russia. Milne's Colonial Defence Committee concluded that they did not have enough information to come to anything other than fairly tenuous conclusions. By the middle of 1879 the prime minister, Benjamin Disraeli, had decided that a Royal Commission of enquiry into the defence of British commerce and possessions abroad was required.[6] The Russian crisis of 1878 had precipitated this and it was established under the stewardship of Lord Carnarvon.

The Commission produced three reports, but it is the evidence of the ship-owners that is crucial to any understanding of the hidden importance of the Carnarvon Commission. The commission sat at the moment that steam was finally superseding sail as the primary means of ship propulsion. In 1879–80 there were 3.97 million tons of steamships on the British register and 3.82 million tons of sailing ships.[7] The career of the American Civil War confederate raider *Alabama* and her effectiveness as a commerce raider greatly exercised the commission, to the extent that she was mentioned over 60 times, but it is the opinions expressed concerning convoy as the primary means of trade protection in wartime that are of real import. All rejected the idea of convoy for trade protection. In the penultimate paragraph of his evidence Alfred Holt, founder of the Blue Funnel Line, stated unequivocally: 'It must be a burdensome vessel that wants a convoy.'[8] Holt was convinced that his fast, fuel-efficient steamers, propelled by compound high-pressure steam engines, would never need a convoy. Charles Maciver of the Cunard line said: 'I don't think any one member of our association would advocate it [convoy] for a moment.'[9] Thomas Ismay of the White Star Line commented: 'I think they [convoys] would be more dangerous to us than advantageous.'[10] Finally William Young, Lloyds insurance member, gave the most resounding rejection of convoy to the commission: 'I think a convoy nowadays as much a question of the past as the old stage coaches and about as useless.'[11]

Many historians have defined the rejection of convoy in terms of laissez-faire economics: there must be no government interference in private enterprise; ship-owners would not tolerate any restrictions on vessel movements in wartime; and any attempt at such restrictions would be economically unacceptable. The real truth is that Victorian ship-owners believed that the new-age steam technology, defined by compound high-pressure steam engines, had rendered obsolete the convoy concept in its entirety. The rejection of convoy as the primary means of trade protection in wartime was to have an important but largely hidden influence on the development of naval strategy.

The Declaration of Paris had terminated the Crimean War and outlawed privateering. In future, attacks on trade would be made by warships alone. Enemy warships would be prevented from attacking trade because ideally they would be blockaded in port. Patrolling cruisers on the trade routes and at focal points on the trade routes would provide the remaining defence of trade.[12] The Carnarvon Commission had recognised the truth of this analysis and in one of the rare statements of Victorian core strategic doctrine had defined the role of the Royal Navy in wartime:

> The Royal Navy is not maintained for the purpose of affording direct protection to sea-ports and harbours, but for the object of blockading the ports of an enemy, of destroying his trade, attacking his possessions, dealing with his ships at sea, and we may add of preventing and attack in great force against any special place.[13]

The three Carnarvon Commission reports were published in 1881 and 1882 but were not available for public scrutiny. In 1880 the Liberals under William Gladstone won that year's General Election and Gladstone, in common with most Whig and Liberal prime ministers of the nineteenth century, held to an unswerving commitment to 'Peace, Retrenchment and Social Reform'. The reports were shelved but as we will see, they were not forgotten.

The Navy and the Nation 1878–87

In retrospect the 1878 crisis was the first of a series that suggested naval weakness and overstretch. The next crisis occurred in 1882, with the bombardment of Alexandria. The third crisis came in 1884–5 and, as in 1878, concerned Russia. In 1884 Russian troops moved towards Afghanistan and took the village of Pandjeh on the Afghan frontier. They also invaded Bulgaria, and this made Gladstone contemplate the same course of action as Disraeli had taken six years earlier – deter Russia by sending a squadron of warships through the Dardanelles straits. A Particular Service Squadron was mobilised for possible Baltic operations; when it appeared ready it was rather publicly inspected by Queen Victoria. The Russians immediately sent a conciliatory note and the crisis passed. In 1878 and 1885 Particular Service Squadrons were mobilised but never deployed and have been largely forgotten as a result. On both occasions they had a huge influence in persuading Russia to back down.

In September 1884 the navy came under the scrutiny of the press in the form of a series of articles in the *Pall Mall Gazette*, under the heading 'What is the truth about the navy?'. This was one of the great early press crusades that caused huge embarrassment to the government and made half the literate population aware of the navy. British naval weakness was greatly over-emphasised and French naval strength magnified out of all proportion. Much of the information used to suggest naval weakness came from the Carnarvon Commission reports, conveniently shelved by the Gladstone government and leaked to the *Pall Mall Gazette* by Captain 'Jacky' Fisher, a man as deeply implicated in the genesis of the pre-dreadnought era as he was in the genesis of the dreadnought era. On 10 November 1884, entirely as a result of this sensational press campaign, Lord Northbrook, Gladstone's First Lord of the Admiralty, announced a £3.1 million naval construction programme. This produced two battleships, seven cruisers, six torpedo cruisers and 14 torpedo-boats.[14] This press campaign showed that press sensationalism could change public opinion. Over the next five years the press would return again and again to the topic of naval weakness. This would become an important factor in the decisions that led to the Naval Defence Act.

Within the Admiralty there was a growing realisation that during the 1878 crisis and after, there was no proper intelligence concerning Russian capabilities or intentions. The second Carnarvon Commission report recommended the establishment of a Foreign Intelligence department. After a certain amount of argument and hesitancy, the Foreign Intelligence Committee (FIC) was established in December 1882. Captain W.H. Hall was the man appointed as head of the FIC and is chiefly remembered today as the father of Admiral Sir Reginald Hall, Director of Naval Intelligence during World War I. W.H. Hall died at the young age of 53 and left no papers, so is almost forgotten today. Under his back-room guidance the FIC grew steadily in influence and by the next Russian scare in 1884–5 it was capable of operating as something close to a naval staff.[15]

Hall wrote two of the FIC's earliest papers and considered the possibility of a maritime war with France or Russia. Few better examples of intelligence reports masquerading as staff appreciations can be found. Hall's first report, on a possible war with France, was delivered in September 1884, just as the *Pall Mall Gazette* press campaign was getting under way. The second was delivered in March 1885 and coincided with the next Russian crisis. Both reports rejected convoy as the preferred method of trade protection:

> With regard to the convoy of merchant-vessels, those most interested in the question, the ship-owners themselves, recognize and admit that such a means of protection would be neither efficient nor practicable now-a-days.[16]

These early FIC reports show clear links back to the Carnarvon Commission and its evidence. As head of the FIC Hall was using the information gleaned from the reports to produce a strategic analysis that demanded a much larger peacetime navy, able in an age without convoy, to take a naval war to a potential adversary on the outbreak of war.

One of the reasons for the changed political climate of the late 1880s that made the Naval Defence Act possible was the partial eclipse of the Liberals over the Irish home rule issue. In November 1885 the Conservatives, led by Lord Salisbury, lost the General Election. Gladstone took office for the third time and was deeply committed to Irish home rule. In June 1886 the Irish Home Rule Bill was lost by 311 votes to 341. In the General Election that followed in July, 77 former Liberals, who now called themselves Liberal Unionists, joined with Lord Salisbury's Conservatives and this gave the Conservatives an election victory. When the Conservatives lost office Gladstone insisted on a change at the head of the navy. Admiral Lord John Hay replaced Admiral Sir Arthur Hood as First Naval Lord. When Lord Salisbury won the July 1886 election the situation was reversed and Hood replaced Hay. This was the last time the professional head of the navy changed with a change of government.

In August 1886 Salisbury appointed Captain Lord Charles Beresford as Junior Naval Lord. Beresford was well known to press and public, largely due to his service at the bombardment of Alexandria in command of the gunboat *Condor*. Beresford joined the Admiralty Board and produced a memorandum on war organisation that recommended the immediate creation of a Naval Intelligence Division (NID) capable of acting as something close to a fully-fledged war staff. The Board considered his views greatly overstated but Beresford, working over the heads of the Admiralty Board, showed the memorandum to Lord Salisbury, who discussed it with three leading admirals and accepted it as true.[17] On 13 October 1886, Beresford leaked the memorandum to W.T. Stead for publication in the *Pall Mall Gazette*. In the face of press criticism, the Admiralty Board backed down and the Naval Intelligence Division came into being, concerning itself not only with foreign intelligence but with mobilisation as well.[18]

Naval History and the *Jeune École*

There were two other major long-term influences on the Naval Defence Act: naval history and the French *Jeune École*. In 1867, John Colomb, a

Royal Marine officer, published a book titled *The Protection of our Commerce and Distribution of our Naval Forces Considered*. There was little immediate reaction to the book but, due to Colomb's persistence, his views came to represent an important element in imperial defence thinking.[19] Colomb asserted that the world position occupied by Britain was directly related to its paramount position as a trading nation. British security depended on three factors: the security of the British Isles; the security of the dependent empire; and the maintenance of maritime communications between the British Isles and both foreign and colonial trade centres.

John Colomb's elder brother Philip was a naval officer who retired as a captain in 1886. A year later he was promoted to rear-admiral on the retired list and to vice-admiral in 1892. On retirement Philip Colomb became a lecturer at the Royal Naval College at Greenwich. He had published various papers, usually presented to the Royal United Service Institution (RUSI) and was in broad agreement with his brother, particularly concerning the importance of trade protection. In 1888 he delivered a bombshell in the form of a paper presented to the RUSI, titled 'The naval defences of the United Kingdom'. This paper rejected outright the conception of invasion defences manned by the army and overseen by invasion experts. He showed that in the eighteenth century, England was kept from invasion by two methods – close blockade of an enemy's ports and alternatively, the defensive waiting with an intact fleet. He pointed out that either system would protect both homeland and moving commerce in the Western Approaches. The requirement for coastal defences and forts simply did not exist. 'Nothing', he said, 'can be done in the way of a territorial attack with a disputed command of the sea'.[20] Colomb had stated in unequivocal terms the parameters of a naval debate in which the steam navy could take care of the entire defence of the Empire, its trade and the mother country itself.

The third naval historian to have considerable bearing on the naval debate of the 1880s was John Knox Laughton. Educated at Cambridge, he started his career as a civilian instructor in the Royal Navy. By 1866 he was lecturing at the Royal Naval College, Portsmouth and he moved to the Royal Naval College at Greenwich in 1873. In 1874 he gave his first naval history lecture, 'The Scientific Study of Naval History' and this topic dominated the rest of his life. Laughton took the view that the scientific study of naval history was what mattered; the past contained lessons for the future.[21]

Laughton's philosophy and outlook appears in the Foreign Intelligence Committee's policy documents of 1884–5. In 'Remarks on a naval campaign', Captain Hall mirrors Laughton's comments, stating that a defensive policy is utterly at variance with the traditions of the British Navy, whose role has always been that of attack, and not defence.[22] Hall was clearly basing his appeal to history and the idea of decisive strength on Laughton's approach to naval history.

Then there was France's contribution to the naval strategic debate in the form of the *Jeune École*. In the late 1870s and 1880s a small group of French men developed an entirely new approach to naval war based on the emerging technology of the time, particularly the torpedo, and it was a strategy specifically designed for the weaker naval power.[23] Its chief advocate and theorist was Admiral Hyacinthe-Laurent-Théophile Aube.

In 1883 he was appointed to an ironclad command and at the same time saw another new-age weapon: the torpedo boat. A year earlier he had met a journalist, Gabriel Charmes, who specialised in foreign affairs reporting. Aube invited Charmes to witness naval exercises and Charmes spent his time on board a 46-ton torpedo boat. This and a sister boat successfully rode out a storm, and the experience resulted in Charmes first naval article, 'Autonomous torpedo boats and the future of the Navy'. Aube was promoted to Rear-Admiral and using Charmes journalistic skills, the two built a complete theory of naval warfare based on two torpedo boats riding out a gale on one occasion.[24]

In January 1886 Aube became Minister of Marine in the radical French republican administration led by Clemenceau. Aube concentrated the French battle fleet at Toulon against Italy. Torpedo craft and coast defence ships defended Cherbourg, while Brest received new-age torpedo cruisers. The redistribution was clearly focused on commercial warfare in the Atlantic and such a strategy could only be aimed at Britain.[25] The central British worry was that France might resort to indiscriminate attacks on trade in wartime.

Aube was not Minister of Marine for very long but his ideas on strategy divided the French Navy for 15 years. Britain's analysis of the *Jeune École* varied from gloomy prognostication, to a reasoned critique that downgraded the perceived threat from the new age torpedo craft.

Nevertheless, the *Jeune École*, with its associated ideas behind torpedo-boat warfare and the consequent threat to commerce, added to the agitation for increased naval expenditure in Britain. It was the ruthlessness of the *Jeune École* that shocked many observers. In an age apparently devoted to the rule of law, the indiscriminate pursuit of the destruction of commerce advocated by Aube and Charmes seemed barbaric in the extreme.

The Naval Defence Act

One of the first intelligence assessments provided by the newly-formed NID was a comparison of the fleets of England, France and Russia in December 1887, and the likely strength of the three fleets four years hence, in January 1891. It showed Britain with a comfortable lead in first-, second- and third-class ships but in 1890 France and Russia would be much closer in first-class battleship strength than in 1887.

In early 1888 there was another 'naval scare' concerning France. On 21 January the London *Standard* carried reports of feverish naval preparations at Toulon, but by 30 January the Foreign Office had established that nothing unusual was going on. In early February, the Italian and German ambassadors informed Salisbury that the French fleet was being mobilised for the Mediterranean. It was quickly established that this was not the case but the agitation in France for a Russian alliance and the fact that the Russians were tapping the French loan market was duly noted in London.[26] By December 1888 the Cabinet was reviewing the necessary construction programme for the years 1889–90 through to 1894–5. The Cabinet was also given an assessment of French policy and naval strength which suggested that unless 'armourclad' building commenced at once, then France and Russia would be in a position to catch up with British programmes.[27]

A further determinant in the development of policies that led to the Naval Defence Act was the introduction of annual fleet manoeuvres. In 1888 the naval manoeuvres examined the feasibility of maintaining an effective blockade of an enemy's squadron and its fast cruisers in strongly fortified ports. An 'enemy' fleet, consisting of five ironclads, commanded by Rear-Admiral Sir George Tryon, was blockaded into Berehaven in Southern Ireland by 'friendly' forces. In the full glare of press publicity, this squadron outwitted the blockading fleet and sailed down both the east and west coasts of England, 'laying waste' the towns, cities and seaports as they passed on their way.[28]

The conclusion was that for a blockade to be effective it should be conducted by a much larger force in proportion to the blockaded fleet than had previously been thought necessary.[29] The blockading force would need to be in a superiority of at least five to three in battleships and two to one in cruisers.[30] The report on the manoeuvres also stated that 'with regard to furnishing convoys for protection of commerce, the days of convoy are past'.[31] The report concluded that the navy was 'absolutely inadequate to take the offensive in a war with only one great power'. It said further that 'supposing a combination of two Powers to be allied as her enemies, the balance of maritime strength would be against England'.[32] The truth behind the Naval Defence Act was a five to three blockade ratio for battleships, and this helped define the parameters of a massive building programme.

In March 1889 the Naval Defence Act was passed, the first and last time naval strength has been subject to an Act of Parliament. In the debate in the House of Commons on 7 March 1889, the First Lord, Lord George Hamilton, stated as a fundamental principle that:

> I think I am correct in saying that the idea has been that our establishment should be on such a scale that it should at least be equal to the naval strength of any two other countries.[33]

This was a powerful restatement of Lord Castlereagh's policy, first promulgated over 70 years earlier in the wake of the Napoleonic wars. It has already been pointed out that the real truth about the Naval Defence Act was defined by the necessity for a five to three blockade ratio for battleships. Under the terms of the act 70 ships were built over a period of five years at a cost of £21.5 million. Eight battleships, the famous Royal Sovereign class, were proposed, with two smaller second-class battleships for the China and Pacific stations. Nine first-class cruisers were provided for, 29 second-class protected cruisers, four smaller cruisers and 18 torpedo gunboats.[34] The two second-class battleships, four of the first-class and 18 of the second-class cruisers were sheathed in wood and coppered for tropical service.[35]

One further question remains to be answered: why specifically parliamentary legislation in the form of the Naval Defence Act? The reason may lie in the politics of the era. Between 1830 and 1885–6 there were 12 General Elections and the Whigs and their successors the Liberals won nine of them.[36] Lord Salisbury wanted to lock some future Liberal administration into higher defence spending with parliamentary legislation whose repeal would leave such a government open to the charge of allowing the country to be woefully undefended.

The Mediterranean Strategic Backdrop

From 1704, when Gibraltar became a British crown colony, the Mediterranean was a British obsession and remained so until World War II and its aftermath. In the nineteenth century successive Mediterranean crises focused British policy on a Mediterranean strategy. In 1827 the Greek War of Independence produced the battle of Navarino, the last great sea fight under sail. In the 1840s Britain, Austria, Prussia and Russia acted in concert against Mehemet Ali, in support of the declining Ottoman Empire. In the 1850s it was the Crimean War, terminated by the largely forgotten but nevertheless important Treaty of Paris. In 1869 the Suez Canal was opened to Britain's immense commercial and imperial advantage. In 1878 the Royal Navy's historic transit of the Dardanelles passage, without the permission of the Sublime Porte and the aftermath in the Congress of Berlin, have already told their own story.

The British fleet in the Mediterranean was not necessarily immensely powerful but it was the largest squadron of operational warships possessed by the Royal Navy. Following France's defeat in the Franco-Prussian War Russia had abrogated the Black Sea demilitarisation clauses of the Treaty of Paris and started to build a Black Sea fleet. This ensured that British naval resources devoted to the Mediterranean effectively doubled in the 1880s as the Russian armoured ships neared completion.

Status quo is an accurate description of Britain's Mediterranean policy in the 1880s and 1890s, and this meant, if not exactly alliance, certainly some sort of accommodation with other Mediterranean powers. Since Italy and France were distinctly hostile to each other, Italy came under consideration as a counterweight to France. Maddelena Island, where three-quarters of a century earlier Nelson had sheltered while blockading Toulon, was now Italian territory, had been fortified and was a naval base. In 1887 the Italian Navy was not the equal of the French but it ranked as the third most powerful navy in the world after Britain and France.[37] In consequence, the prospect of an Anglo-Italian alliance was considered in the London of 1885–6.[38] At this time Italy was developing colonial and imperial interests and wanted Tunis, but this was seized by France in 1881. It was thwarted colonial ambitions that drove Italy towards alliance with Germany and Austria-Hungary.

In February 1887 there was an exchange of diplomatic notes between Britain and Italy respecting the status quo in the Mediterranean. The agreement stated that the status quo in the Mediterranean, Adriatic, Aegean and Black Sea should be maintained as far as possible.[39] Austria-Hungary was also brought into the agreement and in common with Italy was part of the Bismarckian Triple Alliance or *triplice*, established in 1882 between Germany, Italy and Austria-Hungary. This was the closest Britain came to joining the Bismarckian system of alliances. The British agreement with Austria-Hungary was entirely logical; Austria-Hungary had territory in the Balkans and a border with the Ottoman Empire. Austria was a fairly major military power with a small navy capable of punching above its weight. Italy signed the status quo agreement on 14 February 1887, with Austria-Hungary signing on 24 March. It is often said that these agreements were as casual and informal as Lord Salisbury could make them.[40] This is not really the case and a much more strongly worded agreement was signed with Austria on 12 December 1887. It was a considerably longer document, with nine clauses as opposed to four for the earlier February agreement. This stated that the independence of Turkey, as guardian of important interests (independence of the caliphate, the freedom of the straits, etc.), was of paramount importance. What the Anglo-Austrian agreement did not do was to pledge British troops to fight alongside those of Austria in the Balkans. Lord Salisbury wanted no open-ended commitment to Balkan troop deployments in some unspecified future crisis.

Radical Technology Change that Presaged the Pre-Dreadnought Era

Much has been written about the rapidly developing technology of the late Victorian period, often associating the Royal Navy with technological backwardness. In truth the Royal Navy adopted technological innovation partly when it suited them and partly when each new technology step was seen to work. It was a policy best described as cautious conservatism. In terms of the pre-dreadnought era it was steel and electricity allied to triple expansion steam engines, breech-loaded guns and steel armour that made the new-age ships possible.

In general terms a ship's hull constructed of mild steel is 50 per cent lighter than a wooden hull of similar dimensions and tonnage.[41] Mild steel, more properly open-hearth steel, is 25 per cent stronger than wrought iron and this was recognised at the time; by 1877 Lloyds Register of Shipping was recommending a general reduction of 20 per cent in the thickness of plating and frames for steel built ships.[42] Early Bessemer steel was not of high quality; hence the use of Siemens-Martin open-hearth steel – 'mild' steel.

In 1881 open-hearth steel cost £11 per ton as against £7 15s for wrought iron. Ten years later the gap had narrowed to £6 10s against £6 for wrought iron.[43] In 1875 Nathaniel Barnaby, the Royal Navy's Director of

Construction, designed the Royal Navy's first steel built cruisers, *Iris* and *Mercury*. Initially designated despatch vessels, they were built in the Admiralty shipyard at Pembroke from Siemens-Martin open-hearth steel supplied by the nearby Landore steelworks. As a result of the success of the new building material the first six of the nine *Comus* class steel corvettes, effectively small cruisers, were laid down in 1876.[44] In 1879 work started on *Colossus* and *Edinburgh*, the first steel-hulled British battleships, both of which were constructed from open-hearth steel.[45]

Modern electricity generation can be traced back as least as far as the work of Faraday on electromagnetic induction in 1831. By 1858 it had progressed far enough, together with arc lighting, for trials on its use in lighthouses. When the Belgian inventor Gramme's ring dynamo became available in the early 1870s, general purpose arc lighting became economically feasible. Between 1878 and 1880 Swan in England and Edison in the US invented incandescent filament lamps. Britain's first major warship to have electric light was the battleship *Inflexible*.

In some respects the early development of hydraulics was as important as electricity. As guns increased in size it became impossible to work them by hand. Armstrong's devised the first hydraulic handling system, based on the 'Bramah' press. Power was transmitted from an engine by water pressure through a small pipe actuating hydraulic rams.[46]

In the 1860s and 1870s the first high-pressure steam engines were introduced. The two-stage compound steam engine, operating at steam pressures of about 60psi, was a big advance over the earlier 'simple' engines, which operated at low steam pressures, around 20–30psi. Surface condensers allowed fresh water to be used in marine boilers and this ensured that steam pressures could to rise to 60psi. From 1880 onwards, mild steel was introduced for boilers and steam pressures increased further to 90psi. In 1882, with the introduction of corrugated steel furnaces, steam pressures increased again to 130psi. Evaporators ensured that by the late 1880s very pure fresh water was used in the boilers and pressures increased again, to around 155psi.[47]

In the 1880s the advent of the three-stage, triple-expansion steam engine ensured that the battleships of the Northbrook programme, *Victoria* and *Sans Pareil*, laid down in 1885, and the armoured cruisers of the Orlando class were the first large British warships to be fitted with them, as were all the ships of the Naval Defence Act. It needs emphasising that it was the advent of compound and triple-expansion steam engines that finally ended the age of sail.

The early ironclads were protected with wrought iron armour. In 1877 the first compound armour – that is a combination of iron and steel – made its appearance in England. The armour consisted of a wrought iron foundation plate with a rolled steel surface united at welding temperature. This gave a relatively brittle hard steel face supported by a much softer wrought iron backing.

In the 1870s and 1880s gunnery was revolutionised by several technology elements. These included greatly improved slow-burning powder, effective methods of breech loading; an effective means of achieving a gas seal at the breech, known as obturation, and above all else the use of steel for guns. There were various attempts at producing slow-burning powder, mostly involving powder with much larger grain sizes. These included rifled large grain (RLG) powder, followed by prismatic brown (PB) powder and finally slow burning cocoa (SBC) powder, so called because of its colour, introduced in 1884.[48] There were two new-age explosives, guncotton and nitroglycerine, but slowing the explosive detonation for slow-burning as a gun propellant took a long time. France made the crucial breakthrough with Poudre 'B', introduced in 1886; the first successful guncotton propellant, at least three times more efficient than any previous powder and nearly smokeless.[49] In Britain a committee was appointed to examine the potential of guncotton and nitroglycerine. In December 1888 Alfred Nobel submitted an early example of ballistite, based on nitroglycerine. The committee then proceeded to develop its own version of ballistite. The result was named Cordite Mark I and was first referred to as cordite in June 1889. Nobel launched a court action claiming that his patent rights on ballistite had been infringed. He lost the case and the Royal Navy adopted cordite in something like its modern form.[50]

Most accounts of gunnery development state that the problem of breech closure was solved in France, using the interrupted screw method. This is not really the case; the first patents on this type of closure were registered in the United States in 1853.[51] This was heavily developed in France and eventually adopted by most navies of the late nineteenth century, the French Navy adopting it in 1867.[52] The main problem experienced with first-generation breech-loaded guns was that of obturation, obtaining a gas seal at the breech. It was nine years after the French had adopted interrupted screw breech loaders that the problem was finally solved when in 1878 Colonel de Bange introduced a mushroom-shaped obturator.[53]

Implementing the gunnery revolution was to take most of the 1880s and some understanding of ordnance administration is necessary here.

From central batteries to citadels to barbettes.

Alexandra

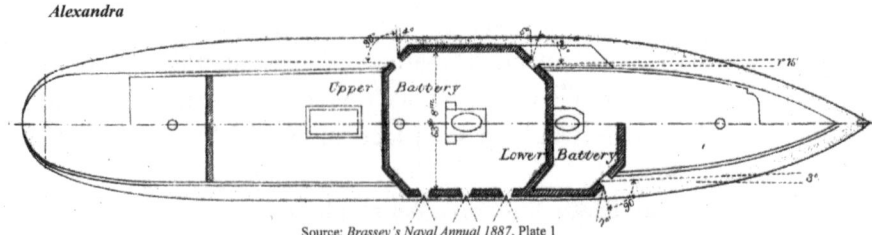

Source: *Brassey's Naval Annual 1887*, Plate 1

Alexandra was the last of the central battery ironclads. Laid down in 1873 she was approaching obsolescence at the time of her completion. *Alexandra* was with Sir Geoffrey Phipps-Hornby's squadron that transited the Dardanelles in 1878. Her central armoured redoubt or battery was split in two. The lower battery, with 12 inches of armour, contained three 10-inch MLRs on each broadside, and the forward section mounted two 10-inch MLRs in the corners. The upper battery, with 8 inches of armour, contained two 11-inch MLRs mounted in the forward corners and two 10-inch MLRs mounted in the aft corners. A heavily embrasured vessel, her ahead fire was two 11-inch and two 10-inch guns. She was propelled by two three-cylinder inverted compound engines, one high-pressure cylinder of 70 inches diameter and two low-pressure cylinders of 90 inches diameter. This ship was Barque rigged, with three masts, and had a sail area of 27,000 square feet. *Alexandra* never made more than six knots under sail alone. Laid down 1873, launched 1875, completed 1877.

Ajax
Agamemnon

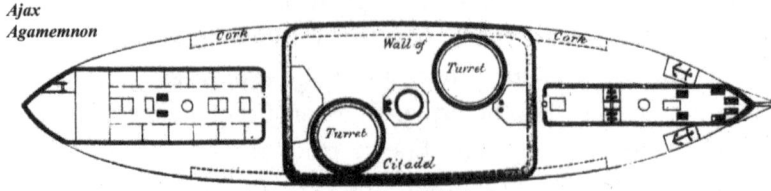

Source: *Brassey's Naval Annual 1887*, Plate 2

These were two of Britain's five *en echelon* ironclad battleships. By common consent they were the least successful *en echelons*. Note the development of the central citadel from the *Alexandra*. Now a central redoubt, the armament is in two turrets with two guns in each. The offset turrets (*en echelon*), combined with the heavily embrasured forecastle and stern upperworks gave nominal ahead and astern fire from both turrets. Cross-deck firing gave (highly theoretical) broadside fire from all four guns. Designed without sails propulsion was by two sets of three cylinder inverted compound engines. Eighteen *en echelons* were built worldwide, for five different navies. These extraordinary ships were arguably the 'missing link' between the broadside and central battery ironclads of the 1860s and 1870s and the developed pre-dreadnought battleships of the late 1880s and 1890s. Laid down 1876, launched 1879 and 1880. Completed 1883.

Collingwood

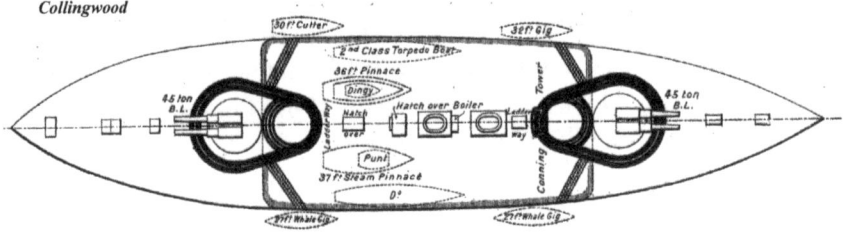

Source: *Brassey's Naval Annual 1895*, Plate 7

The Royal Navy's first true barbette battleship. Her all-steel hull and breech-loaded guns in two turrets, one forward and one aft provided the basic shape of the pre-dreadnought battleship. The guns in open barbettes could only be loaded in the fore and aft alignment and at a maximum elevation of 13½ degrees. In common with both *Alexandra* and *Ajax* she was powered by two sets of three cylinder compound inverted engines. Laid down 1880, launched 1882, completed 1887.

Fig. 1 Armour: from ironclads to pre-dreadnoughts, HMS Alexandra

After the Crimean War it was decided that the Woolwich Arsenal should supply guns to both the army and navy. This was an economy measure designed to prevent duplication of production facilities. On at least two occasions, in 1868–9 and again in 1880–2, the Admiralty resisted attempts to transfer financial responsibility from the War Office to the Admiralty.[54] There were good reasons for this; in the 1870s, in the wake of France's defeat by Germany in the Franco-Prussian war, Britain's naval budget was reduced to its absolute minimum.

In April 1879 an Ordnance Committee was formed to re-examine the vexed issue of breech loading and concluded that the new-age breech loaders were greatly superior to their muzzle-loading equivalents. The decision to move to breech loading was taken, with the concurrence of the War Office.[55] The navy's guns were now very different from those of the army and the decision to use large-calibre breech-loaded guns showed the limitations of the Woolwich system. The construction of the navy's first breech-loading guns was very slow, and numerous ships were delayed in their completion due to late delivery of the new guns.[56] These guns were not very successful; they were a mixture of wrought iron and steel. The battleship *Collingwood*, armed with four 12-inch breech-loading guns, underwent her gunnery trials in May 1886. On firing, the last eight feet of one gun barrel disintegrated. These guns were quickly withdrawn from naval service and replaced by those made entirely of forged steel.[57]

The Birth of the Battleship

The broadside and central battery ironclads of the 1860s and 1870s bore little relation to the pre-dreadnought battleships of the Naval Defence Act. There was a half-forgotten 'missing link' between the ironclads and the pre-dreadnoughts, and that link was the curious naval Neanderthals known as the *en echelon* or diagonal barbette battleships. The tactical assumption behind the curious armament disposition was an ability to operate the full armament in line ahead or line abreast as a fast-moving naval engagement developed. Bernadetto Brin, the chief designer for the Italian Navy, initiated the type with *Duilio* and *Dandolo*, which used the largest guns available, 17.7-inch calibre Armstrong muzzle loaders. The required armour thickness, governed by the possibility of an adversary using the same calibre guns and the consequent massive weight of armour required, was a central armoured citadel less than one-third the length of the vessel.[58] The armour was all steel and was purchased from Schneider of Creusot.[59]

Britain's reply, the *en echelon* HMS *Inflexible*, was laid down in 1874. The guns were 16.25-inch muzzle loaders and the central armoured citadel was exactly one-third of the vessel length, as in the *Duilios*. Her design came to include compound (iron and steel) armour, locomotive torpedoes and also second-class torpedo boats, all fitted before her completion in 1882. Oscar Parkes, with some accuracy, described the *Inflexible* as 'an example of precocious hypertrophy'.[60]

The Italians continued with the *en echelon* type and built a further five, two of which were the much larger *Italia* and *Lepanto*, the latter with an all-steel hull and both fitted with breech-loaded guns.[61] These ships were virtually without armour and with a speed of 18 knots have been called the ancestors of the battle cruisers. Britain built four smaller *en echelons*; *Ajax, Agamemnon, Colossus* and *Edinburgh*. The *Ajax* and *Agamemnon* were the last battleships with muzzle-loaded rifled guns, while the *Colossus* and *Edinburgh* were the first British steel-hulled battleships and also the first with breech-loaded guns.[62] In most respects the *en echelon* ships, with the thickest possible armour and largest-calibre guns, were deeply misguided. In other ways the *en echelons* pioneered much of the new-age technology, characterised by cheap Siemens-Martin open-hearth steel, electrical installations and, in the later ships, breech-loaded guns.

In 1877–8 France laid down the four Terrible-class battleships, armed with two 16.25-inch guns, mounted one forward and one aft.[63] Britain's initial reply was the *Collingwood*, laid down in July 1880. She mounted four 12-inch breech-loaded guns in barbettes, two forward and two aft. All four guns could be deployed on either broadside, with two ahead and two astern.[64] The classic pre-dreadnought gun layout had appeared, very much due to French ships with their gun layout at the ends of the ship. The *en echelon* era was over, but the steel and electricity revolution was continuing apace.

In 1882 the Admiralty laid down the Admiral-class battleships, *Anson, Camperdown, Howe* and *Rodney*. These ships carried the ideas behind the *Collingwood* one step further, were a thousand tons larger and carried four 13.5-inch guns in barbettes. A fifth ship, named *Benbow*, was built with the same barbette disposition as the other Admirals but mounted two massive 16.25-inch guns, one forward and one aft. The gun was not a success.

In 1884, the 'Truth about the Navy' press campaign produced the Northbrook programme, consisting of two battleships, seven cruisers, six torpedo cruisers and 14 torpedo boats. The two battleships were the *Victoria* and *Sans Pareil*, influenced by most of the wrong influences prevalent in Whitehall in the mid-1880s. First, it was decided to mount the 16.25-inch guns developed by Armstrong's for the *Benbow*. Then it was decided to mount the guns in turrets and the consequent weight increase dictated a low freeboard design. These ships were limited in displacement to 10,500 tons so only one turret could be carried, mounted forward, with the two monster 16.25-inch guns. Since there was no arc of fire astern, a single 10-inch gun was mounted aft.

The low freeboard turret type was repeated in the battleships *Nile* and *Trafalgar*. These ships were rather larger at 12,500 tons and mounted four 13.5-inch guns in two turrets, one forward and one aft.[65] There followed a two-year moratorium on battleship building while the naval dockyards were reorganised (discussed later). At the end of the moratorium William White designed the eight battleships of the Royal Sovereign class. Seven of these battleships mounted the same barbette armament as the Admirals and again the advantage of a high freeboard design was emphasised. An eighth ship, HMS *Hood*, was a low freeboard turret ship.

In a paper delivered to the Institution of Naval Architects in April 1889, William White, Director of Naval Construction, reviewed all the battleship types built for the Royal Navy in the preceding 20 years. He also reviewed the French, Russian and Italian battleships already and being built. He stated that four heavy guns should be mounted in two protected stations with training arcs of 260 degrees. He also discussed a powerful secondary armament of 6-inch guns.[66] This paper represented the clearest possible statement of sharply focused design requirements for battleships of the pre-dreadnought type.

Cruiser Development

In the wake of the American Civil War a ship that could run down some future *Alabama* was called for, and the result was a fast, iron-hulled, unarmoured ship designed by Sir Edward Reed.[67] The *Inconstant* was laid down in 1866, displaced 5,780 tons, was armed with ten 9-inch RMLs and had a speed of 16 knots. In every way a successful ship, almost as fast under sail as steam, she was nevertheless an expensive ship to run and at £213,324 her building costs were almost as much as an ironclad.[68] A few more *Inconstant*-type ships were built; the *Shah* and *Raleigh* were very similar and also 16-knot vessels. Smaller versions appeared, such as the *Active* and *Volage*, ships of 3,000-tons and 15 knots speed.[69] The next pair of fast, unarmoured warships have already been touched upon; the *Iris* and *Mercury* were the Royal Navy's first steel-hulled warships. Technically advanced for their day, they were capable of 18 knots and for some years were the fastest ocean-going warships in the world.[70] The nine-ship Comus or 'C' class of 1878 were steel built cruisers of 2,380-ton vessels, fully

Victoria
Sans Pareil

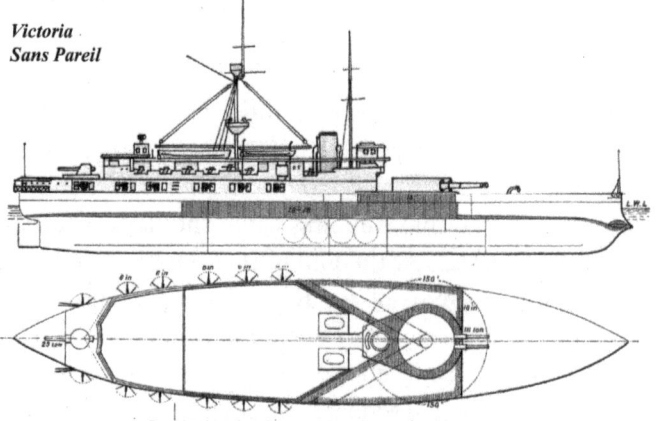

Drawing based on *Brassey's Naval Annual 1895*, Plate 20

Victoria:	Thames Iron Works 21.4.85–9.5.87–8.7.91 £778,650
Sans Pareil:	Elswick 23.4.85–9.4.87–March '90 £844,922
Dimensions:	340 × 70 × 26.6/29 feet = 10,470 tons
Armament:	Two 16.25-inch 110-ton B.L. Guns, one 10-inch 29-ton B.L. gun, twelve 6-inch B.L. Twelve 6-pounders, twenty smaller, torpedo tubes, 1 bow, 1 stern, 2 submerged
Armour:	Belt 18", bulkheads 16", submerged deck fore and aft 3", turret 17", redoubt 18", side to 6-inch guns 3", screen bulkheads to battery 6", conning tower 14"–2"
Machinery:	Two sets Humphreys triple expansion I.H.P 7,500 = 15.3 knots, F.D. 14,000 = 17.2 knots
Coal:	750/1,000 tons, 7,000 miles at 10 knots
Complement:	430, as flagships 550–583

Nile
Trafalgar

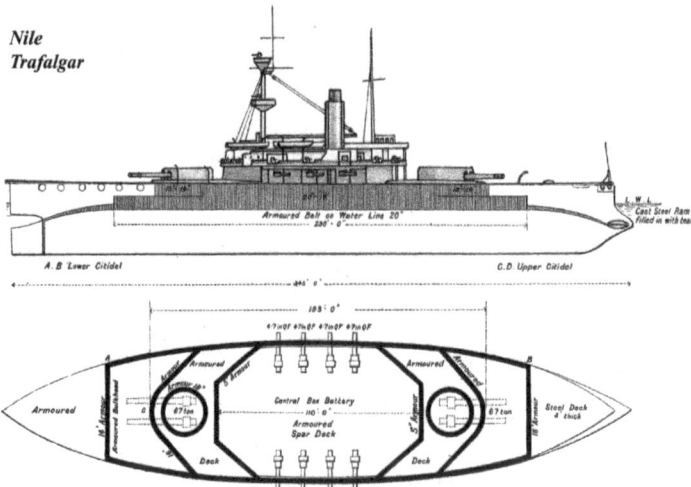

Drawing based on *Brassey's Naval Annual 1895*, Plate 21

Nile:	Pembroke 8.4.86–27.3.88–10.7.91 £885,718
Trafalgar:	Portsmouth 18.1.86–20.9.87–March '90 £859,070
Dimensions:	345 × 73 × 28/29 feet = 12,590 tons
Armament:	Four 13.5-inch 67-ton guns, six 4.7-inch Q.F., eight 6-pounders, nine 3-pounders torpedo tubes, 1 bow and stern, 2 submerged, 2 above water
Armour:	Belt 20" amidships tapering to 14" the ends and 8"–6" at lower edge, bulkheads 16" forward, side 4" Deck throughout 3", skin 2½"–1¾". Total 4,226 tons (33.5%)
Machinery:	*Nile* by Maudslay, *Trafalgar* by Humphreys, two sets triple expansion, IHP. 7,500 = 15.1 knots, 16.75 F.D.
Coal:	900–1,200 tons 6,500 miles at 10 knots
Complement:	558

Fig. 2 Battleships of the late 1880s, Victoria *and* Sans Pareil, Nile *and* Trafalgar.

THE ORIGINS OF THE PRE-DREADNOUGHT ERA 21

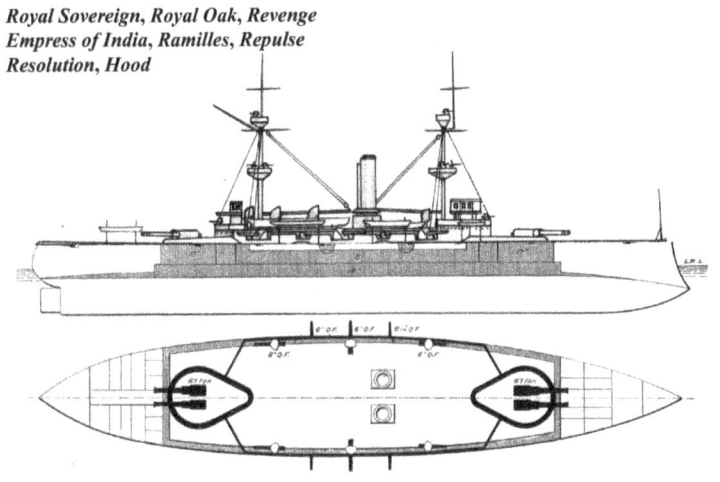

Royal Sovereign, Royal Oak, Revenge
Empress of India, Ramilles, Repulse
Resolution, Hood

Drawings based on *Brassey's Naval Annual 1902*, Plate 14.

Dimensions: 380 × 75 × 27/28 feet = 14,150 tons
Armament: Four 13.5-B.L guns, sixteen 6-pounders Q.F., twelve 3-pounders. Two submerged torpedo tubes forward four tubes above water abeam, one tube above water astern.
Armour: Belt 18"–16"–14" ends, bulkheads 16"–14", deck 3"–2½", barbettes 17"–6"–11", main deck casemates 6" side above belt 4", screen above belt 3", fore conning tower 14". Total 4,560 (32.2%)
Machinery: Two sets 3-cylinder vertical triple expansion H.P. 9,000 = 15.5 knots, forced draught 13,360 = 18 knots
Coal: 900/1,100 tons, 4,720 miles, 10 knots
Complement: 712
Note: An eighth battleship, *Hood*, was a low freeboard turret ship, sometimes referred to as the last of the littoral warfare ships. *Hood* had her main armament turret mounted. Her gun turrets were a deck lower than those in the Royal Sovereigns. The *Hood* had a freeboard of only 11.25 feet. In the Royal Sovereigns the freeboard was 18 feet.

Fig. 3 The Naval Defence Act battleships, Royal Sovereign class

rigged with a 1.5-inch protective deck but a speed of only 13 knots. The Leander class of 1882–3 (four ships), were larger at 4,300 tons and had a better turn of speed at 17 knots. The successor Mersey class were more heavily armed and also had a speed of 17 knots. The protected cruisers of the Naval Defence Act, the 21-ship Apollo class second-class cruisers, all had protective decks, were steel-hulled and armed with two 6-inch and six 4.7-inch breech-loaded quick-firing guns. Of these 21 ships ten were sheathed and coppered for tropical service. In the case of the Apollos they had a true cruiser range of 8,000 nautical miles at 10 knots, made possible with triple expansion engines.[71]

Warship Design and Naval Architects

In the early 1880s the status of naval architects was generally low. When the Royal Naval College was opened at Greenwich the Navy's School of Naval Architecture was moved there. Career prospects for the graduates were generally poor. If they went to the royal dockyards they joined a promotion queue that included many unqualified men senior to them. In consequence, most went to Lloyds Register and the private shipyards. One of the few who stayed the course in the royal dockyards was William White.[72] Born in 1845, he was apprenticed to the Devonport dockyard in 1859. His rise was fairly meteoric and he was largely responsible for the well-designed *Collingwood* and the Admiral-class battleships.[73] In February 1880 White submitted a memorandum recommending the formation of a Royal Corps of Naval Constructors. This suggested that each royal dockyard should have a *corps d'elite* of naval architects capable of designing as well as building ships.[74] In 1883 the Royal Corps of Naval Constructors was formed.[75] The new body embraced naval architects, engineers and, for the first time, people skilled in electrical matters.[76]

In 1885 William White was offered and accepted the post of chief constructor. In October 1885, this post was upgraded to Director of Naval Construction and White was given a seat on the Admiralty Board as Assistant Controller.[77] The First Lord, by this stage Lord George Hamilton, immediately wrote to White asking him to submit proposals for reforming the royal dockyards.[78] White's main objective was nothing less than the total reform of the dockyard system. At this time the armoured cruisers *Imperieuse* and *Warspite* were completing. Both were seriously overweight on completion, partly as a result of design changes during building, partly due to inaccurate design calculations and partly due to inefficient control of construction material.[79] Hamilton was determined to prove that the royal dockyards could indeed build battleships to the standard of the commercial yards. He appointed four committees to inquire into Admiralty and dockyard administration.[80] The committees reported what was suspected, that the dockyards were uneconomic and inefficient. It was suggested that they should be modelled on the management principles that ran the commercial yards. An outstanding naval architect Francis Elgar was appointed Director of Dockyards. He had managed the Earle shipbuilding yard at Hull and been the first professor of naval architecture and marine engineering at Glasgow University. As Director of Dockyards he was equal in rank to the Director of Naval Construction and answered directly to the Controller of the Navy. He made frequent visits to the dockyards and advised on technical and management problems.[81]

The result was the transformation of inefficient naval dockyards into the cheapest and fastest building yards in the world for battleship construction. The ships of the Naval Defence Act were built in naval dockyards that had been reformed from top to bottom, designed by naval architects who belonged to a newly established Royal Corps of Naval Constructors and were backed by an Admiralty Board given detailed technical advice at Board level, all very far from the supposed complacency and technological incompetence of the late Victorian navy.

Perspectives: Crises, Strategic Uncertainties and Technology Changes

Perceptions of strategy changed radically in the 1880s, defined by a series of crises involving the navy. These came one after another in 1878, 1882, 1885 and 1888. Each suggested a Royal Navy in a state of weakness and overstretch, and also technologically backward compared to its principal rivals. The Treaty of Paris terminated the Crimean War and outlawed privateering, but the American Civil War produced deep-felt worries about attacks on trade, and this ensured that the Confederate raider *Alabama* was mentioned nearly 60 times in the evidence to the Carnarvon Commission. Added to this was the almost unanimous opinion that convoy was no longer a viable defence for merchant shipping. Worries and uncertainties about the defence of trade were greatly exacerbated by the *Jeune École*, with its emphasis on commerce destruction.

These uncertainties made successive governments vulnerable to press campaigns and public scares. The political instability of the mid-1880s and the fall of Gladstone's third administration over the vexed issue of Irish home rule need no further comment. Lord Salisbury's political ascendancy was an important factor that made the Naval Defence Act possible. Salisbury had been Foreign Secretary during the latter part of the 1878 crisis and had seen the navy achieve a major foreign policy success without a shot fired in anger. This was the hidden purpose behind the Naval Defence Act – a navy able to achieve foreign policy aims without the use of main force. In other words, a peace-keeping deterrent force.

Added to this was the perception of naval weakness so assiduously promulgated in the press and elsewhere, which quickly gained the ear of a Conservative government eager for a solution that ended an era of strategic uncertainty. The Naval Defence Act may have ended such an era but it initiated one of overt navalism in defence thinking. Defence expenditure on the navy doubled in the 1880s and the other naval powers followed suit. The Naval Defence Act was Britain's unique and probably unnecessary contribution to the international arms race that preceded World War I. In the law of unintended consequences Britain had fired the starting gun.

2

The Pre-Dreadnought Era in the 1890s

Prelude: The Naval Defence Act and the Other European Navies

The passing of the Naval Defence Act had a profound influence on the naval policy of Britain's traditional potential adversaries, France and Russia, and indeed on all the other naval powers. In the case of France the Naval Defence Act coincided with the effective end of the *Jeune École* and its influence on French naval strategy. The arguments about the importance of the *Jeune École* continued for some years into the future, but the battleship *Brennus* was laid down in January 1889, some two months before the Naval Defence Act was passed and France resumed a battleship strategy.[1] Two years later, in 1891, France initiated a major building programme, named after its creator, Admiral Gervais, costing some £37 million and spread over a ten-year period. It was a massive programme, similar to Britain's Naval Defence Act and arguably a direct reaction to it, but larger and to be carried out over a longer period of time.[2] The Gervais programme was not fully carried out and in 1894 only 20 of the 29 ships planned for the first three years had actually been laid down, though this was not readily apparent to the British Admiralty.[3] This was to have hidden consequences when British naval policy was reviewed in 1893.

During the era of the *Jeune École*, Russia also continued with a battleship programme focused on the Black Sea, with three of the four Ekaterina II barbette ships completed in 1889–90.[4] Russia laid down three battleships in the Baltic before 1889, two in 1889 and no fewer than 13 in the ten years after the Naval Defence Act.[5] It needs emphasising that after 1889, Russia became much more focused on battleship building programmes, as did every other navy. The total cost of Russian building programmes in the 1890s amounted to 242 million roubles, about £26.8 million.[6]

The Mediterranean navies of Italy and Austria-Hungary were always included in any British calculation of naval strength. At the time of the Naval Defence Act Italy had seven battleships, each as powerful as anything possessed by France, arguably more powerful in the case of the *Italia* and *Lepanto*, with a further three building.[7]

The rejection of the *Jeune École* just at the moment the Naval Defence Act was passed had a considerable impact not just on French and Italian building programmes but also on that of Austria-Hungary. In 1893 this, the smallest of the European great power navies, scraped together enough money to build three small (5,547 ton) coast defence battleships. The *Monarch*, *Wein* and *Budapest* were too small to be really successful but at the beginning of the 1890s the Austro-Hungarian Navy, influenced by the development of a powerful Italian Navy, moved heavily in the direction of battleship construction.[8]

In August 1893 the First Naval Lord, Sir Frederick Richards, wrote a minute to the Admiralty Board in which he pointed out that while Britain had a distinct lead in battleships, built and building, over the combined totals of France and Russia, if Britain did not continue the construction of yet more battleships, by 1898 the consequences would be serious. Richards also stated that the Gervais programme was France's direct reply to the Naval Defence Act.[9]

In November 1893 William White, Director of Naval Construction, prepared a memorandum for the Admiralty Board which discussed Britain's building programme for the following five years, 1894–9, and the building programmes of the other naval powers. White's memorandum stated that, in view of the French and Russian building programmes, Britain ought to build another ten battleships by 1899.[10] In December 1893 Sir Frederick Richards sent a memorandum to the First Lord, Lord Spencer, in which he described William White's proposals, emphasising that this was a 'minimum programme' giving 'bare ship-for-ship equality in 1898'.[11]

Gladstone, now a very old man, was implacably opposed to increased naval expenditure. Lord Spencer held out in Cabinet against Gladstone, the Chancellor of the Exchequer, Sir William Harcourt and most of the rest of the Cabinet. The Naval Lords threatened to resign as a body if their professional advice was not accepted. Gladstone, with failing eyesight and looking for an excuse to retire, stepped down over the issue of the naval estimates.[12] After a bitter argument the Cabinet, under the new prime minister Lord Rosebery, accepted the draft programme. The nine

THE PRE-DREADNOUGHT ERA IN THE 1890s

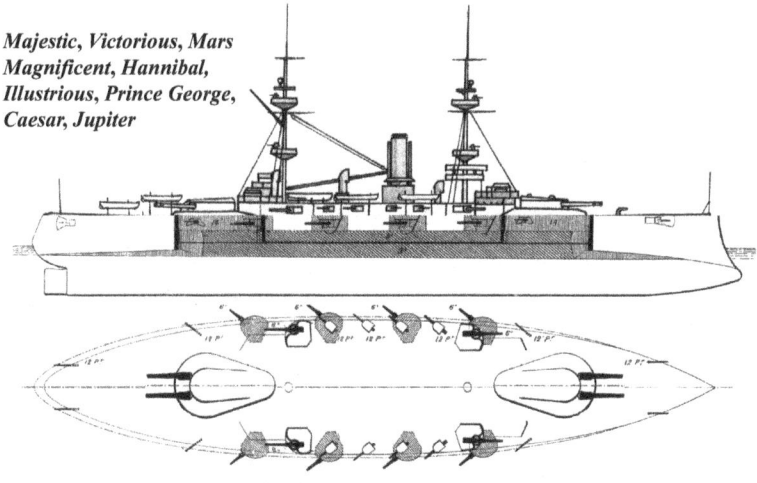

Majestic, Victorious, Mars
Magnificent, Hannibal,
Illustrious, Prince George,
Caesar, Jupiter

Drawings based on *Brassey's Naval Annual 1902,* Plate 15.

Dimensions:	390 × 75 × 26½/27½ = 14,900 tons
Armament:	Four 12-inch 35-calibre guns, twelve 6-inch 40-calibres, sixteen 12-pounders four submerged and one above water torpedo tubes
Armour:	Harvey armour. Belt 9", amidships 14", bulkhead for'd and 12 aft, barbettes 14" × 7", shields 10" casemates 6", decks 4", 3", and 2 ½", conning towers 14" and 3". Total 4,535 tons (30.4%)
Machinery:	Two sets 3-cylinder inverted triple expansion H.P 10,000 = 16.1 knots, F.D. 12,000 = 17 knots
Complement:	672
Note:	The nine ships of the Majestic class represented the largest class of battleships ever built for the Royal Navy

Fig. 4 Majestic class battleships

battleships of the so-called 'Spencer' programme became the Majestic class and were the largest class of battleships ever built for the Royal Navy.

The Spencer Programme

Armour and ordnance developments ensured that the Majestic class battleships were as big an advance over the Royal Sovereigns as they in their turn had been over the Admirals and the Northbrook programme battleships, mostly due to improved armour plate and new ordnance.

A number of attempts were made to carburise – that is, to harden – the face of a steel plate. An American engineer, H.A. Harvey, provided the breakthrough. Harvey carburised the face of a steel plate by keeping it at a high temperature in contact with finely divided charcoal. After cementation the plate was allowed to cool to a dull red heat and then sprayed or quenched in water. In 1887 Captain Tresidder patented a method of rapidly chilling the face of a steel plate by using jets of high-pressure water. Harvey's method of quenching or spraying was less sophisticated than Tresidder's, but steel plates treated by combining the Harvey and Tresidder processes gave about twice the resisting power of wrought iron and were half as good again as compound armour.[13]

In 1892 all-steel Harvey armour was tested at Shoeburyness, and in every case forged steel armour-piercing projectiles were broken up; the Admiralty took the decision to use Harvey armour soon afterwards.[14] With the introduction of Harvey armour plate, 12 inches of compound armour could be replaced with 7½ inches of Harvey armour. In the Majestic class the main armour belt was 9 inches of Harvey armour and this was extended up to the height of the gun deck, about seven feet above the protective deck.[15]

Ordnance did not stop improving with the Naval Defence Act; rather, the Act spurred on further technological development. The 12-inch gun selected for the Majestics was a wire-wound 35-calibre, 46-ton gun, designed by the Royal Gun Factory at Woolwich Arsenal and used cordite propellant charges. Manufacture was shared with the private ordnance companies, particularly Armstrong's.[16] The introduction of armoured shields covering the gun barbettes gave the gun crews a measure of protection.

The last two Majestic class ships, *Caesar* and *Illustrious*, were fitted with a more advanced circular barbette, replacing the older pear-shaped type. This allowed all-round loading, though still at a fixed elevation angle of 13½ degrees and this reduced the firing time from two minutes to 45 seconds. Rapid technological advance in guns did not stop with the Majestics. In the succeeding Canopus class, the last ship of the class, *Vengeance*, was fitted with a Vickers chain rammer, which allowed loading at any angle of elevation. This further reduced the firing time from 45 seconds to 32 seconds. In the subsequent Formidable and London classes a new 40-calibre, 50-ton 12-inch gun was introduced.[17]

In 1894 extra-European factors began to exert a considerable influence on British naval policy. In September 1894 the Yalu naval battle was fought between Japan and China. The Chinese Navy was almost completely destroyed and many of its ships, including a German-built battleship, were captured. At this time there were two battleships building in Britain for Japan. The result was the potential for a Japanese Navy in eastern seas that was considerably stronger than any British squadron ever deployed east of Suez. In March 1895 Sir William White, now knighted, submitted a memorandum to the Admiralty Board with a very detailed analysis of the

Japanese battleships building in Britain, similar to the Royal Sovereigns, though slightly smaller.[18]

White suggested that at least a number of any future first-class battleships should be designed with a shallower draught to transit the Suez Canal. The result was the six ships of the Canopus class (1896–7 estimates), five of which served on the China station. Again there were large technology advances, with the adoption of Krupp cemented armour, a 25 per cent improvement over Harvey armour. The use of Krupp cemented armour needs explanation. Harvey armour had one defect; the back of the plate was not sufficiently tough to break up a shell that had penetrated the glass hard face of the plate. Krupp's experimented with nickel-chrome steel alloys and used the Harvey process to harden the face of the plate. The front of the plate was heated and water-quenched, while the back of the plate was kept at a lower temperature, which helped produce a tough fibrous back to the plate.[19]

The Canopus class represented a major strategic development, modern battleships designed specifically for service on a distant station. Battleship building continued throughout the 1890s with the three ships of the Formidable class (1897 programme), the five ships of the London class (1898 and 1900 estimates) and the six ships of the Duncan class (1898 supplementary and 1899 estimates). The 1898 supplementary estimates were considered necessary to provide a reply to an alleged group of fast Russian battleships. Three Russian ships duly appeared – *Peresviet*, *Osliabia* and *Pobieda* – which turned out to be second-class ships armed with four 10-inch guns. None made above 16 knots sea speed, so the six Duncans armed with four 12-inch guns and a speed of 19 knots can be regarded as very substantially superior.

In 1898 the logic behind the Admiralty desire for yet more battleships can be deduced by counting first-class battleships from the *Collingwood* to the Duncans and arriving at 47 British battleships to 25 Russian and 22 French.[20] After ten years of big building programmes Britain was at exactly the same relative position as she had been before the act was passed. The difference between assessments of naval strength in 1889 and 1898 is that by the middle of the 1890s, the Admiralty and everyone else was thinking in terms of a two-power standard that dealt solely in terms of first-class battleships, now, with the wisdom of retrospective labelling, identifiably pre-dreadnoughts. These strategically important first-class battleships were themselves the end product of a rapidly advancing technology that

**Canopus, Albion,
Goliath, Ocean,
Vengeance, Glory**

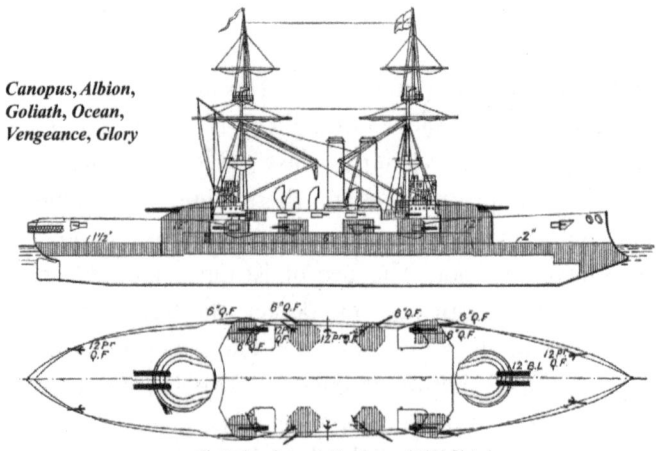

Illustration: *Brassey's Naval Annual 1909*, Plate 4

Canopus:	Portsmouth 4.1.97–12.10.97–Dec '99 £866,516,	*Glory:*	Lairds 1.12.96–11.3.99–Oct '00
Albion:	Thames Iron Works 3.12.96–21.6.98–Jun '01 £858,745,	*Goliath:*	Chatham 4.1.97–23.3.98–Mar '00 £866,006
Ocean:	Devonport 15.2.97–5.7.98–Feb '00 £883,778,	*Vengeance:*	Vickers 23.8.98–25.7.99–Apr '02 £891,217

Dimensions: 390 × 74 × 25.83/26.5 feet = 12,950 tons
Armament: Four 12-inch 35-calibres, twelve 6-inch, ten 12-pounders, six 3-pounders, two maxims, four 18-inch submerged torpedo tubes
Armour: Belt, krupps cemented 6", bow 2", bulkheads for'd 10"–8"–6", aft 12"–10"–6" barbettes (K.C.) 12"–6", shields 8" casemates (H) 6", decks (M) 2" × 1", conning towers (H-N) 12" and 3". Total 3,600 tons
Machinery: *Canopus,* Greenock Foundry, *Goliath,* Penn, *Glory,* Laird, *Ocean,* Hawthorn Leslie, *Albion,* Maudsley, *Vengeance,* Vickers. Two sets 3-cylinder inverted triple expansion H.P. 13,500 18.3 knots
Coal: 800 1,800 tons
Complement: 682

**Formidable, Bulwark,
Queen, Implacable,
Irresistible, London,
Prince of Wales, Venerable**

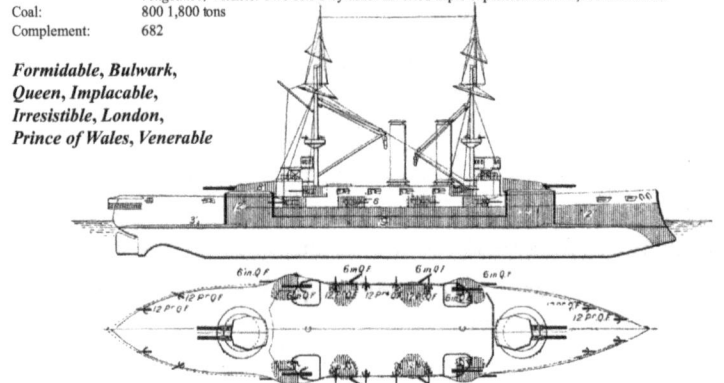

Illustration: *Brassey's Naval Annual 1909*, Plate 4

Bulwark:	Devonport, 20.3.99–18.10.99–Mar '02 £997,846,	*London:*	Portsmouth, 8.12.98–21.9.99–Jun '02 £1,036,393
Venerable:	Chatham, 2.1.99–2.11.99–Nov '02 £1,092,753,	*Queen:*	Devonport, 12.3.01–8.3.02, Mar '04 £1,074,999
Prince of Wales:	Chatham, 20.3.01–25.3.02–Mar '04 £1,193,380,	*Formidable:*	Portsmouth, 21.3.98–17.3.98–Sept '01 £1,022,745
Irresistible:	Chatham, 11.4.98–15.12.98–Feb '02 £1,048,136,	*Implacable:*	Devonport, 13.7.98–11.3.99–Sept '01 £989,116

Dimensions: 431.75 × 75 × 26.833 = 15,000 tons
Armament: Four 12-inch-40 cals., twelve 6-inch, sixteen 12-pounders, four 18-inch submerged TT.
Armour: Belt and lower deck sides 9", K.C. bulkheads 12"–10"–9", barbettes 12"–6", shields 10"–8" casemates 6", conning tower 14", lower decks 2½"–2", middle 3"–2"
Machinery: Two sets 3-cylinder vertical triple expansion H.P. 15,000 = 18 knots
Coal: 900/2,000-tons radius 8,000 miles at 10 knots
Complement: 780 as a flagship 810
Note: Formidable and London classes are put together because they were virtually identical.

Fig. 5 Battleships of the late 1890s, Canopus and Formidable class

THE PRE-DREADNOUGHT ERA IN THE 1890s

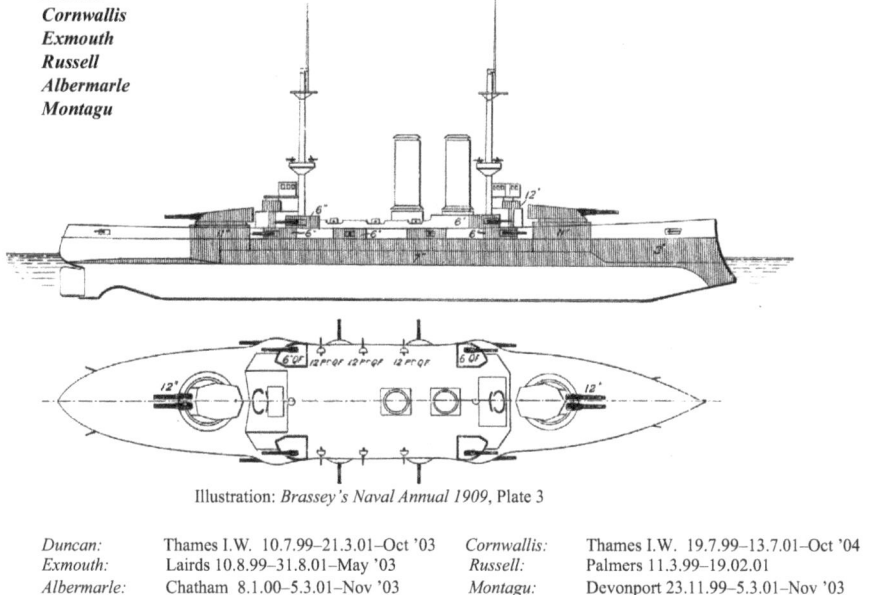

Duncan
Cornwallis
Exmouth
Russell
Albermarle
Montagu

Illustration: *Brassey's Naval Annual 1909*, Plate 3

Duncan:	Thames I.W. 10.7.99–21.3.01–Oct '03	*Cornwallis:*	Thames I.W. 19.7.99–13.7.01–Oct '04
Exmouth:	Lairds 10.8.99–31.8.01–May '03	*Russell:*	Palmers 11.3.99–19.02.01
Albermarle:	Chatham 8.1.00–5.3.01–Nov '03	*Montagu:*	Devonport 23.11.99–5.3.01–Nov '03
Average cost:	£1,093,000		

Other details nearly exactly the same as Formidable class but machinery was two sets of four cylinder inverted triple expansion, which gave an extra knot in speed, H.P. 18,000 = 19 knots

Fig. 6 *The penultimate pre-dreadnoughts, Duncan class*

continually drove older ships to obsolescence and generated the requirement for yet more battleships, each incorporating the latest technology.

The Mediterranean

Exactly why the large 'Spencer' building programme was considered necessary so soon after the huge Naval Defence Act building programme was deeply bound up in Britain's Mediterranean policy. France and Russia went into formal alliance in 1892 and the alliance was an attempt to counterbalance the Triple Alliance of Germany, Austria and Italy, not in fact aimed at Britain. In early August 1893 it became known that a Russian squadron would visit Toulon and that a permanent Russian presence would be established in the Mediterranean.[21]

With the Russian visit to Toulon there was something of a 'naval panic' in Whitehall. France and Russia in alliance and seemingly bent on naval cooperation was, after all, the worst-case British scenario for most of the nineteenth century. In fact, there were only five ships in the squadron that visited Toulon and after the visit was over two of the ships left for Vladivostok via the Suez Canal leaving just three Russian warships in the Mediterranean.[22] In the 1890s there was a growing concern with the Mediterranean, seen as the umbilical cord between Great Britain and her empire east of Suez. *The Times* returned again and again to the vexed issue of naval weakness and the Franco-Russian combination.[23]

In November 1895, the First Naval Lord, Sir Frederick Richards, stated that any Russian occupation of Constantinople would almost certainly result in Russian control of the Dardanelles Straits, denying the Sea of Marmara and the Black Sea to British commerce, or at least making it dependent on Russian goodwill. This would make Russia the predominant power in the eastern Mediterranean. British policy should be aimed at keeping the Russian fleet out of the Mediterranean, and this required increasing the Mediterranean fleet, with a fortified base in the neighbourhood of the Dardanelles. Bearing in mind the Franco-Russian alliance, Richards went on to say that Britain's main regional base, Malta, lay at the apex of a triangle formed by Toulon and the Dardanelles, each containing an enemy fleet within 48 hours' steaming of Malta.[24]

Britain gave up on the Mediterranean agreements in the period 1895–7 and there is a consensus that the reason the agreements proved abortive has never been satisfactorily explained.[25] It has already been stated that Italy built seven *en echelon* battleships in the 1870s and 1880s. The choice of such a large investment in the *en echelon* warship type was unfortunate as this type of ship rapidly became obsolete, being replaced by the pre-dreadnoughts. By the late 1890s Britain had built the eight battleships of the Royal Sovereign class (Naval Defence Act), all completed 1892–5, while the nine Majestic class ships (Spencer programme) were completed 1895–8. By contrast, Italy had just three Sardegna class pre-dreadnought battleships available.[26] At one level the agreement with Italy was given up because the Italian Navy could no longer be considered effective or modern. Technology had overtaken strategy and policy.

The Anglo-Austrian policy was given up for rather different reasons. The agreement only had real value and worth when the British Mediterranean Squadron could transit or force the Dardanelles and anchor before the Sublime Porte. Lord Salisbury returned to office in 1895 and was faced with Armenian massacres in the Balkans. He assumed that the Mediterranean fleet could again be sent up the Dardanelles as it had been in 1878. Sir Frederick Richards, the First Naval Lord, was sent for and told what the Cabinet wanted. He flatly declined to have anything to do with the proposal.[27] His opinion was that if the British forced or transited the Dardanelles, the French fleet might anchor at the entrance to the Dardanelles and the British fleet would be trapped.[28] The considerable numbers of pre-dreadnoughts built and building had made the 1887 agreements obsolete. In view of what happened in 1915 and the Dardanelles/Gallipoli disaster it is also worth recording that in the 1895–7 period, Dardanelles operations were no longer considered possible and the First Naval Lord was prepared to stand up to the prime minister in Cabinet over the matter.

By the mid-1890s sea mines and locomotive torpedoes were a significant threat, and this ensured that the Royal Navy was giving up on littoral warfare. In 1878 and 1885 Particular Service Squadrons had been mobilised for the Baltic using ships specifically designed for littoral warfare, usually referred to as coast defence ships. When the Royal Sovereigns were built, one of them was a low freeboard turret ship built at the express wishes of the then First Naval Lord, Sir Arthur Hood, and named appropriately HMS *Hood*. Eric Grove characterised her as 'the last and greatest low freeboard coast attack ironclad'.[29]

The Cruiser Question in the 1890s

In the 1890s the cruiser question became very complex and in some ways more important and significant than the big battleship programmes. In 1887 the term 'cruiser' was adopted for the smaller naval vessels and the term 'battleship' replaced the term 'ironclad' for the armoured ships.[30] To gain any proper understanding of the late Victorian navy in the years after the passing of the Naval Defence Act the balance between battleship and cruiser programmes needs close examination. It also requires a comparison between the Royal Navy and the navies of the other powers, particularly France and Russia. Between 1879 and 1907 Britain built 62 pre-dreadnought battleships to a Franco-Russian total of 61. The British advantage lay in their lower unit costs; the British ships cost £63 million to a Franco-Russian total of £68.81 million. The tonnage of the respective battleship fleets was also in Britain's favour, 857,729 tons to a Franco-Russian total of 744,940 tons, reflecting the larger and more heavily armed British ships.[31]

In the period 1885–1907 Britain built 151 cruisers to a Franco-Russian total of 77, a figure almost exactly 2:1 in Britain's favour. This 2:1 ratio of cruisers was stated unequivocally in *Brassey's Naval Annual* for 1894.

We must lay down a battleship for every battleship begun by either of the powers that might act in concert against us, and for every cruiser built by them we must build two.[32]

The late Victorian navy did just this; it acquired cruisers in an almost exact 2:1 ratio against France and Russia. Analysis of the costs involved shows another interesting perspective on the reality of the late Victorian navy. The Naval Defence Act spent more on cruisers than battleships, some £10 million on cruisers and £8.4 million on battleships. The spending on cruisers between 1885 and 1907 amounted to £66.7 million, compared to £63 million on battleships. The post-1889 navy was in no sense a battleship navy or even a battleship-cruiser navy but can only properly be called a cruiser-battleship navy.[33]

The British response to the cruisers of France and Russia also needs comment. In the mid-1890s Russia built two very large armoured cruisers whose enormous size seriously worried the Admiralty. The *Rurik* and *Rossiya* were 11,690 tons and 13,675 tons respectively, much larger than their 6,000–8,500 ton predecessors.[34] Britain's reply came in May and July 1895, when the large protected cruisers *Powerful* and *Terrible* were launched. At 14,200 tons they had a battleship displacement. At 520 feet in length, they were considerably longer than any battleship built or building. They cost £750,000, three-quarters the cost of a battleship. Armour was 6 inches for deck, barbettes, turrets and casemates, with a 12-inch conning tower. This gave them 50 per cent of battleship protection. Engines of 25,000 horsepower, using Belleville water-tube boilers, propelled them at 22 knots, almost 2 knots faster than any existing British cruiser. Armament was two 9.2-inch and sixteen 6-inch guns.[35] They were completed just in time to see action in the Boer War and were initially considered a great success by the press and navy. It should be noted that these battleship-sized cruisers were designed and built when Jacky Fisher was Third Sea Lord and Controller, the man responsible for the navy's ships. There were more ominous portents in the *Powerful* and *Terrible*, particularly when seen against the development of the battlecruisers ten years later. In the *Powerful* and *Terrible*, some of the fatal confusion of battleship and cruiser designs can be seen. The big battleship-sized hulls, with the armour at 50 per cent of battleship standard, was ominous if such ships were to work with battleships in some future fleet action.

In 1893 the confusion of purpose concerning cruisers was brought into sharp relief. In a paper presented to the Institute of Naval Architects in

1893, Rear-Admiral Samuel Long discussed the function of cruisers and differentiated between the larger cruisers that might operate with a battle fleet and the smaller cruisers used for trade protection:

> Such a conspicuous difference in the size and offensive powers of cruisers points to the necessity of carefully distinguishing between the parts allotted to them in war, and would, it appears, justify attaching the name of battle-cruisers to many of them [...] There exists, in fact, a class of cruisers analogous to battle-ships. These might advantageously be termed 'battle-cruisers' [...] That powerful cruisers at the end of a telegraph wire will be more conducive to sea power than numerous small ones where ocean routes are concerned.[36]

It is possible that this is the first use of the term battlecruiser, defined as a cruiser able to operate with the battle fleet. As a generic type, the Admiralty continued to build large cruisers in considerable numbers, though not to quite such a size as the *Powerful* and *Terrible*, then France produced a bombshell in the shape of an entirely new-age armoured cruiser. The *Dupuy De Lôme* came close to being a masterpiece of naval architecture. She was laid down in 1888 and launched in 1890, but not completed until 1895 due to problems with her boilers, though she ran her first trials in 1893. In 1893 *Brassey's Naval Annual* described her in some detail:

> She is of 6,300 tons displacement, and her machinery should develop 10,000 horse-power with natural draught, and 14,000 horse-power with forced draught, with a corresponding speed of 20 Knots [...] She is an armoured cruiser in the most complete sense of the word, as she is protected by 4-inch armour over the whole of the hull proper, and over a part of the superstructure [...] the principal armament consists of two 19 cm (7.5-inch) guns and six 16-cm (6.25-inch) quick-firing guns.[37]

The technology elements that allowed such a remarkable warship to be built were the use of Schneider all-steel armour, triple expansion steam engines and breech-loaded guns, quick-firing in the case of the 16-cm (6.25-inch) guns. The strategic purpose of such a ship was not hard to discern; she was built specifically for commerce raiding and independent operations. This ship was proof that the ideas of the *Jeune École* and the desire to bring England to her knees by attacking maritime trade were still alive in French strategic thinking of the 1890s.[38] A further five rather smaller French armoured cruisers were built followed by the relatively enormous

11,092-ton *Jeanne d'Arc*, protected with nickel-steel Harvey armour. She was something of a failure – designed for 23 knots, she never made more than 21.8 knots.[39] Nevertheless, the French had a high opinion of her:

> A comparison between the *Jeanne d'Arc* and vessels of the Powerful and Diadem classes show that the English are less ingenious than ourselves in the matter of naval construction. To know how to unite a powerful armament with sufficient protection and high speed upon a small displacement is a veritable tour de force, and from this point of view it cannot be denied that the *Jeanne d'Arc*, notwithstanding her defects, is a chef d'oeuvre of naval architecture.[40]

The *Jeanne d'Arc* formed the basis for three succeeding classes of large armoured cruisers and the true function and purpose of these big armoured cruisers extended considerably beyond mere commerce raiding and independent operations in distant seas. *Brassey's Naval Annual 1899* discussed the second role for these ships in some detail:

> The role proposed for the Jeanne d'Arc is that of an advanced guard to a fleet of battleships, seeking for and maintaining touch with the enemy. Cruisers of this type are protected against destroyers by their speed and armament, and should be able to fight a battleship for a short time. It is claimed by the French constructors that the Jeanne d'Arc is more powerful than any cruiser afloat.[41]

The statement that cruisers 'should be able to fight a battleship for a short time', picks up on the views of Rear-Admiral Long, given six years earlier. Indeed, it is instructive to see the first stirrings of the battlecruiser role in the late nineteenth century, not just in British thinking concerning the role of large cruisers but also in the views of the Marine Français.

Worries about the weakness of British cruisers led to the building of true armoured cruisers. The Cressy-class armoured cruisers (six ships) were fitted with a six-inch belt (side armour) of Krupp cemented armour, as were the Drake class (four ships).[42] The size and cost of these ships was close to that of battleships. The Cressys were 12,000-ton ships and cost £800,000 each; while the Drakes were 14,000-ton battleship-sized ships costing just over £1 million apiece.[43]

Krupp cemented armour has already been discussed and had something close to two and a half times the stopping power of wrought iron; it was this that made well-protected armoured cruisers possible.[44] Naval

Drake
Good Hope
Leviathan
King Alfred

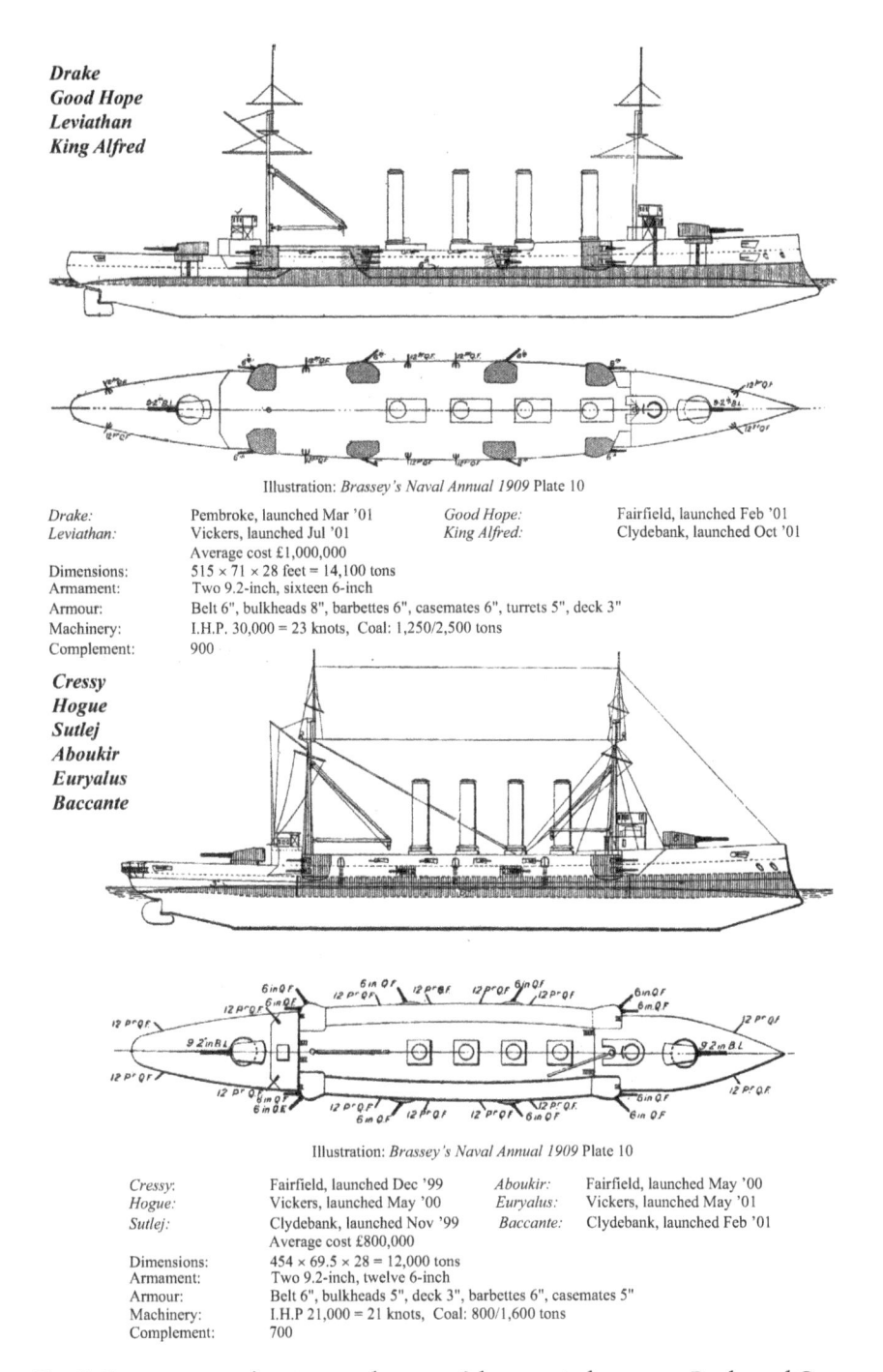

Illustration: *Brassey's Naval Annual 1909* Plate 10

Drake:	Pembroke, launched Mar '01	*Good Hope:*	Fairfield, launched Feb '01
Leviathan:	Vickers, launched Jul '01	*King Alfred:*	Clydebank, launched Oct '01
	Average cost £1,000,000		

Dimensions: 515 × 71 × 28 feet = 14,100 tons
Armament: Two 9.2-inch, sixteen 6-inch
Armour: Belt 6", bulkheads 8", barbettes 6", casemates 6", turrets 5", deck 3"
Machinery: I.H.P. 30,000 = 23 knots, Coal: 1,250/2,500 tons
Complement: 900

Cressy
Hogue
Sutlej
Aboukir
Euryalus
Baccante

Illustration: *Brassey's Naval Annual 1909* Plate 10

Cressy:	Fairfield, launched Dec '99	*Aboukir:*	Fairfield, launched May '00
Hogue:	Vickers, launched May '00	*Euryalus:*	Vickers, launched May '01
Sutlej:	Clydebank, launched Nov '99	*Baccante:*	Clydebank, launched Feb '01
	Average cost £800,000		

Dimensions: 454 × 69.5 × 28 = 12,000 tons
Armament: Two 9.2-inch, twelve 6-inch
Armour: Belt 6", bulkheads 5", deck 3", barbettes 6", casemates 5"
Machinery: I.H.P 21,000 = 21 knots, Coal: 800/1,600 tons
Complement: 700

Fig. 7 Large armoured cruisers at the turn of the twentieth century, Drake and Cressy class cruisers

development in foreign navies, allied to new technology, had forced a very expensive armoured cruiser policy on the British Admiralty. The building of considerable numbers of large armoured cruisers caused *Brassey's Naval Annual* to comment that 'power on the sea has been transferred rather to cruisers than battleships'.[45] A later edition of *Brassey's* gave the final word on the early twentieth-century confusion between battleships and armoured cruisers:

> Our latest armoured cruisers may be classed as battleships. They are the light division of our battle fleet. We are bound to have ships in the British Navy equal in speed to any under foreign flags. These fast battleships will be the defenders of commerce.[46]

The significance of these statements needs little further comment other than to point out that the confusion between battleships and cruisers did not occur suddenly with the first battlecruisers but was made as far back as 1893. Rear-Admiral Long is forgotten today because on 25 April 1893, just a month after presenting his paper, he was killed in a fall from his horse. Had he lived he might well have reached the top of the naval hierarchy and historians today would perhaps talk not of the Fisher era but of the Long era.

Jacky Fisher and the Royal Navy

Jacky Fisher and his wonder ship the *Dreadnought* have been for so long connected, to the exclusion of practically everything else, that it is often forgotten that Fisher's remarkable career was also defined by his deep involvement in the pre-dreadnought era and its origins. Admiral of the Fleet Sir John 'Jacky' Fisher, Earl of Kilverstone, would in his long life be dubbed a genius, a crank, a patriot and a deserter.[47] As his career progressed, his increasingly large numbers of detractors gave him the most unflattering nicknames: radical Jack Fisher, the hobgoblin Fisher, the Asiatic or even the mulatto. Fisher was without question the Royal Navy's most controversial admiral of the twentieth century.

Jacky Fisher was born in Ceylon in 1841, the son of a retired army officer who had taken up coffee planting, with a singular lack of success. The young Fisher was sent home to England at the age of six, never saw his father again and did not see his mother until he was in his twenties. In background he was a true child of the nineteenth-century British Empire. Through the good offices of his godmother Lady Hatton, a friend of Admiral Sir William Parker, the last of Nelson's captains, he obtained his nomination for the navy and joined his first ship *Calcutta* at Plymouth in July 1854. In March 1854, Britain had embarked on the Crimean War and the *Calcutta* was assigned to the Baltic.[48] Here then is the start of the Fisher legend – nominated for the navy aged 13 by the last of Nelson's captains, he saw active service within a year of joining.

In the Baltic, the *Calcutta*, a wooden sailing ship, took little part in events and was soon ordered home. Fisher's next ship was the *Agamemnon* and by May 1856 she was in the Black Sea.[49] In view of the proposed Baltic operations of World War I and the military disaster of the Dardanelles in 1915, operations in which Fisher, as First Sea Lord, participated heavily at the planning stage, it is worth remembering that Fisher was in the Baltic and Black Sea as a highly impressionable youth of 15.

The *Agamemnon* paid off, and Fisher transferred to a steam corvette, the *Highflyer*. For the next five years Fisher served on the China station and saw a good deal of real action at Fatshan Creek and in the taking of the Peiho forts. In January 1860 Fisher gained a first-class certificate in his promotion examinations, from midshipman to mate (mates were later known as sub-lieutenants). His time in China effectively blooded the young Jacky Fisher. He briefly commanded his first ship, the *Coromandel*, at the age of 19, and had proved his worth in countless situations. Now, after five years as midshipman and mate, he was promoted to acting lieutenant and his long march up the naval hierarchy had begun.

Back in England in August 1861, Fisher went on leave and passed his examination for promotion to lieutenant. He was immediately appointed to HMS *Excellent*, the navy's gunnery school. Fisher was more closely associated with HMS *Excellent* than any other navy shore establishment and his successes there marked him for promotion. His first spell of *Excellent* service was as an instructor and lasted until March 1863, when he was appointed gunnery officer of the *Warrior*, the first British ironclad. Fisher's time in the *Warrior* was a great success and he left a year later in March 1864 but was reappointed to HMS *Excellent* in the June of that year. The establishment had just been taken over by Captain Astley Cooper-Key, one of the Royal Navy's first career technocrats and destined to be First Naval Lord 1878–85. For the next few years Fisher attached himself to Cooper-Key and advanced his career as a technocrat.

In the period 1864–7, Fisher was mostly concerned with gunnery and gunnery experiments. In 1867 he turned his attention to torpedoes and mine warfare. These were outrigger 'spar' torpedoes, not free-running Whitehead torpedoes. Fisher immediately concluded that the torpedoes ought to be electrically detonated.

In 1866 Fisher married Francis Katherine Josephine Delves-Broughton, the daughter of the Rector of Bletchley. In 1869, at the early age of 28, Fisher was promoted to commander. He was happily married with two young children and hoped to stay at *Excellent* or the Admiralty. This was not to be, and he went out to China as commander, that is, the executive officer of the *Ocean*, a wooden-hulled ironclad of 3,715 tons. Fisher evidently read his bible a great deal and tended to judge people by their degree of religiosity. In a letter to his wife he passed the following comment on Vice-Admiral Sir Henry Kellett, Commander-in-Chief on the China station 1869–71, he said:

> I feel so very angry with the Admiral [. . .] He hasn't a spark of religion about him, never goes to Church by any chance, and this together with his being an Irishman makes me distrust him.[50]

In January 1872, the *Ocean* returned to England and Fisher was reappointed to *Excellent*, this time in charge of torpedo instruction. HMS *Vernon* was a 50-gun frigate selected as the torpedo school, and trials of the Whitehead torpedo were in progress. In April 1874 Dr Albert Hertz visited *Vernon*. The Hertz horn for mine detonation was in existence and was offered to the Admiralty, who were uninterested.[51] Now, at the age of 33, Fisher was promoted to captain.

From lieutenant to captain, Fisher held only two proper sea-going appointments, as gunnery lieutenant of the *Warrior* and commander of the *Ocean*. His main work had been at *Excellent* as gunnery, torpedo and mine warfare officer. Fisher then had some difficulty obtaining a sea-going appointment; he was a junior captain and young in the rank. The developing Near East Crisis 1876–8 gave him his chance. In November 1876, he was given temporary command of the *Pallas*, a small ironclad ram of 1,794 tons, and spent the next two months in the eastern Mediterranean. In April 1877 Fisher took command of the *Bellerophon*, the flagship of Vice-Admiral Sir Astley Cooper-Key on the America and West Indies station. Fisher handled his command in what became the typical Fisher style. For the first few months, his demonic energy demanded exercises morning, noon and night, then, as the ship came up to his demanding standards, things relaxed and his sense of humour was allowed full rein.

In early 1878 the Mediterranean fleet was sent to Constantinople, as detailed in Chapter 1. At home, a Particular Service Squadron was mobilised under Sir Astley Cooper-Key and Fisher was appointed his flag-captain aboard the ironclad *Hercules*. Afterwards he temporarily commanded the frigate *Valorous* and then *Pallas* again. *Pallas* was so decrepit that chain cable was passed under her to stop her armour plates falling off. In September 1879 he took command of the belted cruiser *Northampton*.[52] She was brand new but rather unsatisfactory in design: too weak to function as an ironclad and too slow for cruiser work.[53] Fisher's command of the *Northampton* was similar to the *Bellerophon*. The first few months were characterised by a shake up and lots of hard work, followed by an easing up and relaxation.[54] Most of the commission was spent on the America and West Indies station.

In January 1881, Fisher at last obtained the vital battleship command he needed if he were to reach flag rank. He was placed in command of HMS *Inflexible*, the first of the Royal Navy's *en echelon* battleships, which had taken seven and a half years to build. The *Inflexible* was a complex ship and shaking her down was a formidable task. Ratings were continually getting lost and a system of internal signposts had to be worked out. The *Inflexible* was the first ship with electric light and this caused early teething problems – one rating was killed by electric shock. Besides the largest guns and thickest armour, two 14-inch locomotive torpedoes were fitted above water and two submerged torpedo tubes were fitted at the bows. Additionally, two second-class torpedo boats were carried; there was much for Jacky Fisher to play with.[55] Then, in July 1882 the bombardment of Alexandria took place.

Fisher distinguished himself in the bombardment and afterwards commanded the Naval Brigade ashore with some distinction, but in the autumn of 1882, he contracted dysentery and was invalided home.[56] After a long period of recovery, he was appointed in command of HMS *Excellent*. Until he reached flag rank in 1891 he was to remain ashore virtually the entire time, and his sea-going career other than as a fleet commander was effectively over. As a captain he had three proper commands, *Bellerophon*, *Northampton* and *Inflexible*. Added to his time as a lieutenant in the *Warrior* and commander in the *Ocean*, these five sea-going spells took him to flag rank.

Fisher the Reformer 1883–96

The four-year period 1882–6 was crucial to Fisher's career as a technical innovator and a naval administrator. The years of naval reform had arrived and at the heart of reform was the vexed issue of naval ordnance. In 1879 the decision was taken that gave the navy breech-loaded guns. As captain of the *Excellent* Fisher was, more than any other individual, responsible for implementing that decision. Such a task could have easily broken the career of a lesser man. It is a measure of Fisher's very real stature that these reforms were carried through with vigour and success.

In November 1886, Fisher became Director of Naval Ordnance (DNO). His second period as a naval reformer now began and was to see the removal of all control by the military over gun supply. In 1879 a committee was set up to supervise gunnery experiments, and in December 1882 it was agreed that the navy should pay for gun mountings out of naval funds. It needs reiterating that the army was not entirely responsible for the gunnery problems; the system of ordnance supply set up after the Crimea was a cost-cutting exercise designed to keep defence spending at the lowest possible limit.[57] In the 1880s, with the emergence of big battleships with large-calibre breech-loaded guns, the post-Crimean ordnance supply system became obsolete.

Fisher was promoted to rear-admiral on 2 August 1890, but remained at the Admiralty as DNO. His last two years as DNO were concerned not only with ordnance for torpedo defence but with torpedo boat developments. Fisher briefly left the Admiralty in 1891 and became Admiral Superintendent of the Portsmouth dockyard. It was largely due to Fisher that the first of the Naval Defence Act battleships, *Royal Sovereign*, was completed in only two years eight months. This was a measure of the very real naval reform that had taken place in the dockyards, compared to the six to seven years building time for the Admiral class.[58]

On 2 February 1892 Fisher became Third Sea Lord and Controller of the Navy, and for the next five years was responsible for the navy's ships. In March that year the tenders for the first torpedo-boat destroyers were put out. Yarrows built *Havock* and *Hornet*, *Havock* having locomotive boilers and *Hornet* water-tube boilers for comparison.[59] *Hornet* proved the faster vessel. Fire-tube boilers consisted of tubes, surrounded by water through which passed the hot gases and the products of combustion. This system was not very efficient because the motion of the hot gases was parallel to the surface of the tubes. The alternative was to pass the water through the tubes and have the hot gases surround the tubes. This method was theoretically much more efficient and was known as the water-tube boiler. As early as 1850 the French boiler manufacturer Générateurs Belleville took out a patent on the water-tube system and fitted the new type of boiler to a small corvette.[60]

The French Navy pursued the water-tube boiler idea with considerable gusto and the battleship *Brennus* was the first battleship to have them.[61] In Britain water-tube boilers were a matter of discussion at both the Institute of Naval Architects and the Royal United Services Institution, with seven papers on water-tube boilers between 1894 and 1897.[62]

In the period 1895–8 further British trials were conducted in which five torpedo gunboats were reboilered with water-tube boilers, each supplied by a different contractor. These were Belleville, Babcock, Niclausse, Du Temple and Mumford.[63] The fact that a different water-tube boiler manufacturer was selected for each vessel shows the extent that the Admiralty were prepared to experiment. As a result of these trials, Belleville boilers were ordered for the large protected cruisers *Powerful* and *Terrible*.[64] This decision was also dictated by the knowledge that the Russian Navy were likely to adopt Belleville boilers for their large cruisers *Rurik* and *Rossiya*.[65]

When Jacky Fisher decided to adopt water-tube boilers the Belleville's were designed in France but built in Britain. They were more complicated than the older fire-tube boilers, needing careful supervision and even more careful stoking. During construction the addition of 'improvements' was never properly explained, causing further problems. For example, French practice taught that lime should be added to the feed water but this was ignored. Stoking the older fire-tube boilers simply involved throwing the maximum amount of coal onto the fire in the shortest possible time. The Belleville's needed small amounts of coal added to the fire on a continuous basis. The early Admiralty manual recommended practices that apparently reduced the horsepower by 25 per cent and only by giving up on the book could engineers obtain a reasonable performance from these boilers.[66] The first British battleships to receive them were the Canopus class, the first of which was laid down in 1896.

With their water-tube boilers the Canopus class battleships were an interesting departure in other ways, and sacrificed armour for speed. Indeed, one writer has termed them 'Queen Victoria's Battlecruisers'.[67] As Third Sea Lord and Controller, Fisher was deeply involved in the design parameters of these ships. On 13 May 1895 a meeting took place in his room at the Admiralty, with Sir William White (DNC) and the Director of Naval Intelligence present.[68] In the case of the Canopus class, Krupp cemented armour was adopted, a 25 per cent improvement over Harvey armour. With a 6-inch belt the Canopus class carried only 3,600 tons of armour compared to the 4,535 tons of the preceding Majestic class. These ships were not sheathed and coppered for tropical service, which gave a considerable saving in weight, and their engines developed 13,500 ihp compared to the 10,000 ihp of the Majestics.[69] This gave a 2-knot speed advantage, 18.3 knots compared to the 16.1 knots of the Majestics.

During his time as Controller, Fisher was happy to see armour sacrificed in the pursuit of speed. The Canopus class, fast but lightly armoured battleships, and the 22-knot battleship-sized cruisers *Powerful* and *Terrible*, faster than any British cruiser built to date, need no further comment. Ten years later Fisher's obsession with speed came to fruition in the battlecruisers, but many of the elements that defined Fisher and the dreadnought era were present in the 1890s. Indeed, any proper understanding of Fisher and the dreadnought era requires a careful examination of Fisher in the pre-dreadnought era.

The first three periods of the Fisher reform era were over. As Captain of *Excellent*, Director of Naval Ordnance and then Third Sea Lord and Controller he had been at the heart of the naval reforms that transformed the Victorian Royal Navy into a steam, steel and electricity navy, the end product of an industrial society.

Fisher as a Fleet Commander 1896–1903

In June 1894, Fisher became a KCB and in May 1896 was promoted to vice-admiral and hoisted his flag in the *Renown*, as commander-in-chief of the America and West Indies station.[70] Fisher remained nearly three years as commander-in-chief. His performance as a fleet commander exactly mirrored his periods as a ship commander. In the initial stages, demonic energy was aimed at bringing every ship up to a high standard of proficiency. Exercises were conducted regularly, with emphasis on fleet evolutions and squadron handling. At this stage Fisher moved towards ideas for more far-reaching naval reforms and actively encouraged officer specialists to give him their comments on improving naval efficiency. In March 1899, Fisher was selected as Britain's naval representative to the Hague Conference. This conference was supposed to limit armaments, mitigate the horrors of war and provide arbitration for the settlement of international disputes.

The conference, in common with most peace conferences, discussed war not peace and nothing very much came out of it. Fisher and Sir Julian Pauncefote, the leader of the British delegation, supported the principle of arms limitation, the mitigation of the horrors of war and international arbitration but no real progress was made towards arms limitation. Agreement in principle that gas shells would not be used was reached but was largely ignored in World War I. The only real benefit to come out of the conference was the setting up of a permanent Court of Arbitration in The Hague.

After the conference, Fisher was appointed Commander-in-Chief Mediterranean, the premier command in the Royal Navy. Fisher was determined to make this the most memorable command of all time. His period in the West Indies had given him vital sea-going experience as a fleet commander after 14 years at the Admiralty. In his first three periods of reform Fisher had been responsible for ordnance, ordnance supply and then fleet equipment. As commander-in-chief he intended to use these new weapons.

All accounts of Fisher's arrival in the Mediterranean agree that it was epoch making. The galvanisation of the fleet began with a cruise to the Levant. Within a year the old obsessions with paintwork, gleaming brass etc. were gone. Fisher is principally remembered today for his concentration on fleet gunnery. In this matter he was strongly supported by many of the rising stars of the expanding navy. In particular, the name of Percy Scott stands out as the man who revolutionised gun practice.

In view of what was to follow in the years 1906–10 and the Fisher–Beresford split, the following incidents must be related. Beresford has already appeared in this story in command of HMS *Condor* at Alexandria and as an injudicious leaker of classified information to the press while Fifth Sea Lord. Now, as a rear admiral, he became second in command to Fisher. Beresford wanted to refresh his memory on fleet manoeuvres. He went ashore early one morning with some of his crew and exercised them on the naval parade ground at Corradino Heights, Malta. The men were spread out, each representing a ship and 'manoeuvred' in line ahead, line abreast etc. Fisher happened to see this and sent a peremptory plain language signal demanding to know why Beresford was ashore without the permission of the c-in-c. The signal was read on the bridge of every ship in the fleet and amounted to a public humiliation for Beresford. The anger and bitterness took a long time to subside. Unfortunately, the 'Corradino' incident was compounded a few months later. On returning to Malta from exercises Fisher would berth first in his flagship *Renown*. He had made it his habit to walk up the 'Barraca' and watch each ship negotiate the entrance to the harbour and turn 180 degrees before berthing. The harbour was narrow and it was a difficult test of nerves and seamanship. Beresford's flag-captain, R.S. Lowry, was not a good ship handler. He was supposed to secure to two buoys in Bighi Bay, the outer anchorage, but made a mess of it and stuck his ship across the harbour entrance. Fisher lost his temper and signalled in plain language: 'Your flagship is to proceed to sea and come in again in a seamanlike manner.'

Fisher had openly reprimanded his subordinates before and Beresford's predecessor, Rear-Admiral Gerard Noel, had suffered the same treatment. Not to be intimidated, he had signalled: 'I am coming to see you in my frock-coat and sword.'[71] In other words a very formal plain language interview was to follow. What was said was not recorded but in the case of Beresford the rebuke left a lasting bitterness between the two men.

During his tenure in the Mediterranean, Fisher achieved three things. He made a 12-knot fleet subject to all sorts of mechanical malfunctions into a 15-knot fleet without breakdowns.[72] He made the first moves towards longer-range gunnery and he gave a good deal of thought to the French fleet at Toulon, with its emphasis on torpedo warfare. The fear was that the numerically weaker French fleet operating in conjunction with torpedo boats in flotilla strength might be an effective match for the British Mediterranean fleet. This fear was further exacerbated by the introduction of gyroscopic control for torpedoes, which effectively tripled their range from 600 to nearly 2,000 yards. Much of the impetus for long-range gunnery came from the belief that battleships should operate outside effective torpedo range.[73]

In 1901 Fisher began to look to his own future. He became a full admiral in 1901 and badly wanted the position of First Naval Lord, but Admiral Lord Walter Kerr obtained the job. Fisher considered retirement or perhaps joining an armaments firm such as Armstrong's but he was looked on favourably by the First Lord of the Admiralty, Lord Selborne, who offered him the job of Second Sea Lord.

Fisher and Naval Reform 1902–6

Fisher was offered the job and accepted his new role as Second Sea Lord, a junior post for a full admiral. He arrived at the Admiralty on 10 June 1902 and commenced his next period of reform. At this time officers entered the navy at the age of 14 to 15-and-a-half. They spent two years at the Britannia training establishment, which consisted of two old wooden battleships, *Britannia* and *Hindustan*, moored on the River Dart below the present Royal Naval College. After two years at Britannia the cadets were appointed as midshipmen to sea-going ships. Surviving RUSI journal articles show just how little agreement there was concerning officer education.[74] Fisher's idea was to lower the age of entry to 13 and bring entry into the navy in line with public school entry, not an unreasonable proposal in the social and political context of 1902.

At this time the status of engineers was low. Over half the complement of a ship might be engine room ratings, yet engineer officers lacked executive status. The recruitment and training of engineers had gone through several stages culminating in 1880 with the establishment of the Royal Naval Engineering College at Keyham. The engineer cadets were recruited from a social level supposedly comparable to deck officers.[75] Students entered between the ages of 14 and 17 and underwent five years of engineering training. Emphasis was placed on sports such as rugby and cricket and each year 'blood' matches were played against deck cadets from *Britannia*.[76] In many respects the engineers received a much better education than their deck counterparts, yet the 'engineer problem' worsened year by year. Engineers had wardroom status but lacked executive status. They enjoyed pay equal to deck officers and high quality training but this did little to compensate for the fact that many seamen officers considered engineers 'lascars with a bottle of oil'.[77]

Fisher's proposal was to give full executive status to engineer officers and to integrate the deck, marine and engineering branches. He also wanted to go one step further and make engineer and deck officers interchangeable with common entry and common training for the first four years. More controversially the Fisher–Selborne proposals entertained the prospect of engineers commanding ships. The first two years of common training would be at Osborne, the Royal residence on the Isle of Wight, now turned into a sort of naval public school. The next two years training would be at Dartmouth, where the old wooden battleships were being replaced by a modern building. As sub-lieutenants, the newly-trained junior officers would be distributed between the three principal branches of the navy: Executive, Engineer and Marine. His proposals may be summarised as follows.

Age

13	Entry into Osborne.
15	Enters college at Dartmouth.
17	Joins training ship for seven months.
17¾	Joins navy for three years.
20¾	Goes through shore courses for sub-lieutenant lasting nine months.
21½ to 22	Finishes courses and goes to sea for a little over a year.
22⅔ to 24	Commences special training in engineering, marine officers' duties, or other specialist work.
24¼ to 27	Goes to sea as a specialist officer.

After about 27½ may present himself for examination as a commander in the executive line.[78]

The idea of common entry and training was just about acceptable to the more conservative senior officers but the notion that engineers could rise to command ships was total anathema, though interestingly this was largely the scheme introduced with great success in the United States Navy. Howbeit, the semi-executive status given to engineers in 1903 was a huge and necessary advance in status.[79] Interestingly, Lord Charles Beresford approved of the scheme:

> There is no reason why Lieutenants (E) should not be just as good and useful experts in their speciality as the gunnery, torpedo and navigating Lieutenants of the present day, without in the slightest degree detracting from their ability to become excellent executive officers. In fact, no reason can be adduced to show that they would not be quite capable of commanding ships and fleets as their brother officers.[80]

In truth the Fisher–Selborne scheme was a failure, with less than 6 per cent of Dartmouth midshipmen volunteering for the engineering branch. The 1914–18 war showed that the amalgamation of the engineering and deck departments was a mistake. It was impractical for an officer to cover all the ground required. Indeed, in 1903 the engineers pointed out that the study and practice of naval engineering needed a lifetime's devotion.[81] The problem with Fisher the reformer was that he could see the necessity for reform and he had a reasonable vision of the final objective. What he could not see were the intermediate steps necessary to arrive at the outcome.

Fisher also introduced reforms for the lower-deck engineers. Engine room artificers (ERAs) were introduced as far back as 1868 and in 1903

Fisher proposed a scheme for training boy artificers. The training consisted of a four-year course after which the boys were rated ERA fifth-class and given the rank of petty officer second class.[82] In addition to the improvement in the status of engineers, 100 senior warrant officers were promoted to lieutenant in the executive, engineer and carpenter branches, something close to revolution in the eyes of many senior officers. As First Sea Lord in 1905, Fisher greatly improved the conditions of ratings. Until 1905, allotments were paid to a rating's dependants while he was away on service. A proportion of this allotment money was retained by the Admiralty as insurance against death or desertion. This iniquitous system was abolished and provision allowances were paid to men on leave. Stokers were given a career structure and could rise to warrant officer rank. Training facilities were provided and mechanicians as a class came into being. Abolition of the system of feeding used at this time gave an able seaman about seven pence a day extra money. On a full rate of 1s 8d a day, this was an effective 35 per cent pay rise. Terms of service and pensions were also greatly improved.[83]

Fisher's reforms in lower-deck personnel and manning were of even greater benefit than those concerning officers. Analysing his lower-deck reforms as a collective whole produces some interesting conclusions. First, they acknowledged the changing world of the 1900s. Seamen were no longer illiterate and many were familiar with trade union and labour representation ashore. The changes to the status of engineers and the rise of warrant officers to commissioned rank acknowledged that in the late Victorian navy a new class of technicians had emerged. These technicians, both officers and ratings, were essential to the working of the steam navy, as ships increased rapidly in complexity.

Fisher at Portsmouth 1903–4

In 1903 Lord Walter Kerr was coming to the end of his term as First Naval Lord and there was a great deal of opposition to Fisher replacing him. Kerr and Fisher did not get on well and many senior officers saw Fisher as a reformer whose ideas were often erratic and ill-conceived. Consequently Fisher accepted the post of Commander-in-Chief Portsmouth. This was a highly paid appointment and carried the highest 'table money' (expenses) of any position in the navy.[84]

At Portsmouth the fledgling submarine service came under his jurisdiction. Much has been made of Fisher's supposed uncanny insight into submarine development, particularly the view that they would become the capital ship of the future. As far back as the 1860s Fisher had been not just a gunnery expert but a torpedo specialist as well; in 1876 he had witnessed trials of a new small torpedo designed by Robert Whitehead himself.[85]

Captain Reginald Bacon was Inspecting-Captain of submarine boats and the first five Vickers-built Holland boats were now operational. Fisher had a considerable amount of contact with Bacon while Second Naval Lord and gained a reasonable grasp of current submarine capabilities as a result. For those who want an example of Fisher's prescience, in May 1903 he delivered a speech to the Royal Academy:

> The submarine-boat and wireless telegraphy. When they are perfected we do not know what a revolution will come about. In their inception they were weapons of the weak. Now they loom large as weapons of the strong. Will any fleet be able to be in narrow waters? Is there the slightest fear of invasion with them, even for the most extreme pessimist.[86]

During his time at Portsmouth, Fisher engineered his appointment as First Naval Lord. He had always been on good terms with royalty, particularly the queen. Fisher's relations with her son Edward VII were even better. In February 1904 Edward VII stayed at Admiralty House Portsmouth. The visit was an outstanding success and Fisher secured the personal support of the monarch in his drive to obtain the position he so desperately wanted. Lord Selborne, the First Lord, was in basic agreement over Fisher's personnel reforms but this was not the reason Selborne wanted Fisher as First Naval Lord. The naval estimates had gone up year by year, from £22.5 million in 1897–8, to £41.7 million in 1904–5. The Chancellor of the Exchequer, Sir Michael Hicks-Beech, was desperate to get the escalating naval budget under control. The Boer War had been hideously expensive and the economy was in recession with tax receipts down. Fisher was able to promise naval economies and this was the real reason he was offered the top job. Fisher was duly appointed professional head of the navy on 20 October 1904, not 21 October, Trafalgar Day, as most sources state. His first action was to change his title from First Naval Lord to First Sea Lord.

Perspectives: The 'New' British Navy of the 1890s

All navies were 'new' in the 1890s, as much as anything else because they were the end product of the steel and electricity technology revolution.

THE PRE-DREADNOUGHT ERA IN THE 1890s

There can be no question that naval competition encouraged the development of naval technology. The demand for improved armour, ordnance and machinery produced battleship classes each of which was a considerable improvement over its predecessors. Constant technological innovation drove ships only ten or 12 years old towards obsolescence and this generated a requirement for yet more battleships.

In the 1890s Britain needed a large Mediterranean Squadron, able to deal with France and Russia in combination, a reasonably large Channel Squadron plus first reserve ships and a battleship orientated China Squadron, with four or five first-class battleships on that station, made necessary by French and Russian ships in eastern seas. It did not matter how many battleships Britain built, there were never enough and each addition to Britain's building programme ensured the expansion of someone else's programme. The Naval Defence Act was supposed to provide Britain with a navy beyond challenge, but in this it signally failed and instead initiated an era of naval competition.

In 1897 the British fleet presented itself for Queen Victoria's Diamond Jubilee review of the fleet. Seventeen new battleships had been completed, eight Naval Defence Act ships and nine Spencer programme ships. From the French point of view every point and detail of weakness in their fleet was exposed for all to see. A French naval engineer Maxime Laubeuf penned a report on the British Navy at the review. The deepest impression made on Laubeuf was the uniformity of the fleet in terms of overall design. On a class-by-class basis, the armament disposition and even the position of masts and funnels did not vary from ship to ship.[87] In the post-1889 period it is unquestionably the case that Britain produced a series of battleship classes that were superior to anything produced anywhere in the world, which explains why they were so widely copied.

As the older ironclads were phased out, so only the first-class battleships were counted towards the two-power standard. This led to a mind set addicted to 'thinking in terms of battleships' and always the insatiable demand for more ships. This mind set was transmitted to Britain's naval rivals, who also built large numbers of new ships, all identifiably pre-dreadnoughts. It has already been stated that in 1898, nine years after the Naval Defence Act and a year in which supplementary naval estimates were considered necessary, Britain possessed, built or building, 47 of the new-age ships to 25 Russian and 22 French. After nine years of battleship building Britain was exactly where she started in regard to the two-power standard. In addition, there were three powerful new navies to be considered, those of America, Japan and Germany.

At Fashoda in 1898, just a year after the Diamond Jubilee fleet review, France chose not to confront Britain over the Sudan issue. Exactly how much this was to do with Britain's 'new' navy is open to question but it can be argued that no European power was ever going to confront Britain over naval and non-European matters.[88] On this basis the Naval Defence Act and the Spencer programme were a considerable overreaction to the position the late Victorians found themselves in. Rather than ending naval competition with a navy beyond reach in terms of overall strength, the Naval Defence Act added fuel to the already expanding world of naval armaments, exactly the opposite of its intent.

Then there was that extraordinary character Jacky Fisher. From the time he leaked information from the shelved Carnarvon Commission reports to the *Pall Mall Gazette*, Fisher was deeply involved in the transformation of the Victorian Royal Navy. As Captain of the navy's gunnery school, HMS *Excellent*, as Director of Naval Ordnance, as Third Sea Lord and Controller, as Commander-in-Chief at Portsmouth, again as Third Sea Lord and Controller and then as a fleet commander on the North America and West Indies station, later in the Mediterranean, he exerted a tremendous influence on the development of the Royal Navy in the pre-dreadnought era.

Fisher was a dynamic character who, at an early stage in his career, had hitched his star to the new-age steel, steam and electricity navy. He had an absolute belief in his ability to understand technology but he was fallible and made mistakes, sometimes serious mistakes. The perhaps too early, if not to say precipitate, adoption of water-tube boilers, the battleship-sized cruisers *Powerful* and *Terrible* and the failure of the Selborne scheme all tell their own story.

3

The New Navies of the 1890s

Prelude: The Development of Extra-European Navies

For three-quarters of a century after Waterloo Britain's main potential adversaries were France and Russia. Neither power was capable, either individually or collectively, of mounting an effective challenge. Maintaining the two-power standard was fairly straightforward and Britain's powerful industrial base ensured that any French or Russian building programme could be countered with ease. This started to change in the 1890s when three new navies appeared on the scene, those of America, Japan and Germany. For the first time there was an extra-European dimension to the world's navies. Exactly how Britain handled this extra-European situation is the subject of this chapter.

The 'Dark Ages' of the American Navy

In America after the civil war there was little real attempt at warship construction. During the late 1860s and early 1870s the American Navy scrapped, sold or mothballed most of its immense wartime fleet of 650 ships. Indeed, the period between the Civil War and 1880 has been called the 'Dark Ages' of the American Navy.[1] In the 1870s Congress would not vote money for new ships, only to repair old ones. In 1874 an attempt was made by the Secretary of the Navy to build five sea-going monitors by replacing the rotten wooden hulls of the four civil war era Miantonomoh class and by completing the monitor *Puritan*. Congress duly voted the funds but a major scandal broke when it was discovered that new ships were being constructed under the guise of repairs. The first of the 'reconstructed' ships did not commission until 1891 by which time the very low freeboard monitor type was effectively obsolete.[2] In an 1881 report by the British naval attaché at Washington, the American Navy was described in the following terms:

> American ordnance is considered out of date. The Dahlgren smooth bore guns were all built prior to 1863. No new vessels have been started since 1867. The wooden ironclads Miantonomah, Monadnock and Terror have become iron vessels. Congress says 'No new vessels' so the US Navy has got around this by completely rebuilding old vessels to obsolete designs. 'Even when there is no plank remaining of the original hull.'[3]

The attaché went on to say that no new vessels were contemplated and no war vessels worth the name were in commission except perhaps the *Trenton*. American naval construction started again in the 1880s at a cruiser level. In 1883 the *Atlanta, Boston, Chicago* and *Dolphin*, known as the ABCD ships, were commenced.[4] The first three ships were in the 4,000-ton range and mounted 8-inch, 6-inch and 5-inch guns.[5] With a speed of 14–15 knots they were a fairly successful attempt at cruiser design and the first steel built ships in the American Navy. It was particularly the case that the design of *Chicago* was heavily influenced by the British twin-screw Leander-class cruisers. Four more cruisers were planned for 1887, the *Newark, San Francisco, Charlestown* and *Baltimore*. These cruisers were approximately the same size as the ABCD ships, and mounted the same calibre armament as their predecessors but with a higher speed of 18–19 knots and a protected deck. These ships were a great improvement over the ABCD ships and again, all were heavily influenced by British designs.

The American Navy and the Development of Strategic Doctrine

In the era before Alfred Thayer Mahan, American naval policy was weighted heavily in favour of *guerre de course*. In wartime the merchant ships of any potential enemy would be subject to capture. There was a strongly held belief that raiders such as the *Alabama* would do much more damage to any potential foe than unwieldy and expensive ironclads. Beyond *guerre de course* the purpose of the navy was coast defence. Home ports would be defended against invasion using monitors and mines. Artillery would be used in conjunction with the coast defence naval forces.[6] In 1889 the Secretary to the Navy, Benjamin Tracy, submitted a lengthy report that for the first time justified an American battle-fleet navy.

The defence of the United States absolutely requires the creation of a fighting force. So far the increase has been mainly in the direction of unarmoured cruisers. These vessels, while useful in deterring commercial states from aggression, and as an auxiliary to secure celerity and efficiency in larger operations, do not constitute a fighting force even when it is intended exclusively for defence. To meet the attack of ironclads, ironclads are indispensable. To carry on even a defensive war with any hope of success we must have armoured battleships [. . .] we must have a fleet of battleships that will beat off the enemy's fleet on its approach.[7]

One may question why in 1889, the American Navy turned suddenly in the direction of a battlefleet navy. In 1894 a British Naval Intelligence assessment of American naval policy from 1883 onwards, quoted the remarks of Mr Herbert, Secretary of the Navy:

The military value of a commerce-destroying fleet is easily overrated. Cruisers directed against an enemy's wealth afloat are capable of doing great damage. They create consternation among merchants and worry the people against whose property they are directed, but unsupported by ships of the line, their operations are, perhaps, never decisive of a war.[8]

Both Tracey's and Herbert's reports directly refuted the traditional American policy of *guerre de course*, attacking an enemy's trade and commerce. From 1889 America was turning decisively towards a battle-fleet navy. An Intelligence Office was established which developed into the Office of Naval Intelligence. Naval attachés were sent abroad to report on foreign progress. Selected American naval cadets were trained in England and by 1885 eight America cadets had trained at Greenwich and Glasgow.[9] There was, in fact, a considerable technology transfer from Britain to America as a result. In 1884 a Naval War College was founded at Newport, Rhode Island. The founders were Rear-Admiral Stephen B. Luce, William T. Sampson and Caspar F. Goodrich. The college studied tactics, strategy, international law, naval history and policy.[10] In 1886 Luce brought Alfred Thayer Mahan to Newport as resident theorist and it is from this time that the American Navy developed doctrine.

Mahan's great contribution to doctrine was building the science of naval warfare in the steam age. He then joined operational doctrine – that is, naval operations – to a national commitment for a big navy. Naval force, naval strategy and national policy were conjoined. Mahan aligned operations with culture, geography and economics and this ensured that the American Navy could focus on the building of a battle-fleet navy. In the age of Mahan the American Navy became embedded in the political and social context of the nation.[11]

In 1890 the first of his books, *The Influence of Seapower upon History*, was published. This was followed by *The Influence of Seapower upon the French Revolution and Empire*, in two volumes (1892). Mahan's arguments and ideas were designed to encourage a sceptical American public that investment in a big navy was a good idea, with substantial long-term benefits. A large battle fleet was the essential element, used either against the enemy battle fleet or as a weapon of blockade. Mahan's arguments can be best presented from his own words:

> Seapower [...] belongs to the unchangeable or unchanging order of things, remaining the same, in cause and effect, from age to age. They belong, as it were, to the order of nature, of whose stability we hear so much in our own day; whereas tactics, using as its instruments the weapons made by man, shares in the change and progress of the race from generation to generation. From time to time the superstructure of tactics has to be altered or wholly torn down; but the old foundations of strategy so far remain, as though laid upon a rock.[12]

To the growing band of late nineteenth-century navalists, the idea of sea power unchangeable and unchanging was particularly attractive and a justification for a large navy. Then there were the arguments about the instruments, the manufactured weapons. This further reinforced the need for more, better and bigger battleships. In Mahan's view, 'command of the sea' did not imply actual ownership of the oceans. Logically, this was impossible and strategically unnecessary. No nation can 'own' the sea. The sea cannot be developed or bought. The sea is a medium through which one travels. In Mahan's own words:

> The first and most obvious light in which the sea presents itself from the political and social point of view is that of a great highway; or better, perhaps, of a wide common, over which men may pass in all directions, but on which some well worn paths show that controlling reasons have led them to choose certain lines of travel rather than others.[13]

To preserve a nation's traffic along these well worn paths, to deny the paths to the enemy is to possess 'command of the sea'.[14]

A modern reading of Mahan suggests that he believed naval supremacy, then and in the future, would be wielded by a transnational consortium of naval powers acting in defence of a global system of free trade to the mutual benefit of the participating powers.[15] Mahan saw the transnational consortium as very much an Anglo-American affair and in 1902 he wrote that, 'The British Empire is in external matters our natural though not our formal ally'.[16] It is interesting that Mahan did not consider attacks on trade totally irrelevant, rather they were modes of naval warfare that were inferior to the role of the battle fleet. The true role of the battle fleet was interdiction of the enemy's trade, preferably through the medium of blockade. He argued that it was not:

> the taking of individual ships or convoys, be they few or many, that strikes down the money power of the nation; it is the possession of that overbearing power on the sea which drives the enemy's flag from it, or allows it to appear only as a fugitive; and which be controlling the great common, closes the highways by which commerce moves to and from the enemy's shores.[17]

It is also interesting to note that Mahan, almost alone amongst the naval theorists of the late-nineteenth century, did not reject convoy as the primary means of trade protection:

> A convoy is doubtless a much larger object than a single ship, but vessels thus concentrated in place and time are more apt to pass wholly unseen than the same number sailing independently, and so scattered over wide expanses of sea.[18]

The First American Battleships

In 1883 the Brazilian Navy took delivery of an *en echelon* battleship built in Britain to an advanced design by Samuda, at Poplar. The *Riachuelo* was just over 6,000 tons full load displacement. She mounted four 9.2-inch guns placed *en echelon* amidships in the manner of HMS *Inflexible*. The hull was entirely steel. Steel-faced compound armour gave her a belt 11 inches thick and 250 feet in length.[19] This one ship was something of a technological tour de force, as good as anything possessed by the Royal Navy. A second *en echelon* ship named the *Aquidaban* was also built and the Brazilian Navy took delivery in 1887, four years after the *Riachuelo*.[20] When completed these two ships were, by a significant margin, the most powerful warships in the western hemisphere. They made a deep impression on American thinking in the mid-1880s.

There could be no question of America allowing this situation to continue and the result was the first real attempt at battleship construction, the *Texas* of 1886. Designed by John Barrow in England (the John Barrow of Barrow Shipbuilding), she mounted two 12-inch guns each in two *en echelon* turrets, very similar to the *Riachuelo* and *Aquidaban*, and at 6,500 tons was very nearly the same size as the Brazilian ships.[21] She was not completed until 1895, when the *en echelon* type was obsolete in European navies.[22] Her half sister the *Maine*, similar in size to the *Texas*, really an armoured cruiser version of the battleship, was armed with four 10-inch and six 6-inch guns. When she blew up in Havana harbour in 1898, almost certainly due to unstable cordite in her magazines, this was taken as the *casus belli* for the Spanish-American war.

In 1890, Congress voted money for three 'coast-line, sea-going battle-ships', *Indiana, Massachusetts* and *Oregon*.[23] In these ships the classic late-Victorian battleship form was adopted, a vessel with two twin turrets, one forward and one aft. These were ships of 10,228 tons, armed with four 13-inch and eight 8-inch guns. Over-gunned for their displacement and lacking a counterweight to offset the gun barrels, these ships listed in the direction the guns were trained. They were not very successful, with too much attempted on a limited displacement, but with forced draught they could make 17 knots. The freeboard forward was only 11 feet 4 inches.[24]

The Chilean civil war (January to August 1891) nearly involved the United States through the medium of a steamer the *Iata*. The *Iata* was sent to the United States to collect armaments but arrived in San Francisco before permission had been given for the arms shipments to be loaded. A United States marshal was placed onboard but *Iata* slipped her moorings, proceeded to sea, took the arms from the schooners and put the official ashore. The Americans took this as a violation of their flag rights and the United States government arrested the *Iata*.[25] The significance of the Chilean civil war on American naval policy lay in the fact that the Chilean Navy was equipped almost entirely with British-built ships of often superior design to anything possessed by the United States.

Shortly after the end of the Chilean civil war a Brazilian naval revolt occurred. The revolution did not succeed but the revolutionaries managed to interfere with neutral trade. The result was the threat of intervention by the United States. Once again the United States had nearly been drawn into conflict in South America, her navy facing powerful, technically advanced warships built in Britain, in the form of *Riachuelo* and *Aquidaban*.

One further American battleship was completed before the Spanish-American war, the *Iowa*, a distinct improvement on the *Indiana* and at 11,410 tons with the same armament, she had a forecastle deck extending to the rear of the after 12-inch turret. Five more battleships were laid down, none of which was ready by 1898 and the Spanish-American war. The *Kearsage* and *Kentucky* were ships of 11,500 tons armed with four 13-inch and four 8-inch guns. The 8-inch turrets were fixed on top of the 13-inch turrets, a very unsatisfactory arrangement, as the 8-inch guns had to be trained with the 13-inch. The reason for this was a desire to keep the draught of these ships to 23 feet, so that they could operate in the shallow waters of the Gulf of Mexico. These two ships were the first US battleships to make extensive use of electrical machinery for everything, including gun training.[26] The next three ships, *Alabama*, *Illinois* and *Wisconsin*, were slightly larger at 11,552 tons, armed with four 13-inch and fourteen 6-inch guns.

The Spanish-American War

With the magazine explosion of the *Maine* in Havana harbour came the Spanish-American War and the vexed issue of Cuba in American politics. From the time of Jefferson, America had regarded Cuba as a legitimate American interest, to be purchased or taken by main force.[27] With the loss of the *Maine* in Havana harbour, the Americans at last had an excuse to invade. At the outbreak of the war the US had 53 modern warships, with five battleships built and five building. The Spanish government had made no real preparations for a naval war and in 1898 had only three armoured cruisers.[28] At the start of the war the battleship *Oregon* was in San Francisco and had to sail 13,400 miles around Cape Horn to the West Indies. The point was not lost that, had a Panama Canal been in place, the steaming distance would have been just 4,600 miles.[29]

Naval operations took place in both the Atlantic and Pacific. In the Pacific Commodore Dewey commanded the Asiatic fleet and knew before the war even started that the Philippines would be his first target. His was primarily a cruiser force consisting of six ships.[30] At the outbreak of war he was at Hong Kong and the British, hearing of the declaration of war, politely asked him to leave, thus preserving their neutrality.[31] Arriving at Manila Bay the American task force and the Spanish fleet were soon closely engaged. Dewey took his small fleet past the Spanish guns five times at ranges from 5,000 to 2,000 yards. In fact neither side had any real hitting ability and Dewey's ships only started to score hits at close range. In less than five hours of fighting the Spaniards surrendered.[32]

In the Atlantic the Americans took Cuba by blockading its western side and Havana. The Spanish sent out a relieving force consisting of four armoured cruisers and three destroyers. Another squadron was ready to support the Philippines, revealing the real Spanish difficulty, the need for two task forces plus sufficient ships for the coast defence of Spain itself. The relieving squadron made it to Cuba and slipped through the American blockade lines only to be bottled up in harbour. After six weeks, at the end of which the US army ashore was able to bombard the Spanish ships from land, the Spanish made a break for freedom. They aimed to go to Puerto Rico for coal. In fact they were caught by the Americans and the Spanish force was destroyed completely.[33]

In the peace negotiations that followed the United States took Cuba, Puerto Rica and the Philippines. They annexed the Hawaiian Islands, Eastern Samoa and Wake Island.[34] In the 1890s the American Navy became a formidable force to be reckoned with. The best American warships were every bit as good as their European counterparts. In a surge of naval enthusiasm, the Americans doubled their battleship strength; six in 1898 became 12 by 1905, with 13 more built by 1908.

British Policy Towards the United States

By the 1880s American trade was growing rapidly. The continental United States was now settled and becoming heavily industrialised. By 1890 there were 166,703 miles of railroad.[35] The Civil War had shown just how powerful the United States was becoming. The size of the Union army dwarfed Britain's army and Canada could no longer be held in the face of a sustained American hostility. Such a war was not considered possible and would have been financially disastrous to both sides.

In the 1880s the rapidly developing American steam navy required coaling bases. In 1878 America signed a treaty with Samoa and established a coaling base. A trading agreement was also made and in 1879 Germany and Britain obtained the same trading rights. The interests of the three powers often conflicted, and in 1889 America found herself in a diplomatic imbroglio with Britain and Germany over Samoa.[36] In January 1889 British, German and American warships were all in Apia harbour, Samoa, when a hurricane struck. Only HMS *Calliope* escaped. With full power on her compound steam engines she was just able to work her way to windward and escape, and as a result, throughout the rest of her long career was known as 'hurricane jumper'. Of the six German and American warships, four were wrecked, with some loss of life.[37] Later in the year at a Berlin conference the three powers agreed to the neutrality of the islands and established a tripartite protectorate.[38]

Britain had a long history of difficult relations with America. The burning of the White House in the war of 1812 was still remembered. There were real Anglo-American diplomatic problems over certain specific issues the first of which was the American Civil War Confederate raiders *Alabama*, *Florida* and *Shenandoah*. The *Alabama* was the most famous and captured some 65 vessels, valued with their cargoes at $4 million dollars. The *Alabama* was built in Britain at Laird's shipyard and completed in 1862, but not actually armed there and at the time this was technically legal.[39] The *Alabama* was about to be detained in Britain but made good her escape before she could be detained. The subsequent career of this one ship almost brought the Federal United States into conflict with Britain. The Union felt itself entitled to compensation for the damage inflicted on American property. The Americans felt that the British government had been remiss in allowing the *Alabama* and other Confederate cruisers to depart and supplying them with coal.[40] In 1871 a commission met in Washington and agreed to impartial adjudication in Geneva. The tribunal met in December 1871 and Britain was ordered to pay £3,229,166.[41] Britain accepted the adjudication and in doing so adopted a diplomacy aimed at rapprochement with the United States.

The next diplomatic imbroglio was Venezuela. From the 1860s onwards, British banks and financial institutions lent large sums of money to Venezuela which endlessly defaulted on the loan repayments. In 1895 the American president, Grover Cleveland, took up the case of Venezuela and its claim to approximately one half of the neighbouring British colony of British Guiana. Cleveland demanded that Britain submit the dispute to impartial arbitration and then invoked the Monroe Doctrine, which forbade European powers from acquiring new colonies in the western hemisphere. Lord Salisbury answered in two parts, first accepting the Monroe Doctrine in its entirety and stating that it did not apply to Canada or the West Indies or to any other British possessions already extant. The second part suggested that some land might be ceded, based on a Royal Geographical survey of 1841–3, but that most Venezuelan claims were based on the extravagant claims of Spanish colonial officials in the eighteenth century. Cleveland then gave a bellicose speech stating that it was the duty of the United States to resist the appropriation of any lands by Britain that the United States had independently decided actually belonged to Venezuela. It was a moment of real crisis, only brought to a sudden finish when the realisation of a potential war between Britain and the United States caused a massive fall on the New York Stock Exchange.[42] Thereafter the dispute fizzled out but it was a marker for the future. Europeans would, in future, have to take the Monroe Doctrine very seriously indeed.

The next potential impasse in diplomatic relations concerned Alaska. The Russo-British treaty of 1825 defined the boundary between Canada and Alaska, along the crest of the mountains except where the crest lay more than ten marine leagues from the coast, in which case the line should run at that distance. In 1867, Russia sold Alaska to the United States and in 1898 the great Klondike gold rush took place. Canada now claimed that the boundary should be measured from the tips of the promontories rather than from the windings of the coast. In 1903 arbitration was agreed. Six impartial jurists deliberated and decided in favour of the United States. There were further problems between the US and Canada over fur sealing in the Bering Sea. The US regarded the Bering Sea as a *mare clausum*; that is a closed sea under the dominion of the state. This, it was claimed, had been the case under the Russians and the US had succeeded to the Russian rights.[43]

Britain, America and the Panama Canal

At the same time as the Alaska boundary question, the proposed construction of a trans-isthmian canal came to the fore. Canal projects had been around for a long time and numerous projects, chiefly involving the Nicaraguan route, were started and failed in the first half of the nineteenth century. In 1846 America acquired California, Nevada, Arizona and New Mexico. The importance of any canal project increased and America became ever more sensitive in regard to rival ambitions in Central America. America concluded a treaty with New Granada (Columbia) and a Panama railway was constructed across the isthmus. Anglo-American rivalry produced the Bulwer-Clayton Treaty, concluded in 1850. John M. Clayton was the American Secretary of State at the time and Sir Henry Bulwer was British minister in Washington. This treaty was concerned primarily with a canal along the Nicaraguan route, that is, 'between the Atlantic and Pacific Oceans by way of the river San Juan de Nicaragua and either or both of the lakes of Nicaragua or Managua to any port or place on the Pacific Ocean'. Article VIII of this treaty said that it established 'a general principle relating to any waterway across the isthmus between North and South America'. Both sides agreed that neither should exercise exclusive control over the canal nor fortify any such canal when built. The treaty existed for 50 years and became a real stumbling block in Anglo-American relations.[44]

Ferdinand de Lesseps, of Suez Canal fame, now took an interest and in 1879 an International Engineering Conference was held in Paris and decided on the Panama route, as opposed to the Nicaraguan route. The French attempt at constructing a Panama Canal was a complete failure, with malaria and disease wiping out virtually the entire construction workforce. In 1888 the de Lesseps company went into bankruptcy. In 1893 the company assets were taken over by a new corporation known as the New Panama Canal Company. This attempt at a canal was directly against the terms of the Bulwer-Clayton Treaty. In February 1900 the first negotiations concerning abrogation of the Bulwer-Clayton Treaty took place. John Hay, the American Secretary of State, and Lord Pauncefote, the British Ambassador in Washington, agreed an accord which was some way short of total American control of the proposed canal but the Senate rejected it. Amendments were introduced and the treaty was eventually ratified in December 1900. However, the treaty in its new form was unacceptable to Lord Salisbury's government in London and it lapsed. In November 1901 a new agreement which specifically superseded the Bulwer-Clayton Treaty, known as the Hay-Pauncefote Treaty, was ratified. The treaty provided for the construction of a canal 'under the auspices of the government of the United States'. It further stated that the United States was 'to have and enjoy all the rights incident to such construction, as well as the exclusive right of providing for the regulation and management of the canal'.[45]

Why then did Britain accept the new treaty with a fair degree of alacrity? The answer is not too difficult to find. America had just fought her first colonial war, with Spain, and won. The coincidence of the Venezuelan dispute, the Alaskan boundary dispute and the Boer War had put British resources under great strain. A large naval deployment in the Caribbean or off the coast of South America was out of the question; Britain bowed to the inevitable and accepted American great power status.

Britain and America in the Pre-Dreadnought Era

Against this background of fairly aggressive American imperialism one may question what America really thought of Britain in this period. In

November 1889 *Scribner's Magazine* carried an article written by Russell Soley, who had been Assistant Secretary to the United States Navy. The subject matter concerned the effect on American commerce of an Anglo-Continental war. The article pointed out that a European war presented no particular problem to the United States unless Britain was involved, in which case the problems became massive, due to the sheer size of the British mercantile marine – about 60 per cent of the world total, with a large North American trade. It went on to say that in a modern war *Alabama* had shown how easy it was to attack commerce and how difficult to defend it. If both sides in a modern war had a dozen or so *Alabamas*, the major disadvantage lay with the state in possession of the largest mercantile marine: Britain.[46] In 1887 Britain imported £118 million of food, all by sea. Fairly obviously, in a maritime war Britain would suffer more than any other belligerent.

The argument was then developed that if marine insurance rates climbed high, Britain might reflag her enormous mercantile marine under neutral colours. The United States, circumscribed by navigation laws that did not allow a foreign-built vessel to be owned by an American citizen, could not participate but would watch as huge quantities of American goods, carried in neutral ships, fell to the belligerent at war with Britain.[47] The arguments presented came down heavily on Britain's side.

> No right-minded American can view a serious calamity to England otherwise than as a calamity to his own country and to the world. Apart from sentiment, the ties of blood and language, and all such considerations, which are perhaps stronger now than ever, Americans can never lose sight of the fact that England stands today in European politics for the same idea of Constitution and liberty that they themselves believe in – which, indeed, they inherited from her, and which is markedly different from that which prevails in France, and still more from that of Germany.[48]

The article concluded that the present United States Navy was:

> An absurd little fleet of half-a-dozen warships to which our navy has dwindled counts for nothing in the preservation and vindication of neutral tights [...] With the United States today there need be no question of fighting if it pursues its true policy of armed neutrality – if it brings its fleet up to the old normal standard of 80 to 100 vessels of war. But so long as its sea-coast cities and its immense maritime interests remain unprotected as at present, its population, its area, its credit, its wealth, and in all other elements of

potential strength, will serve but little purpose in securing a respectful hearing from belligerent aggressors.[49]

The argument that the United States needed a large navy to protect neutrals carrying American goods in wartime is interesting in a number of ways. It anticipated by some years the argument developed by Mahan; that in a future naval war, naval supremacy would be wielded by a transnational consortium of naval powers.[50]

Given the difficult situation vis-à-vis the Franco-Russian alliance and the consequent need for a strong Mediterranean fleet, from the 1890s onwards Britain could never have realistically deployed a large battle fleet in the Caribbean and did not want to.[51] Britain kept a close eye on the development of the American Navy, as successive annual reports show.[52] In reality, the great advantage that accrued to Britain from the development of a large American Navy was the ability of the United States Navy to make armed neutrality a force to be reckoned with, if Britain was involved in a war with a European belligerent.

For Britain, the emergence of the United States of America onto the world stage was not serious – indeed can be described as advantageous. Britain had a nominal duty to defend Canada and the West Indies. In truth, if America had invaded either, it is doubtful if anything could have been done. In the relations between Britain and the United States there was little real difficulty when a strong American Navy arrived on the world stage. Britain tacitly admitted the reality of American power in the Gulf of Mexico and Caribbean, and focused her diplomacy accordingly, but what would be her reaction to the other extra-European power: Japan?

The Japanese Backdrop

In 1542 the Portuguese were the first Europeans to come into contact with Japan. The early Western rivalry in Japan was between the Portuguese and the Dutch, and this came to a head in 1640 with the expulsion of the Portuguese. Thereafter the Dutch traded unmolested for two centuries. In 1853 the American Commodore Perry arrived in Japan with a squadron of ships and more or less demanded a treaty that opened up Japan to America. Seven months after his first visit Perry returned and a goodwill treaty was signed. Shimoda and Hakodate were opened as treaty ports and England, Holland and Russia soon obtained similar treaties.[53] For centuries, Japan was ruled by a feudal oligarchy composed of territorial lords (*daimyo*) and a warrior caste (*samurai*).⁵⁴ At the head was the shogun, notionally under the emperor, who had no real power. The arrival of Commodore Perry precipitated a crisis that resulted in civil war, the abolition of the shogunate, the birth of modern central government and the restoration of the emperor's power.⁵⁵

In 1868 the Maiji dynasty heralded the new age. In the last 30 years of the nineteenth century Japan industrialised rapidly and effectively. By the first years of the twentieth century Japan was the first industrialised Pacific economy.⁵⁶ Japanese engineers and students were sent overseas and quickly learnt the ways of an industrial society. Two hundred and fifty years of isolation from or at best minimal contact with the West put Japan at a serious technological and strategic disadvantage; by contrast European ships had traversed the world and set up trading and naval bases. Then in 1862 an incident took place that caused a major rift in Anglo-Japanese relations. Local *samurai* murdered a British businessman, Charles Richardson. The British government demanded recompense but none was forthcoming. The following year a British fleet sailed into Kagoshima Sound and reduced the port to a smoking ruin.⁵⁷

Britain and Japan: A Developing Relationship

This is not to say the relations between Britain and Japan were usually bad. In the main they were quite good and the British made constant use of Japanese dry-docks and other naval resources. In the period 1860–85, British warships on the China station were powered by 'simple' steam engines, with one stage of steam expansion and had insufficient bunkers to steam from Singapore to Hong Kong or from Hong Kong to Japan against the monsoon. The China station flagship and its consorts not assigned to other duties usually sailed north with the spring monsoon, dry-docked in Japan at Yokohama or Nagasaki and then visited Russian Siberia. They returned southwards in the autumn propelled by the north-east monsoon. It was an unvarying routine that could hardly have been altered in time of war; this was the strategic reality of the China station in the sail and steam era.

The use of dry-docks in Japan needs explanation. The Hope dry-dock at Aberdeen, Hong Kong was designed to take the British warships on the China station and had been built with an Admiralty subsidy. However, it had drawbacks, principally that the dock entrance had only 20 feet of water over the sill. This ensured that ships had to be lightened, all stores removed, including coal, and also masts and yards, excepting the lower masts. The dock was difficult to get into and Aberdeen itself was considered unhealthy, hence the preference of British admirals for docking in Japan.[58] In truth, Hong Kong may have been the main trading entrepôt on the China coast but Hong Kong's value to the Royal Navy as a base was somewhat limited.

The arrival of Commodore Perry and the British bombardment at Kagoshima made the Japanese realise how intensely vulnerable they were to maritime aggression. The Japanese were aware, perhaps brutally aware after Kagoshima, of Britain's naval predominance and it was to Britain they turned for help in educating and training the officers and men of their new navy, and the first British instructors arrived in 1870. The Japanese government decided that the system of naval education should be British and in 1871 Royal Navy style uniforms were adopted for cadets. Not all naval officers were trained in Britain and most continued to be educated at the Royal Naval College at Tokyo. British naval attachés were not slow to see the potential of the developing Japanese Navy.

> Some of the officers are obviously very able and well informed men and the course of study at the Royal Naval College, Tokio [sic], shows that as regards theoretical studies they are desirous of being on a par with other nations. The naval force available could be readily concentrated at either of the principal ports. I am of the opinion that in their own waters and in proportion to their strength they would be found obstinate enemies.[59]

The Birth of the Japanese Steam Navy

The Japanese were not capable of building a large ocean-going navy before 1900, so in the 1870s, 1880s and 1890s many warships were built abroad. The first three such ships were the *Fuso*, *He-yei* and *Kongo*, all built in Britain in the 1870s.

The *Fuso* was a central battery ironclad of 3,717 tons, the *Kongo* and *He-yei* armoured corvettes of 2,200 tons. All three ships were steam driven and barque rigged. Japanese navigation and technical skills were very limited and British crews brought them to Japan with only a few Japanese on board. In the 1870s the Japanese Navy consisted of little more than these three ships, plus an assortment of older vessels captured from the shogunate in the civil war and units loaned to the emperor by loyal clans. These included an ironclad ram *Adzuma*, built in France for the American Confederates during the American Civil War. The gunboat *Chiyodogata* was of particular interest as the first warship built in Japan. In addition there was a corvette, four paddle wheel steamers and four old sailing ships.

In 1882 the first Navy Expansion Bill was passed which voted 26,670,000 yen for naval construction. Forty-eight vessels were planned over an eight-year period. The bill also provided funds for shipyard development and for the training of officers and men. Many naval officers were to be trained in Britain.

The Japanese Navy was strongly influenced by the *Jeune École* and had a fully-rigged protected cruiser, the *Unebi*, built in France at Forges et Chantiers, Le Havre. At 3,625 tons she was not large and mounted four 24-cm Krupp guns in two sponsons on each beam. With a heavy spread of canvas and so much weight out on the beam this ship was probably unstable under sail and she disappeared between Singapore and Japan in October 1887. Three slightly larger protected cruisers were built to French designs, two in France, *Itsukushima* and *Matsushima*, and one in Japan from French material, *Hashidate*. The first Japanese armoured cruiser was the 2,400-ton *Chiyoda*, laid down at Clydebank in 1888 and completed in 1890; she mounted ten 4.7-inch guns.[60]

In terms of doctrine there were two British naval officers who had a decisive influence on the Japanese Navy of the 1880s and early 1890s. The first was Lieutenant-Commander L.P. Willan, who from 1879 taught gunnery and navigation, also tactics and fleet movements.[61] The second was Captain John Ingles, who arrived in 1887 and over the next six years took up the naval controversies of the day, the most important was his advocacy of line ahead tactics. The main arguments against line ahead tactics were torpedo and ramming tactics by the enemy. Ingles showed that superior speed, superior firepower and superior gunnery could overcome these disadvantages. As more and more cruisers joined the Japanese Navy, so fleet manoeuvres became increasingly important.[62]

The Sino-Japanese War

From 1881 onwards China made a considerable effort to become a naval power. A Sino-Japanese war was a possibility in 1881 but neither side had the ships for such a conflict. Initially China acquired a number of gunboats, capable of operating on her great rivers.[63] In 1881 China ordered two 7,500 steel hulled battleships, *Chen Yuen* and *Ting Yuen*, both built in Germany by Vulkan, launched in 1882 and completed in 1884. They were armed with four 12-inch Krupp guns in two barbettes placed *en echelon* forward.[64]

Vulkan also built two armoured cruisers of 2,900 tons, *King Yuan* and *Lai Yuan*, both armed with two 21-cm guns. China also acquired five protected cruisers, four of which were built in Britain, and six unprotected cruisers, four of which were built at Foochow and two in Germany by Howaldt.[65]

The Korean peninsula had traditionally been dominated by China but Japan had been working to take over her weaker neighbour. In 1894 an insurrection broke out in Korea and China sent troops to quell it. The Chinese government sent a note to the Japanese government and used the term 'tributary state' to describe Korea. Japan replied denying the 'tributary state' note and informed China that she was sending 4,000 troops to Korea immediately. Japan justified her actions by stating that she had a legal right to send troops to Korea if China had already done the same and claimed this under the terms of the Chemulpo Convention.[66]

The action started on 20 July 1894. Two Chinese warships, the protected cruiser *Tche Yuen* (*Chi Yuen*) and the 1,000-ton torpedo gunboat *Kwang Yi* (*Kuang Yi*) were steaming from Asan in Korea.[67] Off the island of Phung-Do they met a Japanese squadron consisting of three protected cruisers *Naniwa*, *Yoshino* and *Akitsushima*. The Japanese cruiser *Naniwa*, commanded by Captain Togo, had been ordered to sweep the Gulf of Asan and to check if Chinese ships were landing troops on the Korean coast. China and Japan were not yet officially at war so Togo was not sure what to do when the Chinese warships hove into view.[68] The *Tche Yuen* had never been a ship that steered well, her steering gear broke down and she inadvertently bore down on the Japanese ships as if she was attacking.[69] Togo had already ordered his men to action stations and he opened fire. The British trained gunners were soon scoring hits on the Chinese ships. The *Yoshino* and *Akitsushima* joined in and one of the very few ironclad era naval battles was under way.[70] Eventually the *Tche Yuen* rigged for hand steering and limped off to Wei-hai-Wei. The *Kuang-Yi* attempted to use her torpedoes but was unsuccessful. On fire, with most of her crew killed, she reached land and was destroyed on the beach by the Japanese.[71]

At this stage Togo could see two more ships entering the Gulf from seawards.[72] One was a British merchant ship and the other a Chinese naval escort. The Japanese knew of the British ship *Kowshing* but two shots were fired across her bow and the *Kowshing* stopped. The *Naniwa* ordered *Kowshing* to follow her, but the Chinese onboard *Kowshing* wanted to return to Taku. After four hours of negotiations Togo advised the British onboard to leave the ship and ordered *Kowshing* to be torpedoed. The torpedo missed, so he fired a broadside that hit in the engine room and five minutes later the ship began to sink. Most of the Europeans jumped overboard and were rescued by *Naniwa*, then Togo machine-gunned the unfortunate Chinese struggling in the water. The legality of the attack on the *Kowshing* was a matter of controversy in its day but it was established that Japan was in her legal rights to stop the *Kowshing*.

On 16 September the Chinese Admiral Ting left Talien Bay (Darien) and headed for the Yalu River. He had with him the two *en echelon* battleships, *Ting Yuen* and *Chen Yuen*, and three armoured cruisers, the *King Yuen*, *Lai Yuen* and *Ping Yuen*. Two smaller protected cruisers *Chi Yuen* and *Tsi Yuen* were also present, as were four even smaller ships. In terms of speed this was a 16-knot fleet. On reaching the Yalu River in the evening, the fleet anchored 12 miles out to sea with fires banked; ready for action.[73] Compared to the Japanese fleet Ting had a larger more powerful force with a number of British, German and American advisers.[74]

The Japanese fleet, commanded by Admiral Ito, appeared the next day and battle commenced. Admiral Ito had four 18-knot protected cruisers as a flying squadron. The main fleet consisted of three protected cruisers, the armoured cruiser *Chiyoda* and the now elderly *Fuso* and *Hiei*.[75]

Admiral Ting chose to engage in line abreast with a strong centre and weak flanks. This was the logical deployment with his two powerful *en echelon* ships. The Chinese fleet, though nominally the stronger, was poorly handled by Admiral Ting, who fought entirely to a pre-arranged plan. This was in marked contrast to the Japanese, who fought by signals throughout.[76] The Japanese crossed the Chinese front and turned in succession, eight points to port, opening fire at 3000 yards.

It was a dangerous manoeuvre and the Chinese almost succeeded in cutting the Japanese line. As it was, three Japanese ships, the *Fuso*, *He-yei* and *Akagi*, were all badly damaged. If the Chinese fleet had been better handled, this initial advantage could have been exploited, indeed from the Chinese viewpoint the battle was half won, but after the opening manoeuvres the battle became a melee, with the Chinese ships losing all formation.[77] Japanese fire concentrated on the battleships *Chen Yuen* and *Ting Yuen* and both were hit repeatedly. If Ting had increased speed from a desperately slow 6 knots he might have broken Ito's line.[78] He did not do so because of the increasing chaos in his ships. Nevertheless, the Japanese-protected cruiser *Matsushima* was heavily damaged by shots from *Ting Yuen*, with 100 officers and men killed. This forced Admiral Ito to shift his flag to *Hashidate*, as his flagship limped out of action.[79]

In the first phase of the action four of the Chinese ships were sunk or driven off. One fled and her captain was later beheaded for cowardice.[80] The range of most of the fighting was around 2,500 yards, yet Ito did not press his advantage and allowed the two battleships *Ting Yuen* and *Chen Yuen* to escape. Both ships were in something approaching a sinking condition and could have been finished off with torpedoes. There were several good reasons for Ito not pursuing the attack. He had been unable to sink the Chinese battleships and several Japanese ships were badly damaged. Nevertheless, his caution cost him a decisive victory and Ting was able to return to Port Arthur, having lost five ships. After the battle the Japanese were left holding the seas. Ting eventually took his ships to Wei-Hai-Wei, where the Japanese fleet blockaded them and this further enhanced Japanese morale.[81]

Japanese efforts then centred on Port Arthur and it fell to them on 20 November 1894. Japanese troops occupied the Liaotung Peninsular and China was forced to recognise the 'independence' of Korea, which now became an area of Japanese influence. The treaty of Shimonoseki ceded the Liaotung Peninsular to Japan but Western pressure soon forced Japan to give up this prize.[82]

Britain, Japan and Russia After the Sino-Japanese War

For more than 30 years Russia had wanted an ice-free port in the Pacific. The 1858 Treaty of Aigun had ceded Vladivostok to Russia. In 1872 Russia established a main fleet base for their Pacific fleet at Vladivostok, much to the annoyance of Japan, because Vladivostok was ice-free for nine months of the year. After the Sino-Japanese War, in the face of a potential war with Imperial Russia the Japanese backed down and Port Arthur was ceded to Russia, who at long last gained an ice-free port in the Pacific.

By 1903 the trans-Siberian railway linked Port Arthur to European Russia. Japan was now faced by an immensely powerful Russian fleet that could easily strike at the heart of Japan.[83] For Britain there was then the prospect of a Dual Alliance member with a greatly enhanced Pacific fleet potential. Matters were further complicated by French ambitions in the Far East. The French already possessed Indo-China (Viet-Nam) and were intent on furthering their influence in China itself. With French ambitions in Indo-China complicating matters, the Germans also decided to interfere and in their actions may be seen the first stirrings of a German blue-water naval strategy. A German fleet went to the Bay of Kiaochow and forced the Chinese to cede them a base at Tsingtau in Shantung province.[84]

Britain, Japan and Wai-Hai-Wei

After the Sino-Japanese War Britain decided to reinforce her Far Eastern fleet heavily. Germany and Russia had doubled their naval strength in the region and Britain was forced to keep three, four or even five first-class battleships on the China station.[85] Japan had taken Wei-Hai-Wei in the war with China but had never made a great deal of use of it. Britain had looked at the prospect of large Russian, German and French navies in the region and found it daunting. A *modus vivendi* with Japan, the strongest regional power, was logical. A naval base in the Gulf of Pecheli was even more logical, with Russia at Port Arthur and Germany at Tsingtau. Approaches were made to Japan and in 1898 Britain took a lease on Wei-Hai-Wei. There was considerable disagreement in Whitehall concerning the need for a base in the area. Politically, to Lord Salisbury's Conservative government, the German and Russian bases demanded a British reply. Wei-Hai-Wei was opposite Port Arthur, only 60 miles distant. The Admiralty do not appear to have been much consulted over the need for a base and service opinion was sharply divided about its usefulness.[86] The original intention was to fortify the base and create a viable coaling station. In the event, the Anglo-Japanese naval agreement five years later obviated the need to fortify the base, and this greatly reduced the development costs. What emerged was a useful little dockyard, unsuitable for a large fleet.

Before the *modus vivendi* with Britain over Wei-Hai-Wei, Japan had already turned to Britain for new warships. The time had come for Japan to acquire a true battleship navy. Under Admiral Yamamoto Gombei a Japanese fleet of 65,000 tons in 1894 became a fleet of 260,000 tons by 1905.[87] Battleships were ordered from British yards, including the *Fuji* and *Yashima*, built respectively by the Thames Ironworks and Armstrong's at Elswick and both launched in 1896. The Thames Ironworks and Armstrong's also built the *Shikishima* and *Hatsuse*, launched in 1898 and 1899. The *Asahi* was built at Clydebank and *Mikasa* by Vickers at Barrow.[88] Finally the *Kashima* and *Katori* (Elswicks and Vickers). These last two ships were 16,400 tons displacement, armed with four 12-inch and four 10-inch guns and every bit as good as their contemporary British counterparts of the King Edward class.[89] The others all conformed to the late Victorian

British practice and mounted twin 12-inch gun turrets, one forward and one aft. A heavy secondary battery of 6-inch guns was carried exactly mirroring British practice of the period. Six large armoured cruisers were built, *Asama, Tokiwa, Iwate, Izumo, Azuma* and *Yakumo* and eight protected cruisers.[90]

The Anglo-Japanese Naval Treaty

In spite of the acquisition of a large modern navy, Japan still had a central unresolved problem. Russia was in alliance with France and Japan was still not strong enough to take on the combination. Britain had a rather similar problem defined by the First Lord of the Admiralty, Lord Selborne in a memorandum dated 17 January 1901.

> In a few months time Britain will have four first class battleships and sixteen cruisers in Chinese waters as against a combined French and Russian strength of seven first class and two second class battleships and twenty cruisers [...] For us the odds of nine battleships to four would be too great, and we should eventually have to add to our battleships on the China station. The effect of this would be twofold. It would leave us with little or nothing more than a bare equality of strength in the Channel and Mediterranean, and a bare equality at the heart of the Empire is a dangerous risk [...] Great Britain and Japan together would next year be able to show eleven battleships against the French and Russian nine, as well as a preponderance of cruisers.[91]

Britain and Japan had essentially similar interests in needing to counter German and Franco-Russian moves on the China coast. Britain was building Japan's warships and the Japanese Navy was heavily modelled on the Royal Navy, so what could be more natural than the alliance of these two powers. In 1895 Lord Salisbury as Prime Minister thought the strategic and military interest being shown in Japan by many was greatly over-estimated, 'She may no doubt be of use in hindering Russia from getting an ice-free port'. Russia occupied Port Arthur and Salisbury began to look more favourably on the idea of an Anglo-Japanese alliance.[92]

The result was the Anglo-Japanese naval agreement signed on 30 January of 1902. There were six articles in the treaty. Article one recognised the independence of China and Corea (Korea, spelt Corea at the time). It also recognised the right of either power to interfere in these countries if their interests were threatened or if another power interfered. Article two guaranteed the strict neutrality of both Britain and Japan if either was at war with another power. Article three was the interesting one. It guaranteed that if either Britain or Japan was at war with a combination of two other powers, each would come to the assistance of the other. If France and Russia were at war with Japan, Britain would come to the aid of Japan and vice versa. Article four stated that neither Britain nor Japan would enter into other treaty agreements with other powers without consulting each other. Article five stated that when either party's interests were in jeopardy they would inform each other. Article six stated the time period of the original treaty; five years.[93]

The treaty is interesting in other ways. The Japanese wanted 20,000 tons of best Welsh steam coal per annum. Japanese lump coal was low quality bituminous. This coal burnt off huge quantities of black smoke and had a low heat value. During the Sino-Japanese War this lump coal had been used and had reduced the speed of ships. For war purposes the Welsh steam coal was essential.[94] Most of the larger ships were now fitted with radio and long lists of call signs and code words were worked out, to allow communications across the language barrier. Every few months, deployments were worked out between the two navies, allowing a concentration in the Gulf of Pechili that substantially outgunned any combination of two other powers.[95]

Even with the naval base at Wei-Hai-Wei and the naval agreement with Japan, Britain was stretched in the late 1890s and the early years of the twentieth century. The generally tense situation in the Far East demanded five first-class battleships on the China station, ships that could have been more usefully deployed closer to home. Despite disagreements over policy and associated arguments between the Admiralty and Foreign Office the moves made by Britain were essentially correct; Japan was becoming the strongest regional naval power and the mutual interests of Britain and Japan neatly coincided, especially where checks to German and Franco-Russian ambitions were concerned.

The fact that Japan was not yet able to build battleships and armoured cruisers of her own was steadily being rectified. The four principal dockyards at Yokosuka, Tokyo, Kure and Sassebo were rapidly developed. By 1905, the number two dock at Kure and the number two dock at Yokosuka were able to take the largest battleships in existence. Each dock was over 500 feet long and could easily berth the *Kashima* and *Katori* at 455 feet in length.[96]

The Russo-Japanese War

The war with Russia, when it came, was a direct outcome of the Russian ousting of Japan from Port Arthur and the Russian occupation of Manchuria. Both Vladivostok and Port Arthur were now connected to European Russia via the trans-Siberian railway. Russian dominance of the coastline of the Sea of Japan was an obvious and direct threat to Japan itself. By 1902 Japan had six battleships and six armoured cruisers, an extremely homogenous force. Russia sent a stream of battleships to the Far East but did not expand its dockyards on the Pacific coast. Her warships represented a much less homogenous group and this was to have important consequences in the future.

The Russian staff had considered various war plans and concluded that the purpose of their fleet was to 'secure command of the Yellow Sea and South Korean waters'. The main body of the fleet was stationed at Port Arthur to command the Yellow Sea. The defeat of the Japanese fleet was not considered.[97] This was in marked contrast to the Japanese, who were determined to deal with the Russians once and for all. In the months before the war Russia was slow to recognise that war was inevitable, even after the sinking of the Russian cruiser *Variag* and the gunboat *Korietz* in the so-called 'Chemulpo' incident.[98] The Russians sought refuge in diplomatic delays but the Japanese broke off all talks abruptly and mounted a surprise attack on Port Arthur. At midnight on 8 February 1904, a Japanese destroyer flotilla crept into Port Arthur Bay and torpedoed the battleships *Retvisan* and *Tsarevitch*, also the cruiser *Pallada*.[99] The next morning the Japanese again approached Port Arthur with battleships commanded by Admiral Togo. At noon they started a slow bombardment of the ships in Port Arthur. Far from being disorganised, the Russians came out in line abreast supported by their shore batteries. The Japanese, not wanting to risk their valuable battleships, withdrew. Having failed in their first attempt on Port Arthur, the Japanese tried to disable the port with blockships but this failed on two occasions. Togo tried another tactic and on 12–13 April mined the waters outside the harbour.[100]

To boost the Russian effort, the dynamic Admiral Makarov was sent to the Far East. He succeeded in raising Russian morale and the day after the mines had been laid took a small force out of Port Arthur led by the battleship *Petropavlovsk*. Makarov was killed when the battleship *Petropavlovsk* struck one of the mines and blew up. The Russians in their turn resorted to mine warfare and in May 1904 laid a minefield off the

Liaotung Peninsula, an area frequented by Japanese warships. On 15 May the Japanese battleships *Hatsuse* and *Yashima* struck mines and were sunk. Japan had lost one-third of her battleship strength in a single day.

The Russians twice tried to escape to Vladivostok but failed. The skirmishing of 1904 reached its climax with a substantial battle on 10 August. The Russians sustained severe damage to the flagship *Tzesarevitch* and Admiral Vitgeft was killed. The Russians withdrew to Port Arthur in confusion. Then, on the 18 August, a second battle took place and this time it was the Vladivostok squadron that was badly mauled. The armoured cruisers *Rurik* and *Gromoboi* were heavily damaged, with many men killed. Having achieved local naval mastery the Japanese then intensified their attacks on Port Arthur. In October 1904 they closed in from the land and destroyed the Russian fleet by howitzer fire. Seven battleships, one armoured cruiser, five protected cruisers and 29 smaller vessels were destroyed or captured.[101]

This heavy defeat was not to be tolerated by the Russians. They made the historic decision to deploy their Baltic fleet in the Far East. The Baltic fleet, commanded by Admiral Rodjestvenski, started its historic voyage around the world. Leaving the Baltic, they entered the North Sea and encountered the Hull fishing fleet off the Dogger Bank. Mistaking the trawlers for Japanese torpedo boats, they opened fire, sinking several trawlers. This incident brought the Russians and British to the brink of war. Eventually the incident was smoothed over and the Russian fleet continued its amazing voyage. This turned out to be a nine-month ordeal marked by mutiny, international protests and unintelligible instructions from home.[102]

Eventually the Russians entered the South China Sea and steamed towards the Straits of Tsushima and Japan. Japanese cruisers soon made contact and using radiotelegraphy were able to report the position of the Russian fleet. Rozhestvensky was steaming at ten knots, almost his maximum fleet speed. The main Japanese advantage was speed, 15 knots for the Japanese fleet but above all else, the Japanese fleet was a homogeneous group of warships able to work together in a highly coordinated manner. The Japanese fleet was painted a uniform grey, which made the ships less distinct. By contrast the Russian ships with bright yellow funnels were easily distinguished. Nearly all the Japanese ships were equipped with wireless telegraphy.[103]

The main action took place on 27 May 1905. The Second and Third Russian Baltic squadrons were deployed in two columns, line ahead. At

1400 hours the main Japanese squadron headed south-west and made as if to cross the Russian fleet at right angles. Togo chose, rightly, to engage in line ahead with his most powerful battleships in the van and the weaker armoured cruisers to the rear. To Togo's amazement, the Russians made no real effort to target the Japanese ships at their turning point, when they were most vulnerable.[104] At 1408 hours the Russians opened fire at a range of 7,000 yards. The Japanese waited a little longer and commenced action at 6,600 yards. The Russian ships at the head of the port column soon sustained heavy damage.[105]

The Russians were defeated not just heavily but devastatingly. Of the 38 Russian ships, 20 were sunk and six captured. Two were sunk later when it was realised they were damaged beyond repair. Six were disarmed and interned in neutral ports and only two ships escaped. Seven Russian battleships were sunk outright and four captured. Raising and repairing the cruisers sunk at Port Arthur further enhanced the strength of the Japanese fleet. Of the nine Russian cruisers present at Tsushima four were sunk and three escaped to Manila. Another was wrecked and one only escaped to Vladivostok.[106]

Perspectives: The Lessons of a Naval War in the Pre-Dreadnought Era

The lessons of this fleet action were many and varied. This was the only naval battle fought between late Victorian battleships and was a test of ideas about naval tactics as much as ideas about construction. The Japanese fleet, largely British built and adhering to British tactics, won a decisive victory over a Russian Navy using essentially French ideas and technology. The quality of Japanese materiel made itself felt and a hail of fire from large and medium-calibre guns overwhelmed the Russian ships.

At Port Arthur, mines did terrible damage to the Russian fleet but the Russians had also used mines to good effect and sunk two Japanese battleships, the first time covert weapons had sunk battleships. The fact that mines could sink battleships tended to force capital ships on the defensive. The ideas about speed conferring overwhelming advantage were accepted and this was to have a profound effect on British ship design in the years ahead.[107]

From Britain's viewpoint the outcome was entirely satisfactory. The endless worries about Russian encroachment in the Pacific were over; the chosen ally had annihilated the Russian fleet. Britain had witnessed a huge strategic change where, in a period of less than 20 years, a relatively stable naval world with Britain facing France and Russia had been transformed into a world with two new very powerful extra-European navies, those of the United States and Japan. The destruction of the Russian Navy by Japan, Britain's chosen ally, shows just how powerful Japan had become.

4

Fisher and the Dreadnought

Prelude: Fisher as First Sea Lord

When Fisher became First Sea Lord in October 1904 he brought to the Admiralty a number of schemes for both ship construction and fleet redistribution. These ideas were not hastily thought out, they were the result of years of quiet deliberation, aided by an informal committee of experts that included naval officers, engineers and constructors from private shipyards. Fisher wanted battleships and armoured cruisers of 16,000 tons. The battleships would have a speed of 21 knots and the cruisers 25 knots. Destroyers of 750 tons would be built and armed with 4-inch guns. Submarines of 350 tons would form the basis of a balanced underwater fleet.[1] The idea behind a super battleship was by no means confined to Fisher. In 1904, while Commander-in-Chief at Portsmouth, he was writing to the naval journalist Arnold White:

> Sir Andrew Noble, the head of the Elswick firm, came all the way from Newcastle to see me yesterday about a new design for a battleship that will 'stagger humanity'.[2]

Fisher's redistribution of the fleets has been the subject of much comment. The First Lord of the Admiralty, Lord Selborne, in a memorandum dated 6 December 1904 and written by Fisher, gave the reasons for the proposed fleet redistribution. He pointed out that Britain had now built or was in the process of building 26 armoured cruisers, whereas four years earlier there had been none. These ships had changed the nature of naval warfare and France had built or was building 25 such ships, with 12 completed in the period 1902–4. In both navies the armoured cruisers were fast enough to overtake most other vessels, or to escape from a more heavily armed opponent. Their armour was adequate against most other warships and their armament the equal of some older battleships. It was particularly the case that the new-age armoured cruisers, both French and Russian, were far superior to most of the small second- and third-class cruisers that constituted Britain's naval presence in distant waters. It was also the case that these second- and third-class cruisers were no match for the larger, newer trans-oceanic liners that could be fitted out as armed merchant cruisers in wartime. Selborne went on to point out that the current fleet distributions on foreign stations dated from the pre-electric telegraph era and the age of sail.[3]

It was proposed to change the name of the Home Fleet to the Channel Fleet, based in home waters with 12 battleships. The Channel Fleet was renamed the Atlantic Fleet, based on Gibraltar with eight battleships. Each fleet would have an armoured cruiser squadron attached consisting of six ships. The Mediterranean Fleet, with eight battleships would also have an attached armoured cruiser squadron. All three cruiser squadrons were considered detachable for special service duties and showing the flag in impressive force. In some respects the armoured cruiser squadrons presaged the battlecruisers of a few years later, ships designed for worldwide deployment and the defence of empire. The cruisers on overseas stations were divided into three groups. Those in eastern seas comprised the cruisers on the China, Australia and East Indies stations. The Cape of Good Hope squadron was the connecting link between either the eastern group and the Mediterranean cruisers or the eastern group and the western group.[4] The South Atlantic command was abolished altogether and the older sloops and gunboats were ordered home as their fighting value was very limited.

Ships in the Home and Channel fleets were not commissioned for any particular period of time, rather they had 25 per cent of their crews changed every six months and made up with fresh entries from the depots. Even ships on three-year commissions had so many personnel changes that it seriously degraded operational efficiency. In future all commissions would be for two years, without personnel changes. The first reserve ships would have two-fifths (nucleus) crews onboard, including all the technical specialists.

It was assurances on naval economy that gave Fisher the top job. To obtain the necessary economies, 154 ships were struck off the effective list. With so many ships withdrawn from foreign stations, the subsidiary dockyards that supported them were no longer necessary. The naval bases at Halifax, Jamaica, St Lucia, Ascension and Esquimalt were abolished.

Fisher did reduce the naval estimates, as the figures given here clearly show: 1904–5 – £36,889,000, 1906–7 – £31,869,500.[5]

At exactly which point Fisher, the Royal Navy and the British political establishment became anti-German needs careful analysis. From 1901 onwards, surviving documents (dealt with in the next chapter) show growing concern with the German Navy and its building programmes. The view expressed by Arthur Marder, that Fisher's fleet redistribution was markedly anti-German, has been strongly refuted, most notably by Ruddock Mackay.[6] Mackay pointed out that the Atlantic Fleet, based at Gibraltar, was effectively a strategic pivot. A memorandum from the Director of Naval Intelligence, Rear-Admiral Prince Louis of Battenberg, dated 14 November 1904, suggested that the new King Edward class battleships then completing should go to the Atlantic Fleet.[7] At the time of their completion these ships were fast (18.5 knots) and powerful, armed with four 12-inch, four 9.2-inch and ten 6-inch guns.[8] Battenberg went on to say that the Atlantic Fleet could reinforce British battle fleets either in home waters or in the Mediterranean. In the Mediterranean the French Navy was about to commission the first three République class battleships, and these needed to be covered by British ships of the latest type. In the north, the French Navy was, as always, seen as the principal threat. The German Navy was indeed in the equation but Battenberg pointed out that most of its battleships had a weak armament of 24-cm (9.4-inch) guns as opposed to the 12-inch guns of the British battleships.[9] Given the speed of the King Edwards, these Gibraltar-based battleships were four days steaming from the North Sea and two days from Malta. At this point in history the Admiralty's response to the various potential threats was entirely flexible.

Fisher and the Genesis of the Dreadnought Idea

In early 1904 Fisher wrote of ship design:

> In approaching the important question of ship design the first essential is to divest our minds totally of the idea that a single type of ship as now built is necessary [...] strategy not tradition should govern the types of ships to be designed.[10]

Lord Selborne's memorandum of 6 December 1904 proposed a committee on designs composed of naval officers and also scientific and technical experts, who would decide the principal features of any new warships.[11]

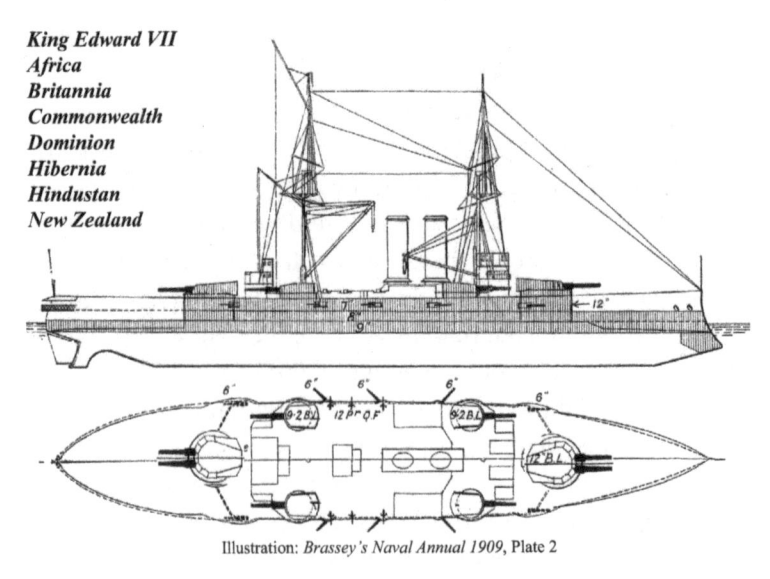

King Edward VII
Africa
Britannia
Commonwealth
Dominion
Hibernia
Hindustan
New Zealand

Illustration: *Brassey's Naval Annual 1909*, Plate 2

King Edward VII:	Devonport, 8.3.02–23.7.03–Feb '05 £1,382,675
Dominion:	Vickers, 23.5.02–25.8.03–July '05 £1,364,318
Commonwealth:	Fairfield, 17.6.02–13.5.03–Mar '05 £1,302,127
Hindustan:	Clydebank, 25.10.02–19.12.03 Jul '05 £1,320,127
New Zealand:	Portsmouth, 9.2.03–4.2.04–Jun '05 £1,1,335,975
Africa:	Chatham, 27.1.04–20.5.05–Nov '06 £1,382,970
Britannia:	Portsmouth 4.2.04–10.12.04–Sep '06 £1,347,620
Hibernia:	Devonport, 6.1.04–17.6.05–Jan '07 £1,347,620
Dimensions:	453.775 × 78 × 24.5/26.75 feet = 16,350 tons
Armament:	Four 12-inch, four 9.2-inch, ten 6-inch, fourteen 12-pdrs
Armour:	Belt 9"–4", bulkheads 12"–8", barbettes 12"–6", battery 7", conning tower 12", battery 7", Deck 2½"–2"
Machinery:	Two sets four cylinder vertical triple expansion, contract ships engined by builders. *King Edward* and *Hibernia* by Harland and Wolf. *Britannia* and *New Zealand* by Humphreys and Tennant. H.P. 18,000 = 18.5 knots
Coal:	950/2,200-tons Radius 7,000-miles at 10 knots
Complement:	777

Fig. 8 The last pre-dreadnoughts or semi-dreadnoughts, King Edward class

The design committee was appointed on 22 December 1904 and consisted of seven naval officers and seven civilians, all best described as Fisher men. The first consideration was gun armament calibre and range.

Fisher appears to have been surprisingly uncertain about the calibre of gun to be adopted for any new ships. He had used the second-class battleship *Renown* as his flagship both on the North America and West Indies station and in the Mediterranean. He liked the four 10-inch guns, with a higher rate of fire than the 12-inch guns of the first-class battleships. He also liked her higher top speed: 18 knots. During his time in the Mediterranean the Italian Navy had laid down the four battleships of the Vittorio Emanuele class. They mounted two 12-inch and twelve

8-inch guns. With a speed of 21–2 knots, they were virtually armoured-cruiser/battleship hybrids.[12] Fisher, ever the speed enthusiast, took a keen interest.

After 1900 the Royal Navy, and indeed the navies of the other powers, steadily modified the 'standard' pre-dreadnought battleship design. A main armament of four 12-inch guns and a secondary of twelve 6-inch gave way to ships with a powerful intermediate armament of 8-inch or, in the case of Britain, 9.2-inch guns. When Fisher became First Sea Lord two further battleships, *Lord Nelson* and *Agamemnon*, were planned, armed with four 12-inch and ten 9.2-inch guns. The question then arose, which was more important, gun power (the battleship) or speed (the armoured cruiser)? Two years earlier, in January 1902, the senior officers' War Course at Greenwich had assessed the value of gun power versus speed by comparing two potential battleship designs, one armed with four 12-inch and eight 8-inch guns, designated 'Type A', the other with four 10-inch and sixteen 6-inch guns, designated 'Type B'. The more heavily armed ship had a speed of 18 knots and 12-inches of belt armour, while the other had a speed of 22 knots, but only 5-inch belt armour. In fact, these were the design proposals for the United States battleships, *Louisiana* and *Connecticut* (Type A), and the four armoured cruisers *North Carolina*, *Montana*, *Washington* and *Tennessee* (Type B). The War Course assessment suggested that fire would be opened at a range of some 6,000 yards closing to 3,000 yards and the 12-inch gun would penetrate the armour of the 10-inch armed ship at almost any range. In this scenario, gun power was much more important than speed, though at long range three of the more lightly armed ships could hold their own against two of the more heavily armed.[13] The arguments about the value of speed versus armour and guns were further complicated by two battleships building in Britain for Chile. The *Constitution* and *Libertad* mounted four 10-inch and fourteen 7.5-inch guns; belt armour was seven inches of Krupp cemented and at 19 knots they emphasised speed over gun power, almost identical to the Type B ships described above. The Chilean treasury hit problems and at launch in January 1903 they were sold to the Royal Navy to prevent them being purchased by Russia. The price was £2,432,000 and they became HMS *Triumph* and HMS *Swiftsure*, completed in June 1904 just as Fisher was about to become First Sea Lord.[14]

Selborne's memorandum of 6 December 1904 also referred to the war raging in the Far East between Russia and Japan and stated that the

Admiralty Board could benefit from the lessons of the war.[15] Earlier in the year, on 10 August 1904, the war in the Far East came to a head with a gunnery duel opening at a range of 17,000 yards with much of the action at 7,000–12,000 yards, and the Japanese had the better of it.[16] Such a long-range gunnery duel was unprecedented and Fisher concluded that any new battleship built for the Royal Navy would have to fight at these much longer ranges. Therein lay a major problem, the inability to hit at long range.

The Embryonic Mechanisation of Gunnery Fire Control

In the period 1899–1900 the Mediterranean Fleet carried out firing trials at ranges of 5,000 to 6,000 yards and the results of these experiments were turned into a series of articles by Captain Edward Harding, a Royal Marine officer. Control positions were established onboard the ships and the fall of shot could be observed. By 1902 it was becoming accepted that spotting the fall of shot had to be done from a position aloft and that this was the only way to obtain and keep ranges.[17]

A report from the Director of Naval Ordnance dated 13 January 1904 analysed battle-firing practice for the battleship *Vengeance* and the cruiser *Eclipse*. At 6,000 yards *Vengeance* scored four hits with 202 shots.[18] HMS *Eclipse* devised a two-observer system for range taking. This was the work of Midshipman Hardy, the most junior midshipman onboard.

> There is a station in each top in which the angle between the fore and aft line of the ship and the line from the top to the object is observed. These two angles are signalled down to the lower station. There are, in this station two slotted bars, pivoted at a certain distance apart. These bars are set to the angles signalled down from the tops, and the distance between the intersections of the threads in the centre of each slot and the pivot is the range.[19]

Whether this system could have been developed into a practical system is a matter of fascinating speculation, as is the effort required to make the basic instrument to the design of a junior midshipman. Long-range gunnery experiments were carried out in both the Mediterranean and home waters. In April 1904 it was concluded that ranges of 8,000 yards were possible, with fire opened at 9,000 or 10,000 yards.[20]

From 1898 onwards some attempt had been made to devise methods for accurate hitting at ranges from 3,000 to 6,000 yards. The only way to establish the range of the target was to fire salvoes, not single shots. The splash from the fall of shot was observed to be either over or short of the target and corrections were made until a straddle was obtained. A long series of trials showed that for salvo firing to work one calibre of gun only was essential. Most of the early experiments in salvo firing involved the 6-inch secondary armament of battleships.[21]

As far back as 1892 Professor Barr had designed a rangefinder with a baseline length of four feet six inches and an accuracy of 1 per cent at 3,000 yards. This was a coincidence rangefinder with two separate lines of sight. Coincidence rangefinders use a right angle at one end of the instrument and at a particular range there will be an oblique angle at the other end. To find the range, the displaced image formed by the oblique angle is aligned with the centred image produced by the right-angled end of the instrument, hence 'coincidence'. To increase the accuracy of the rangefinder or to achieve an increase in range the baseline must be increased. By 1906 9-foot baseline rangefinders were available and accurate to 1 per cent at 7,000 yards. The mirrors at either end of the coincidence instruments were replaced by pentagonal prisms, whose two reflecting surfaces cancelled alignment shifts in the coincidence plane.[22] Using this principle, range-finders with a baseline length of 15 feet became a practical proposition.

In 1902 Lieutenant John Saumarez Dumaresq devised a trigonometric slide rule calculator, named after him, which recorded the target course, speed and bearing; also the change of range, rate and deflection when given the ship's own speed and estimates of the enemy course, speed and bearing. Dumaresq's fundamental insight was very simple, that range rates (across and along) did not depend on the range, only on target course and speed. In 1903 Captain Percy Scott had suggested a clock mechanism that indicated the best current estimate of the changing range. Vickers took the idea and devised the Vickers clock. Information from the Dumaresq updated the Vickers clock, which calculated the changing range based on a set range rate.[23]

The various trials with long-range firing were reviewed by Scott and he concluded that firing should be controlled from the fore upper and main lower tops. At each control point there would be five people – a control officer, a rangefinder operator, an operator to work the Dumaresq, a stopwatch operator to call out 50 yard range changes based on the rate and an operator for a range and deflection transmitter. How far this was necessary when the Vickers range clock was in use is unclear. When fire was opened the fall of shot was observed to correct the range and deflection figures.[24] It should be noted that both first generation fire control instruments were devised by naval officers and can be regarded as 'in house' attempts at improved fire control.

Fisher and the Further Development of the Dreadnought Idea

A further consideration in deciding on the design of any new ship was the danger from torpedoes and the conclusion that in future, battleships should operate outside effective torpedo range, about 5,000 to 6,000 yards in 1905. Fisher took the torpedo menace very seriously indeed, possibly because he had been deeply involved with torpedoes as far back as the 1870s. His most unequivocal statement on the issue, made early in 1904 is quoted here:

> I tell you I had a man standing in this office a few days ago who had seen a Russian torpedo hitting a small target time after time at 3,000 yards and at 24 knots. We can only do 2,000 yards at 18 knots. Soon it will be 5,000 yards, and then where is your gunnery going to be.[25]

Much the same thing was said in his HMS *Untakeable* memorandum dated October 1904:

> Another reason that leads to long ranges is the dread of the torpedo, which limits the closeness of approach to 3,000 yards. But in large ships with good-sized turning circles, to ensure not approaching within 3,000 yards, the manoeuvring distance will be at least 5,000, otherwise in an unappreciable time the two squadrons get within torpedo range.[26]

Fisher probably overestimated the torpedo threat. During the Russo-Japanese War, hundreds of torpedoes had been fired and very few hits had been scored. *Brassey's Naval Annual 1905* carried a long assessment of the war and use of torpedoes. The author of the report was Cyprian Bridge, a former Director of Naval Intelligence, who severely downgraded the threat from torpedoes:

> The conclusion should be that it is a weapon of limited efficiency; to be depended on only in special circumstances of infrequent occurrence. To found on it a system of tactics, a plan of campaign, or even a type of ship design would be paralleled by founding a system of artillery tactics on the employment of the sabres carried by the gunners. It is not too much to say that experience of the late campaign, confirming as it does the arguments

of students of tactics in these days of long-range guns, justifies a demand that torpedoes should be withdrawn from the armament of cruisers and battleships.[27]

In the summer of 1904 Fisher gave the problem of future ship design a great deal of thought. He was helped by W.H. Gard, the chief constructor at Portsmouth dockyard and Alexander Gracie, managing director of Fairfield Shipbuilding and Engineering. By May 1904 outline designs for HMS *Dreadnought* were ready, with the sketch design prepared by October 1904, when Fisher became First Sea Lord.[28] Fisher remained undecided about the armament and until almost the last minute favoured the largest number of 10-inch guns. Naval attaché reports of the Japanese naval operations stressed the importance of long-range hitting and the much greater effect of 12-inch guns compared to smaller calibres. Howbeit, in October 1904, just after becoming First Sea Lord, Fisher submitted a comparison of two fundamentally different battleship designs, one produced by Armstrong's armed with sixteen 10-inch guns, the other with eight 12-inch guns.[29] It was only in November 1904, almost certainly as a result of the August battle between Japan and Russia, that he finally accepted the 12-inch gun as the primary armament of the new ship. Various layouts were considered and eventually design 'H', with an armament of ten 12-inch guns in five twin turrets, was selected, with three centreline turrets, fore, aft and amidships, and two wing turrets. The wing turrets had theoretical firing arcs ahead, so six guns could fire ahead and eight on each broadside.

The use of wing turrets needs explanation. Oscar Parkes stated that as far back as 1880, with the genesis and building of the battleship HMS *Collingwood*, end-on fire had been discarded and that in future battleships would operate in line ahead, with guns trained on the broadside.[30] This is a dangerously misleading statement. *Brassey's Naval Annual* for 1906 stated the real truth behind the wing turrets of the *Dreadnought*.

> On the forecastle will be mounted two 12-inch guns in a barbette, the centre line being considerably above the water-level. On each side, a short distance to the rear, there will be two other pairs of 12-inch guns on the upper deck level, and in order to enable these guns to fire ahead an embrasure is formed at each side of the forecastle, so that all six 12-inch guns may take part in a running fight.[31]

The idea of end-on fire and a 'chase' action was still alive in 1906 in both the British and German navies. The secondary armament was practically nonexistent and consisted of twenty-four 12-pounders. The *Dreadnought* and a cruiser version which became HMS *Invincible* were to be turbine powered and to have speeds of 21 and 25 knots respectively.

The decision to use turbine propulsion in any new battleship was indeed revolutionary but not necessarily quite as revolutionary as suggested in numerous other accounts of the *Dreadnought* and *Invincible*. In fact, turbine propulsion for large ships, particularly Atlantic liners, was under consideration some three years earlier. A large ferry steamer had been built in 1901 and was turbine powered. The *King Edward* was in every respect a successful ship.[32] The 1903 edition of *Brassey's Naval Annual* discussed the *King Edward* and went on to say:

> It will be of interest in connection with this part of the subject to give here some of the chief elements of a design for an Atlantic liner with turbine machinery, which has been prepared at the Wallsend yard of the Parsons Marine Steam Turbine Company. The vessel is to be 540 ft long by 63 feet wide, 41 feet moulded depth, and 25 ft 6 in draught [...] The displacement is put down at 15,000 and the I.H.P. 23,000, and this gives an estimated speed of 21½ to 22 knots.[33]

The 1904 edition of *Brassey's* gave further details of the new turbine powered Atlantic liners:

> Since we last wrote on the subject it has been decided to place the Parsons turbine in vessels of the ocean liner type. The proprietors of the Allan line have ordered from Messrs. Workman, Clark and Co., of Belfast, a vessel for the Liverpool-Canadian mail service.[34]

The Allan line had two liners built, *Victorian* and *Virginian*. Ordered in October 1903, the first was the *Victorian*, a 10,635-ton ship, 540 feet in length, triple-screwed and powered by three Parsons direct acting turbines of 15,000 horsepower to give a speed of 18 knots. A high-pressure turbine was attached to the centre shaft and low pressure turbines were used on the wing shafts. *Victorian* entered service on 23 March 1905, while *Virginian* started her maiden voyage on 6 April 1905. She set up a new record of five days 20 hours, 40 minutes for the Liverpool–Rimouski (Canada) crossing. These ships made their maiden voyages four and five months respectively before the keel plates of the *Dreadnought* were laid.[35] If the turbine machinery had failed outright or had proved unworkable the Admiralty would certainly have known of it. The first Cunard liner to be turbine powered was RMS *Carmania*, launched 21 February 1905, with her maiden voyage commencing 2 December 1905, some nine months after *Virginian* and two months after *Dreadnought* had been laid down.

The Royal Navy had some limited turbine experience with small destroyers and a 'scout' class cruiser, HMS *Amethyst*. *Amethyst* was laid down in 1903 and commissioned in March 1905, at almost exactly the same time as *Victorian*. By the time *Dreadnought* was laid down there was indeed some turbine experience in newly-commissioned Atlantic liners and in an admittedly small third-class 'scout' cruiser.

Fisher and the Building of the *Dreadnought*

Dreadnought was laid down at Portsmouth in October 1905 and was launched by Edward VII on 10 February 1906, thus breaking the tradition that launches were performed by females.[36] *Dreadnought* made her steam trials in October 1906, a year and a day after her laying down. She was completed in a blaze of publicity and press headlines. This remarkable building achievement owed more to showmanship than to anything else. During his time at Portsmouth Fisher had ensured a stockpile of materials to ensure hasty construction. Pre-fabrication work had started in May 1905 and some 6,000 weeks of labour costing £41,295 had been put into her before keel-laying on 2 October 1905.[37] The extra 12-inch gun turrets were taken from the *Lord Nelson* and *Agamemnon*, which were late completing in consequence. By taking every short cut possible and giving the *Dreadnought* priority over all other construction, she was completed sensationally fast. Nevertheless, though ready for steam trials, the *Dreadnought* was not fully completed for another three months. In view of the big increase in speed, the hull form was very different from any previous battleship and was fully tank-tested. It is widely stated that the *Dreadnought* had a ram bow. The original design had a straight bow but Fisher did not like it and tank-testing showed that any curved shape gave at least half a knot speed advantage compared with a straight bow.[38] The curved shape was not in fact a ram.

With Fisher's constant prompting *Dreadnought* was ready for steam trials on 29 September 1906, commissioned on 11 December and started her maiden voyage on 5 January 1907. The 11 December date is probably her real completion date.[39] A quadruple screw design was adopted that developed 23,000 horsepower and gave a speed of 21 knots. Two high-pressure turbines were fitted to each wing shaft, one for steaming ahead and

Lord Nelson
Agamemnon

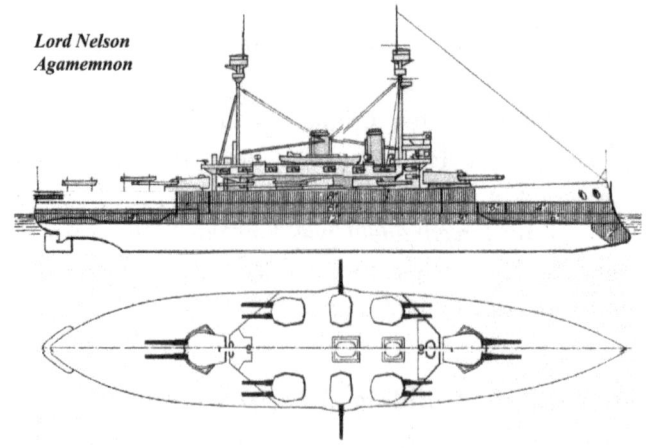

Based on *Brassey's Naval Annual 1914* Plate 5

Lord Nelson:	Palmer, Nov '04–Sept '06–1908 £1,500,000
Agamemnon:	Beardmore, Oct '04–June '06–1907
Dimensions:	435 × 79.5 × 27 feet = 16,500 tons
Armament:	Four 12-inch 45 cal., ten 9.2-inch 50 cal.
Armour:	Belt 12", amidships 6", forward 4", aft, deck 2", barbettes 12", turrets 8", lower deck side 8"
	Secondary turrets 7", conning tower 12", battery 7", secondary turrets 7"
	conning tower 12". Total 4,200 tons (25.45%)
Machinery:	Two sets 4-cylinder vertical triple expansion 2 screws 15 Yarrow or Babcock boilers, IHP 16,750 = 18.5 knots
Coal:	900 tons normal, 2,000 tons max, 400 tons oil
Complement:	865
Comment:	The design of these two ships so closely resembles the Japanese *Aki* and *Satsuma* that it must be concluded that the Japanese were given access to British designs.

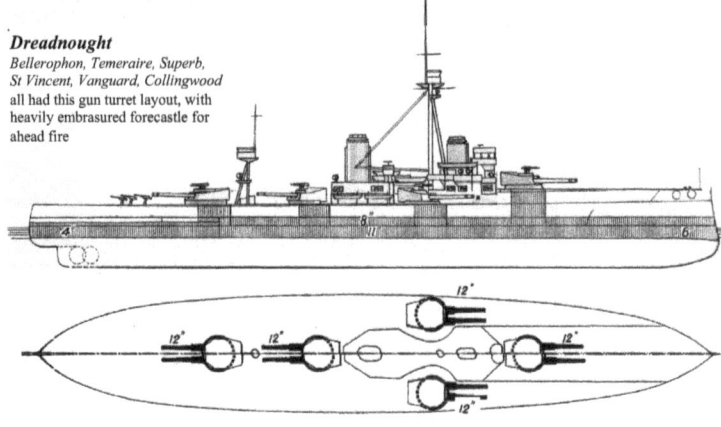

Dreadnought
Bellerophon, Temeraire, Superb,
St Vincent, Vanguard, Collingwood
all had this gun turret layout, with
heavily embrasured forecastle for
ahead fire

Based on *Brassey's Naval Annual 1914* Plate 4

Dreadnought:	Portsmouth, Dec '05–Feb '06–Oct '06
Dimensions:	520 × 82 × 31 feet = 17,900 tons, full load 22,200 tons
Armament:	Ten 12-inch 45 cal. twenty-four 12-pounders
Armour:	Belt 11" amidships 6" forward 4" aft, deck 2¾", barbettes 11", turrets 8"
	Fore conning tower 12", after conning tower 8". Total 5,000 ton (27.93%)
Machinery:	Parsons turbine 4 screws, 18 Babcock boilers
	SHP 23,000 = 21 knots
Coal:	900 tons normal, 2,000 tons maximum
Complement:	800

Fig. 9 British semi-dreadnoughts and the Dreadnought *herself*

the other for going astern. The two inner shafts each had three low-pressure turbines; one for cruising, one for going at speed and one for going astern. The steam from the high pressure turbines fed the low-pressure units on the inner shafts. There was no complicated valve linkage for timing the high pressure or low pressure stages as in reciprocating engines, so high speed steaming was possible with much greater reliability and less vibration than previously.

Protection was rather less than *Dreadnought*'s predecessors *Lord Nelson* and *Agamemnon*. Instead of the 12-inch belt of the *Lord Nelson* class an 11-inch belt was adopted. The protection scheme distinguished clearly between the upper and lower armour belts and the upper belt was only eight inches thick. This ensured that the rather narrow 11-inch belt was often submerged in a seaway. During World War I, running under full load wartime conditions, virtually the entire main belt armour was submerged most of the time.[40] Torpedo protection was given very careful consideration. Internal armoured screens were fitted over the magazines and partial torpedo bulkheads were used. Since the later dreadnoughts had complete torpedo bulkheads, these 'partials' need explanation. At this time there was a good deal of emphasis on venting the gas caused by a torpedo exploding. An armour deck covering an empty explosion chamber might resist the gas and force it deeper into the hull, exactly the opposite of the desired effect. In consequence, there was no armour deck outboard of the partial torpedo bulkhead.[41]

Naval reaction to the *Dreadnought* was very mixed. Influential naval thinkers such as Sir William White, Admiral Custance, Lord Brassey and A.T. Mahan condemned her out of hand. They argued that a greater number of smaller ships was both necessary and preferable. A strong secondary armament would smother a target in a hail of fire that could not be sustained by larger slower firing guns. The battle analysis of Tsushima was very contradictory. Custance and Mahan denied any need for speed while Lieutenant-Commander Sims of the United States Navy, destined to command the American naval forces in Europe during World War I, argued that speed allowed the Japanese to choose the range and time of battle. In terms of gunnery, the engagement was decisive at 6,000–8,000 yards, exactly the range the *Dreadnought* was designed to fight at. Sims also showed that the most hits were scored when the rate of range change was least.[42]

It may be questioned whether Fisher was right in going for a radical new type of battleship but there can be no doubt that other nations were building ships with very heavy intermediate batteries and that at some time in the future they would have made the step to a *Dreadnought* type. The *Dreadnought* concept was not exclusively British nor a uniquely Fisher product. In 1903, *Jane's Fighting Ships* carried an article by the Italian naval constructor Vittorio Cuniberti, titled 'An ideal battleship for the British Navy'. He proposed a 17,000-ton ship armed with twelve 12-inch guns, protected by 12 inches of armour with a speed of 20 knots. This combination of armament, protection and speed would bring an overwhelming concentration of fire into action at a decisive battle range. In America, where experiments with heavy intermediate batteries were greatest, the experiments with all big gun layouts were carried further at an earlier stage than in Britain. In 1903, plans were drawn up for two battleships with eight 12-inch guns. Two turrets were carried forward and two aft, with one turret superimposed over the other in each case. The *Michigan* and *South Carolina* were planned well before the *Dreadnought*.[43] Taken with Japanese and Italian ideas for battleship construction, it was clear that the move to a uniform main armament was going to be taken in the years 1905–9.

The sea trials of the *Dreadnought* were a great success and the 1906–7 programme provided for four more dreadnoughts. The incoming Liberal government cut this to three, not unreasonable in 1906–7. The *Bellerophon*, *Temeraire* and *Superb* were nearly exact replicas of the *Dreadnought*. The only differences were an upgrading of the secondary armament from 12-pounders to 4-inch guns. The bridgework of the early dreadnoughts has been much criticised over the years, particularly the placing of the foremast behind the funnel. At any speed the control top was smoked out and rendered uninhabitable. The reason for this was twofold; partly the belief that top weight had to be kept down to an absolute minimum and if the funnel formed the bridge supporting structure this reduced weights. It was also the case that the boat handling derrick could be part of the mast structure. At least in part, the lengthy time it took to evolve a satisfactory bridge/foremast/funnel arrangement was due to Rear-Admiral Jellicoe's obsession with boat handling arrangements.[44] Fisher's second wonder ship was, of course, the dreadnought cruiser *Invincible*, a ship evolved for radically different reasons than those that produced the *Dreadnought*.

Fisher and the First Battlecruisers

Fisher took the view that, in an age when battleships could be sunk by torpedo craft and submarines, the battleship was of diminishing utility.

The new type of battleship (*Dreadnought*), designed for high speed, was justifiable only if the ship was a glorified armoured cruiser.

> This new battleship will not only be a battleship but a first class cruiser superior to any but the very latest, hence for years to come she will be useful since whether battleships are or are not used in the future her speed will always make her of the greatest value.[45]

The confusion of purpose over the exact role of the battleship and armoured cruiser was discussed in Chapter 2, and it was pointed out that as far back as 1893, Rear-Admiral Long had used the term battlecruiser to describe the larger first-class cruisers. The large armoured cruisers of the late 1890s and early 1900s were perceived to fulfil many of the functions of battleships and indeed could on occasion be considered fast battleships. There is no doubt Fisher wanted a fusion of the battleship and armoured cruiser types, but accepted that this was not yet possible and said so:

> There is good ground for enquiry whether the naval supremacy of a country can any longer be assessed by its battleships. To build battleships merely to fight enemy battleships, so long as cheaper craft can destroy them, and prevent them of themselves protecting sea operations, is merely to breed Kilkenny cats unable to catch rats or mice [...] This at once forces a consideration as to how a battleship differs from an armoured cruiser. Fundamentally the battleship sacrifices speed for a superior armament and protective armour. It is this superiority of speed that enables an enemy's ship to be overhauled or evaded that constitutes the real difference between the two. At the present moment naval experience is not sufficiently ripe to abolish totally the building of battleships so long as other countries do not do so. But it is evidently an absolute necessity in future construction to make the speed of a battleship approach as nearly as possible that of the armoured cruiser.[46]

Further confusion concerning the exact role of the battleship and armoured cruiser was added by Japan and her building policy, known in detail in London through the medium of the Anglo-Japanese naval treaty. Even before Tsushima, the Japanese were planning four very powerful new ships with both battleship and armoured cruiser characteristics, close to Fisher's 'fusion' concept. The battleships *Aki* and *Satsuma* were laid down at Kure and Yokosuka respectively, in March and May 1905, five months before the *Dreadnought* was commenced. Each mounted four 12-inch and twelve 10-inch guns, making them ships that come under the heading of semi-dreadnoughts. It was originally intended that *Satsuma* would be the world's first all big gun battleship, predating the *Dreadnought* by some months, but the cost of the Russo-Japanese War brought Japan close to financial ruin, so the cheaper armament was adopted. These were the first battleships built in Japan and took nearly five years to build as Japanese engineers grappled with the complexity of battleship construction. *Aki* was powered by Curtis turbines and had a speed of 20 knots, while *Satsuma* retained the more conventional triple expansion machinery, with a speed of 18.25 knots. At the same time, two cruiser versions of these ships were planned, *Kurama* and *Ibuki*, each mounting four 12-inch guns, with a lighter secondary battery of eight 8-inch guns. *Ibuki* was powered with Curtis turbines and *Kurama* triple expansion engines. Laid down in August 1905 and May 1906, they had a speed of 21.25 knots and 22 knots respectively. The 1914 edition of *Jane's Fighting Ships* calls them armoured ships and in brackets, 'Battle Cruisers'. Japan had two other large armoured ships building, *Tsukuba* and *Ikoma*, laid down in January and March 1905. They were armed with four 12-inch and twelve 6-inch guns. With a speed of 20.5 knots and weak 7-inch armour, *Jane's Fighting Ships* was apparently unable to classify them and referred to them simply as 'armoured ships'.[47] In truth, these ships came close to the cruiser/battleship 'fusion' type so favoured by Fisher.

As conceived, Britain's first battlecruisers, the three Invincible class ships, had three roles: as the fast wing of a battle fleet, able to engage battleships in the manner described by Admiral Long as far back as 1893; as super-cruisers able to press home a reconnaissance in the face of enemy armoured cruisers; and also as trade protection by sinking any armoured cruiser or armed merchant liner in existence. The armed merchant liner used as a commerce destroyer will be examined later and represents an important but hidden reason for the first battlecruisers.

At the time the first battlecruisers were conceived, Germany was just becoming a perceived adversary and her mercantile marine had several large fast ocean liners that might be used as armed merchant cruisers in wartime. Writing in the late 1920s, Admiral Bacon, Fisher's first biographer, put it well:

> The Invincible had a totally different genesis from the Dreadnought. She was designed in order to meet a want that had long been felt but never supplied, namely, a ship fast enough to hunt down any armed merchant ship afloat.[48]

Writing in the late 1930s, Vice-Admiral K.G.B. Dewar directly contradicted this view and said that 'Fisher's introduction of the battlecruiser type was open to more severe criticism, because it fulfilled no strategic or tactical need'.[49] John Roberts puts the two statements side by side, and in doing so shows the disagreements about the role and purpose of the battlecruisers.

In terms of trade defence in 1901, the Naval Intelligence Division established a new section to plot the flow of trade to and from Britain. This gave the Admiralty a day-by-day analysis of the position of British registered merchant vessels. Information was provided by local consuls, shipping agents and even, on occasion, secret agents. Lloyds of London also supplied a vast amount of intelligence on shipping movements. The now vast telegraph cable network was used to supply the Admiralty with much of this information. In 1906 a War Room was established in the Admiralty and plotted both British and foreign warships and merchant ships. In this context the first battlecruisers, wireless equipped, were a rapid deployment force, designed to go to any future trouble spot, based on accurate intelligence.[50]

The detailed design of the *Dreadnought* was finally decided in May 1905 and the armoured cruiser in July 1905.[51] Great secrecy was attached to the new cruiser design and the 1906–7 edition of *Jane's Fighting Ships* suggested an armament of eight or ten 9.2-inch guns.[52] Fisher wanted to abandon the use of the words battleship and cruiser, substituting the term armoured vessel to describe both types.[53] He appointed a second design committee, known as the 'fusion' committee, but stated the parameters of the new ship; 25.5 knots and a 12-inch gun armament. What emerged was an armoured cruiser version of the *Dreadnought*.[54] The ship HMS *Invincible* had the same calibre guns as the *Dreadnought* but one turret fewer, one turret forward, one aft and two *en echelon* amidships. The reintroduction of *en echelon* mounted turrets can only be satisfactorily explained if it is remembered that back in 1881 Fisher had commanded the *en echelon* battleship *Inflexible* and wanted a fusion of the *Inflexible* and *Devastation* gun layouts. The nominal cross-deck firing to give a full broadside of eight 12-inch guns was very nominal. Battleships and battlecruisers with *en echelon* mounted turrets tore up their decks in cross-deck firing to such an extent that it was virtually never done in peacetime. *Invincible* was turbine powered with quadruple screws, and had a speed of 25 knots. She could outrun any ship she could not outgun. She had no fewer than ten turbines developing 41,000 shp, two high pressure and two low pressure ahead turbines; the high pressure turbines on the outer shafts, the low pressure on the inner shafts, two high pressure and two low pressure astern turbines and two cruising sets, with steam provided by 31 boilers. Her armour scheme was very similar to the Minotaur-class armoured cruisers laid down in 1905 and consisted of a 6-inch belt, 7-inch to 2-inch bulkheads, 7-inch barbettes and turret faces 10 inches.[55] The 3,460 tons of armour protection amounted to 19.9 per cent of displacement compared to the 5,000 tons of armour in the *Dreadnought* (27.6 per cent).[56] The armour scheme of the *Invincible* and her sisters *Inflexible* and *Indomitable* has been the subject of a great deal of negative criticism over the years:

> Admiral Schofield remembers that when he joined *Indomitable* as a midshipman in 1912, the weakness of the deck armour was a matter of common knowledge among the officers. Beneath the thin deck plating amidships lay a transverse magazine which served the two *en echelon* wing, 12-inch gun turrets. The magazine, which lay across the full beam of the ship, contained at full load, fifty tons of high-explosive cordite and some 400 shells. Above this magazine, the diesel dynamo room was situated. This was ventilated by a large air trunk to the upper deck, across was fitted a grating, so, in fact, there was nothing to stop a plunging shell from penetrating straight through to the magazine.[57]

Some of the more severe criticism of the three Invincibles' armour is unfair. At the time they were laid down, France had 25 armoured cruisers, built or building, mostly armed with 19-cm (7.6-inch), 16-cm (6.4-inch) and 14-cm (5.5-inch) guns. Germany had eight armoured cruisers, built or building and all save one were armed with 21-cm (8.2-inch) guns. Russia had seven armoured cruisers, with three building, mostly armed with 6-inch guns. All were armoured with belts of four to six inches thickness.[58] Against such opponents the first battlecruisers were indeed adequately protected. What Fisher did not anticipate, and perhaps he should have, was that Germany would build battlecruisers of her own. Finally, the term battlecruiser was adopted in November 1911, to describe the ships of the Invincible class and, later, to distinguish them from the older armoured cruisers.[59]

The Armed Merchant Liner Cruiser Concept

The idea that the larger liners might be used as armed merchant cruisers in wartime was not new. It was recognised from the early days of steam that

Invincible
Indomitable
Inflexible

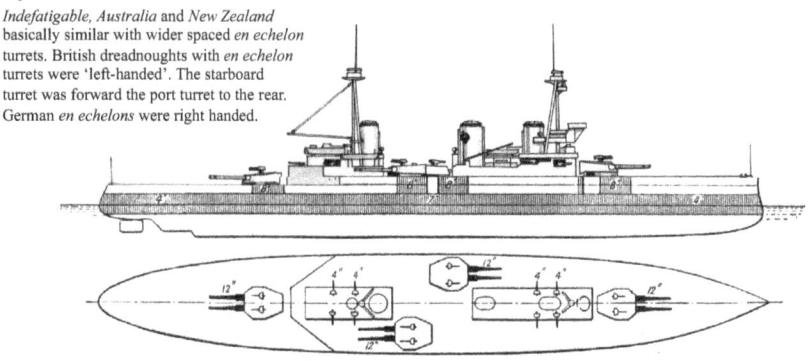

Indefatigable, Australia and New Zealand basically similar with wider spaced *en echelon* turrets. British dreadnoughts with *en echelon* turrets were 'left-handed'. The starboard turret was forward the port turret to the rear. German *en echelons* were right handed.

Brassey's Naval Annual 1914, Plate 10

Invincible:	Elswick, Apr '06–Apr '07–'08	£1,662,337
Indomitable:	Fairfield, Mar '06–Mar '07–'08	£1,677,515
Inflexible:	Clydebank, Feb '06 Jun '07–'08	£1,635,739
Dimensions:	560 × 78.5 × 26.5/30 feet = 17,250 tons, 20,000 tons full load	
Armament:	Eight 12-inch 45 cal., sixteen 4-inch	
Armour:	Belt 6" amidships 4" bow, bulkheads 7"–6", barbettes 7", gunhouses 7" conning tower 10" (fore) 6" (aft), main deck 1"– ¾", middle deck 1½", lower 2½" Total armour 3,460 tons (20.05%)	
Machinery:	Parsons turbines 4 screws, S.H.P. 41,000 = 25 knots	
Coal:	1,000 tons normal, 3,080 tons max.	
Complement:	837	

Fig. 10 The first dreadnought battlecruisers, Invincible class

the larger, faster steamships had considerable military value. As far back as 1839–40 the Admiralty had signed contracts with Cunard, the Royal Mail Steam Packet Company and the Peninsular and Oriental Company for these companies to provide the Admiralty with their best steamers in wartime.[60] Germany had two major shipping lines, North German Lloyd and Hamburg-America; until the 1890s neither was much competition to the British. In 1897, just as the German Navy was moving towards the First Navy Law and fleet expansion, North German Lloyd laid down the *Kaiser Wilhelm de Grosse*. At the time of her completion she was the largest and fastest liner in the world, 14,350 tons and 22½ knots. In 1900 Hamburg-America eclipsed her with the *Deutschland*. Soon North German Lloyd held nearly a quarter of the North Atlantic passenger trade, and Hamburg-America was never far behind. Further liner building gave Germany *Kaiser Wilhelm II*, *Kronprinz Wilhelm* and *Kronprinzessin Cecilie*.[61] All were good for 22½–23 knots, as fast as any armoured cruiser afloat.

Worries about German ocean liners were voiced by Lord Brassey who stated as far back as 1902 that, of the 11 liners built since 1895 and capable of steaming at 20 knots or more, only one, the *Oceanic*, was British registered. Brassey's answer was to subsidise high speed merchant ships rather than the slower mail boats. Reginald Custance, as Director of Naval Intelligence, opposed the idea of subsidies and wanted all resources devoted to the battle fleet. His successor as DNI, Prince Louis of Battenberg, disagreed. In a report of 1903 he analysed the fast German liners and concluded that they were superior to British Liners.

> It cannot be denied that at the present time the Germans have four ships which have probably a faster continuous sea speed than anything we can oppose to them [...] or that these four ships acting in concert with their heavy armaments, fitted with wireless telegraphy [...] could seriously interrupt our trans-Atlantic imports [...] It is clear that we are outmatched both in speed and in armaments, if our vessels of this class are able to catch and fight any which our possible enemies can send out [...] Most of them are several knots slower than the four great German liners.[62]

The North Atlantic liner trade was further complicated when J.P. Morgan, the acknowledged railway king of America and one of the richest men in history, appeared on the scene. Morgan tired of railways and bought the American steel industry. In what was at the time the largest private financial transaction in history; he bought out Andrew Carnegie and the result was US Steel, the world's first billion-dollar corporation. Morgan soon tired of steel and decided to buy the North Atlantic liner trade. In 1902, with a capital of $120 million, he founded International Mercantile Marine (IMM) and started to buy shipping lines. Within a very short time companies such as Red Star Line and Leyland Line came under his control. Then he bought the entire capital stock of the White Star Line for $25 million. Next he approached Cunard and offered them 80 per cent over the market price for their shares.

When J.P. Morgan attempted to buy the North Atlantic liner trade, the real alarm felt in London concerned American-owned British registered ships. In wartime these ships could be conveniently sitting in American ports, indefinitely delayed if there was the remotest possibility of them being commandeered as auxiliary cruisers. If Morgan 'owned' the North Atlantic, one of the main methods of trade protection in wartime – the ability to use fast liners as auxiliary cruisers – was removed. As far as the Admiralty was concerned, and indeed British opinion, British flag registration should mean British corporate ownership as well. Cunard turned down Morgan's offer, but thought they might reconsider if the offer was increased. The government waited with bated breath to see what would happen. Cunard wanted capital for new large fast ships and they wanted it badly; J.P. Morgan already owned close to half the North Atlantic liner tonnage and wanted it all. If Cunard sold out, the largest and most lucrative shipping trade in history would fall under American domination.[63]

In 1902–3 Rear-Admiral Battenberg (DNI) was recommending subsidies for merchant ships with speeds over 22 knots and it was unacceptable to have German liners that could not be pursued in wartime.[64] As a result of the deliberations concerning fast merchant ships, Cunard were given a loan of £2.6 million to build two new super-ships and a mail subsidy of £150,000 per annum. The Admiralty loan (subvention) covered the cost of strengthened deck plates to support 6-inch naval guns in wartime and allow fast conversion to auxiliary cruiser status. The subsidy was more than ten times larger than any subvention previously paid to a ship-owner. The *Mauretania* and the *Lusitania* were supremely important. The *Mauretania* held the Blue Riband, that is, she was the fastest ship on the North Atlantic for 25 years. The *Lusitania*, torpedoed in 1915 with the loss of more than 1,000 lives, many of them American, was a major cause of American entry into World War I on the allied side.

These liners were turbine powered, and in addition to the enormous government subsidy Cunard benefited from the cutting edge warship technology defined by *Dreadnought* and *Invincible*. Their direct drive turbines developed 68,000 shp. The liners' semi-warship construction included double-skinned sides and coal bunkers designed to absorb shellfire. They were designed for 24$\frac{1}{2}$ knots but made 26–7 knots in service. At just over 30,000 tons they were half as big again as any other liners in existence. J.P. Morgan had lost his battle to buy the North Atlantic liner trade and Britain had two liners that in wartime could run down any German liner in existence. Fisher's 'fusion' committee had concluded that only the fastest merchant ships were worth subsidising:

> The speed of modern cruisers absolutely precludes the use of any vessels for trade protection or destruction not possessed of very high speed. The only ships with the necessary speed are the two new Cunarders.[65]

Mauritania became an armed merchant cruiser in World War I. Paradoxically her enormous size and massive coal consumption made her wholly unsuitable for the task, yet it was the armed merchant cruiser concept that had, in part at least, produced the original government subsidy that built her.

It may be concluded that the *Invincible* was built not just to run down every armoured cruiser built but also any liner built, since these liners could be armed merchant cruisers in wartime. Fisher's idea of asserting worldwide naval supremacy was based on Rear-Admiral Long's belief, stated as far back as 1893, 'that powerful cruisers at the end of a telegraph wire will be more conducive to sea power than numerous small ones, where ocean routes are concerned'.[66]

Entente Cordiale and British Naval Policy

After the Anglo-Japanese Treaty Britain started the process of improving her relations with neighbouring great power states. Joseph Chamberlain was Colonial Secretary from 1895 to 1900, and one of the first politicians to realise that 'splendid isolation' was no longer valid. He wanted an Anglo-German alliance and from 1898 onwards said so in public. He worked towards this objective in both public and private until 1901 when Prince Bülow and Baron Holstein rebuffed his efforts. Chamberlain then turned to France and initiated talks between Paul Cambon and Lord Lansdowne, who became Foreign Secretary in 1900. These talks developed into the *entente cordiale*. Britain needed the *entente* as much as anything else because of her alliance with Japan. If Japan was attacked by two powers (France and Russia in alliance since 1893), the third power (Britain) would immediately have to declare war on these two powers. The *entente* was really a reinsurance treaty, with the prospect of France mitigating the effects of Russian aggression, particularly in the Far East. The *entente* was also concerned with other extra-European questions, particularly Egypt and Morocco, with an agreement that Britain was paramount in Egypt and the Sudan, and France in Morocco.

1905 was a year that radically changed the strategic landscape for Britain. The *entente cordiale* with France the previous year and the testing of the *entente* by Germany over Morocco in the spring of 1905, combined with the near annihilation of the Russian Navy at Tsushima, had ended the almost century-long British strategic appreciation that France and Russia were her potential adversaries in some future conflict.

The Development of British Defence Policy from 1903

Having considered the immediate effects of the *Dreadnought*, a larger analysis of defence policy and how policy was determined can be attempted. At the start of the Boer War the army's performance in the field mirrored the worst bungling of the Crimean campaign 45 years earlier. Against the Russians in the Crimea and against Boer commandos, the British Army found warfare a salutary experience. After the Boer War, the Elgin Commission was appointed to inquire into the early stages of the army's efforts in South Africa. Largely as a result of the Elgin Commission, in March 1903 the Committee for Imperial Defence was formed. Lord Esher wanted a root and branch reform of the War Office. In Esher's view, the post of commander-in-chief should be abolished and replaced by an army council. In September 1903, Esher, Fisher, and Balfour were guests of Edward VII at Balmoral and the Committee of Imperial Defence (CID) was discussed in detail. The committee included Lord Esher, Fisher and the secretary of the committee, Sir George Clarke (Lord Sydenham).

At this time, Fisher wanted a joint Cabinet head for the army and navy, effectively a Minister of Defence, as in Austria-Hungary. In reality Fisher's idea of a joint army/navy minister in the cabinet was an army subordinated to naval control.[67] The army, in Fisher's view, should be assigned limited roles, particularly amphibious roles. The navy estimates could be held steady while defence costs fell, presumably at the expense of the army. The army reforms at this time were largely sensible and the General Staff system was extended to the entire army and not just the War Office. An Expeditionary Force was established, consisting of one cavalry and six infantry divisions, a total of 120,000 men. In July 1907 the Territorial and Reserve Forces Act became law. This merged the yeomanry and volunteers into 14 divisions and 14 mounted brigades, all equipped up to regular army standards. The role of the Territorials would be home defence at the start of a war and after several months training, a place alongside regular units in action.

Esher was offered the post of Secretary of State for War. He turned it down in favour of the post of Lieutenant and Deputy Governor of Windsor Castle, preferring a socially prestigious role at Court and the opportunity to manipulate events behind the scenes to the more obvious trappings of power.

As the years passed and the nemesis of 1914 approached, so the importance of the CID increased. Apart from the short premiership of

Sir Henry Campbell-Bannerman, it was the premierships of the Conservative Arthur Balfour and the Liberal Herbert Asquith that dominated the early years of the twentieth century. Despite their different political affiliations, these prime ministers took a rather similar approach to defence matters. Each knew enough about the complications of defence policy not to want any direct involvement unless absolutely necessary. This ensured that when a complicated defence problem was presented to the prime minister, he promptly formed a sub-committee of the CID. The sub-committee then deliberated and reported back in the course of time. It is probably unkind to suggest that these sub-committees were a useful method of shelving unpalatable problems with difficult solutions; nevertheless the byzantine workings of the CID and its sub-committees had a vitally important influence on the development of government in the twentieth century. In due time, a young Royal Marine officer, Captain Maurice Hankey, became secretary of the CID and in 1916 the committee became the basis for the Cabinet Office Secretariat with Hankey as Cabinet Secretary. Thus, the office for the implementation of prime ministerial control came into being, not through Civil Service wishes but out of a committee formed to consider the nation's defences as a result of army bungling in the Boer War.

Perspectives: Fisher Derailed, Dreadnoughts and a Fast Changing World

The *Dreadnought* has been variously described as either a blunder or a stroke of genius.[68] In truth it was neither and the view taken by David Brown and others, that this was simply a ship whose time had come, is closest to the truth.[69] All the technology elements that made the *Dreadnought* work, including turbines, wireless telegraphy and the beginnings of automated gunnery fire control systems existed in 1905–6. Other nations, particularly the United States and Japan, were already moving in the direction of advanced semi-dreadnought types and the coming of the *Dreadnought* or something like it was probably inevitable. What Fisher did not seem to realise was that he had totally reversed traditional British Admiralty policy that had served the navy and the nation well for decades. Before the Naval Defence Act Admiralty policy was reactive and responded to naval innovation by other powers; it did not of itself initiate change. Fisher reinforced the proactive policy and did not consider the consequences of initiating radical naval change. The Fisher *Dreadnought* policy, designed initially as an economy measure to cut naval expenditure, led quickly into an enormously expensive naval arms race with Germany. It can be argued that the Fisher policy was, to quote John Brooks, 'risky, insufficiently considered, ill-informed and unnecessary'.[70]

Fisher's wonder ship *Dreadnought* was conceived as a result of astute reading of the foreign competition and an analysis of the war between Japan and Russia in the Far East. It is particularly the case that the battle fought on 10 August 1904 ensured that the *Dreadnought* was armed with 12-inch guns. The Anglo-Japanese naval treaty ensured that Britain had full access to the reports of the naval war and British naval attachés served with the Japanese fleet. The *Dreadnought* was not specifically anti-German in nature and no surviving document concerned with the *Dreadnought* mentions the German Navy.[71]

The confusion of purpose concerning the exact role of the battleship and cruiser was by no means limited to Fisher and ran back into the genesis of the armoured cruiser in the 1890s. Fisher, as with so many other ideas concerning the development of navies, picked up on the idea of a 'fusion' ship and ran with the concept. The result was the new testament ships, the first battlecruisers. It is interesting to note that the *Dreadnought* was built in the royal dockyard at Portsmouth while the first three battlecruisers were built in private yards, *Invincible* at Elswick, *Inflexible* at Clydebank and *Indomitable* at Fairfield. The cancellation of ships building in private yards would have had huge political ramifications for the incoming Liberal government. It may be suggested that Fisher placed the orders in private yards to forestall any cancellation by the incoming administration. It also shows his deep-rooted commitment to the idea of the battleship/cruiser, the true fusion ship.

The 1905 Morocco crisis identified Germany as the most likely adversary in a future war and her navy was a decidedly battleship navy. There were, of course, German armoured cruisers but they were many fewer than their French counterparts. There was also the matter of large, fast German liners, capable of operating as merchant cruisers in wartime. Nevertheless, in this new context of North Sea operations lightly armoured battlecruisers had little further role. Germany aimed to fight in the North Sea and if battlecruisers were to be used as a fast scouting wing of the battlefleet, they needed to be armoured to 80 per cent of battleship standard. The *Invincibles* were fair enough in their way but continuing the concept was a huge mistake. The battlecruisers vitiated Britain's response to the German threat, and this can be laid directly at the feet of Jacky Fisher.

Fisher's four great successes were the nucleus crew system, the scrapping policy for older less effective ships, the fleet redistribution made possible by the annihilation of the Russian Navy in the Far East and, finally, the *Dreadnought*. The negatives included the failure of the Osborne scheme, already discussed, and the idea that engineers might one day command ships. Fisher's biggest mistake was his failure to realise that other navies, particularly the German Navy, might build battlecruisers of their own.

5

The Imperial German Navy (Kaiserliche Marine)

Prelude: The German Navy Before Tirpitz and the Kaiser

At the dawn of the twentieth century Germany emerged as a first-class naval power, mainly due to Alfred Von Tirpitz's advocacy of the German Navy as the instrument of *Weltpolitik*, that is, Germany as a world power. In this vision he was strongly supported by Kaiser Wilhelm II and a man destined to be German Chancellor, Bernard Von Bülow. In the 1860s, the Kingdom of Prussia had a small navy, the navy of the North German Confederation – really only a coast defence force. This navy was smaller than that of Italy or Austria-Hungary and ranked clearly as a minor power navy. The German empire grew rapidly and the Franco-Prussian War established Germany as a military power of the first order with the Kaiserliche Marine, or Imperial Navy, formally constituted in 1871. The Franco-Prussian War eclipsed French naval and military strength and ensured that throughout the 1870s German interest in a navy was minimal. At the time of the Franco-Prussian War the North German Navy had five ironclads, three built in Britain and two in France. Bismarck and Moltke did not consider navies important; armies were all. The German Navy as a force was subordinated to the army and considered an adjunct to a larger land-based strategy. As a largely coast defence force, the German Navy existed to protect the Baltic and North Sea coasts.

In the years following the Franco-Prussian War, it was generals who commanded the German Navy. In 1872, Lieutenant-General Von Stosch became the first chief of the Imperial Admiralty and introduced a ten-year plan. His plan was not ambitious and was never fully carried out.[1] In the 12 years he commanded the German Navy, ten ironclads were acquired.

These included three central battery ironclads, two of which, *Kaiser* and *Deutschland*, became the last British built ironclads in the German Navy. A total of seven central citadel ironclads were acquired, all built in Germany as her shipbuilding industry got under way.[2] The German Navy also acquired several fast cruisers of around 5,000 tons, with a respectable turn of speed, at 18–20 knots.

At this time many German naval officers had entered the navy via the merchant marine. Von Stosch did not approve of these men and of the 20 senior officers in 1872, half were gone by 1878; all had a merchant marine background.[3] Officer entry in future would be similar to the army, with emphasis placed on family and background. A Marine Engineer Corps was established but applicants had to demonstrate an ability to speak both English and French, a device effectively excluding common machinists from advancing to engineer officer status. Stosch also introduced infantry drill as part of a sailors' training and is remembered today as the man who 'militarised' the German Navy.[4]

For Germany, the first impulse towards an oceanic navy was the building of cruisers and the acquisition of overseas territory in Africa and the Pacific. Bismarck issued a 'White Book', entitled *German Interests in the South Seas*. This publication considered how Germany could expand her trade in the South Sea Islands. German explorers, backed by warships reconnoitred the coasts of New Guinea and New Britain, hoisted the German flag. Many large and small islands fell under German control and this included most of the Solomon Islands, while the islands to the north of New Guinea became the Bismarck Archipelago.[5]

By the end of the 1870s most German cruisers were being sent to East Asian and South Pacific destinations. In 1879 eight of their 12 active cruisers were in the Far East, in 1880, ten of 12; in 1881, eight of 11; in 1882, seven of ten and in 1883 seven of 12.[6] Activity centred around Samoa and at one point in the 1880s American and German warships came close to war over Samoa. The net result of these deployments was an officer corps with an increasing amount of trans-oceanic experience. In 1881 Germany negotiated a contract with China and built the battleships *Ting Yuen* and *Chen Yuen*, already discussed.[7]

The great crisis of the Von Stosch era occurred in May 1878, when three German ironclads, *König Wilhelm*, *Grosser Kurfürst* and *Preussen*, were steaming down the English Channel in close formation. In avoiding a merchant ship the *König Wilhelm* managed to ram the *Grosser Kurfürst*, which sank in just 15 minutes, taking 276 of the crew of 500 to the bottom of the sea.[8] The resultant court martials, enquiries etc. left Von Stosch badly damaged but still in charge.

In 1883 General Caprivi became chief of the Admiralty. Caprivi believed in *guerre de course* and war against an enemy's commerce, using torpedo boats backed by cruisers. He recognised the need for some form of battle fleet, and work started on the Kiel Canal, linking the Baltic with the North Sea.[9] Influenced by the *Jeune École* in the Caprivi era, the German Navy purchased a great many torpedo-boats. In 1886 a British naval attaché, Captain Kane, made an assessment of the officer in command of the torpedo-boats, Captain Alfred Tirpitz:

> Captain Tirpitz commands the Flotilla and has made torpedo boats his speciality [...] He has steamed against gales of wind with them, he has manoeuvred them in all weathers, day and night, he has steamed 18 knots for 6 hours with a whole Flotilla of 12 boats, without one losing station.[10]

Jeune École tactics and torpedo-boats gave an emerging generation of young officers some proper sea-going and command experience, in addition to that gained on the cruisers stationed overseas. Captain Kane also commented on the help and assistance given to him by the German Navy:

> The Admiral Commander-in-Chief of the Baltic station was absent when I arrived at Kiel; and the officer in temporary command, not feeling sure of what he ought to do, wrote to the Minister of Marine for instructions. General Caprivi replied that I was to be shown everything; that the standing orders about foreign officers held good, but that a special exception was made in my case, in consequence of the very friendly manner in which the German Naval Attaché was treated in England.[11]

The Anglo-German naval antagonism lay some years in the future. Between 1878 and 1883 no armoured ships were laid down, partly due to the emphasis placed on torpedo warfare and *guerre de course* influences and, one suspects, doubts about the advisability of building large, expensive armoured ships following the *Grosser Kürfurst* disaster. The battleship *Oldenburg* was laid down in 1883 and in 1888 the first of the Siegfried class coast defence ships was laid down. There were eight of them, at the time much the largest class of armoured ships built for the German Navy. At 3,691 tons they were too small to be battleships and too large to be gunboats. They were armed with three 24-cm (9.4-inch) guns, essentially a cruiser armament, but with a speed of 14½ knots they were too slow to be cruisers.[12]

Then, in June 1888, Kaiser Wilhelm ascended the throne and everything changed. In July the Kaiser replaced Caprivi with Vice-Admiral Count von Monts, the first professional navy man to command the German Navy. The first impulse towards the creation of a larger navy was the expansion of the Russian Baltic fleet. In 1890 this caused Germany to lay down four battleships of 10,000 tons each, the first proper capital ships built for the German Navy. The *Brandenburg, Weissenburg, Wörth* and *Kurfurst Friedrich Wilhelm*, all mounted an unusual arrangement of six 28-cm (11-inch) guns. Four 28-cm guns were mounted in two twin turrets fore and aft and a third twin turret was mounted amidships. This third turret carried two 'short' 28-cm guns, 35 calibres in length as opposed to 40 calibres for the fore and aft guns.[13] Monts did not live to see these ships built; he died after just six months in office and the Kaiser appointed Vice-Admiral Max Von der Goltz to succeed him.

From 1871 to 1889 the German Admiralty answered directly to the Kaiser. Kaiser Wilhelm altered the administrative structure and effectively divided the authority of the Admiralty into three sections, the Supreme Command (Oberkommando der Marine), the Reichsmarineamt (Imperial Naval Office or RMA) and the Naval Cabinet (Marinekabinette). The Kaiser performed his role as commander-in-chief through the Supreme Command headed by Von der Goltz. The Supreme Command was also responsible for ship types and design. The naval cabinet was responsible for all personnel matters and the secretarial aspects of the Kaiser as commander-in-chief. The RMA was the official ministry anticipating naval needs into the future, dealing with the Reichstag and supervising construction. Admiral Hollmann was in charge of the RMA from 1891 to 1897 and it can be said that in these years RMA policy lacked direction. The Kaiser wanted a much larger navy to support his image of Germany as a world power, but there was no clear vision of how this was to be achieved.[14]

Kaiser Wilhelm, Alfred Tirpitz and the German Navy

It was now that Alfred Tirpitz appeared as a policy maker. He was the Baltic station chief of staff 1890–2 and rapidly made a name for himself as a tactician and torpedo strategist. Exactly when he rejected *Jeune École* torpedo tactics and embraced the battle fleet concept is unclear but it was probably coincident with the publication of A.T. Mahan's *The Influence of Sea Power upon History*.[15]

Kaiser Wilhelm first met Captain Alfred Tirpitz in 1890 or 1891. It was a moment of real destiny for both men and at last gave the Kaiser what he was looking for, someone who had a clear conception of naval policy. Tirpitz was ten years older than the Kaiser and had served in the navy since 1865. From 1892 to 1896 he was Chief of Staff to the High Command and deeply involved with exercises that attempted to relate strategy (ends) to tactics (means). In June 1894 he wrote a memorandum, 'Service Memo IX', that stated the case for a strong German Navy:

> A state which has oceanic or world interests must be able to uphold them and make its power felt beyond its own territorial waters. National world commerce, world industry [. . .] world intercourse and colonies are impossible without a fleet capable of taking the offensive. The conflicts of interests between nations, the lack of confidence felt by capital and the business world will either destroy these expressions of the vitality of a state, or prevent them taking form, if they are not supported by national power on the seas and therefore beyond our own waters. Herein lies by far the most important purpose of the fleet.[16]

Then there was the extraordinary business of the Jameson raid and German support for Kruger, in the form of a telegram sent on 3 January 1896 and signed by the Kaiser:

> I express my sincere congratulations that, supported by your people without appealing for the help of friendly powers, you have succeeded by your own energetic action against armed bands which invaded your country as disturbers of the peace and have thus been able to restore peace and safeguard the independence of the country against attacks from outside.[17]

In England there was outrage. The *Morning Post* summed up the attitude of the British press:

> It is difficult to speak calmly of this telegram. The fitting retort would be the ordering of our Mediterranean Fleet to the North Sea. England will not forget it, and her foreign policy will in future be strongly influenced by the remembrance.[18]

The Times said: 'England will concede nothing to menaces and will not lie down under insult.'[19] For Tirpitz the Jameson raid was the opportunity he had been waiting for. He was able to say that the Kruger telegram had awakened the nation to the necessity for a fleet, a view heavily reinforced by the seizure of the German ship *Bundesrath* at Delagoa Bay. This ship and others were searched, suspected of carrying contraband for the Boers.[20] In June 1897, after a year in command of the German East Asiatic Squadron, Tirpitz was appointed secretary of the Reichsmarineamt.

Kaiser Wilhelm

It must be rated one of the strangest quirks of history that Queen Victoria's two eldest children should have played such prominent, if inadvertent, roles in the story of the Anglo-German naval rivalry. Her eldest child, Princess Victoria, married Crown Prince Frederick, the son of the German emperor and became in due course, Kaiser Bill's mother, while Albert Edward, Prince of Wales, became Edward VII and gave strong support to Jacky Fisher in the great naval expansion of the dreadnought era.

The birth of Friedrich Wilhelm Victor Albrecht, known as Fritz, was a difficult and damaging forceps delivery. As a result his left arm was paralysed, the shoulder socket was torn away and the surrounding muscles damaged beyond repair by the delivery forceps. At first, the disability appeared worse: the left leg hardly responded at all, the child had pains in the left ear and left side of the head.

Nonetheless, this physically disabled child appeared reasonably intelligent and might have led a normal life had he not been born a Prussian prince and heir to the throne of Imperial Germany. He had to learn to ride so that he might join the Prussian cavalry. He learnt to support his left arm in his belt or pocket and to slip the reins from his right to his left hand. The trouble was, he practised so hard his right arm became extremely over-developed, causing him to lose balance and fall off his horse on the right side.

His mother apparently showed little compassion for her disabled son and almost appeared to bear a grudge against him. She quite openly preferred the company of her younger, healthier offspring. Few children could ever forget such a rebuff and in Wilhelm's case he came to hate his mother, her liberal views and her English ways. Wilhelm turned to Prussian authoritarianism.

At 18 he was enrolled in the Prussian cavalry. 'Never', wrote Hinzpeter his tutor, 'was a young man enrolled in the Prussian cavalry who seemed so physically unfitted to become a keen and brilliant cavalry officer'. Wilhelm persevered and was soon able to ride at the head of his regiment in his glittering uniform and astonished his elders with his apparent prowess. At 25 he was a major and at 29, in name at least, a general.[21]

Throughout his childhood and early manhood, the old Emperor Wilhelm I ruled Germany. It was demonstrably the age of Bismarck, the Iron Chancellor who welded Prussia and the Germanic states into Imperial Germany. In the 1880s, the nonagenarian emperor ruled on and on. He could recall his youthful days brilliantly. He had known Talleyrand and entered Paris after Waterloo. In short, he was positively the last of the Waterloo generation and representative, moreover, of a Prussia that defeated Napoleon in alliance with England.

His son, the Crown Prince Frederick, waited and chafed but still his ageing father lived on. In March 1887, Edward Prince of Wales went to Berlin to celebrate the birthday of the old Kaiser and the Crown Prince showed signs of hoarseness. A few weeks later, the trouble was diagnosed as cancer of the throat. A huge medical row ensued and Frederick's wife refused to allow anyone to examine him except an English surgeon.[22] A tracheotomy was performed, but the cancer remained. Edward Prince of Wales saw his brother-in-law at San Remo in February 1888 and he was fading rapidly.[23] William I died in March 1888; his son followed him on 15 June after a reign of just 99 days.

Wilhelm came to the throne at the age of 29. As emperor, Wilhelm was confronted by Bismarck, now an old man with a foreign policy aimed at restraining Austria and Russia from any Balkan attacks or adventures. In 1872 he had formed the *Dreikaiserbund*, or three emperors alliance, between Germany, Austria-Hungary and Russia, aimed at neutralising the Balkan ambitions of Austria-Hungary and Russia. The Balkan rivalries of Austria-Hungary and Russia forced Bismarck to come down rather too heavily on the side of Austria-Hungary, thus alienating Russia. A second *Dreikaiserbund* was established in 1881 and lasted three years. It was renewed in 1884 but finally lapsed in 1887, to be succeeded by the triple alliance, or *triplice*. Germany and Austria-Hungary were in formal alliance, and Italy joined them in 1882. Britain, through the medium of the Mediterranean agreements of 1887, came near to being a partner in the *triplice* and this was as close as Britain came to being an alliance partner with

Bismarck's Germany. With the final failure of the *Dreikaiserbund* Bismarck concluded a secret reinsurance treaty with Russia that, roughly stated, ensured Germany would not go to war with Russia over an Austrian attack in the Balkans. Germany would only support Austria if Austria were attacked first.[24]

Bismarck always regarded England as a mystery, outside the European sphere almost, but by 1888 he had come to believe that England should be obliged, by continental developments, to seek German support, hence his secret delight at Britain's willingness to enter into those Mediterranean agreements.[25]

Conflicts between the young Kaiser and Bismarck ensured that he resigned in disgust, on 18 March 1890 after 28 years as German chancellor. Count Caprivi was appointed chancellor. The trouble was that, just as Bismarck resigned, the secret treaty with Russia was about to be renewed. The Kaiser, Caprivi and the ruling clique felt that if the treaty became known in London or Vienna it might break up the Triple Alliance, so the treaty was not renewed.[26]

For whatever reasons – his disability, his alienation from his parents, particularly his English mother, and coping with the rigours of Prussian military life – at a psychological level, Kaiser Bill was a highly-strung character. His acute nervousness might better be described as neurasthenic. He can be seen to best advantage on his yacht *Hohenzollern*, built in the second year of his reign for 4.5 million Goldmarks.[27]

> It was a kind of floating casino and the tone was to match. In the mornings it amused him to make members of his suite, including the oldest Adjutants-General, do open-air exercises and gymnastics on deck, and while they were bending their knees or squatting, he would take the opportunity of giving them such a push that they sprawled all over the place. (The old boys professed to be greatly delighted by this attention, but clenched their fists in their pockets and afterwards abused the Emperor like fishwives).[28]

> A holiday cruise with William II was a trying experience. There was a great deal of false heartiness, noise and exuberance, mixed with dirty stories, schoolboy pranks and all the intrigue of a court entourage.[29]

Between 1893 and 1914 the *Hohenzollern* spent about 1,600 days, or four and a half years, at sea with the Kaiser on board.[30] For Wilhelm, when the era of Bismarck passed and Germany started to build a fleet and pursue a policy of *Weltpolitik* (world power), it fulfilled a deep psychological need, as indeed did his yacht.

The German Navy Laws of 1898 and 1900

In an age when public interest in a big German Navy was minimal, Tirpitz proved to be a propagandist *par excellence* in promulgating the idea of a strong German Navy. A technical journal, *Marine-Rundschau*, was turned into a popular magazine about naval affairs. *Nauticus*, a naval annual, was started and the press were briefed by a news bureau within the Navy Office. Rallies demanding naval expansion were held; industrialists and politicians attended naval reviews. The German academic community supported the idea and soon some 270 'fleet professors' (*flotten-proffessoren*) were writing in favour of a greatly expanded German Navy. Mahan's classic works were translated into German and placed onboard every German warship.[31]

The Kaiser had read Mahan from cover to cover but had not thought out a naval policy; Tirpitz had done just this. Immediately after his appointment as head of the Reichsmarineamt he produced a 22-clause memorandum. Clauses two, three, four and six tell their own story and were directly anti-British.

> For Germany the most dangerous naval enemy at the present time is England. It is also the enemy against which we most urgently require a certain measure of naval force as a political power factor [...] Commerce raiding and transatlantic war against England is so hopeless, because of the shortage of bases on our side and the superfluity on England's side, that we must ignore this type of war against England in our plans for the constitution of our fleet [...] Our fleet must be so constructed that it can unfold its greatest military potential between Heligoland and the Thames [...] The military situation against England demands battleships in as great a number as possible.[32]

Unlike most naval officers, Tirpitz was a skilled speaker, very good at explaining his ideas quickly and simply. Above all, he knew how to handle the difficult and prickly Kaiser. If state papers had to be taken to the Kaiser when he was involved in his endless round of entertainment, for example a stag shoot, then Tirpitz would arrange with the head forester that no cry of 'a stag' would occur in the critical few minutes needed to transact business. If a certain glint in the Kaiser's eye revealed extreme nervousness or irritability, then Tirpitz knew it was not the day to promulgate some new naval enterprise.[33]

In formulating naval policy Tirpitz had two slogans, 'emergency fleet' and 'danger zone'. Taken together, these two elements formed the notorious 'risk theory' (*Risikogedanken*). 'Risk theory' stated that the German fleet must be powerful enough to inflict unacceptable damage on the strongest naval power, obviously England. If England were to attack the German Navy, England would undoubtedly win, but at such a cost that her position vis-à-vis the other naval powers would be seriously compromised. In the case of the German Navy, the risk theory relied on the creation of an 'emergency' or 'sallying fleet' (*Ausfallflotte*). It was called the 'emergency fleet' on the basis of some future crisis, an emergency, causing a British attack on Germany. To create this emergency fleet, Germany had to pass through the danger zone, when her fleet was still not strong enough to inflict serious damage on the British fleet and might be 'Copenhagened' by it. This was a reference to Admiral James Gambier's seizure of the Danish fleet in 1807 in order to prevent it joining France, voluntarily or otherwise. At this time, there were very few battleships in the North Sea and Tirpitz believed, wrongly, that the British would be unable to concentrate a large naval force in northern European waters. The inherent contradiction in the 'risk theory' was the view that Britain would do nothing about her own building programmes. If Britain increased her naval estimates year by year and matched the German programmes, the danger zone would become everlasting.

The first German navy law was announced to the German public in November 1897. The Reichstag passed it in March 1898. The voting was 212 votes to 139. Tirpitz had wooed the Reichstag very carefully indeed and had persuaded the large Catholic centre party to vote for the navy law. Henceforward, the German fleet would consist of 19 battleships, 12 large and 30 small cruisers and eight armoured coast defence battleships. The total cost of this programme was 400 million Goldmarks, 20 million sterling equivalent, spread over the period 1898–1903, almost exactly the size of the British programme under the Naval Defence Act nine years earlier.[34] The size of the German Navy was increased by 30 per cent and of course the new construction programme attracted a great deal of attention. The hidden factor was the replacement of battleships after 25 years, large cruisers after 20 years and small cruisers after 15 years.[35] This automatic replacement policy (*ersatz*) written into law ensured that any future Reichstag was not in a position to reduce the naval budget. Tirpitz now had carte blanche to replace all small old ships with large expensive new ones.

Taken in combination, the Tirpitz memorandum of 1897 and the first navy law of 1898 gave the German Navy a direction and logic that had been singularly lacking in the ten or so years before the Tirpitz era. The focus on England suggested by Tirpitz made the entire plan fall into place and the navy became the diplomatic and military tool the Kaiser so desperately desired.[36] In terms of ships the Kaiser class (five ships) were the last ordered in the Hollmann era. They were 11,000 tons but reverted to a main armament of four 24-cm (9.4-inch) guns with eighteen 15-cm (5.9-inch) guns as the secondary armament. The 24-cm was the largest calibre of gun capable of 'quickfiring'. German thinking favoured a hail of fire from medium guns rather than the much slower rates of fire from large-calibre heavy guns. These five ships, built in the 1890s, were markedly inferior to their British counterparts and were really coast defence ships for Baltic service. The first navy law produced the five Wittlelsbach class battleships, slightly larger with the same cruiser armament on a nominally battleship hull.[37] The 19 battleships defined by the first navy law, in addition to those already discussed, included the central battery ironclad *Oldenburg* and the four Sachsen class central citadel ironclads. This gave a total of 19 battleships. The heavy cruisers included three old ironclads rebuilt as cruisers *König Wilhelm, Kaiser, Deutschland*; also the *Kaiserin Augusta*, the five-ship Hertha class, the *Fürst Bismarck* and *Prinz Heinrich*. The building of the *Prinz Adalbert* brought the numbers up to 12.[38]

In 1899 the High Command of the navy was replaced by an Admiralty Staff (Admiralstab), responsible for strategic planning, the training of officers and naval intelligence. In time of war it would assume overall command and direct naval operations. The commanders of the Baltic naval station, the North Sea naval station, the cruiser squadron and the First Battle Squadron were given equal status with the RMA and Admiralstab; all had direct access to the Kaiser.[39] In addition, independent ship commanders in foreign waters and the training inspectorate also had direct access to the Kaiser. All of this was of huge benefit to Tirpitz. The influence of the Admiralty Staff was removed from naval planning and the RMA was left to its own devises. Tirpitz was now answerable only to the Kaiser and he made sure that all matters related to naval policy, finance and construction found their way to the Kaiser through himself. The 1899 reorganisation cannot be regarded as a success. The divided command structure ensured that endless misunderstandings took place. A good example of this occurred in 1904 when the Kaiser decided to take the new armoured cruiser *Friedrich Karl* to the Mediterranean as escort for his protracted summer cruise. The Chief of the Imperial Naval Cabinet did not bother to inform the Admiralty Staff, who only found out about the deployment when a casual request to arrange coaling facilities at Gibraltar was received. If mobilisation had taken place in 1904 a powerful new cruiser would have been unavailable and the Admiralty Staff would not have known about it.[40]

If the first navy law was reasonable enough and was very much an expression of Germany's considerable industrial and commercial prowess, the second navy law was an entirely different matter. In October 1899, notice of the new law appeared in the German press and it was laid before the Reichstag in January 1900. These proposals coincided with the Boer War and the search of German vessels taking 'contraband' to the Boers. Tirpitz and the Kaiser could not hope for better arguments to justify their cause. Under the second navy law, the fleet was expanded to 38 battleships, though this number included the eight small Siegfried class (3,691 tons), coast defence ships, reconstructed 1898–1904. Under the terms of the navy law these were upgraded to battleships and could in due time be replaced by *ersatz* battleships – indeed nearly half the German dreadnoughts were *ersatz* Siegfrieds. In addition there were 14 large and 38 small cruisers.[41]

The second navy law went far beyond the scope of the first. It ensured that the German Navy and its expansion were built into the structure of the German state. Tirpitz intended to spend £80 million on ships and £13 million on dockyards and harbours. He hoped to raise £38.5 million in loans and to pay the balance, some £54.5 million, by increased taxation. From 1900 onwards, German navy law became fixed and immutable to an extent not realised in Britain.[42] Tirpitz was now raised to the rank of Prussian Minister of State and became one of the most powerful men in Germany.

This law proposed a programme of construction that demanded the laying down of three battleships a year for 16 years. German shipyards could only expand their building capacity on the basis of a guaranteed stream of orders. When the Naval Defence Act was passed in Britain, this was by no means the case. Shipyards were nothing like so dependent on warship orders and a far smaller proportion of shipbuilding capacity was devoted to warship construction. It was with the second navy law battleships *Braunschweig*, *Elsass*, *Lothringen*, *Hessen* and *Preussen* in 1902–4 that Germany built ships that were comparable with their British counterparts. These five ships mounted four 28-cm (11-inch) and fourteen 17-cm (6.7-inch) guns. The five ships that followed – *Deutschland*, *Hannover*, *Pommern*, *Schlesien*, and *Schleswig-Holstein* – had the same armament, designated SK, 'Schnelladenkanonen', or quick-firing, with a firing rate of two rounds per minute for the 28-cm guns and a range of 18,800 m.[43] It should be noted that Germany and the United States both acquired almost exactly the same number of pre-dreadnoughts, 24 German to 25 American.

It was with the second navy law that the British at last realised the nature and danger of risk theory. Tirpitz managed to conceal the real purpose of the first navy law, particularly 'risk theory', with considerable skill, but his hand was forced in the debates over the second navy law. *Brassey's Naval Annual 1900* gave the full text of the second naval law:

> Under the existing circumstances, in order to protect Germany's sea trade and colonies, there is one means only, viz., Germany must have a fleet of such strength that, even for the mightiest Naval Power, a war with her would involve risks as to jeopardise its own supremacy. For this purpose it is not absolutely necessary that the German Fleet should be as strong as that of the greatest sea power, because generally, a great Sea Power will not be in a position to concentrate all its forces against us. But, even if it should succeed in confronting us in superior force, the enemy would be so considerably weakened in overcoming the resistance of a strong German Fleet that, notwithstanding a victory gained, the enemy's supremacy would not at first be secured any longer by a sufficient fleet.[44]

How far Britain recognised this as a statement of intent and indeed of 'risk theory' is difficult to assess, but Tirpitz was the first modern strategist to conclude that the new German Navy was an instrument designed to achieve diplomatic realignments.[45] For Britain, the German Navy posed particularly difficult problems. The second navy law of 1900 left Germany holding the balance of power between Britain and the Dual Alliance of France and Russia. The assumptions behind the Naval Defence Act were now no longer valid. To ensure Britain's naval supremacy in European waters, a three-power navy would be necessary.

The First German Dreadnoughts

When *Dreadnought* was commissioned at the end of 1906 Germany was still building pre-dreadnoughts. The five ships of the Deutschland class were commissioned between August 1906 and July 1908, the last nearly two years after the *Dreadnought* was completed. In 1904 Tirpitz was planning a 16,000-ton 'semi-dreadnought' battleship with a heavy intermediate armament. This was based on the logic that the largest ships able to transit the Kiel Canal would be in the 16,000-ton range. The battleships *Nassau* and *Westfalen* were ordered in May and October 1906 as *ersatz* replacements for the now elderly *Bayern* and *Sachsen* launched in 1875 and 1876 respectively. The proposed armament was four 28 cm (11-inch) guns and eight 24 cm (9.4 cm), guns all in twin turrets. Two other battleships were to follow, *Posen* (*ersatz Baden*) and *Rheinland* (*ersatz Württemburg*). Only the *Nassau* had been laid down when news of the *Dreadnought* filtered through. The Germans were surprised, to say the least; to proceed with the *Nassau* would have resulted in ships that were obsolescent on completion.

All work ceased on the *Nassau* and work did not restart until July 1907, a full year later.[46] For most of the summer of 1906 Tirpitz buried himself in the Black Forest and avoided the Kaiser. Tirpitz was deeply disturbed by news of the new battleship, as well as the three cruisers building and rapidly concluded that the German Navy had no option but to compete. Not to do so would have meant the de facto acceptance of permanent British naval superiority and the effective end of the Tirpitz plan. His dilemma was that German dreadnoughts would make it clear to Britain that Germany was directly in competition with the Royal Navy and the projected costs for any new dreadnought-type ships were horrendous.[47]

By August 1907, Germany had prepared her answer to the dreadnought a design with twelve 28-cm (11-inch) guns and a secondary battery of twelve 15-cm (5.9-inch) guns. The four Nassaus mounted their twelve 28-cm guns in six twin turrets; one mounted forward, one aft and four on the beam as wing turrets. It is often stated that the beam turrets were made necessary because steam reciprocating engines were physically tall and took up a great deal of space amidships as opposed to turbines which lay flat. This is not really the case in ships the size of battleships, but the idea that a reserve of gun power on the lee side of a battleship in action was an advantage only applies to pre-dreadnoughts fighting at short range. At long ranges, plunging fire made any turret as vulnerable as any other turret. With four wing turrets as opposed to two in the *Dreadnought*, a great deal of weight was carried far out on the beam. To counteract this, the Nassaus were designed with a high metacentric height of 2.33 m (7.65 ft). In fact, the roll period of the Nassaus was coincident with North Sea waves and bilge keels had to be fitted as roll compensation.[48] Slow ships were slowed still further as a result.

The heavier armament of 12 as opposed to the *Dreadnought*'s ten guns also requires comment. The German 28-cm (11-inch) gun used a shell that weighed 305 kg (675 pounds). These 'Schnelladenkanonen' quickfiring guns could at a pinch fire three rounds a minute as opposed to the two

Westfalen
Nassau
Posen
Rheinland

These two classes of German dreadnoughts were powered by triple expansion machinery, not turbines. Germany did not have any turbine manufacturing capability. The use of Parsons steam turbines would have involved a royalty payment of one million Goldmark per ship.

Westfalen:	Weser, Bremen, Jul '07–Jul '08–Oct '09
Nassau:	Wilhelmshaven, Jul '06–Mar '08–Oct '09
Posen:	Krupp, Jul '07–Dec '08–Mar '10
Rheinland:	Vulkan, Stettin, Aug '07–Sept '08–Mar '10
Average Cost:	£1,838,000 (37.3–37.9 million Goldmark)
Dimensions:	470 × 89 × 27.25 feet = 18,900 tons
Armament:	Twelve 11-inch 45 cal., twelve 6-inch 45 cal.
Armour:	Belt 11½" amidships 6", bow 4", aft barbettes 11", turrets 11", lower deck redoubt 8" battery 7", conning tower 12" Total armour 6,650 tons (35.18%)
Machinery:	3 sets 3-cylinder triple expansion Boilers 12 Schulz-Thorneycroft I.H.P. 20,000 = 19.9 knots
Coal:	950 tons normal 2,700 tons max. 200 tons fuel oil
Complement:	957–966

Illustration: *Brassey's Naval Annual 1914*, Plate 35

Thuringen
Helgoland
Ostfriesland
Oldenburg

These 22,000-ton ships were much larger than the *Nassaus*. This size increase was made necessary by the move to 30.5-cm (12-inch) guns. There was also a big leap in costs from 37.9 million to 46 million Goldmark. These ships might have been turbine powered by Parsons, but as with the *Nassaus* this would have incurred a royalty payment of 1 million Goldmark per ship.

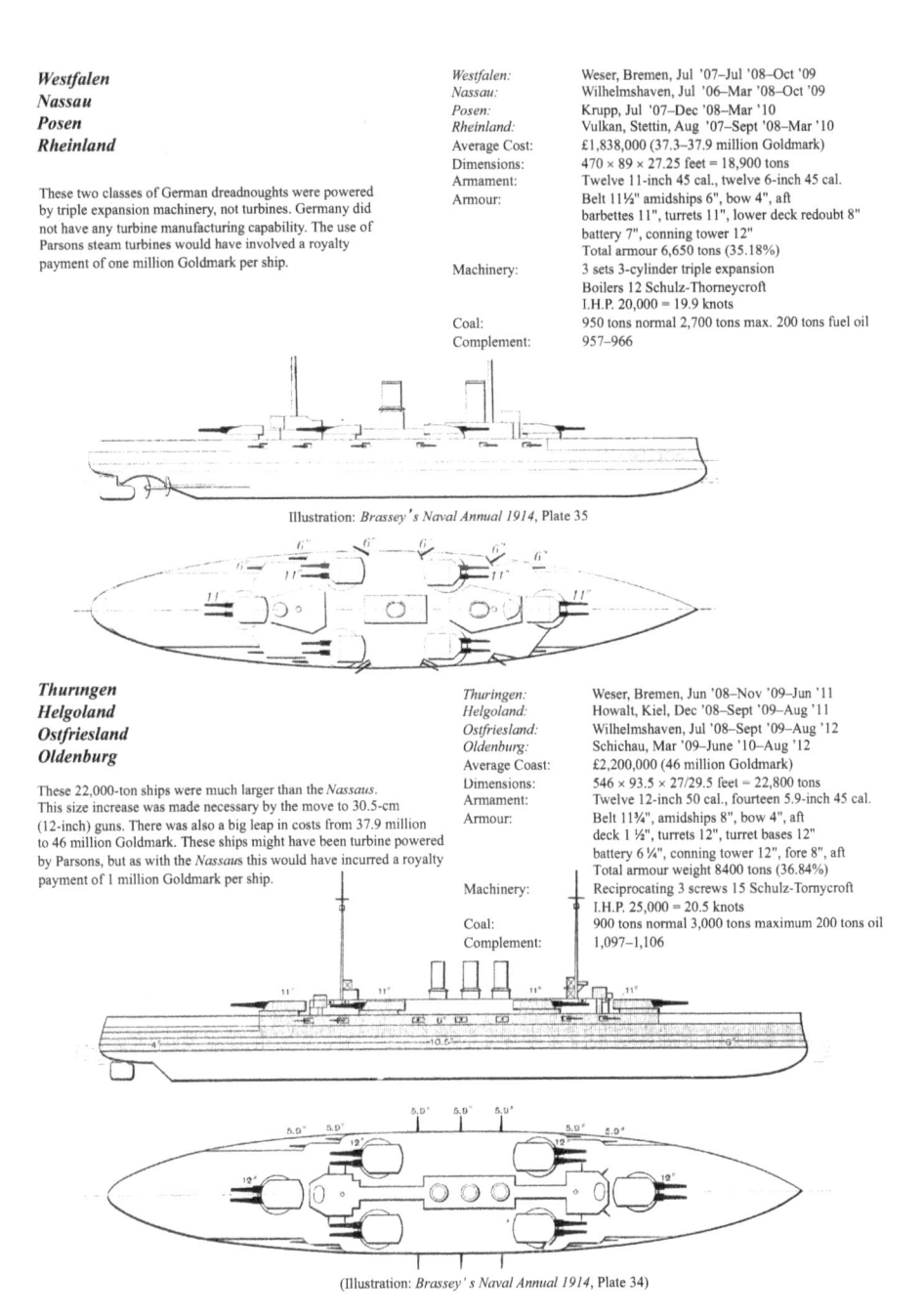

Thuringen:	Weser, Bremen, Jun '08–Nov '09–Jun '11
Helgoland:	Howalt, Kiel, Dec '08–Sept '09–Aug '11
Ostfriesland:	Wilhelmshaven, Jul '08–Sept '09–Aug '12
Oldenburg:	Schichau, Mar '09–June '10–Aug '12
Average Coast:	£2,200,000 (46 million Goldmark)
Dimensions:	546 × 93.5 × 27/29.5 feet = 22,800 tons
Armament:	Twelve 12-inch 50 cal., fourteen 5.9-inch 45 cal.
Armour:	Belt 11¾", amidships 8", bow 4", aft deck 1 ½", turrets 12", turret bases 12" battery 6¼", conning tower 12", fore 8", aft Total armour weight 8400 tons (36.84%)
Machinery:	Reciprocating 3 screws 15 Schulz-Tornycroft I.H.P. 25,000 = 20.5 knots
Coal:	900 tons normal 3,000 tons maximum 200 tons oil
Complement:	1,097–1,106

(Illustration: *Brassey's Naval Annual 1914*, Plate 34)

Fig. 11 The first German battleships, Nassau class

of the British 12-inch gun.[49] At this stage in history, Germany could not design and manufacture steam turbine machinery and the development of such machinery had never been encouraged by Tirpitz. Three sets of triple-expansion engines were used and developed 20,000 horsepower for a speed of just less than 20 knots. Each was compartmentalised as a separate system, each propulsion system driving one screw. The Nassaus and the last of the pre-dreadnoughts, the Deutschlands, used Schulz-Thorneycroft small tube boilers. Eight boilers were used in the Deutschlands and 12 in the Nassaus. The use of small tube boilers gave a saving in weight and space of about 30 per cent. This did not alter the fact that that *Dreadnought* was only 10 per cent larger than the last of the British pre-dreadnoughts, whereas the Nassaus were 43 per cent larger than the Deutschlands. There was also a big price jump from 24.481 million (£1.198 million) to 37.399 million Goldmark (£1.83 million).

There were other factors that distanced the Nassaus from their British counterparts. They were cramped to an almost ludicrous degree and for most of the time a large percentage of the crew lived ashore in barracks. In reality, these ships were over-gunned for their displacement, hastily designed as a reply to the *Dreadnought* and distinctly inferior to their British counterparts. Jacky Fisher, in so neatly anticipating the opposition and taking the next step forward in battleship design, had ensured a considerable British advantage that would be difficult for Germany to counter.

The new-age dreadnoughts, if Germany decided to build such ships, would be unable to transit the Kiel Canal. Germany needed the Baltic as a safe training ground and if necessary, to be able to deploy her battle fleet against the Russian Baltic fleet. In wartime the Skagerrak and Kattegat could be easily mined. Widening the Kiel Canal was possible but a hugely expensive project. The Kiel Canal is 61 miles in length and was built when the largest battleships were about 12,000 tons. In the event, at enormous cost, the canal was widened and finally completed in August 1914.

When the *Nassau* was laid down in July 1906 *Jane's Fighting Ships* credited her with an armament of fourteen 28-cm guns;[50] *Brassey's Naval Annual* credited her with 16.[51] German secrecy over the building of their first dreadnoughts was extreme and the British Admiralty had no real information about them. Eventually, just before the launch of *Posen*, the last of the Nassau class, Captain Reginald Hall, son of W.H. Hall, the first Director of Naval Intelligence and destined to be Director of Naval Intelligence in World War I, came up with a plan to obtain information. Hall and two other officers dressed as engine room artificers took the Duke of Westminster's fast private motor launch to Germany. They raced up Keil harbour to Krupp's building yard, simulated engine failure and took a series of photographs through the conning tower. In the following year Oscar Parkes, a medical student destined to be a long-serving editor of *Jane's Fighting Ships*, managed to photograph the Nassaus fitting out.[52]

The worst features of the Nassaus were overcome in the successor class, the Helgoland class of 1908–9, *Helgoland* (ersatz Siegfried), *Oldenburg* (ersatz Frithjof), *Ostfriesland* (ersatz Oldenburg) and *Thüringen* (ersatz Beowulf). The same armament layout was used but the displacement jumped from 18,570 to 22,440 tons. Length was increased from 451 ft (137.7 m) to 548 ft (167.2 m) and beam from 89 ft (26.9 m) to 93.5 ft (28.5 m). Guns of 30.5-cm (12-inch) calibre replaced the 28-cm (11-inch) of the Nassaus and shell weight was increased from 305 kg to 405 kg (891 pounds). The main belt armour was 30 cm in thickness. Steam turbines were considered but only Parsons turbines were available and would have cost a one million Goldmark royalty payment per ship. In spite of this a speed of 20.5 knots was obtained, again using a triple screw reciprocating machinery arrangement.[53] In considering the first four German dreadnoughts, the Nassaus, they had fairly serious defects largely ironed out in the Helgoland class that followed.

The First German Battlecruisers: *Blücher* and *Von der Tann*

Jane's Fighting Ships 1906–7 credited the three new cruisers *Invincible*, *Inflexible* and *Indomitable* with an armament of eight or ten 9.2-inch guns.[54] Based on this wrong information, which appears to have been planted by Jacky Fisher, the German Navy laid down the most powerful armoured cruiser ever built. They were just completing two other armoured cruisers, *Scharnhorst* and *Gneisenau*, armed with eight 21-cm (8.2-inch) guns and both destined to be sunk by the British battlecruisers *Invincible* and *Inflexible*. Their half sister the *Blücher*, also destined to be sunk by British battlecruisers, was a 15,590-ton monster armed with twelve 21-cm (8.2-inch) guns. The guns were carried in twin turrets, disposed in the same manner as the Nassaus, one turret forward, one aft and four wing turrets. By the time it became known that the three British dreadnought cruisers would be armed with 12-inch guns it was too late to alter the design and the *Blücher* was completed with her comparatively light main armament.

The British had little real idea what was going on in the German shipyards and in 1908 *Brassey's* credited *Blücher* with ten 28-cm guns but thought this improbable on a displacement of 15,000 tons and went on to suggest that six or eight 28-cm guns was more likely. The 1909 edition got it right with twelve 21-cm guns.[55]

Blücher was comparatively lightly armoured with an 18-cm (7-inch) belt, roughly comparable to the Invincibles. *Blücher* was a triple screw ship with three sets of four cylinder triple-expansion engines. On trials in 1909, the *Blücher* developed 43,886 ihp, the highest power ever achieved by a reciprocating-engined warship and achieved a close to battlecruiser speed of 24$\frac{1}{2}$ knots.[56] Despite the light gun armament and armour, *Blücher* always operated with the German battlecruisers and can be counted a semi-battlecruiser.

When it became apparent that the three *Invincibles* would be armed with 12-inch guns the German reply came in 1907–8 with the laying down of the *Von der Tann*. Several design proposals were put forward and in September 1906 it was decided to use a modified version of the 28 cm (11-inch) double turret used in the Nassau class battleships. The main arguments concerned the exact role of the new ship. Admiral von Heeringen stated that this new cruiser should be capable of employment against the enemy's battle line. Tirpitz believed the opposite and the new cruiser should be used only against enemy cruisers. On 22 June 1907 the Kaiser authorised the construction of cruiser named after Freiherr Ludwig von und zu der Tann-Rathsamhausen, a Bavarian general from the Franco-Prussian War.[57]

Armed with eight 28-cm (11-inch) guns disposed in the same manner as the Invincibles, including *en echelon* midships turrets she appeared, on paper at any rate, to be a direct reply. Detailed appraisal of her design shows this not to be the case. When compared to the *Invincible*, the only disadvantage to the German design was a lack of freeboard. Tirpitz and the German Admiralty defined the role of the *Von der Tann* very differently from that perceived by Fisher for the *Invincible*. In the final analysis the German Navy ignored the overseas deployment role but accepted the fast scouting role in its entirety. It was assumed that the dreadnought cruiser, or battlecruiser, might take heavy punishment from enemy capital ships. Consequently protection was 80 per cent of battleship standard, not the 50 per cent of the Royal Navy's first battlecruisers. The figures speak for themselves.

Blücher

On trials in 1909 *Blücher* developed 43,886 IHP, 27% over designed IHP. This made *Blücher* the most powerful reciprocating-engined warship ever built

Blücher:	Kiel, launched 1908, £1,349,000
Dimensions:	489 × 80.33 × 27 feet = 15,500 tons
Armament:	Twelve 8.2-inch, eight 6-inch
Armour:	Belt 6", turrets 6"
Machinery:	I.H.P 32,000 = 24.5 knots
Coal:	900/2,300 tons
Complement:	847

Brassey's Naval Annual 1914, Plate 41

Von Der Tann

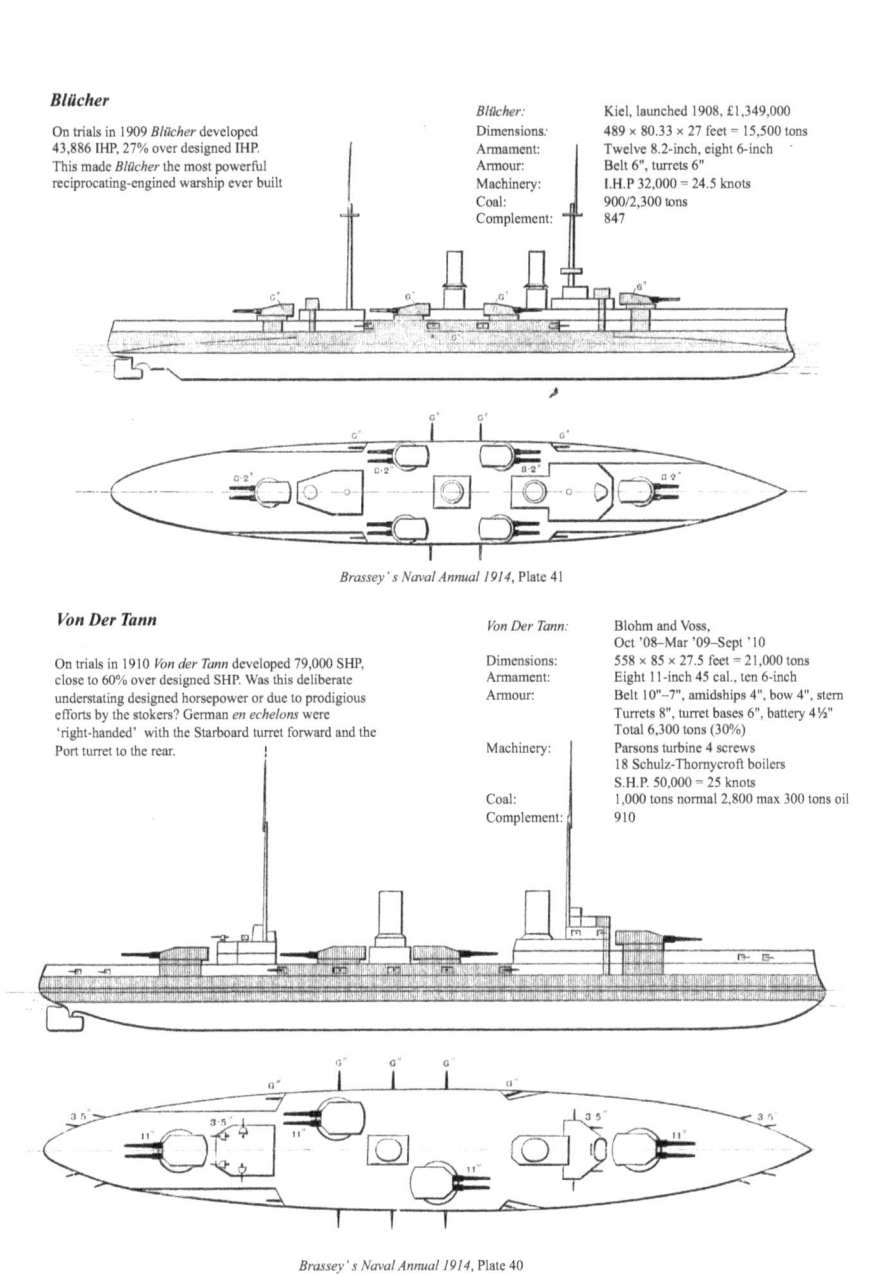

On trials in 1910 *Von der Tann* developed 79,000 SHP, close to 60% over designed SHP. Was this deliberate understating designed horsepower or due to prodigious efforts by the stokers? German *en echelons* were 'right-handed' with the Starboard turret forward and the Port turret to the rear.

Von Der Tann:	Blohm and Voss, Oct '08–Mar '09–Sept '10
Dimensions:	558 × 85 × 27.5 feet = 21,000 tons
Armament:	Eight 11-inch 45 cal., ten 6-inch
Armour:	Belt 10"–7", amidships 4", bow 4", stern Turrets 8", turret bases 6", battery 4½" Total 6,300 tons (30%)
Machinery:	Parsons turbine 4 screws 18 Schulz-Thornycroft boilers S.H.P. 50,000 = 25 knots
Coal:	1,000 tons normal 2,800 max 300 tons oil
Complement:	910

Brassey's Naval Annual 1914, Plate 40

Fig. 12 Kriegsmarine: From Armoured Cruiser to Battlecruiser, Blücher *and* Von Der Tann

Nassau	Belt: max. 30 cm (11.75 inches). Total armour weight 6,650 tons (35.24 per cent).
Von der Tann	Belt: max. 25 cm (9.80 inches). Total armour weight 6,100 tons (31.49 per cent).
Dreadnought	Belt: max. 28 cm (11 inches). Total armour weight 5,000 tons (27.6 per cent).
Invincible	Belt: max. 15 cm (6 inches). Total armour weight 3,460 tons (19.88 per cent).[58]

The final percentages are the percentage of displacement devoted to armour. The *Von der Tann* had a greater percentage of displacement devoted to armour than the *Dreadnought*, and indeed a greater overall weight of armour, while the *Invincible*, with less than 20 per cent of displacement devoted to armour, tells its own story. A further advantage enjoyed by all the German *grosse kreuzers* from *Blücher* onwards was an armoured torpedo bulkhead. In the case of *Von der Tann* this was 25-mm (1-inch) thick. The torpedo bulkhead covered the length of the citadel from the bow turret to the stern turret and was set back by four metres from the outer hull skin. The intervening space was divided in two by a gangway longitudinal bulkhead, the inner section of which was used to store coal. This greatly limited damage from torpedoes. The Iron Duke class battleships were the first British capital ships to have this type of anti-torpedo protection.[59]

The question then arises, exactly what was sacrificed to build a battle-cruiser with something close to 80 per cent the armour of a battleship. The unexpected answer is very little. The Invincibles were designed for 25 knots but made 27 knots in service. The *Von der Tann* was designed for 25 knots but on trials developed 79,000 shaft horsepower with Parson's steam turbines and made 27.4 knots.[60] This was just a year after the *Blücher* had become the most powerful reciprocating-engined warship ever built. In German pre-dreadnoughts and dreadnoughts three sets of machinery and triple screws were used but in *Von der Tann* quadruple screws were adopted. High pressure turbines worked the outer shafts and low pressure the inner shafts. Each turbine developed 19,700 shp and drove each shaft separately. The *Von der Tann* achieved everything the Invincibles set out to do and adopted a respectable armour scheme capable of absorbing heavy battle damage. German battleships and battlecruisers all used Schulz-Thorneycroft small tube boilers, 18 in the case of *Von der Tann*; these were considerably lighter and took up about one-third less space than the British large tube Babcock or Yarrow boilers.[61] In the case of the German battlecruisers, with the saved space and weight devoted to armour, they had been approaching a decisive advantage over their British counterparts. The German reply to the Invincibles was a masterstroke of warship design and as a result the German Navy gained a huge advantage when the battlecruisers were tested in World War I. Jacky Fisher always wanted a 'fusion' between the battleship and cruiser; the German Navy achieved it.

In the case of the *Invincibles* an enormous sacrifice in armour achieved a 1.5-knot advantage in service and this gave little or no significant edge to the battlecruisers in action during World War I. Filson Young later recorded in *With the Battlecruisers*:

> We never really caught up with the German Battlecruisers when they were running away from us at full speed. It takes a long time, and a huge distance to be covered, if a ship going at high speed is to be overtaken by a slightly faster one of which she has the start. In the case of a ship steaming at 24 knots, having a twenty miles start of a ship steaming at 26 knots, it would take five hours, and 130 knots would have to be covered in a stern chase, before the twenty miles were reduced to ten – the beginning of effective gunnery range.[62]

After the success of the *Von der Tann*, enlarged versions were laid down as part of the 1910 programme. The *Moltke* and *Goeben* were armed with ten 28-cm (11-inch) guns, with a superimposed turret worked in aft, a turret disposition exactly the same as the British Neptunes. Parson's turbines developed 70,000 shp and this gave a speed of 27 knots.[63] The belt armour was increased from 25 cm (9.8 inches) to 27 cm (10.6 inches), 80 per cent of comparable German battleship scale and on a direct par with the 10-inch belt armour of the British Neptunes. All German battleships and battlecruisers were armed with bow, stern and broadside torpedo tubes. This was arguably a mistake; these tubes never scored a hit and the bow tubes involved a relatively large unenclosed space forward. At Jutland the battlecruiser *Lützow*, fitted with 60-cm (23.6-inch) torpedoes, sustained a heavy hit forward and her large torpedo flat filled with water. Progressive flooding forward eventually brought the stern and the propellers out of the water and the ship was abandoned.

The German Navy was now acquiring one battlecruiser a year, and exactly how this was done needs explanation. The navy law of 1900 was curtailed by the Reichstag which had struck out six large and seven small

Moltke
Goeben

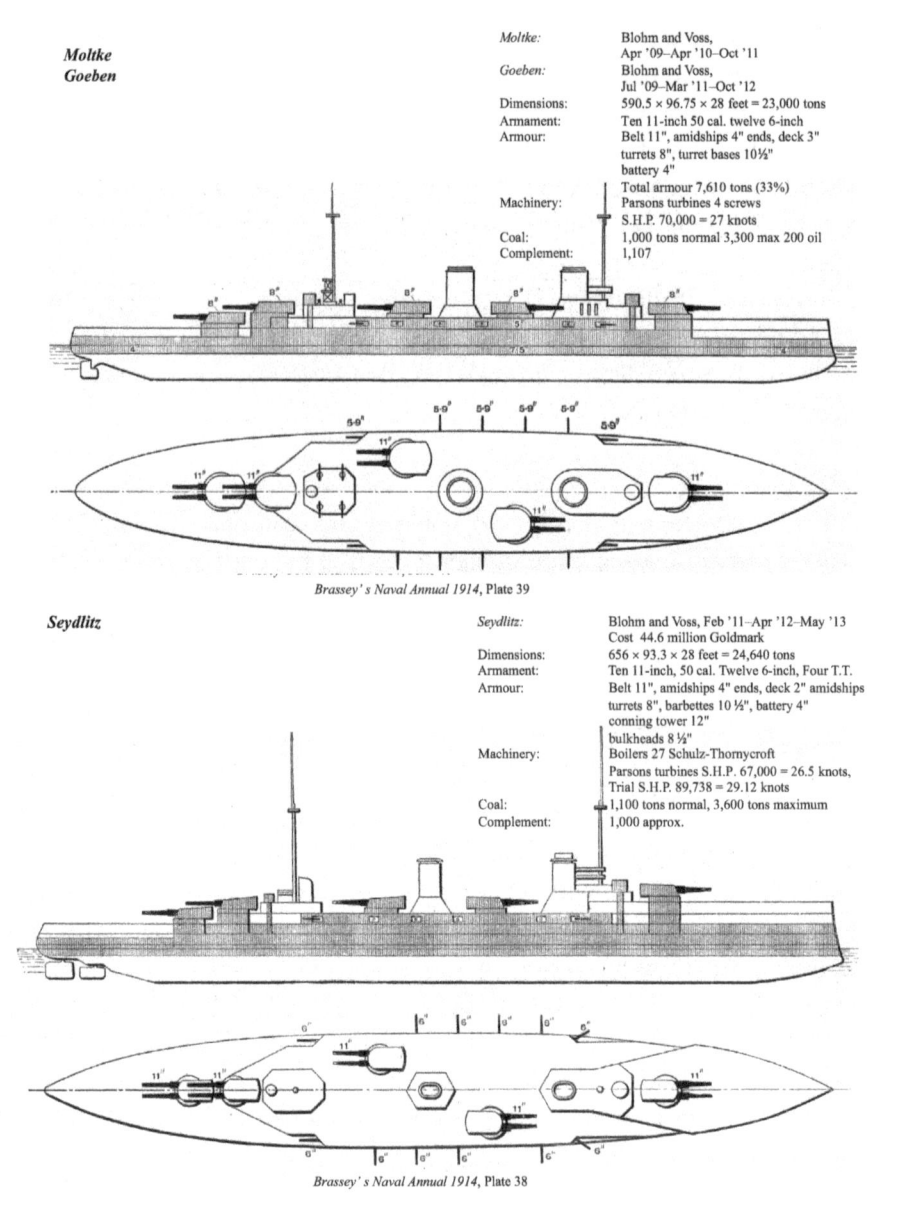

Moltke:	Blohm and Voss, Apr '09–Apr '10–Oct '11
Goeben:	Blohm and Voss, Jul '09–Mar '11–Oct '12
Dimensions:	590.5 × 96.75 × 28 feet = 23,000 tons
Armament:	Ten 11-inch 50 cal. twelve 6-inch
Armour:	Belt 11", amidships 4" ends, deck 3" turrets 8", turret bases 10½" battery 4" Total armour 7,610 tons (33%)
Machinery:	Parsons turbines 4 screws S.H.P. 70,000 = 27 knots
Coal:	1,000 tons normal 3,300 max 200 oil
Complement:	1,107

Brassey's *Naval Annual 1914*, Plate 39

Seydlitz

Seydlitz:	Blohm and Voss, Feb '11–Apr '12–May '13 Cost 44.6 million Goldmark
Dimensions:	656 × 93.3 × 28 feet = 24,640 tons
Armament:	Ten 11-inch, 50 cal. Twelve 6-inch, Four T.T.
Armour:	Belt 11", amidships 4" ends, deck 2" amidships turrets 8", barbettes 10 ½", battery 4" conning tower 12" bulkheads 8 ½"
Machinery:	Boilers 27 Schulz-Thornycroft Parsons turbines S.H.P. 67,000 = 26.5 knots, Trial S.H.P. 89,738 = 29.12 knots
Coal:	1,100 tons normal, 3,600 tons maximum
Complement:	1,000 approx.

Brassey's *Naval Annual 1914*, Plate 38

Fig. 13 The three German battlecruisers, Moltke class

cruisers. It was not originally intended to start these cruisers until the battle fleet was complete. In 1906, a *Novelle* (modification to the navy law) was introduced, that reinstated the cruisers. These additional cruisers appeared first as armoured cruisers, then as battlecruisers.[64] As cruisers they did not have *ersatz* numbers, rather letter designations – *Blücher* was 'E', *Von Der Tann* 'F', *Moltke* 'G', and *Goeben* 'H'.

Germany as a Potential Adversary

From the 1880s onwards, German colonial ambitions had caused a certain amount of friction with Britain. During the second Boer War German public opinion became virulently anti-British and to a considerable extent this was orchestrated by the German government. An example of the excesses of the German press included a picture of Queen Victoria supposedly presenting a Victoria Cross to a 13-year-old boy soldier who had allegedly 'outraged' eight Boer women.[65]

In late October 1901 Lord Selborne sent a lengthy document to his father-in-law, Lord Salisbury. It contained a very detailed assessment of Britain's naval expenditure in the previous 20 years and a closely argued analysis of Britain's potential adversaries. Selborne pointed out that at the time of the Naval Defence Act, France and Russia were Britain's main adversaries, with the Italian Navy rather larger than that of Russia. By 1901 the situation had changed radically. France remained the second naval power to Great Britain while Italy had sunk to sixth place. He went on to say that Russia, Germany and the United States had risen to the ranks of great naval powers and Japan had become an important one. Towards the end of his memorandum, perhaps for the first time, the navy of Germany was considered.[66]

> The naval policy of Germany, on the contrary, is definite and persistent. The Emperor seems determined that the power of Germany shall be used all the world over to push German commerce, possessions, and interests. Of necessity it follows that the German naval strength must be raised so as to compare more advantageously than at present with ours. The result of this policy will be to place Germany in a commanding position if ever we find ourselves at war with France and Russia, and at the same time to put the Triple Alliance in a different relative position to France and Russia in respect of naval strength to that which it has hitherto occupied. Naval officers who have seen much of the German Navy lately are all agreed that it is as good as can be.[67]

In the following year Hugh Arnold-Foster, now Parliamentary Secretary to the Admiralty, visited Germany and Wilhelmshaven. He compiled a detailed report on the German Navy and started by saying that Germany would very likely take over the Dutch Empire, either by war or by agreement. He went on to define Britain's considerable geographic advantage over Germany. If the Straits of Dover were closed to German warships they would have to steam over a thousand miles around the north of Scotland to arrive off the Scilly Isles, typically burning at least 400 tons of coal before commerce raiding could begin. Their nearest overseas coaling base was in the Cameroons, making commerce raiding very difficult if not to say impossible.[68] He went on to analyse the first navy law battleships of the Wittelsbach class and concluded that they were exceedingly powerful, with remarkably powerful ahead and astern firepower. He described the four primary armament guns as 9.6-inch calibre, whereas they were 24 cm (9.4 inch) and fired a shell that weighed 309 pounds.[69] His comparison of British and German battleships is detailed but somewhat flawed, assuming that their 24-cm guns were in some way comparable with British 12-inch calibre guns, presumably because they were quick-firing. Nevertheless, Eric Grove believes that because of their high rate of fire – three to four rounds a minute these ships – cannot be considered second class.[70] Arnold-Foster finished his report with a detailed description of the German Navy at Wilhelmshaven and concluded that it was very efficient, with much to teach the Royal Navy.[71] The report had much to commend it and taken with Lord Selborne's memorandum of the previous year, these documents represent two of the early detailed attempts to assess Germany as a potential adversary.

In June 1904 King Edward VII visited Kiel. Rather against the advice of Von Bülow the Kaiser paraded the German Fleet for inspection. The impression was lasting and ominous.[72] In November the British press, in the form of the magazine *Vanity Fair*, published an editorial hinting at a preventative war against Germany before she became too strong:

> The real enemy is Germany [...] There are men at the British Admiralty today who understand that naval victory against an efficient enemy depends largely on the success of the first blow [...] Germany is the enemy. The German Fleet is built and maintained for no other purpose than to profit by English disaster [...] Do not let us be under any illusion as to the reality of German enmity to this country.[73]

This article and others in *Vanity Fair* and the *Daily Mail* added to German concerns that a surprise attack might be made on them. The German naval attaché in London, Captain Coerper, forwarded an article suggesting a preventative war against Germany and the German ambassador was summoned to Berlin with his staff. The Ambassador did not think an attack likely but explained that British opinion was becoming nervous about the German fleet.[74]

The first Morocco crisis took place when Arthur Balfour's Conservative government was still in office. British commercial interests in Morocco were considerable and between 1899 and 1901 44.7 per cent of Moroccan imports were British. The comparable figures for France and Germany were 22.1 per cent and 11.6 per cent.[75] Morocco was the last independent territory in the region and France wanted to expand westwards from Algeria. In support of this France signed two bilateral agreements, with Britain in April 1904 and Spain in October 1904, allowing the establishment of a French protectorate over Morocco. Germany was angered by the *entente cordiale* and the apparent carve-up of North Africa between France and Britain. Apart from anything else, Germany could no longer play off the jealousies of the two Western powers when she wanted to secure colonial advantages. Bülow and Baron Holstein, the grey eminence of the German Foreign Office, decided to break the *entente* in the most spectacular manner possible. They persuaded the Kaiser to visit Morocco.

The arrival of the Kaiser in Tangiers on 31 March 1905 caused consternation. In his 'open door' speech he stated that he looked on the Sultan of Morocco as the ruler of a free and independent state and that he would always negotiate directly with the Sultan. The Kaiser expected Germany to have the same trade advantages as other countries and wanted an independent Morocco. It was a provocative challenge to France that could not be ignored. It was also the case that under the terms of the *entente*, France was promised British diplomatic support over Morocco, in return for French support for the British position in Sudan. The Foreign Office suspected that Germany wanted a base in Morocco, probably Mogador.[76] Lord Lansdowne, Foreign Secretary in Balfour's government, had authorised the preparation of Anglo-French naval and military talks about action against Germany. These talks had taken place between Fisher and the French naval attaché on the one hand, with Sir James Grierson, Director of Military Operations, and the French military attaché on the other. As a result Britain and France were able to work together and the Moroccan crisis produced a peace conference in the town hall at Algeciras, held in January 1906, by which time the Liberals were back in office. In advance of the talks, the French foreign minister was promised a fair degree of support by his opposite number, the Liberal Foreign Secretary, Sir Edward Grey.[77] The conference ran from January to April 1906 and Germany found herself isolated, with only Austria-Hungary, of the 13 nations represented, supporting her. Eventually a face-saving compromise was reached whereby France was awarded a controlling interest in Moroccan affairs, but guaranteed equality of trade and economic freedom to all the signatories to the agreement. In return Germany took a part of the French Congo, which was added to the German Cameroons.[78]

Germany had no real intention of going to war over Morocco; they had merely wanted to test Anglo-French resolve. As the diplomatic moves were made, the naval and military leaders were forced to work out their options in the event of an Anglo-French war with Germany. Rather than breaking the *entente* between Britain and France, the Kaiser and Morocco welded the *entente* powers into a much tighter bond, standing against Germany. It also initiated the process of bringing Russia into *entente* with Britain. By 1909 the triple alliance of Germany, Austria-Hungary and Italy now faced a triple *entente* of Britain, France and Russia. Morocco considerably worsened the tensions between the two developing power blocs.

In the wake of the Morocco crisis Captain Edward Slade, the captain of the War College at Portsmouth, carried out a detailed appraisal of a potential war with Germany. He concluded, as Arnold-Foster had, that Germany was likely to absorb Belgium and Holland, possibly by forcing them into a customs union; this was after all the mechanism that Bismarck had used to unify the disparate German states. The report also said that when the Emperor Francis Joseph died Austria would also be absorbed into the German Empire. Britain would be drawn into a war with Germany over the issue of Belgian neutrality; it was absolutely unacceptable for Britain to allow a German-dominated coast facing Britain to extend as far as Dunkirk. Slade went on to suggest that in a war with Germany, Britain should seize an island off the German coast.

> We must have a base close to the German ports from which we can act, and for this purpose we must occupy the islands at the mouth of the Ems river [...] The situation of Borkum is a very good one, as it cannot be bombarded from the main land, the nearest point being 25,000 yards distant [...] Borkum is the only one of the Frisian Islands that is entirely surrounded by water at all states of the tide, and is therefore only accessible to that power which can control the communication, or in other words has the command of the sea.[79]

It was the start of the Royal Navy's pre-World War I obsession with Borkum and Baltic enterprises. In January 1907 a Foreign Office official Eyre

Crowe, later Sir Eyre Crowe, penned a memorandum on the present state of relations between Britain, France and Germany. He quoted Herr von Tschirschky:

> Germany's policy always has been, and would be, to try to frustrate any coalition between two States which might result in damaging Germany's interests and prestige; and Germany would, if she thought that such a coalition was being formed, even if its actual results had not yet been carried into practical effect, not hesitate to take such steps as she thought proper to break up the coalition.[80]

In other words, Germany's attempt at breaking the *entente* was the result of seasoned policy, no mere whim of the moment. Crowe went on to say that England's foreign policy was determined by the immutable conditions of her geographical position on the ocean flank of Europe. He also said that with a vast overseas empire, England was dependent on preponderant sea power, as stated by A.T. Mahan.[81] Five years earlier, in 1902, Mahan wrote of Germany and her geographic position:

> For all communities east of the Straits of Dover it remains true that in war commerce is paralysed and all the resultant consequences of impaired national strength entailed, unless decisive control of the North Sea is established. That effected, there is security for commerce by the Northern passage; but this alone is mere defence. Offence, exerted anywhere on the globe, requires a surplusage of force, over that required to hold the North Sea, sufficient to extend itself west of the British Islands [. . .] This is Germany's initial disadvantage of position, to be overcome only by adequate superiority of numbers.[82]

1905 appears to have been the key year – the year in which Japan annihilated the Russian Navy, the year of Fisher's fleet redistribution policy, the year in which the *entente* with France was tested and the year in which, as a result Britain, started the process of working out her position in a European war with France as an ally and Germany the belligerent.

Perspectives: The Anglo-German Antagonism

The Anglo-German antagonism is very difficult to analyse coherently; apart from anything else there was no one single element to it. In the mid-1890s Britain was under pressure from several directions. During the unsuccessful early stages of the Boer War German commentators were quick to place a question mark over the future of the British Empire. Yet within a few years Britain's navy had been expanded and overhauled, the army was being reformed and diplomacy had reached understandings with Washington and Paris.[83] Britain's ally Japan had annihilated the Russian Navy and Britain's five first-class battleships were withdrawn from the Far East. Britain was now in a position to heavily reinforce her naval position in home waters, something Tirpitz had not thought possible.

This was demonstrably the age of imperialism; aggressive imperialism was 'the spirit of the age', suggested Arthur Marder.[84] Another author writing in 1914 said of the Anglo-German antagonism:

> The moral origins of the sentiment of antagonism between England and Germany are thus obvious enough – the confrontation of two States, each dowered with the genius for empire; the one, the elder, already sated with the experience and the glories of empire; the other, the younger, apparently exhaustless in resources and energy, baulked in mid-career by 'fate and metaphysical aid,' and now indignant.[85]

Reviewing the 1890s, *Schlesische Editing* said of England:

> In Angra Pequena and New Guinea and East Africa and China and Mesopotamia? From Zanzibar to Samoa! An unbroken line of disappointment. The German People is gradually coming to recognise that England is Germany's worst enemy.[86]

To the conflicts of imperialism may be added the strongly social-Darwinist views and opinions of numerous writers, politicians and intellectuals. That ardent navalist Lord Esher said:

> There is no doubt that within measurable distance there looms a titanic struggle between Germany and Europe for mastery. The years 1793–1815 will be repeated, only Germany, not France will be trying for European domination. She has 70,000,000 of people and is determined to have commercial pre-eminence. To do this England has got to be crippled and the Low Countries added to the German Empire.[87]

In his famous memorandum of 1907 Eyre Crowe said of German attitudes and opinions that they believed 'the world belongs to the strong'.[88] In truth Social Darwinism transformed a German idealist tradition 'into a particularly noxious doctrine of relentless struggle and mastery'.[89] Nearer our own time, the German historian Gerhard Ritter noted in the preface to the second volume of his work *Staatskunst und Krieghandwerk* that during his studies of the Wilhelmine era he had become aware of much darker shadows than his generation and that of his academic teachers had considered possible.[90]

6

The Politics and Diplomacy of Naval Policy

Prelude: The Liberals, Fisher and the Royal Navy

When the *entente cordiale* with France was tested over Morocco, Germany came to the fore as potentially Britain's major adversary and this raised the question of Britain's position in a future European war. The Selborne Memorandum of December 1904 discussed naval building programmes and stated that in future British programmes would to some extent take note of German programmes. In March 1905 Lord Selborne resigned his post as First Lord and became Britain's High Commissioner in South Africa. The Earl of Cawdor was appointed his successor. Cawdor's term of office lasted only from March to December 1905 and he was dogged by ill health throughout.[1]

As First Lord, the Earl of Cawdor is remembered for one thing only, the Cawdor Memorandum. In November 1905 a parliamentary paper was prepared, 'A Memorandum on Admiralty Work and Progress', which discussed shipbuilding programmes in some detail.[2] Particular attention was paid to shipbuilding times and a strategic requirement of four large armoured ships laid down every year was defined. Since building times were around two years, eight capital ships would be under construction at any time.[3] This strategic requirement was considered to be the 'irreducible minimum', the absolute minimum requirement for national security in the face of foreign naval competition. A more modern analysis suggests that it was in fact the absolute maximum programme.[4] This was a highly political document designed to leave an incoming Liberal administration wrong-footed.

In December 1905, Arthur Balfour resigned as prime minister. This was unusual in that the Liberals under Sir Henry Campbell-Bannerman took office before the General Election. Balfour knew he would lose the election and hoped to show the Liberals split and disunited over the issue of naval expenditure. It did not work and in January 1906 the Conservatives lost the General Election badly and were cut to a rump of just 156 members. Opposing them were 379 Liberals, 52 Labour members and 83 Irish Nationalists. The Liberal majority over the Conservatives was 223.

Jacky Fisher was due to retire on 25 January 1906, when he reached his sixty-fifth birthday. The only way for him to remain as First Sea Lord was promotion to Admiral of the Fleet. One of Balfour's last acts as prime minister was to sign an order in council that raised Fisher to this rank.[5] Fisher's position as First Sea Lord was secure into the foreseeable future. With Russia defeated in the Far East and France now an ally under the *entente cordiale*, the Liberals seemed poised to do what they had done on every occasion they had assumed office since 1830. Policies of retrenchment, social reform and cuts in naval expenditure would be the order of the day. In fact, the *Dreadnought* policy was pushed hard as an Admiralty exercise in economy, not extravagance. With her uniform main armament and the standardisation of design, Fisher showed that 30 dreadnoughts could be run for the cost of 29 *Lord Nelsons*. Fisher was able to show Lord Tweedmouth, the incoming Liberal First Lord, a decrease in the naval estimates for 1905–6 and a projected further decrease in 1906–7.

The Liberals had come into office at the end of the fiscal year and had no option but to accept the naval estimates for 1906, which they did in the March of that year. The three Invincible class battlecruisers were provided under the previous year's (1905) estimates and were laid down between February and April 1906, with the *Dreadnought* herself launched at Portsmouth in the February of that year. At this time Herbert Asquith was Chancellor of the Exchequer and demanded big cuts in the 1907 programme. Fisher, desperate to keep his construction programmes intact, suggested that the 1907–8 estimates be kept to the same level as the 1906–7 estimates. Asquith would have none of it and demanded further heavy cuts on the basis that current naval strength went far beyond any reasonable two-power standard. Tweedmouth attempted to justify his case by stating that a modern battleship usually became obsolete after just 15 years.[6] It was an ineffective approach that resulted in a 50 per cent cut in the capital ship construction programme for the following year, provided an agreement on armament reduction was reached at the second Hague Conference. Fisher was surprisingly pragmatic about working with the Liberal government.

THE POLITICS AND DIPLOMACY OF NAVAL POLICY 137

He appears to have supported the cuts, and said so in a letter to Lord Tweedmouth in September 1906.

> In dropping the one Dreadnought this year we are only doing what has been done in the preceding two years [...] it is simply stupid to talk of the loss of our naval supremacy. 1 Dreadnought built; 3 to be laid down this year; 3 next year (because the Hague Conference will be futile); 3 'Invincibles' building (in my opinion superior) to Dreadnoughts. 10 Dreadnoughts practically built or building in two years!!![7]

The 1906 (Conservative) programme included four dreadnoughts. This was cut to three and the *Bellerophon*, *Temeraire* and *Superb*, virtually repeat dreadnoughts, were laid down between December 1906 and February 1907. The Admiralty were able to answer Asquith by saying that three were necessary to make up, with *Dreadnought* herself, a tactical group of four dreadnoughts.[8]

Some six weeks after his letter to Tweedmouth Fisher was guest of honour at the Lord Mayor's Banquet, 9 November 1907. He assured his listeners that they could sleep quietly in their beds.[9] It was unfortunate rhetoric because on 3 October the British naval attaché in Berlin was reporting an acceleration in the rate of German shipbuilding.[10] The speech was ill-judged in other ways because the suggestion of overwhelming naval strength was seized on by the radical liberals as a justification for big spending cuts in the naval budget.[11]

Liberals, Dreadnoughts and Kaiser Wilhelm

In the following year, 1907–8, only two dreadnoughts were proposed, the 50 per cent reduction agreed in 1906. No naval agreement was reached at the Second Hague peace conference and a third ship was included in the programme. The 1907–8 programme consisted of three ships, *Collingwood*, *St Vincent* and *Vanguard*, again nearly repeat dreadnoughts, with the same turret layout.[12] The first four German dreadnoughts, the Nassaus, were due for completion in 1910, when Britain would have ten completed, a comfortable lead. It was the estimates for the following year, 1908–9, that caused a major political row. In November 1907 138 backbench Liberals petitioned the prime minister for massive cuts in defence expenditure. By late November the Cabinet were telling the Admiralty that no dreadnoughts should be laid down in the next fiscal year. The Sea

Lords presented Tweedmouth with a memorandum protesting at the high-handed way they were being treated and there was also a verbal threat of resignation by the entire board. To avoid such a public clash, which would undoubtedly have an impact on the government's popularity, in January 1908, Campbell-Bannerman overruled the Treasury and agreed the Admiralty's own estimates, which included two dreadnoughts. Unfortunately, before Tweedmouth could present the revised package to the Cabinet Campbell-Bannerman had a massive heart attack. Asquith was appointed deputy leader and by February 1908 had made the Admiralty's estimates null and void. Fisher was called before the Cabinet and informed that the estimates were to be reduced by £1,340,000. The Cabinet then agreed an increase in the estimates of £900,000 and declared the matter closed.

The revised 1908–9 programme included just one dreadnought and an armoured cruiser armed with 9.2-inch guns. In March Asquith during a debate in the House of Commons described this ship as a 'battlecruiser'. Fisher pounced and the 15,500-ton armoured cruiser with eight 9.2-inch guns became a large 18,500-ton battlecruiser armed with eight 12-inch guns. The difference in price more than made up for the February cuts. Asquith could do nothing – he had after all described the ship as a battle-cruiser.[13] In spite of the extra dreadnought cruiser (the term battlecruiser was only adopted formally in 1912), there was a large press clamour against the small building programme. 'Is Britain going to surrender her maritime supremacy to provide old-age pensions?', demanded the *Daily Mail*. At this time the Imperial Maritime League was making great headway, with Admiral Lord Charles Beresford at its head. The Fisher–Beresford feud (to be discussed later) was at its height and the League wrote to Lord Esher asking him to join. On 6 February 1908 Esher published his reply in *The Times*. Esher said that 'there is not a man in Germany, from the Emperor downwards, who would not welcome the fall of Sir John Fisher'. The Kaiser read the letter and replied to it, writing personally in a hand-written nine-page letter addressed to Lord Tweedmouth.[14]

> If England built 60, 90 or 100 battleships, there would be no change in the German building plans. It was unpleasant for Germans to notice that in discussions about the British programmes of construction, there was always some reference to the German navy. People would be very thankful over here if [. . .] Germany were left out of the discussion.[15]

Tweedmouth was amazed and flattered to receive a personal letter from an unfriendly head of state and showed it to his friends. The letter was answered by King Edward and by the Foreign Office. Tweedmouth then wrote a private letter to the Kaiser, giving prior information of Britain's naval estimates, information not yet available to parliament. *The Times* got wind of it and in a leader said:

> If there was any doubt about the meaning of German naval expansion, none can remain after an attempt of this kind to influence the Minister responsible for our Navy in a direction favourable for German interest.[16]

Tweedmouth was considered to have been recklessly indiscreet and was dismissed almost immediately, to be replaced by Reginald McKenna. In the summer of 1908 there were increasing concerns about German naval building programmes. Then in October came the extraordinary affair of the Kaiser and the *Daily Telegraph* interview. The Kaiser sometimes stayed with an English friend, Colonel Stuart-Wortley, and in the autumn of 1907 told him that he (the Kaiser) had done so much for England, and was badly misunderstood. Stuart-Wortley saw the Kaiser again in September 1908 and the Kaiser asked that as much publicity as possible be given to what he regarded as his anglophile views and opinions. Stuart-Wortley wrote a rough draft of an interview designed for publication in the *Daily Telegraph* and submitted it to the Kaiser. The Kaiser considered the article well written and sent it to Von Bülow, who was on holiday at Norderney and thought it merely a typical Kaiser-speech, so did not bother to read it. Von Bülow sent it back to Berlin for any necessary revisions. In Berlin it was opened by an under-secretary, Stemrich, who also did not read the typescript and sent it to a privy councillor. Councillor Klehmet actually read the typescript and thought it 'very dubious', but felt it was not the job of the Foreign Office to contradict the Kaiser. The letter was sent back to Stemrich, who again did not read it and sent it to Norderney, where it was received by Von Müller, Chief of the Naval Cabinet, who also did not read it and gave it to Von Bülow, who gave it a cursory glance, signed it and sent it back to Berlin, from where the Kaiser sent it to Stuart-Wortley and the *Daily Telegraph*.[17] The article was published on 28 October 1908 and across the passage of a century still makes interesting if not to say hilarious reading.

> You English are, mad, mad, mad as March hares. What has come over you that you are so given over to suspicions quite unworthy of a great nation? What more can I do than I have done? [...] To be forever misjudged, to have my repeated offers of friendship weighed and scrutinized with jealous, mistrustful eyes, taxes my patience severely.[18]

He went on to say that he was a friend of England but that the German people were generally hostile and were prepared to go to war with England. He then astounded *Daily Telegraph* readers by stating that during the Boer War he had written to the British General Staff and told them how to win it.[19] He claimed that at the height of the Boer War France and Russia had urged him to join a tripartite alliance to humiliate England; it was only the intervention of the Kaiser that prevented this.[20] Finally he addressed the vexed issue of the German Navy and its strategic purpose. The Kaiser stated that the German Navy was built to defend Germany's now vast worldwide trade and suggested that it might even be used against Japan. How German battleships, notoriously lacking in coal-carrying capacity, based in the Baltic and North Sea, could easily be deployed in the Far East does not seem to have occurred to him.[21]

The article managed to offend Britain, France, Russia and Japan. France and Russia denied there had ever been a suggestion of a tripartite alliance against England. The Japanese wondered what crisis could produce a naval war with Germany. Reactions in Britain ranged from outrage to amusement. Bülow claimed to the end of his days that he had not read the article due to pressure of other work and that the Foreign Office was to blame. Nevertheless, Bülow was Chancellor, he knew the Kaiser's foibles well and his position was weakened by the extraordinary *faux pas* of his Emperor. A diplomatic dispatch from Germany to Sir Edward Grey, Britain's Foreign Secretary, stated the following.

> From what Count Hohenthal said I gathered that he considered the Emperor to be hopelessly erratic, and there was no hope of altering or controlling his impulsive character and action, and that there was equally little hope that any other Chancellor would have been more successful in doing so than Prince Bülow had been. In fact the situation was hopeless, and, as a Bavarian friend said to me, using a graphic Bavarian expression: 'es wird eben so weiter gewurstelt', i.e 'We shall go muddling on in the same old way'.[22]

In 1909 Bulow retired and was replaced by Bethmann-Hollweg who found serious alarm in the Foreign Office over the growing estrangement with England. There was also a realisation that German fleet building was pushing Britain towards France and Russia, but the Foreign Office could not override the Kaiser, whose private cabinets were very important and 'civilians' were excluded. The German Ambassador to Britain, Count Paul von Wolff-Metternich, suggested to Tirpitz:

There is an idea in our naval circles that once we have taken some decided step towards the further construction of our fleet, England will submit to the inevitable and we shall become the best of friends It is a disastrous mistake [...] it will set England in arms against us.[23]

In 1908 the net effect of the Kaiser's two interventions, apart from the chaos they produced in German foreign policy, was to focus attention on naval building programmes. Exactly how Britain would respond to Germany will be seen later, particularly when the German naval building programmes were reviewed.

Alfred Tirpitz and the German Bid for Naval Supremacy

Tirpitz did not actually accelerate the time it took to build a battleship, but it needs to be clearly understood that he did make a bid for naval supremacy. The second navy law of 1900 upgraded the eight small coast defence ships of the Siegfried class to battleships, discussed in Chapter 5. When the second *novelle* (modification to German navy law), was introduced in November 1908 the *ersatz* (replacement) time for battleships was altered from 25 years to 20 years and these eight ships could be added to the *ersatz* list of new hulls. The *ersatz* date started from the first payment for a ship under construction and it is this that brought the eight Siegfrieds into the picture and enabled Tirpitz to step up the tempo of warship building. The four Brandenburg class battleships laid down in 1890 could also be added to the *ersatz* list. The addition of the central battery ironclad *Oldenburg* gave Tirpitz the potential for 13 new battleships, in addition to the four Nassaus building. It has already been noted that the first *novelle* of 1906 had upgraded the large cruisers of the second navy law to armoured cruisers and later battlecruisers. Tirpitz was now in a position to lay down three battleships and one battlecruiser a year. The 1908–9, 1909–10, 1910–11 and 1911–12 programmes would define the parameters of a German Navy with nearly the same number of dreadnoughts as Britain. The total dreadnought programme, including the battlecruisers, now stood at 21 ships. From Britain's point of view, the questions that needed answering concerned the speed with which the German programme could be completed and the nature of the British response to the Tirpitz challenge.

The Admiralty and the Foreign Office had a number of sources of intelligence, including diplomats, consulates and naval attachés. The attachés were by far the most important, possessing the sort of detailed knowledge concerning navies that diplomats lacked. The two British naval attachés assigned to the Berlin Embassy in this period were Commander (later Captain) Philip Dumas, 1906–8, and Captain Herbert Heath, 1908–10. Dumas was deeply concerned about German naval building capability. In 1906 he visited the Germania and Imperial Dockyards at Kiel, the Imperial and Schichau dockyards at Danzig and Elbing, the Vulkan yard at Stettin, Krupps works at Essen, and the dockyard at Wilhelmshaven.[24] In a report of 3 October he concluded that Schichau at Danzig could build six battleships, deliver the first in 25 months and one every four months thereafter. Vulkan at Stettin could lay down five battleships at once, while the Germania yard at Kiel could build a battleship in just two years. Blohm and Voss could deliver four ships of the largest size in $3^1/_2$ years and Weser at Bremen were capable of building two large cruisers and delivering them in 25 to 30 months.

> To sum it all up it will be seen that the great shipyards of Germany could reasonably be expected to build and deliver nine battleships and three cruisers of the largest size in 33 months allowing twelve 28 cm guns for the former and eight 28 cm guns for the latter [. . .] at my lower estimate Krupp could produce 88 in the given time and at the greater estimate could produce 132 which latter number would be just sufficient.[25]

Throughout 1907 Dumas kept the Admiralty and the Foreign Office informed of naval developments in Germany. Dumas alerted the Admiralty to the second *novelle* on 3 October 1907 and said that by 1920 Germany would possess 38 battleships of 20 years old or less.[26] In a report of 23 October 1907 he reviewed in some detail the *ersatz* programme for the years ahead. All 17 possible replacements discussed earlier were identified, with their replacement dates. Dumas remained as attaché until July 1908 and in a succession of reports warned of the big German building programmes.

In July 1908 Dumas was replaced by Captain Herbert Heath, who went about his work in much the same way as Dumas and started his period as attaché by visiting the various shipyards and commenting on them in some detail. By late October 1908 he was becoming convinced that Tirpitz was accelerating his naval building programmes. In a report dated 21 October 1908 he stated that two of the contracts for the 1909–10 programme had already been placed, six months before the money for their construction had been voted by the Reichstag.[27] A further report dated 16 November stated that by October 1911 the German Navy might have ten dreadnoughts and three battlecruisers completed.[28] This was overstated, as the actual number was seven dreadnoughts and two battlecruisers.[29] By March 1909 Heath was reporting that by the beginning of 1912 Germany would have 13 battleships and battleship-cruisers ready for service.[30] Britain would have 14 plus the ships of the 1909–10 programme. The attachés overestimated the building capacity of the German shipyards but rang some very necessary alarm bells. It is also clear that a 'sweetheart' relationship existed between the RMA and the shipyards. The shipyards knew well in advance of the orders being given that they would be awarded the contracts and were able to start new hulls in a leisurely way, minimising overtime payments and using common stock materials such as steel purchased at the previous year's prices, thus maximising profits.

There were important differences in the way German and British attachés worked. The German naval attaché in London, Korvettenkapitän Widenmann, answered directly to Tirpitz and the Kaiser, not to the ambassador and the Kaiser endlessly backed the attaché against the ambassador. In the case of Britain, attachés held full diplomatic status and all attaché reports were submitted to the ambassador before onward transmission, not to the Admiralty, but to the Foreign Office. There were other worrying features that surfaced in 1908. In 1907 Britain had concluded an *entente* with Russia and in October 1908 Austria-Hungary annexed Bosnia and Herzegovina, backed by Germany. In the face of Austro-German unity, Russia, still recovering from her disastrous war in the Far East, was not prepared to go to war in defence of Balkan Slavs, but was not likely to forget the humiliation and unlikely to step down in some future Balkan crisis. Britain, France and Russia were now strongly united against Germany.

Krupp's produced all the heavy guns for German dreadnoughts and in July 1908 had floated a loan of £2.5 million. Most of this money was spent on the Essen works, extending its gun-making capacity by at least 30 per cent. The British assessment concluded that Krupp's could produce the main and secondary armament of eight ships per year.[31] The building time for a dreadnought depended as much on the availability of guns and armour as on the actual laying down date. The Admiralty were convinced that material for the four ships of the 1908–9 and the four ships of the 1909–10 programmes was being collected and that these ships would be completed in 24 months. On 15 December 1908, the First Lord, McKenna, asked the German naval attaché in London, Widenmann, when the construction programme for 1909–10 came into effect. The answer was, of course, 1 April 1909. Why, McKenna asked, had two of the ships already been laid down, one at Schichau and the other at Vulkan? Widenmann replied that this information was based on mistaken inferences and was being exploited in a tendentious and anti-German manner.[32]

On 4 January 1909, Grey again tried to obtain a statement from the German ambassador. Grey spoke of three 'sphinx-like riddles' that were worrying the British Admiralty. These 'riddles' concerned the construction, in advance of their dates, of the battleships *Oldenburg* and *Friedrich der Grosse*, at Schichau and Vulkan respectively. Grey went on to say that, at the normal rate of building, Germany would have 13 dreadnoughts by February 1912. If material for four further ships was collected well in advance of the navy law timetable, then 17 dreadnoughts would be ready by February 1912. Building at the limit of speed and capacity, Germany could conceivably have 21 dreadnoughts by April 1912. The British programme, decided in March 1909, would have to take these building projections into account. Metternich replied that navy law determined the German shipbuilding programme and that a sudden use of the entire shipbuilding capacity of the country to shorten times of construction was thereby excluded. In fact, Metternich accepted the first of Grey's figures, 13 dreadnoughts by February 1912, but not the conjectured 17 or 21 ships.[33]

During the winter of 1908–9, an Argentine naval mission arrived in Europe with a view to ordering dreadnoughts from a shipyard in Britain, France or Germany. The mission arrived in Britain on 1 March 1909 and its leader, Admiral Garcia, told Fisher that the level of access to the German shipyards had been unprecedented. The mission had counted something close to a hundred 28-cm (11-inch) and 30.5-cm (12-inch) guns completed or under construction and that there were 12 keels under construction. Fisher concluded that Germany might have 12 or 13 dreadnoughts completed by April 1911; with the possibility of as many as 21 dreadnoughts by April 1912 if their programmes were heavily forced. If this was indeed the case, Britain would need to lay down eight ships in 1909.[34]

In December 1908 Asquith informed King Edward that the acceleration in German shipbuilding times meant that the Admiralty was asking for six dreadnoughts in the 1909–10 programme, not the four originally proposed. In Cabinet McKenna was a much more effective First Lord than Tweedmouth and fought the navy's case there with great skill. He argued strongly for the six ships but was overruled. Asquith never accepted that Germany could have 21 dreadnoughts by 1912, but by early March considered that they might have 17 to Britain's 20. The Admiralty were now demanding eight ships for 1909–10 so Asquith allowed the first four ships and postponed a decision on the second four ships until July. In the event the second four ships were allowed, partly because of the worsening diplomatic situation in Europe, caused by Austria-Hungary's annexation of Bosnia-Herzegovina and partly because a constitutional clash was developing between the Commons and Lords, with the near inevitably of a general election. In this situation the Liberals did not wish to appear weak and vacillating on defence matters.[35]

The Arms Race Goes Critical

The decision to lay down eight ships in one year was a complete *volte face* compared to the previous year's programme cuts. It was made necessary by the apparent acceleration in the German programmes. In fact, no acceleration in building times had taken place but the *ersatz* replacements for the eight Siegfrieds allied to the first and second *novelles* contributed to a large expansion in the German Navy that Britain could not possibly ignore. If Britain's stance was inevitable, how far was the German Navy 'offensive' and the British navy 'defensive'? Britain had no military conscription, a small standing army and a liberal political tradition that militated strongly against heavy defence spending in peacetime. If Germany had the largest navy and army in Europe, it would have achieved European hegemony without a shot being fired in anger. Britain's tiny peacetime army could never stand against Germany, so the German Navy was almost, by definition, offensive in nature. To later generations, these arguments appear simple and deterministic, yet they were real enough in their day. Sir Edward Grey, the Foreign Secretary, speaking in the House of Commons debate on the naval estimates, on 29 March 1909, said:

> No superiority of the British Navy over the German Navy could ever put us in a position to affect the independence or integrity of Germany because our Army is not maintained on a scale which, unaided, could do anything on German territory. But if the German Navy were superior to ours, they maintaining the Army, which they do, for us it would not be a question of defeat. Our independence, our very existence would be at stake [. . .] Two things would produce conflict, one is an attempt by us to isolate Germany. No nation of her standing or position would stand a policy of isolation assumed by neighbouring powers. Another thing, which would certainly produce conflict, would be the isolation of Britain, the isolation of England attempted by any great continental power so as to dominate and dictate the policy of the

continent. This has always been so in History. The same reasons which have caused it in History would cause it again, but between these two extremes of isolation and domination there is a wide space in which two nations can walk together in a perfectly friendly way.[36]

There was other apparent evidence for an acceleration of the German programmes. In December 1908, the Admiralty had access to the German naval estimates for 1909–10. The payments for capital ships showed a very large increase indeed. Payments for capital ships were made in four instalments. The first two instalments for the four ships of the 1908–9 programme, £1.13 million, were only £90,000 less than the amount of the first three instalments for the capital ships of the 1906–7 programme. This increase implied either larger ships or accelerated construction. In fact, the four Helgoland ships were considerably larger than the preceding Nassau class ships and mounted 30.5-cm (12-inch), not 28-cm (11-inch) guns.

There was also the evidence of British engineers and others who visited Germany. The Danzig yard at Schichau received its first battleship order for the dreadnought *Oldenburg*, belonging to the 1909–10 programme. Any ship of that year's estimates was supposed to be laid down after 1 April 1909, that is, the date on which the credits for new construction were voted by the Reichstag. Yet a Briton skating over the ice of the frozen Baltic saw her ribs rising above the graving berth in the early weeks of 1909, months before she was supposed to be laid down.[37] Mr Mulliner, managing director of the Coventry Ordnance Works, in numerous visits to Germany, concluded that Krupp's huge extension at Essen implied a large increase in production of heavy guns and mountings. Moreover, he backed his suspicions with considerable evidence of what was going on. As far back as 1906, he had warned the War Office of accelerated German building times, and this information was duly passed to the Admiralty. The Admiralty chose to ignore this evidence and suspected him of giving tendentious information in the hope of getting large orders for his firm. Nevertheless, the big German naval expansion and Britain's probably inevitable reply to it turned an era of intensifying naval competition into a full-blooded naval arms race.

The Fall of Fisher

In the period 1906–9 Fisher made numerous enemies both within and outside the armed forces. Indeed, the most authoritative biography of Fisher

1 HMS Dreadnought *after her completion in 1906.*

2 HMS Dreadnought *and ship's cat. The cat was called Togo and was treated with great affection by everyone from the captain downwards.*

3 HMS Dreadnought, *underway in 1907 as flagship of the Home Fleet.*

4 HMS Orion, *the first of the super-dreadnoughts, armed with ten 13.5-inch guns.*

5 *HMS* Inflexible, *first generation battlecruiser of the Invincible class.*

6 *HMS* Bellerophon *at sea.*

7 *HMS* Neptune *at anchor.*

8 *HMS* Birmingham, *5,400 tonnes, sister of cruiser Nottingham. Both ships were completed in 1914.*

9 *HMS* Nottingham, *5,440 tonnes, sunk by a U-boat on 19 August 1916.*

10 *The two fore turrets of HMS* Iron Duke *during rough weather in the North Sea.*

11 *England's sea power, HMS* Iron Duke.

12 *Battleship HMS* Iron Duke *photographed early in the war.*

13 Another view of HMS Iron Duke, *super-dreadnought armed with ten 13.5-inch guns and twelve 6-inch guns. Flagship of Sir John Jellicoe 1914–16.*

14 HMS Centurion, *super-dreadnought armed with ten 13.5-inch guns.*

15 *The ill-fated battlecruiser HMS* Queen Mary, *which blew up at Jutland with the loss of 1,266 men. Her loss tended to condemn the battlecruiser type.*

16 *The battlecruiser HMS* Tiger, *the most elegant of the British battlecruisers.*

17 *Admiral Jellicoe climbs to the bridge of* Iron Duke.

18 *Admiral Scheer, German Commander-in-Chief.*

19 Admiral Beatty.

20 Admiral Hipper, German battlecruiser commander.

21 *HMS* Warspite *in 1917.*

22 *Admiral Beatty, the King and Queen of Belgium, Admirals Goodenough, de Brock and de Robeck on board* Queen Elizabeth.

23 *The German Cruiser* Emden, *3,600 tonnes, completed in 1908.*

24 *The destruction of the* Emden *as seen from HMAS* Sydney, *one of the great early triumphs of the Royal Australian Navy.*

25 *The naval battle in Heligoland Bight, during the sinking of the* Mainz, *as seen from the deck of a British cruiser. The Heligoland Bight battle (28 August 1914) was a considerable though chancy British success.*

26 *The Dardanelles: A barge full of soldiers passing a man-o-war in the Straits. The battleship is either HMS* Irresistible *or HMS* Implacable. *Sister ships, both served in the Dardanelles.* Irresistible *was sunk by a mine 18 March 1915. This is probably* Implacable, *which survived long enough to have her picture taken. Both ships were pre-dreadnoughts dating from the 1898–9 period.*

describes the years 1906–10 as the 'years of dissention'.[38] In 1907, almost immediately after the building of the *Dreadnought*, Cabinet ministers began to question the wisdom of the dreadnought policy. David Lloyd George described the policy as 'wanton and profligate ostentation'.[39] Campbell-Bannerman as prime minister complained to Asquith, when the latter was Chancellor of the Exchequer, that he resented paying out so much for these very large experimental ships.[40] The *Manchester Guardian* termed the *Dreadnought* Fisher's one great mistake.[41]

The story of the creation of the Home Fleet shows the level of dissention created by Fisher. In 1906 Fisher, to keep alive his building programme and achieve cuts in the naval Estimates, decided to reduce the number of ships in full commission. This included seven battleships and four armoured cruisers, all to be placed in nucleus crew reserve. These ships were assigned to the so-called 'Home Fleet' and were crewed with 60 per cent of their full complement. Fisher did not inform the fleet commanders in advance of these cuts and they were leaked to the press. Press hostility to Fisher and the 'Home Fleet' concept allowed his somewhat disparate enemies to coalesce around this vexed issue.[42]

The origins of the Fisher–Beresford contretemps have already been traced back to the Corridino and other incidents at Malta in 1900. Beresford was a younger son of the Marquis of Waterford; hence the honorary title 'Lord'. He joined the navy in 1859, aged 13. His first appointment was to the flagship of the Mediterranean Squadron and then to HMS *Galatea*. He entered parliament as a Conservative in 1874 and represented County Waterford until 1880. In the same year that he entered parliament, he accompanied the Prince of Wales to India and royal patronage ensured he was promoted to commander in 1875. Appointed to command HMS *Condor*, a 780-ton gun vessel, he took part in the bombardment of Alexandria and distinguished himself working close inshore. From 1885 to 1888 he was again a Member of Parliament, this time for Marylebone East. He was Junior Naval Lord in Lord Salisbury's second administration and resigned over the vexed issue of naval expenditure. He was captain of the cruiser *Undaunted* from 1889 to 1893, was promoted to rear-admiral in 1898 and again entered parliament, this time for York. In December 1899 he was made second-in-command of the Mediterranean Squadron.

In reality, at the time of promotion to rear-admiral he had very little actual sea time. His service as a lieutenant can only be described as limited. He was promoted early to commander and served as second-in-command of exactly one ship before further service in a royal yacht. He had indeed commanded the gunboat *Condor*, but of his 14½ years sea service since promotion to lieutenant, 6½ were in royal service or as a flag lieutenant. This gave him a mere 5½ years of proper sea service.[43]

Beresford was Member of Parliament for Woolwich from 1902 to 1903. Later, back at sea he commanded the Channel Fleet. When the Russian Baltic Fleet fired on British trawlers in the North Sea, mistaking them for Japanese torpedo boats, asked what he would have done if war had been declared Beresford stated that he would have engaged the Russians at Tangier with half his battleship force. Why he should have used just half his available force was not explained. The Admiralty were understandably incensed at such an amateurish attitude, and to show his displeasure Fisher wanted Beresford relieved of his command early.

From 1905 to 1907 Beresford was Commander-in-Chief Mediterranean and took up an attenuated command of only eight battleships, compared with the 12 of Fisher's day.[44] He corresponded regularly with the First Lord, Tweedmouth. Fisher complained bitterly that this was unprecedented conduct, yet he had done exactly the same while commander-in-chief. Admiral Sir Arthur Wilson was Commander-in-Chief Channel Fleet, based at Portland, and Fisher took great pleasure in putting Beresford under Wilson's command for joint exercises. Needless to say, Beresford was not told in advance.

In 1907 Beresford's term as Commander-in-Chief Mediterranean drew to its close and he was offered command of the Channel Fleet in succession to A.K. Wilson. Beresford accepted the Channel Fleet on the understanding that he would hold the senior naval command in home waters. Initially his command included 17 battleships, nine cruisers and 36 destroyers. The trouble was that the seven battleships discussed earlier were about to be placed in reserve. Three of these ships came from the Channel Fleet, reducing its strength from 17 to 14. At the same time the Atlantic and Mediterranean fleets were each reduced from eight to six battleships. Beresford's Channel Command was, therefore, greatly attenuated when he took over in April 1907.[45]

The seven reserve battleships, manned with three-fifths crews, would be based on Chatham and Dover, along with four armoured cruisers. In addition to the other fully crewed battleships, the newly completed dreadnoughts went to this command and not to the Channel Fleet, giving a total of 16 battleships in the Chatham-Dover command. This huge battlefleet, with all its attendant cruisers and destroyers, was commanded by Rear-Admiral Bridgeman. The now small Atlantic and Mediterranean fleets and the attenuated Channel Fleet were all commanded by senior vice-admirals or full admirals, yet the biggest single concentration of warships was commanded by a junior rear-admiral.[46] Beresford was understandably furious at his attenuated command and did everything in his power to denigrate Fisher. It can be argued that Fisher's naval dispositions in home waters were not the result of the inexorable rise of the German Navy but rather the inexorable feud between the two leading admirals of the day. Towards the end of Beresford's time in command of the Channel Fleet Prince Louis of Battenberg, very much a swimmer in the fishtank, writing to another 'Fisherite', George King-Hall:

> J.F. was determined that Beresford would not have so big and honourable a command [as Wilson held]. I think C.B. has been badly treated, although he is not a patch on Arthur Wilson [...] You know how much I admire J.F. He is a truly great man, and almost all his schemes have benefited the Navy [...] His hatred of C.B. has led him to maintain for the past two years an organisation of our home forces that was indefensible.[47]

Beresford was already a wealthy man but in November 1906 an immensely rich brother died and left him a fortune. With practically limitless money at his back he could afford to keep open house at his London residence in Grosvenor Street and turn aristocratic society against Fisher. Fisher believed Beresford could do more with his chef than by talking.[48] He entertained lavishly and was the darling of aristocratic ladies, led by Lady Londonderry. In addition there was a considerable number of discontented admirals who wanted Fisher ousted and these people formed a 'syndicate of discontent'. When Vice-Admiral Bridgeman became Second Sea Lord he paid Beresford a courtesy call because he had served under Beresford in the Mediterranean. Thinking he was part of the 'syndicate of discontent' the butler showed him into the library where he found, seated around a table, a number of embarrassed admirals, obviously engaged in plotting against Fisher and the Board of Admiralty.[49]

Fisher had support from J.L. Garvin, editor of the *Observer* newspaper, and the *Times* and *Telegraph* newspapers.[50] By judicious leaking of information, the Fisher viewpoint was usually well represented. Against aristocratic society opposition, Fisher had the King's ear and easy access to Court circles.

In November 1907 the 'paintwork' affair involving Beresford and his subordinate Rear-Admiral Percy Scott, who commanded the First Cruiser Squadron, became the juicy scandal of the year. The Kaiser was visiting the Channel Fleet and Beresford obviously wanted his fleet smartly turned out, so ordered his ships into port. Scott was performing gunnery exercises and ordered his armoured cruisers into port, with the rather ill-considered signal: 'Paintwork appears to be more in demand than gunnery so you had better come in to make yourself look pretty.' Initially nothing happened but two days later Lieutenant Lionel Dawson from Beresford's flagship was in the wardroom of Scott's flagship *Good Hope* and learned of the message.[51] He did not have to inform Beresford but did so in an act of gratuitous mischief-making. Scott was publicly rebuked by Beresford, who wanted him dismissed from his command. Fisher refused but the press got to hear of it and as a result the Fisher–Beresford feud became known to the public.

In May 1908 Fisher penned a long memorandum to McKenna, evaluating Admiralty relations with Beresford. In it he quoted some of Beresford's more outrageous statements:

1. The Home Fleet is a fraud upon the public and a danger to the Empire.
2. We have an emasculated Channel Fleet.
3. The *Dreadnought* indicates a decadent tendency to rely on powerful material rather than on skill and grasp of the art of war.
4. There never has been, with the exception of the Mediterranean Fleet, formulated a proper war plan for the British Navy.[52]

Fisher went on to explain that relations with Beresford were so bad that in time of war this would be a positively dangerous situation. He explained that the Channel and Home Fleets were to be conjoined into a single unified command and this was the moment for Beresford to come ashore, conjecturing March 1909 as the appropriate date.[53]

On 11 May 1908 came the levée incident. While waiting for the King to appear at a court reception, Fisher chatted to Winston Churchill and David Lloyd George. Beresford went past and shook hands with Churchill and Lloyd George but when Fisher put out his hand Beresford turned his back on him. In June Beresford wrote to McKenna and levelled six charges against Admiralty policy. He charged that the allocation of fleets in home waters was all wrong, that the constitution of the Home Fleet was nonsense and that there was no war plan agreed between the Admiralty and the senior commander-in-chief afloat. There was a shortage of small cruisers, a shortage of destroyers for North Sea operations and no properly defended North Sea base. Beresford's claim that there were no war plans was strongly refuted by Fisher.[54]

Beresford's command was terminated in March 1909 but it was unfortunate that Beresford should have come ashore just as serious alarm was being expressed concerning the German construction programmes. He consulted Balfour, the Tory opposition leader, and warned Asquith, the prime minister, that he intended to do everything in his power to demand an inquiry into the policy and conduct of the Board of the Admiralty since the day Fisher became First Sea Lord.[55] In April 1909 he sent a letter to Asquith attacking the administration of the Admiralty on two fronts. These concerned the redeployment of the fleets in home waters, which had led to his Channel Fleet command being diminished and then terminated, and the lack of war plans. Asquith found himself in a difficult position and under such strong pressure that he was forced to appoint a committee of enquiry into the administration of the navy. It was a massive victory for Beresford and humiliation for Fisher.[56] The enquiry took the form of a sub-committee of the CID and was composed of Asquith, Lord Crewe, Lord Morley, Grey and Haldane. Asquith also wanted Sir Arthur Wilson, Beresford's predecessor in command of the Channel Fleet, and Lord Esher to sit on the committee, but Beresford objected to both as they were known to be pro-Fisher. Evidence was heard from Beresford, McKenna, Custance, Sir Arthur Wilson and from Captains H.H. Campbell and A.R. Hulbert, both officers in the NID. It transpired that both these officers, working in the war and trade sections, had quite illegally supplied Beresford with confidential information. After the commission had reported both officers were sacked and the Trade Division was abolished. The War Division was integrated into the mobilisation department but this left the Naval Intelligence Division severely weakened at just the moment it was moving towards the nucleus of a properly constituted Naval Staff.[57]

Beresford had drawn up charges against the organisation and distribution of the fleet in home waters, against the shortage of small craft, particularly destroyers, and the lack of war plans and intelligence.[58] An example of the extent to which Fisher would not take Beresford into his confidence and the lengths to which Beresford would go to obtain information occurred when Admiral Bridgeman asked for one of the Channel Fleet captains, the Hon. (later Admiral the Hon. Sir) Alexander Bethell, as his Chief of Staff. Fisher told Beresford no more than that Bethell was to be relieved of his command. At the same time he advised Bethell to keep his coming transfer to the Home Fleet secret from his c-in-c. When Bethell was away at sea Beresford paid a social call on his wife, to discover what Fisher was up to, as hopefully she would disclose her husband's next appointment. The Flag Lieutenant made a similar and, as it turned out, vain approach to Bethell's 9-year-old daughter.[59]

The Beresford Enquiry consisted of 15 meetings held over six weeks and the report was issued on 12 August as a Parliamentary Paper. It consisted of two volumes, 328 pages of proceedings and 245 of appendices, including 2,600 questions.[60] On the vexed issue of war plans, Beresford said that two years earlier the Admiralty had told him that war with Germany would involve a distant blockade. Beresford maintained that this was a defensive policy and proposed an attacking policy, with destroyers off the German ports, and the battle fleet behind. Under cross-examination he admitted that he had been given war plans but felt they hardly merited the name. He condemned the scrapping of small cruisers that could be used for blockade duties, missing the point that large, fast armoured cruisers had rendered the old small cruisers obsolete. In truth, to implement Beresford's plan would have required about 300 light craft.[61]

Fisher hardly spoke at the enquiry, except to answer questions put to him. McKenna as First Lord gave a staunch defence of the Fisher Admiralty. He stated that during Beresford's time in command, the fleets in home waters were being slowly organised into a single unitary command but this had taken time and there was as yet no North Sea harbour able to accommodate the Home Fleet.[62] The general conclusions of the committee were diplomatically worded to avoid offending either party and supported the Admiralty's arrangements for war.[63] The report stated that there were sufficient small craft, principally destroyers and that a lack of these craft did not constitute a risk to the safety of the country.[64] The report was only a qualified vindication of Fisher and apparently Asquith had gone out of his way to protect Beresford's reputation. The problem was that Beresford's critique of Admiralty policy had only been refuted by two recent measures; the amalgamation of the Channel and Home Fleets and Beresford's dismissal. The report also said that the Naval Intelligence Division should be expanded into a Naval Staff. Beresford hailed the report as a victory for himself, very far from the truth. Fisher described the report as 'a most cowardly production' and was certainly badly damaged by it. The remarks about a Naval War staff were in his opinion a 'red herring'.[65] Within days Beresford had circulated a letter to an army of journalists expressing 'great satisfaction' at the outcome of the commission. Fisher knew he was now mortally damaged, as did Asquith and McKenna. By October it was decided that he should retire on his sixty-ninth birthday in January 1910. The one consolation was that he was raised to the peerage.[66]

The Committee for Imperial Defence 1902–12

Central to understanding how British defence strategy developed in the decade or so before World War I is the operation of the Committee for Imperial Defence. Amongst the topics discussed in its early years was the possibility of invasion and the part played by the army and navy in countering invasion. Under some pressure from the League at the beginning of 1903, the prime minister, Arthur Balfour, asked the service chiefs to assess the possibility of the French capturing a port on the south coast as a precursor of invasion. Up to this time the navy had regarded coast defence as an army function. In the wake of the ruinously expensive Boer War and the desire for expenditure cuts in the service budgets, the navy, anticipating an axe being taken to their budget, changed tack and claimed that they could take care of the entire defence of the United Kingdom from attack or invasion.

Captain George Egerton, head of the navy's torpedo and mine warfare school, considered that the defence of coasts and ports was much better left to the navy. He thought that submarines and torpedo-boats were well suited to such work. There was some argument about this – submarines were very crude affairs in 1903 – but Selborne as First Lord considered the idea sound. The War Office wanted a home army of 350,000 men, to which the Admiralty replied that the worst-case invasion situation was a raiding party of perhaps 5,000 men. In the discussions that took place at this time the Admiralty comprehensively demolished the War Office arguments for a large field army for home defence.[67] As prime minister, Arthur Balfour unequivocally accepted the idea that the navy could guarantee the British Isles against seaborne attacks on a much larger scale than mere raids.[68] From 1903 onwards it was accepted that submarines were a very effective *defence mobile* for naval harbours, narrow channels and the coast line. A few boats would be deployed at Portsmouth, Sheerness, Plymouth, Malta, Hong Kong, Queenstown and Pembroke. Others would be stationed at Dover and Gibraltar, making the passage of the respective Straits very hazardous.[69]

Of course, the War Office were opposed to any reduction in their role in home defence but in March 1905 the Admiralty, with Fisher in control, scored a decisive victory over the War Office at a CID meeting. At the end of 1905 Sir George Clarke was secretary of the CID and asked the recently appointed Director of Naval Intelligence, Captain Charles Ottley, to outline the Admiralty's war plans. He said that the reserves would be mobilised and the Atlantic Fleet deployed in home waters. It was doubtful if the Channel Fleet could go to the Baltic early in the war and he did not think a landing in Schleswig-Holstein practicable (though apparently Fisher did). He thought a landing in Denmark possible if Denmark agreed. In 1905 these ideas were not considered stupid or dangerous and Clarke had always supported the idea of amphibious operations. The problem was the possible German violation of Belgian neutrality and the War Office, with its General Staff, had concluded that two army corps could be landed in Belgium by the twenty-third day from mobilisation. In the development of strategy in this era the Admiralty and the War Office held increasingly divergent views. The Director of Military Operations, Major-General Grierson, told the French military attaché that any Admiralty Schleswig-Holstein plan was 'ridiculous'. The French attaché agreed that such an operation was 'très delicate'.[70]

When Balfour was prime minister the CID had sided with the Admiralty on every important issue. The Liberal administration was less inclined to do so, particularly when the larger and more important warships had become so expensive. From early 1906 Fisher became increasingly reluctant to co-operate with any CID discussion concerning the navy.[71] In December 1905 a small group of naval and military officers had formed a sub-committee on amphibious warfare, with Ottley as a member. It quickly became clear that discussions had already taken place with the French and both sides had concluded that in a war with Germany the British Army should support the left flank of the French Army. A furious Fisher, to demonstrate Admiralty opposition to this policy, withdrew Ottley from the committee and concluded that Clarke was trying to manoeuvre the CID into a position of authority over the Admiralty.[72] For his part Clarke wanted (probably reasonably) an integrated approach to defence planning with the War Office and Admiralty each understanding the role of the other in national defence, certainly not the case in 1906.

Towards the end of 1907 Fisher's enemies, including Beresford and *The Times* military correspondent Colonel Repington, demanded a yet further invasion enquiry. In February 1908 Fisher and his Director of Naval Intelligence, Captain Slade, again scored a significant debating victory over the army, showing that a British amphibious force of some 60,000 troops would deter any German invasion. From the army side, General Sir William Nicholson asserted that the British had no monopoly of amphibiousness. Fisher and Slade destroyed Nicholson's arguments with consummate ease, claiming that any large-scale invasion attempt could not hope to evade the navy. Nicholson had been humiliated at the 1903 invasion enquiry and his second defeat at the hands of Fisher had the effect of creating yet another important enemy for the First Sea Lord.[73] In the run-up to the enquiry, it is amusing to note that, writing to Lord Esher, Fisher twice referred to Sir William Nicholson as Sir William Beelzebub.[74]

In late 1906, in preparation for the CID invasion inquiry, Fisher had Captain George Ballard head a committee to draw up war plans, with the emphasis on amphibious operations. This work was done at the War College at Portsmouth. The basis of staff training that emerged had started in 1900 when Captain H.J. May, largely on his own initiative, organised the first War Course for senior officers at Greenwich. This course became accepted as a valuable asset and in 1905 was moved to Portsmouth, at Fisher's behest.[75] Ballard examined the feasibility of a number of amphibious ideas such as landing British forces in Denmark and Schleswig-Holstein and capturing Heligoland as a forward base for a close blockade of the German North Sea coast. In a lengthy paper Ballard concluded that such schemes were 'utterly impracticable'.[76]

A second group, known as the Whitehall Committee, was established in early 1907 and considered roughly the same topics, including the capture of various North Sea islands as well as the close blockade of German naval bases. Nicholas Lambert is probably right in concluding that these 'war plans' were not so much examples of poor strategic planning but rather strategic studies.[77] To complete the story of amphibious operations, in 1908 Fisher set up a third committee, this time to examine the feasibility of seizing the islands at the entrance to the Baltic and paralysing all German initiative as a result. Almost everyone involved with the project was doubtful if such operations could ever be carried out.[78]

Deeply integrated with the idea of amphibious operations was the idea of blockade, the ancient and venerable weapon of the eighteenth and early nineteenth centuries. By 1903–4 close blockade had effectively received its *coup de grâce*.[79] Another conclusion of the Ballard Committee was that the only way to bring effective pressure to bear on Germany was a distant economic blockade with blockading cruisers sealing the North Sea entrances. The trade division of the Naval Intelligence Division made a fairly detailed assessment of Germany's vulnerability to economic blockade and the idea of distant blockade was accepted in the period 1905–8.[80]

The final twist in the story of blockade and the seizure of some point on the German coast came in August 1911. Against the background of the Agadir crisis, Asquith convened a meeting of the CID and wanted to know the Admiralty war plan. Fisher's successor as First Sea Lord was Admiral of the Fleet Sir Arthur Wilson, known throughout the navy as 'old 'ard Art', an extremely obstinate man renowned for his inflexibility, and like Fisher opposed to the idea of a Naval Staff. On 23 August 1911 he expounded a war plan that involved the close blockade of the entire German North Sea coast, with the battle fleet in close support. In 1905 Wilson had supported the idea of landings on the Frisian Islands and the capture of Heligoland, and had expressed this view to a CID committee at the time.[81] It was then that yet again the clash of personalities made itself felt. General Nicholson, who had been humiliated by Fisher at the 1903 invasion inquiry, had always claimed that 'his day would yet come to conquer'.[82] This was indeed his day and he was able to claim that Wilson's war plans, especially the capture of Heligoland, were madness and that the amphibious schemes might have been valuable about a hundred years earlier.[83] Wilson's views are all the more extraordinary because, in his evidence to the Beresford Enquiry, he had openly castigated the idea of working on the German coast.[84]

Until recently historians have cited Wilson's evidence to the CID as proof that he was an exceptionally poor strategist. Nicholas Lambert has suggested a different approach; that despite his renowned inflexibility, between 1909 and 1911 Wilson, having accepted distant blockade in the 1907–9 period, changed his mind about close blockade. The reason was the rapid development of the submarine into an effective, lethal war weapon. Warships operating a distant blockade would not be able to stop submarines leaving their bases. Close blockade at least gave a reasonable chance that the submarines would be caught leaving port and sunk before they could do any serious damage to British ships. In 1913 Wilson was to reiterate his changed views concerning close blockade and stated unequivocally that 'the advent of the submarine is the reason which makes the close blockade absolutely necessary'.[85] Lambert is probably correct in his view of Wilson's *volte face* on close blockade, but the older view, that both Fisher and Wilson continued to believe in amphibious and Baltic operations right up to World War I, should not be ignored.

If Lambert is essentially correct in the belief that Fisher wanted a 'flotilla defence' role for the navy in the North Sea, it may be questioned exactly how far Fisher had really thought this through.

> Two violently contrasting themes certainly recurred in his mind; the offensive idea of an expedition to the Baltic and the daunting anticipation of the coming dominance of the submarine [...] The latter theme tended to nullify the first.[86]

Towards a Naval Staff

The final thread in defence thinking concerns the development of a Naval Staff. In the 1880s Beresford had been instrumental in turning the Foreign Intelligence Committee into the Naval Intelligence Division. He did this by adding a mobilisation section to the existing Foreign Intelligence Committee. He also advocated the creation of a third section – war plans. In other words, Beresford was advocating a naval war staff, or something close to it, long before anyone else. In 1899 Rear-Admiral Reginald Custance was appointed Director of Naval Intelligence. As far back as 1886 he had worked for the Foreign Intelligence Committee so was already experienced in the relatively new field of naval intelligence. Under his superintendence the department grew from an intelligence-gathering organisation to one which also dealt with strategy and war plans. At this time the Intelligence Division had no executive power and its role was advisory.[87] It is interesting to note that at the time Fisher went to the Mediterranean as commander-in-chief with Beresford his second-in-command, Custance was Director of Naval Intelligence. Fisher knew Custance reasonably well; both men had served in the Admiralty at the same time and appeared to have been on good terms. In the autumn of 1900 the Mediterranean Squadron carried out manoeuvres that resulted in Fisher asking for a doubling of his destroyer flotillas. Custance was opposed and Fisher knew this through an old friend the Naval Secretary, Rear-Admiral Wilmot Fawkes. In March 1901 the First Lord, Selborne, visited Fisher at Malta accompanied by the Naval Secretary, the First Sea Lord, Sir Walter Kerr, and Custance. Fisher refused to accommodate Custance at Admiralty House and a 'frank and acrimonious exchange of views' made the breach between Fisher and Custance permanent.[88]

Beresford sent a letter condemning the state of the Mediterranean Squadron to Arnold White who had it published in the *Daily Mail*. In view of the fact that Custance had opposed reinforcing the Mediterranean Squadron, he fell out badly with Beresford. The open enmity between Beresford and Custance helped divide opposition to Fisher's reforms. It was only in 1907, when Beresford and Custance came together in the Channel Fleet, that the two men recognised their value to each other in attempting to drive Fisher from office.[89]

During the visit to the Mediterranean by Selborne, Kerr, Custance and Fawkes, Fisher appeared to believe strongly in a Naval War College and discussed it in some detail with Selborne. This is corroborated in a letter to his wife dated 20 July 1901.

> I have had another great point conceded by the Admiralty in the establishment of a Naval War College, which I urged ferociously when they were at Malta. I feel sure Lord Selborne was convinced, but the others would not have it at any price.[90]

In August 1901, writing to Selborne, Fisher reiterated what he had said previously. 'We shall never be right till you have a Naval War College and a Naval "Von Moltke" at the head of it! He will be hated by both the First Lord and the First Sea Lord.'[91]

In the autumn of 1901 Captain Prince Louis of Battenberg arrived in the Mediterranean in command of the new battleship *Implacable*. He had been Assistant Director of Naval Intelligence under Custance and got on well with Fisher. In the first half of 1902 Fisher sent him numerous memoranda concerning proposed naval reforms and possible war scenarios such as war with France or war with France and Russia. Interestingly, Germany is not mentioned as a potential foe, though a German–American alliance was considered. Battenberg was able to assure Fisher that under Custance's superintendence a Defence Division had been added to the NID dealing with plans of campaign and strategy for peace and war.

Battenberg argued that the NID, with its newly added Defence Division, was in outline at least a Naval Staff in all but name, and in a letter to Fisher said so.

> We thus have the skeleton ready to hand – it only wants clothing, and placing on a higher pedestal. Quite recently we have added to it indirectly by the establishment of the 'War Course' at Greenwich, already crowned with excellent results.[92]

As First Sea Lord Fisher ensured that the NID remained purely advisory and the drafting of war plans (strategic exercises) was delegated to the

War College. Lord Selborne certainly thought that Fisher was on course to establish a Naval Staff and in 1911 said so in a letter to Winston Churchill when the latter became First Lord.

> I bequeathed that task [forming a War Staff] as an urgent legacy to Fisher nearly seven years ago and gave him all the material for its fulfilment. To my surprise and disgust on my return from South Africa [in 1910] I found he had done nothing; I say surprise because I thought it would have been a job after his own heart, but obviously I was wrong.[93]

Fisher apparently accepted the idea of a Naval General Staff in 1901–2 but rejected it as First Sea Lord, arguably because of his feud with Beresford, which came to include the former Director of Naval Intelligence, Sir Reginald Custance. It can be argued that Beresford was only offered the Channel command to keep him out of parliament and that Fisher appointed Custance as Beresford's second-in-command because they had fallen out badly in the Mediterranean. The fact that they patched up their differences and worked together for Fisher's downfall came as a nasty surprise. Beresford and Custance were both advocates of a Naval General Staff, and this may account for Fisher's change of mind.

In truth, Fisher and his successor Wilson were genuinely undecided how a future naval war would be fought and neither wanted a Naval Staff. Wilson was quickly replaced by Bridgeman and, again, Bridgeman did not want a Naval Staff. In October 1911 McKenna was replaced as First Lord by Winston Churchill, who quickly retired Bridgeman on the slightly bogus grounds of 'ill health'. Prince Louis of Battenberg succeeded Bridgeman as First Sea Lord and a Naval Staff was created on 8 January 1912. There were three divisions, operations, intelligence and mobilisation.

There were two significant contributions made by the War Staff in the period 1912–14 and both concerned blockade, discussed earlier. By April 1912 the idea of an intermediate blockade had been substituted for close blockade. Naval exercises showed the weakness of an intermediate blockade and in 1913 Ballard suggested a distant blockade. This would include a cordon across the Dover Straits and across the Orkney–Norway gap. The northern blockade would be upheld by the main British fleet in a Scottish base.[94]

The earlier assessments of the development of the Naval Staff, particularly those that condemn the Staff 1912–14, are wide of the mark. The Staff did evaluate the major elements of any future naval war – blockade and fleet engagement. The major defects in planning can be laid at the feet of

Fisher and his successor, Arthur Wilson. They delayed the establishment of a Naval Staff, which left too little time for fully competent war planning to be in place by 1914.

Perspectives: The Fisher Era

More than any other individual Fisher took the Victorian and Edwardian Royal Navy from its days as a peacekeeping deterrent force towards the reality of a war-ready navy. The building of the *Dreadnought* was an important way station on the road. Fisher did not, as so many accounts suggest, drag the Victorian and Edwardian Royal Navy 'kicking and screaming' into the twentieth century. There were Fisher-era mistakes, sometimes serious mistakes, detailed in previous chapters.

Fisher's attitude to the creation of a War Staff shows his limitations and lack of strategic grasp. Fisher's principle focus prepared the Royal Navy for the outbreak of war but did not provide plans for its prosecution.[95] This was not all Fisher's fault. It has already been pointed out that the Beresford Commission resulted in the abolition of the trade division and the amalgamation of the war division with the Mobilisation Department, thus stymieing the development of the Naval Intelligence Department into a Naval Staff. In the final analysis, the late establishment of a Naval Staff was the greatest failure of the Fisher-era Admiralty.

7

From Dreadnoughts to Super-Dreadnoughts

Prelude: The Last 12-Inch Gunned Dreadnoughts

In 1907–8 just three dreadnoughts were laid down, including *Vanguard*, built by Vickers in just 22 months, the fastest building time since the *Dreadnought* herself. The principal difference from the Bellerophons was the adoption of 50-calibre guns as opposed to the 45 calibres of the earlier dreadnoughts. The 50-calibre guns were not an unwarranted success; the higher muzzle velocity caused muzzle-wobble, which reduced accuracy at longer ranges.[1]

The 1908–9 programme included just one dreadnought, HMS *Neptune*, and represented the first real departure from the *Dreadnought* design. The Admiralty knew that the second pair of American dreadnoughts, *Delaware* and *North Dakota*, carried ten 12-inch guns all mounted on the centreline, to give a broadside of all ten guns, as opposed to eight in the early British dreadnoughts. Dreadnoughts building for Argentina and Brazil had twelve 12-inch guns with superfiring turrets fore and aft and *en echelon* turrets amidships. To increase the broadside fire without a massive increase in length, the *Neptune* was the first British dreadnought with a superimposed turret and in consequence was only ten feet longer than the *St Vincent*. One turret was mounted forward, two *en echelon* amidships and two aft, the one superimposed over the other. The superimposed turret aft caused interference with the sighting ports on the lower turret and could fire only within about 30 degrees of the fore-and-aft axis. *Neptune* was fitted with flying bridges for boat storage, and these connected the fore, midships and aft superstructures and again helped limit length. In reality these decks were a serious hazard to the *en echelon* turrets beneath. If damaged or destroyed in wartime the flying bridges would have collapsed onto the turrets. The fore part of the flying bridges was removed in 1914–15. The *en echelon* turrets were not a great success. The cross-deck arcs of fire were severely restricted and trials revealed the deck beneath sagging badly as a result of blast damage. The deck was heavily reinforced with extra pillars and 'Z' bars as a result.[2]

The second ship of the 1908–9 programme was the battlecruiser *Indefatigable*. This was the ship that should have been an armoured cruiser, armed with 9.2-inch guns, but was upgraded after Asquith made an error in a House of Commons debate and described her as a battlecruiser. The design details were completed in November 1908 and she was laid down at Devonport in February 1909. The first battlecruiser *Invincible* went to sea in June 1908 and started her formal trials in October of that year. This meant that there was little or no feedback from the earlier ship to the new design.[3] In fact the *Indefatigable* was a slightly enlarged version of the *Invincible*, some 18 feet longer, which allowed the midships *en echelon* turrets wider (70 degrees) cross-deck firing arcs. Rather than developing a new design, the *Indefatigable* emphasised the weaknesses of the *Invincible* design. The armament was exactly the same as the *Invincible*, eight 12-inch 45-calibre guns. If anything the armour was even less than the *Invincible*, with the six-inch belt extending for only 298 feet amidships. The total weight of armour was 3,735 tons (19.92 per cent of displacement), compared to the 3,460 tons of armour (19.88 per cent of displacement) for the *Invincible*.[4] This meagre amount of armour was really only appropriate to an armoured cruiser of a few years earlier. Fisher had originally intended that battlecruisers should overwhelm the enemy's scouting forces and if necessary engage their battleships for a time. It does not seem to have occurred to him that the enemy might also possess battlecruisers.[5] In truth, the *Indefatigable* was the weakest design to emerge from the Fisher-era Admiralty and arguably should never have been built. The fact that two sisters were added later compounded the error.

The 1909–10 estimates produced the eight ships of the 'we want eight' programme. Three designs were used and the first two battleships, *Colossus* and *Hercules*, were very similar to the *Neptune*. Both were laid down in July 1909 and completed more or less exactly two years later. Both were built to contract, *Colossus* by Scotts and *Hercules* by Palmers. The upper deck layout was changed; there was only one mast, and the after mast and control positions were omitted as these were smoked out in *Neptune*. Armour was improved and an 11-inch belt was included, increased from the

10 inches of the *Neptune*. Total armour weight was 6,570 tons compared to the 5,700 tons of the *Neptune*.[6] The gun armament was identical to the *Neptune*, with ten 12-inch 50-calibre guns. These were the last battleships with 12-inch calibre guns and the last to use the unsatisfactory *en echelon* turret arrangement.

Super-Dreadnoughts

It was the four battleships of the Orion class that represented another large technical leap, almost as great as that from pre-dreadnoughts to dreadnoughts. The name ship was laid down at Portsmouth in November 1909. Displacement was increased from 17,900 tons to 22,500 tons made necessary by the adoption of 13.5-inch guns.

Increasing the gun calibre by 1.5 inches might seem relatively insignificant, but it produced a 60 per cent increase in shell weight. The 12-inch gun fired an 850-pound shell, the 13.5-inch a 1,250-pound shell or a 1,400-pound 'heavy' shell. These guns had a lower muzzle velocity than the 12 inch, the reduction from 2,852 feet/second to 2,491 feet/second greatly lengthening the barrel life. The old 12-inch gun turrets had an elevation of 15 degrees, and this was increased to 20 degrees in the *Orion*. With a lower muzzle velocity a higher elevation was needed for a given range. The range of the new guns was also increased, from 21,200 yards in the 12-inch 50-calibre gun to 23,750 yards in the 13.5-inch 45-calibre gun. The propellant weight was reduced, since a lower muzzle velocity was required. In fact, only 293 pounds were required, whereas 307 pounds were needed in the 12-inch 50-calibre weapon.[7]

The disposition of the turrets was a radical departure and five twin turrets were mounted on the centre line, with turrets superimposed fore and aft (super-imposed, hence super-dreadnought) and an amidships turret. The designation for the five turrets from fore to aft was 'A', 'B', 'Q', 'X', 'Y'. A big increase in offensive power was not the only feature of these ships; belt armour was increased to 12 inches, with a strake of armour carried up to foredeck level. This, combined with the superimposed turrets, raised the centre of gravity and necessitated a beam increase of three and a half feet, pushing towards the beam limits for British dockyards.

Machinery was the now standard Parsons turbines, giving a shaft horsepower of 27,000 and a speed of 21 knots. Three oil sprayers were fitted, operating at 300 pounds pressure. In all these pre-World War I ships, oil spraying was an adjunct to coal burning, used for raising steam quickly and facilitating high speed steaming. Once again the bridge, funnel and mast arrangement left a good deal to be desired. The fore funnel and bridge structure were integrated with the mast abaft the funnel. The man responsible for this unsatisfactory arrangement was the Controller, Rear-Admiral John Jellicoe, destined to command the Grand Fleet at Jutland.[8]

The estimates for 1909–10 had provided for four ships plus four 'contingent' ships and three further Orion type super-dreadnoughts, *Monarch*, *Conqueror* and *Thunderer*, were all laid down in April 1910. All were contract built ships; *Conqueror* (Beardmore), *Monarch* (Armstrongs) and *Thunderer* (Thames Iron Works). At an average cost of £1.88 million each, warship costs were obviously rising fast. *Thunderer* was the last major warship built on the Thames.[9]

The final two ships of the 'we want eight' programme were the battlecruiser equivalent of the Orions and the increase in displacement was no mere 2,500 tons. From the last dreadnought battlecruiser *Indefatigable* to the super-dreadnought battlecruisers there was an increase of 7,550 tons. The *Lion* and *Princess Royal* displaced 26,350 tons, up to 29,680 tons full load displacement. From now on, battlecruisers would be £2 million ships of nearly 30,000 tons and in every case their size would considerably exceed their battleship equivalents.

In assessing battlecruiser development, an explanation is needed for the enormous size of these ships, now considerably larger than battleships. The answer lies in the requirement for speeds well in excess of 25 knots. In 1908, it was known that the German battlecruisers would be capable of 25 knots and the first requirement for Britain's 1909–10 battlecruisers was a speed of 27 knots. This ensured an increase in length of 120 feet over the Orions and a length to beam ratio of 7.45:1. The horsepower required to raise the speed from 21 to 27 knots was phenomenal, from the 44,000 shp the *Indefatigable* to 70,000 shp in the *Lion*.

In addition to the size and speed requirements, the new ships were to carry eight 13.5-inch guns, the same calibre armament as the Orions but one turret less. Two twin turrets were mounted forward and one aft. Instead of suppressing 'Q' turret and mounting two turrets aft, 'Q' was retained and 'X' turret was omitted. The huge increase in boiler capacity ensured a third funnel was worked in between 'Q' and 'Y' turret. The bridge structure was again integrated with the fore funnel and the heat generated by the enormous boiler capacity rendered the control top uninhabitable. Eventually, on the express instructions of the First Lord, now Winston Churchill, the bridge, mast and funnel were remodelled, with the

FROM DREADNOUGHTS TO SUPER-DREADNOUGHTS 165

Lion
Princess Royal
Queen Mary
The 'Splendid Cats' had their funnels heightened and bridge and mast arrangements changed just before World War I

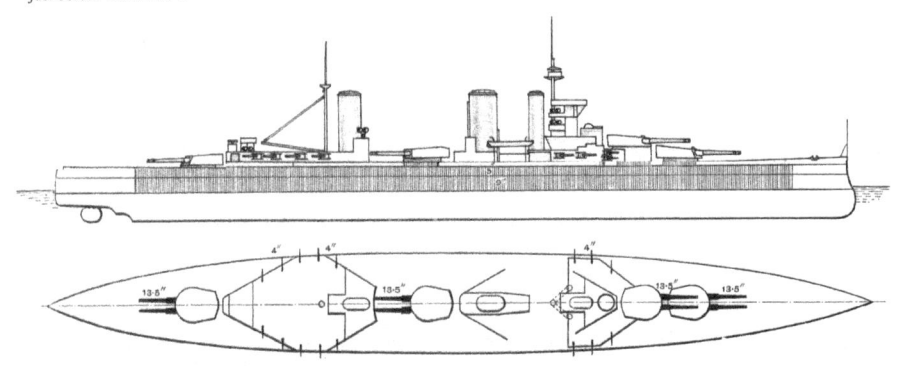

Brassey's Naval Annual 1914, Plate 9

Lion:	Devonport, Nov '09–Aug '10–May '12 £2,086,458
Princess Royal:	Vickers, May '10–Apr '11–Nov '12 £2,089,178
Queen Mary:	Palmers, Mar '11–Mar '12–Sept '13 £2,078,491
Dimensions:	660 (700) × 88.5 × 27.67/31.67 feet = 26.350 normal, 29,700 tons full load.
Armament:	Eight 13.5-inch 45 cal. sixteen 4-inch 50 cal. two 21-inch T.T.
Armour:	Lower belt 9"–6"–5", upper belt 6"–5"–4", bulkheads 4", barbettes 9"–8" gunhouses 9", conning tower 10" upper deck 1", lower deck 1½"–1", amidships 2½" ends. Total 6,595 tons (25%)
Machinery:	42 boilers, Parsons turbines S.H.P. 70,000 = 28 knots
Coal:	1,000 tons normal, 3,500 tons maximum, 1,135 tons oil
Complement:	1,085–1,061

Fig. 14 The super-dreadnought battlecruisers, Lion class

bridge set back from the conning tower with a light pole mast. All three funnels were heightened and the classic asymmetric profile of the 'splendid cats' emerged. The name ship *Lion* was laid down at Devonport in November 1909 and was followed in May 1910 by *Princess Royal*, built by Vickers.

Armouring ships with an overall length approaching 700 feet caused the irreconcilable problem of all British battlecruisers. Even if a reasonable percentage of displacement was allotted to protection, it could be only spread thinly on such a huge hull. In fact, 6,200 tons of armour was provided, representing 23 per cent of displacement. This compared with 3,500 tons of armour (19.5 per cent) on the Invincibles. On such a massive hull only a thin 9-inch belt was possible, fined to six inches and then further reduced to four inches at the ends. This compared ominously with the German battlecruisers *Moltke* and *Goeben*, fitted with 28-cm (11-inch) belts and only 1.5 knots slower in service. Even more ominously, a 9-inch belt could be penetrated by high velocity German 28-cm (11-inch) shells at almost any probable battle range.

More and More Super-Dreadnoughts

Five more super-dreadnoughts were planned for 1910–11. The *King George V*, *Centurion*, *Ajax* and *Audacious* were virtually repeats of the Orions. The bridge arrangements were more sensibly defined and large flat funnels gave a more satisfactory, symmetrical appearance.[10] The *Queen Mary*, the third Lion class ship, was the battlecruiser equivalent of the *King George V*.

In addition to the five ships of the 1910–11 programme, two further battlecruisers were built, one paid for by Australia and one by New Zealand. These were sisters of the unsatisfactory *Indefatigable*. The *Australia* was to serve as flagship of the Royal Australian Navy and the *New Zealand* was an outright gift to the Royal Navy. These ships were not laid down until June 1910, by which time British designs had moved on to *Lion* and *Princess Royal*. By this stage a good deal was known about German construction plans and building yet more poorly-armoured battlecruisers was a major mistake. Fisher's influence was at work, hence the choice of battlecruisers rather than battleships.[11]

The ships of the 1909–10 and 1910–11 programmes provided the Royal Navy with 15 more dreadnoughts to add to the 12 already built or building. The building programmes for two years more than doubled the navy's dreadnought strength. Against this doubling in 1909–10 and 1910–11 the navy's margin of superiority had hung on a single year's programme and excessive focusing on very large battlecruisers tended to vitiate the importance of the battleships that were necessary to counter German moves. This was the moment that an era of intensifying naval competition became a full-blooded arms race. The following year's programme (1911–12) again included four battleships and one battlecruiser. The Iron Duke class (*Iron Duke*, *Marlborough*, *Benbow* and *Emperor of India*) were, at 25,000 tons, slightly larger than their predecessors, mounted the same armament of ten 13.5-inch guns and re-introduced a powerful secondary battery of twelve 6-inch guns. The reason for this change was the belief that in misty North Sea conditions, the enemy might be found close at hand and a hail of fire from the 6-inch guns could be decisive and at the very least help confuse enemy range-taking and gun-laying.[12]

The secondary battery was not a great success. It was casemate mounted as in the pre-dreadnoughts and was sufficiently far forward to be washed out in any seaway. Secondary batteries distributed along the length of the ship, close to the waterline, were not just dangerous because of flooding, but also because of potential fire and explosion. The secondary battery could only be given medium armour, 6-inch in thickness and this could be penetrated by main armament projectiles at almost any range. Behind this meagre protection there was ready to use ammunition with more in transit from magazines and shell rooms. These enhanced secondary batteries were expensive, unlikely to score hits and any exposed ammunition could endanger the ship.[13]

The battlecruiser *Tiger* was the battlecruiser equivalent of the *Iron Duke*. At 28,500 tons, she was 3,500 tons larger than the *Iron Duke* and the only British battlecruiser with a casemate mounted secondary armament of twelve 6-inch guns. With 9-inch belt protection and a total of 7,400 tons of armour, 25 per cent of displacement, she was easily the best of the pre-war battlecruisers. The armament remained the same as the Lions, eight 13.5-inch guns, but the gun layout was changed and 'Q' turret was mounted behind the three funnels but considerably forward of 'Y' turret. This ensured that 'Q' could fire over 'Y' and was sufficiently far away from 'Y' not to be knocked out by a shell that could disable both turrets, as happened to the German battlecruiser *Seydlitz* at the Dogger Bank battle in 1915.[14]

Just as the 1909–10 estimates produced the first super-dreadnoughts, an enormous improvement over the dreadnoughts, so the 1912–13 estimates produced battleships that were almost as large an improvement over the first super-dreadnoughts. The five Queen Elizabeth class ships (*Queen Elizabeth*, *Warspite*, *Barham*, *Valiant* and *Malaya*), were 27,500 tons and 600 feet in length. They mounted eight 15-inch guns in four turrets, two superimposed forward and two aft. Each gun fired a shell that weighed 1,920 pounds, considerably more than twice the weight of a shell from a 12-inch gun. The reason for the increase in gun calibre was partly that Japan and the United States were known to be developing 14-inch (35.6-cm) guns, but also the (mistaken) belief that Germany intended to fit such guns to her König class battleships. Churchill, as First Lord, decided to go one better and pushed for the development of 15-inch guns. The 15-inch gun possessed 30 per cent more energy and 50 per cent greater destructive power after penetration than the 13.5-inch gun. The maximum range of

Iron Duke
Marlborough
Benbow
Emperor Of India

These ships reintroduced the casemate mounted battery of twelve 6-inch guns, arguably a mistake.

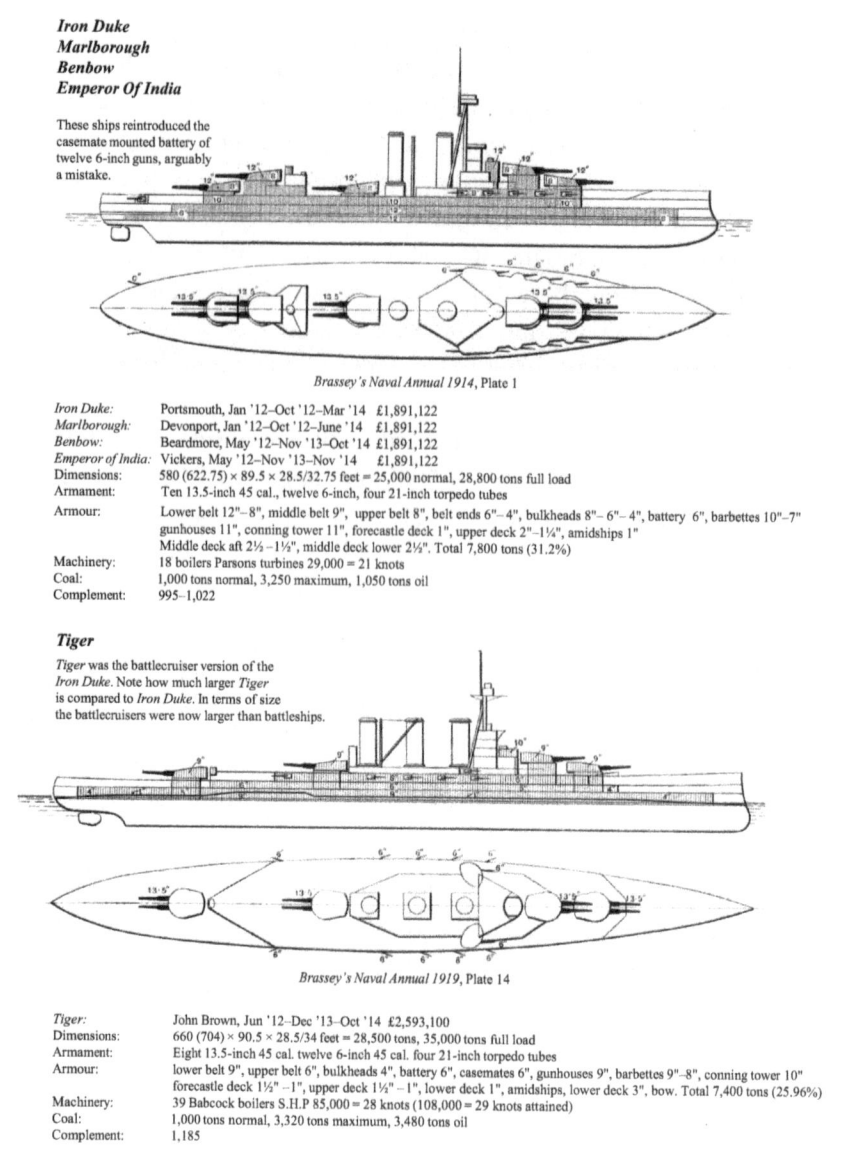

Brassey's Naval Annual 1914, Plate 1

Iron Duke:	Portsmouth, Jan '12–Oct '12–Mar '14 £1,891,122
Marlborough:	Devonport, Jan '12–Oct '12–June '14 £1,891,122
Benbow:	Beardmore, May '12–Nov '13–Oct '14 £1,891,122
Emperor of India:	Vickers, May '12–Nov '13–Nov '14 £1,891,122
Dimensions:	580 (622.75) × 89.5 × 28.5/32.75 feet = 25,000 normal, 28,800 tons full load
Armament:	Ten 13.5-inch 45 cal., twelve 6-inch, four 21-inch torpedo tubes
Armour:	Lower belt 12"–8", middle belt 9", upper belt 8", belt ends 6"–4", bulkheads 8"–6"–4", battery 6", barbettes 10"–7" gunhouses 11", conning tower 11", forecastle deck 1", upper deck 2"–1¼", amidships 1" Middle deck aft 2½–1½", middle deck lower 2½". Total 7,800 tons (31.2%)
Machinery:	18 boilers Parsons turbines 29,000 = 21 knots
Coal:	1,000 tons normal, 3,250 maximum, 1,050 tons oil
Complement:	995–1,022

Tiger

Tiger was the battlecruiser version of the *Iron Duke*. Note how much larger *Tiger* is compared to *Iron Duke*. In terms of size the battlecruisers were now larger than battleships.

Brassey's Naval Annual 1919, Plate 14

Tiger:	John Brown, Jun '12–Dec '13–Oct '14 £2,593,100
Dimensions:	660 (704) × 90.5 × 28.5/34 feet = 28,500 tons, 35,000 tons full load
Armament:	Eight 13.5-inch 45 cal. twelve 6-inch 45 cal. four 21-inch torpedo tubes
Armour:	lower belt 9", upper belt 6", bulkheads 4", battery 6", casemates 6", gunhouses 9", barbettes 9"–8", conning tower 10" forecastle deck 1½"–1", upper deck 1½"–1", lower deck 1", amidships, lower deck 3", bow. Total 7,400 tons (25.96%)
Machinery:	39 Babcock boilers S.H.P 85,000 = 28 knots (108,000 = 29 knots attained)
Coal:	1,000 tons normal, 3,320 tons maximum, 3,480 tons oil
Complement:	1,185

Fig. 15 British super-dreadnought of the 1912 programme, Iron Dukes and Tiger

these guns was 23,400 yards. Fire control was based on a 15-foot range finder mounted on top of the conning tower, and 15-foot range finders mounted locally on each turret.[15]

Protection was heavier than in any previous British battleship and the main belt armour was 13 inches in thickness. A total of 8,600 tons of

Queen Elizabeth
Warspite
Valiant
Barham
Malaya

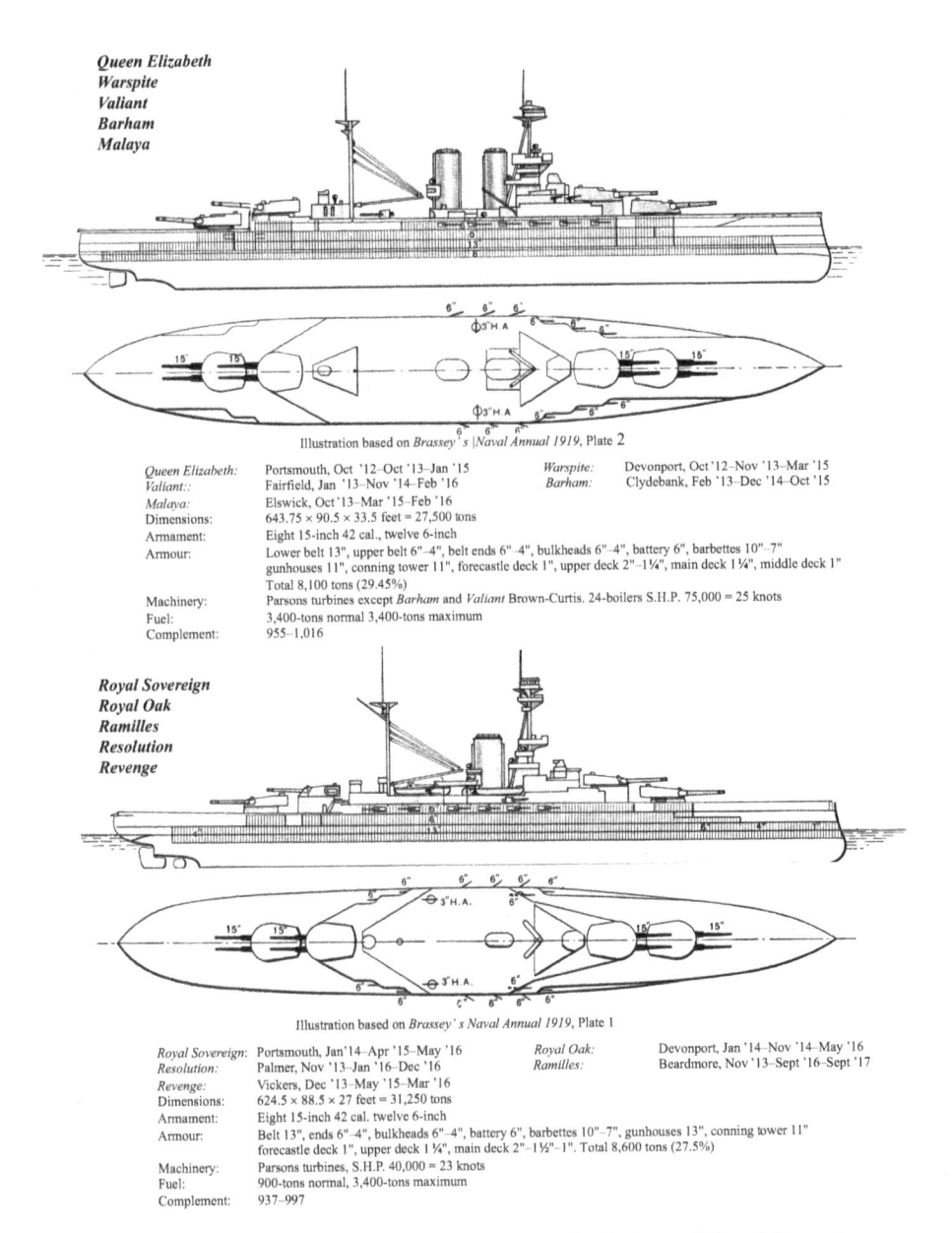

Illustration based on *Brassey's Naval Annual 1919*, Plate 2

Queen Elizabeth:	Portsmouth, Oct '12–Oct '13–Jan '15	*Warspite:*	Devonport, Oct '12–Nov '13–Mar '15
Valiant::	Fairfield, Jan '13–Nov '14–Feb '16	*Barham:*	Clydebank, Feb '13–Dec '14–Oct '15
Malaya:	Elswick, Oct '13–Mar '15–Feb '16		
Dimensions:	643.75 × 90.5 × 33.5 feet = 27,500 tons		
Armament:	Eight 15-inch 42 cal., twelve 6-inch		
Armour:	Lower belt 13", upper belt 6"–4", belt ends 6"–4", bulkheads 6"–4", battery 6", barbettes 10"–7" gunhouses 11", conning tower 11", forecastle deck 1", upper deck 2"–1¼", main deck 1¼", middle deck 1" Total 8,100 tons (29.45%)		
Machinery:	Parsons turbines except *Barham* and *Valiant* Brown-Curtis. 24-boilers S.H.P. 75,000 = 25 knots		
Fuel:	3,400-tons normal 3,400-tons maximum		
Complement:	955–1,016		

Royal Sovereign
Royal Oak
Ramilles
Resolution
Revenge

Illustration based on *Brassey's Naval Annual 1919*, Plate 1

Royal Sovereign:	Portsmouth, Jan'14–Apr '15–May '16	*Royal Oak:*	Devonport, Jan '14–Nov '14–May '16
Resolution:	Palmer, Nov '13–Jan '16–Dec '16	*Ramilles:*	Beardmore, Nov '13–Sept '16–Sept '17
Revenge:	Vickers, Dec '13–May '15–Mar '16		
Dimensions:	624.5 × 88.5 × 27 feet = 31,250 tons		
Armament:	Eight 15-inch 42 cal. twelve 6-inch		
Armour:	Belt 13", ends 6"–4", bulkheads 6"–4", battery 6", barbettes 10"–7", gunhouses 13", conning tower 11" forecastle deck 1", upper deck 1¼", main deck 2"–1½"–1". Total 8,600 tons (27.5%)		
Machinery:	Parsons turbines, S.H.P. 40,000 = 23 knots		
Fuel:	900-tons normal, 3,400-tons maximum		
Complement:	937–997		

Fig. 16 Oil burning super-dreadnoughts, Queen Elizabeths and Royal Sovereigns

armour was worked into the design (31 per cent of displacement). These battleships were true 'fast' battleships and were designed for 24 knots, developing 75,000 shp. The *Queen Elizabeth*, *Warspite* and *Malaya* were the first battleships with reaction type geared cruising turbines. In a sense these ships were Fisher's 'fusion' concept, the amalgamation of the battleship and battlecruiser type into a true fast battleship. In consequence, no battlecruiser equivalent was included in the 1912–13 programme, just the five battleships. The fifth battleship, *Malaya*, was the gift of the Federated Malay States. Arguably these were the best tactical group of battleships produced by any nation in the dreadnought era and, also arguably, British battleship design, despite mistakes in previous classes, now moved ahead of German designs.

The Great Gunnery Fire-Control Controversy

The early dreadnoughts benefitted from the first generation of mechanical fire control instruments described in Chapter 2. The serious limitation to the Dumaresq was the absence of any means of measuring the target course and speed, which were simply estimated. The Dumaresq and Vickers clock working in combination were equally limited and unable to account for changes in the change of range rate. Even if the firing ship and target ship courses and speeds were constant, the range could not only remain unchanged or change at a constant rate, but could also change at a rate that was itself changing at a constant rate. The change of range rate, computed literally by stopwatch methods, could easily result in a highly inaccurate setting of the Vickers clock.

With the advent of *Dreadnought* sight setting became part of a centralised system known as 'fire control'. Slide rule technology allowed the calculation of corrections to calculated target ranges. All of these corrections were limited by the constantly changing range rate problem which produced inherent errors in the range data produced by the Vickers clock, when the range was changing rapidly these manual calculations were just too slow.[16] In the years before 1914 two distinct approaches to fire control were developed; the highly sophisticated Pollen system, named Argo, and the rather simpler Dreyer system. One interpretation is that the Argo system was a synthetic system, the Dreyer, a virtual rate plotting system.

Range-finder spans became inaccurate at longer ranges and measuring bearings from your own ship, which is liable to yaw as much as six degrees in two or three seconds, degraded the results to the point where they were virtually meaningless. The introduction of gyrocompasses might have solved some of the problems, but in all except flat calm weather the problem of yaw remained.[17] Two men realised that even fairly inaccurate target ranges and bearings could be used to produce a reasonably accurate estimate of target course and speed. These men, a civilian, Arthur Hungerford Pollen, and Lieutenant Frederic Dreyer, took radically different approaches to what became known as plotting.

Pollen was socially well connected and was managing director of the Linotype Company on whose board sat Lord Kelvin. At the behest of a naval officer cousin, Pollen first witnessed a naval gunnery practice at Malta in 1900 and was amazed that the guns could not reliably hit the target at ranges of less than a mile.

Between 1901 and 1906 Pollen's ideas centred around a two-observer system that proved a failure. Pollen's next attempt used a plotting unit to calculate the target's position and relative motion, and needed a gyroscope to allow for yaw.[18] It took time to develop the plotting unit and several early experiments were failures. Plotting was performed manually and proved slow and unreliable, the bearing transmission system was flawed and yaw proved a major problem. Nevertheless, Pollen persevered and he understood the significance of range rate. Pollen saw plotting as a means of visualisation and calculation; future ranges could be calculated from the plot of firing ship and target ship's courses. This was true-course plotting.[19]

Pollen revamped his system and presented it to the Admiralty. The Controller, Rear-Admiral Jackson, was not much in favour of it on the grounds that it was a technically complicated system that would be much more difficult and expensive to build than Pollen anticipated. Eventually a compromise was worked out whereby the change of range machine would be developed only after the gyro corrected plotting instrument had been proven on trials. By 1907 work on an automatic plotting devise and a gyro-stabilised range-finder were all well advanced. At this juncture the DNO was Reginald Bacon and his assistant was Lieutenant Frederic Dreyer. Both were firmly opposed to Pollen's ideas and Dreyer believed he could build a manual fire control plotting system superior to Pollen's automated system.[20]

In late 1907 the famous, or perhaps infamous, *Ariadne* trials took place under the supervision of Admiral of the Fleet Sir Arthur Wilson. After inspecting the installation Wilson complained that Pollen's instruments lacked any means of getting data to the guns.[21] In early December the first trials of the system proved that automatic plotting was entirely feasible, even in heavy sea conditions with a large amount of yaw but Wilson, with Dreyer as his assistant, proposed an entirely manual plotting system. Ranging and training were performed by separate operators and a torpedo director was used in conjunction with a Barr and Stroud range-finder. Range and bearing data were transmitted to a plotting station where the information was used to give a diagram of the relative movements of the firing and target ships. This plotting method produced a 'virtual' plot where the firing ship was stationary for all plotting purposes. The target's virtual course and speed and the change of range rate could then be read off using a standard Admiralty Dumaresq calculator. A Vickers clock would then give the corrected target range. The major defect of this system was that it ignored the effect of yaw. A series of extremely biased comparative trials then took place on board the battleship *Vengeance*. The trials were conducted in nearly perfect weather conditions when the effect of yaw was minimal. Visibility was perfect and Dreyer's well-trained 16-man team performed faultlessly. There was virtually no rate of range change between the *Vengeance* and the target ship *Ariadne*. Pollen and his assistants were suddenly supposed to work the Admiralty Dumaresq calculator and the Vickers clock, instruments with which they were totally unfamiliar. The final set of trials was run on 15 January 1908 and involved the two test vessels on the same course at the same speed. After 50 minutes Wilson decided that the Dreyer system was superior to that of Pollen's and the trials were ended.[22] Pollen was paid £11,500 for his work and in return guaranteed absolute secrecy for 18 months.[23] Pollen's reply was to found the Argo Company and to proceed with the construction of a vastly improved gyro mounting. Designs for the clock, that is, the computer, were also finalised. By March 1909 Pollen's redesigned system was ready for testing.

Wilson was appointed First Sea Lord in succession to Jackie Fisher and Dreyer, with considerable support from Wilson and Bacon, continued to develop his system. In fact all Dreyer's early trials were failures and he was forced to acknowledge the problem of yaw. This resulted in his adoption of a gyro-stabilised range-finder, the very sort of mechanical instrumentation his manual plotting system was supposed not to use.[24]

Against this background of Dreyer's failures Pollen managed to obtain an interview with Reginald McKenna, the First Lord. By March 1909 the Admiralty had agreed to test the complete Aim Correction system which included the 'clock'. In October 1909 the armoured cruiser *Natal* was used for trials. Captain Ogilvy the *Natal*'s commanding officer took a close interest in the gyro-stabilised range-finder and bearing indicator. He also commented at length on the automatic true course plotter and concluded that in battle it would be necessary to plot the target position while the firing ship was turning. Pollen had considered this helm-free option and become convinced that this was the next step forward. On 10 November Pollen's engineers were ordered off the *Natal* on grounds of secrecy. Pollen asked for and got an interview with Bacon and eventually an agreement was reached on cooperation between the navy and the Argo Company. Pollen then experienced a disastrous piece of bad luck. He presented Ogilvy and his officers, who all believed in the Argo system, with a gift of oysters, which proved to be contaminated with typhoid. Ogilvy died as a result and Pollen lost an influential supporter. Pollen's position was further weakened by the advent of Wilson as First Sea Lord and Bacon's replacement by Rear-Admiral Archibald Moore. Bacon had slowly come round to Pollen's point of view and had finally accepted the need for an automated fire control system. At the end of his time as Director of Naval Ordnance he had even placed an order for 45 gyro-stabilised range-finders. Moore immediately reduced the order to 15. A further set of trials was held in June 1910 and the modified change of range machine, the Argo Clock Mark I, was tested. Pollen's engineers were again ordered off the ship and there were constant breakdowns during trials as a result. Nevertheless the trials supervision committee concluded that Pollen's Aim Correction system, with its emphasis on true course plotting, was vastly superior to Dreyer's virtual course plotting technique.[25]

In spite of the setbacks Pollen continued to improve his instruments and moved towards a true helm-free fire control system with the Argo Clock Mark II. To solve the second order differential equations necessary to compute the rate of range change while the ship was under helm, a disk-ball-roller mechanism was adopted. James Thompson had designed a tide gauge using a ball disc and cylinder differential analyser and this type of analogue computer was suggested as the basis of an entirely new approach to gunnery fire control. In its final form, in 1912 the Argo Mark IV was tried onboard HMS *Orion*, the first of the super-dreadnoughts. The problems of a fleet action fought with large range rate changes was not considered at all and despite the success of the Argo Mark IV the Admiralty finally rejected it in favour of the Dreyer fire control system based on virtual rate plotting.[26]

Both tables relied on the Barr and Stroud optical rangefinder, which in the murky conditions of the North Sea had its limitations. Extravagant claims have been for the Pollen system but in reality, though it was the better system it was nothing like as superior as some more recent authorities have claimed. In the end the Royal Navy adopted the 'in house' system as opposed to that of an erratically brilliant inventor.

By contrast, the German Navy used stereoscopic range-finders as opposed to coincidence range-finders. The operators had to have identical vision in both eyes. They placed a 'wandermark' over the target, which could be as ill defined as a smudge of smoke. The Zeiss optics were superior to the Barr and Stroud optics and this gave the German Navy something of an advantage in range-finding. The Zeiss range-finders were susceptible to vibration and the concussion of near misses with the resultant hull judder was enough to degrade their range-finding ability.[27] A crucial part of range-taking and firing was finding the exact range as quickly as possible.

German Super-Dreadnoughts

The five battleships of the Kaiser class showed a design competence lacking in Germany's first two dreadnought classes. These ships were the *ersatz* replacements for the remaining five Siegfried class coast defence ships. The name ship was *Kaiser* (ersatz *Hildebrand*), the others *Friedrich der Grosse* (ersatz *Heimdall*), *Kaiserin* (ersatz *Hagen*), *König Albert* (ersatz *Ägir*) and *Prinzregent Luitpold* (ersatz *Odin*). These were the first turbine powered German battleships and used the now standard three-shaft arrangement, with ten boiler rooms and three sets of turbines in six engine rooms. Three of the ships used Parsons turbines, while the *Friedrich der Grosse* was powered by AEG-Curtis turbines and the *König Albert* by Schichau turbines. *Prinzregent Luitpold* was supposed to have been fitted with a diesel engine for cruising but this was never completed, so she was completed as a twin-screw ship, capable of 21.7 knots. Her sisters made from 22 knots to 23.4 knots on trials.[28]

These ships used the same gun layout as *Moltke* and *Goeben*, and the British Neptunes, with one turret forward, two *en echelon* amidships and two aft, the one superimposed over the other. The battlecruisers used ten 28-cm (11-inch) guns while the Kaiser class were armed with ten 30.5 cm (12-inch) guns. The main belt armour was 35 cm, nearly 14 inches. This compared ominously with the *Neptune*'s 10-inch (25-cm) belt and *Colossus* with an 11-inch (28-cm) belt. The German ships had close to 10,000 tons of armour worked into the design, compared to the 5,700–6,570 tons in the British ships.[29] The Kaiser class were bigger than their British contemporaries at 24,330 tons, but needed considerably more propulsive effect to obtain 21 knots. This was to be a feature of all dreadnoughts. The British were tank testing hull forms at an earlier stage than Germany and British designs usually needed about 20 per cent less propulsive effect than their German counterparts. The five Kaisers were all laid down in 1909–10 and completed in 1912–13, taking an aggregate 36 months for each ship. The slower building times for the German ships shows clearly that the acceleration in German programmes was not concerned with accelerating building times but with having large numbers of *ersatz* ships on hand for replacement.

The next four German super-dreadnoughts, all completed by November 1914, were the four battleships of the König class. These were the only German battleships with an all centre-line gun turret arrangement, very similar to the British super-dreadnoughts, with ten 30.5-cm (12-inch) guns as opposed to the British ten 13.5-inch (34.3-cm) guns. In terms of their *ersatz* numbers the ships were replacements for the Brandenburg class battleships of the early 1890s and designated as follows, with one additional ship over the *ersatz* programme, as an addition to naval strength. The extra ship designated 'S' became *König*, next *Grosser Kurfürst* (*ersatz Kurfürst Friedrich Wilhelm*), *Markgraf* (*ersatz Weissenburg*) and finally *Kronprinz* (*ersatz Brandenburg*). *König* and *Kronprinz* were powered by Parsons turbines, while *Grosser Kurfürst* used AEG-Vulcan turbines and *Markgraf*, Bergmann turbines. It was pointed out in Chapter 5 that all German dreadnoughts and battlecruisers used Schulz-Thorneycroft small tube boilers and the saving in weight and space was used in additional protection. The belt armour on these ships was again 35 cm (14 inches). It was a wider, thicker main belt than on any British battleship and a total of 10,118 tons of armour was carried compared to the 6,400–7,800 tons on the British Orion, King George V and Iron Duke classes.[30]

The final class of German battleships were the four ships of the Bayern class, only two of which were completed. The name ship *Bayern* was considered an addition to naval strength and designated 'T', while the sister *Baden* was *ersatz Wörth*. The other two were slightly different in design and were launched but never completed. The *Württemberg* was *ersatz Kaiser Wilhelm II* and *Sachsen*, *ersatz Kaiser Friedrich III*. These German super-dreadnoughts were the only German battleships to mount 38-cm (15-inch) guns, eight being carried, disposed exactly as in the British Queen Elizabeth class, in twin turrets, two forward and two aft. German dreadnoughts all had a secondary battery of twelve to sixteen 15-cm (5.9-inch) guns.

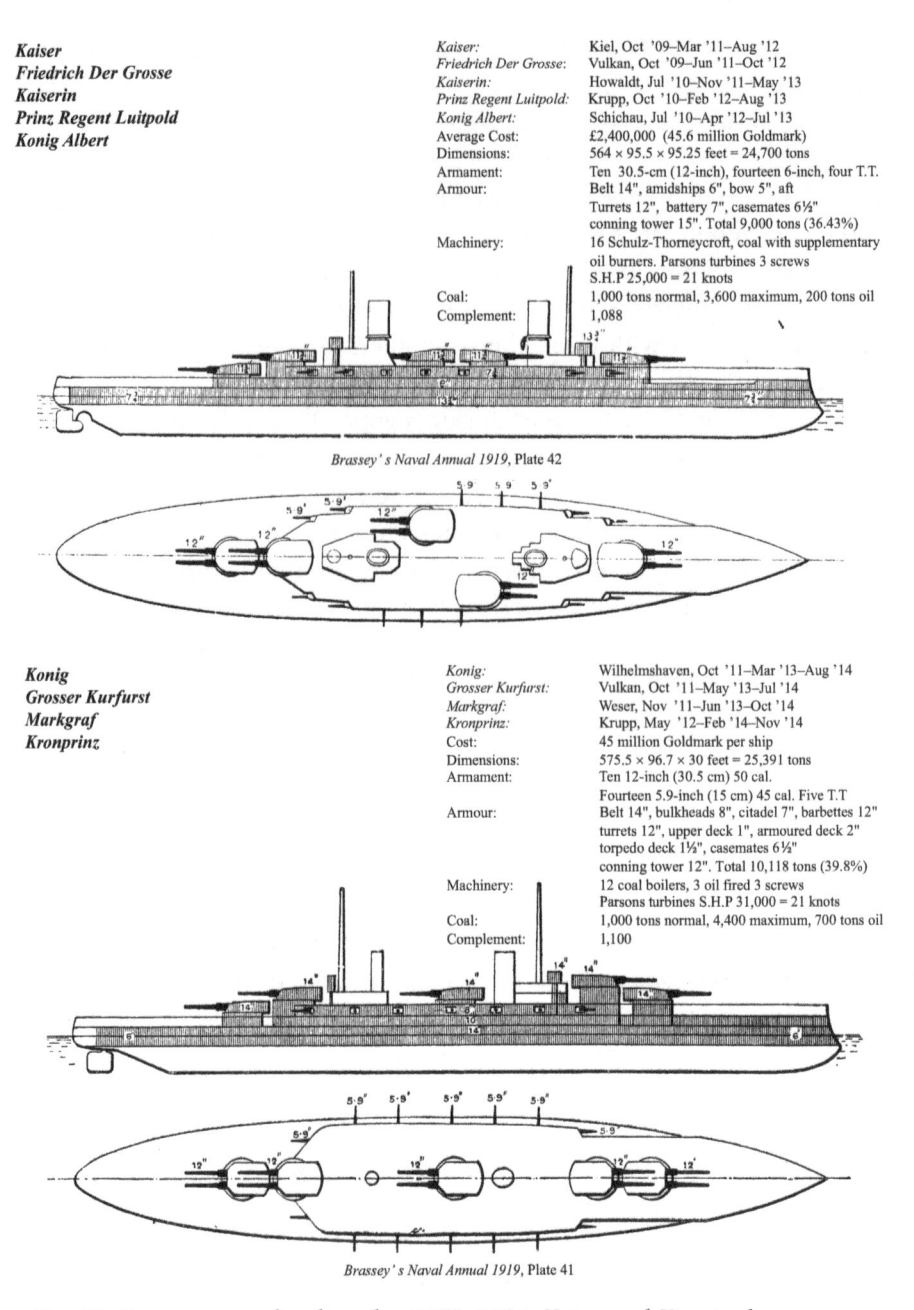

Kaiser
Friedrich Der Grosse
Kaiserin
Prinz Regent Luitpold
Konig Albert

Kaiser:	Kiel, Oct '09–Mar '11–Aug '12
Friedrich Der Grosse:	Vulkan, Oct '09–Jun '11–Oct '12
Kaiserin:	Howaldt, Jul '10–Nov '11–May '13
Prinz Regent Luitpold:	Krupp, Oct '10–Feb '12–Aug '13
Konig Albert:	Schichau, Jul '10–Apr '12–Jul '13
Average Cost:	£2,400,000 (45.6 million Goldmark)
Dimensions:	564 × 95.5 × 95.25 feet = 24,700 tons
Armament:	Ten 30.5-cm (12-inch), fourteen 6-inch, four T.T.
Armour:	Belt 14", amidships 6", bow 5", aft
	Turrets 12", battery 7", casemates 6½"
	conning tower 15". Total 9,000 tons (36.43%)
Machinery:	16 Schulz-Thorneycroft, coal with supplementary
	oil burners. Parsons turbines 3 screws
	S.H.P 25,000 = 21 knots
Coal:	1,000 tons normal, 3,600 maximum, 200 tons oil
Complement:	1,088

Brassey's Naval Annual 1919, Plate 42

Konig
Grosser Kurfurst
Markgraf
Kronprinz

Konig:	Wilhelmshaven, Oct '11–Mar '13–Aug '14
Grosser Kurfurst:	Vulkan, Oct '11–May '13–Jul '14
Markgraf:	Weser, Nov '11–Jun '13–Oct '14
Kronprinz:	Krupp, May '12–Feb '14–Nov '14
Cost:	45 million Goldmark per ship
Dimensions:	575.5 × 96.7 × 30 feet = 25,391 tons
Armament:	Ten 12-inch (30.5 cm) 50 cal.
	Fourteen 5.9-inch (15 cm) 45 cal. Five T.T
Armour:	Belt 14", bulkheads 8", citadel 7", barbettes 12"
	turrets 12", upper deck 1", armoured deck 2"
	torpedo deck 1½", casemates 6½"
	conning tower 12". Total 10,118 tons (39.8%)
Machinery:	12 coal boilers, 3 oil fired 3 screws
	Parsons turbines S.H.P 31,000 = 21 knots
Coal:	1,000 tons normal, 4,400 maximum, 700 tons oil
Complement:	1,100

Brassey's Naval Annual 1919, Plate 41

Fig. 17 German super-dreadnoughts 1909–1914, Kaiser and Koenig class

The main armour belt was again 35 cm (14 inch), with a total of 11,335 tons of armour built into the design, as opposed to 8,600 tons in the Queen Elizabeths. *Baden* and *Bayern* used three shaft Parsons turbines, allied to 14 Schulz-Thorneycroft boilers. They developed 48,000 shp for a speed of 21 knots, compared to the 77,000 shp and 24 knots speed of the Queen Elizabeths.[31] It can be suggested that the balance of qualities between ordnance, armour and machinery was better in the Queen Elizabeths.

All the German battlecruisers used Parsons steam turbines allied to four screws. Tirpitz did not believe in turbine propulsion for battleships and the Reichsmarineamt did nothing to encourage turbine development. In 1902 the British Parsons Company opened its own German branch, the 'Turbinia' Deutsche Parsons Marine AG. There were challenges from North German Lloyd, Krupp, Siemens-Schuckert and MAN who explored the Swiss Zoelly turbine system. AEG and Vulcan conducted joint research but the Parsons was the only fully developed turbine system.[32] By the time the Kaiser and König class battleships were built there were German alternatives to Parsons turbines, AEG Curtis and Schichau turbines, also AEG-Vulcan and Bergmann turbines. In truth, German development of turbines lagged seriously behind Britain and it was only the use of Parsons turbines that made the German battlecruisers possible.

After the *Moltke* and *Goeben* the next German battlecruiser was the *Seydlitz*, ordered in 1912. She was armed exactly as the *Moltke* (eight 28-cm/11-inch guns), but was a larger ship at 24,594 tons, with her length increased from 186.5 m (612 ft) to 200.5 m (658 ft). The beam was reduced from 29.5 m (96.75 ft) to 28.5 m (93.5 ft), to gain a further speed increase; the only occasion the Germans reduced beam to increase speed. Underwater protection was improved and her forecastle was one deck higher compared to the *Moltke*. This increased freeboard and seakeeping qualities. *Seydlitz* became the worst damaged surviving capital ship at Jutland and in terms of buoyancy was probably saved by the increased freeboard forward. Schulz-Thorneycroft small tube boilers were used, with the usual saving in weight and space. In *Seydlitz* and a number of other ships the material used in the boiler tubes had a tendency to pitting and this made frequent re-tubing necessary. Armour included a 30-cm (11.8-inch) belt, with a total of over 7,500 tons of armour worked into the design.[33]

Three further battlecruisers were laid down in 1912–13, *Derfflinger*, *Lützow* and *Hindenburg*. These were the German Navy's super-dreadnought battlecruisers. Armed with eight 30.5-cm (12-inch) guns, two turrets superimposed forward and two aft, they were 26,180-ton ships,

210.4 m (690 ft) in length. They were flush-decked vessels with a pronounced sheer forward. The armour in these ships was, as usual, superb, with a 30-cm (11.8-inch) belt and 9,838 tons of armour worked into the design.[34]

Two further classes of German battlecruisers were planned. Three reached launch stage but were never completed, while the fourth was never launched. Their intended names and *ersatz* designations were as follows, *Mackensen* (ersatz *Victoria Louise*), *Prince Eitel Friedrich* (ersatz *Freya*), *Graf Spee* (ersatz *Blücher*) and *Fürst Bismarck* (ersatz *Friedrich Carl*). These would have been 30,000-ton ships armed with eight 35-cm (13.8-inch) guns and had a designed speed of 28 knots. Three further battlecruisers. ersatz *Yorck*, ersatz *Gneisenau* and ersatz *Scharnhorst*, were planned but only one was laid down and work was halted when about 1,000 tons of steel had been put into her.[35]

Light Cruisers and Destroyers

Light cruisers were not really descended from the small, protected cruisers of the late Victorian navy but from the 'Scout' class cruisers built in the first years of the twentieth century, the last of which, the 2,640 ton *Adventure* and *Attentive*, were laid down in January 1904. Fisher believed, wrongly, that all small cruisers were obsolete. Protection of trade could be left to the battlecruisers and scouting for the fleet to destroyers. It rapidly became clear that destroyers were too small and frail for scouting duties and that a larger vessel was required.[36]

The first light cruiser, *Boadicea*, was laid down in July 1907 and the second, *Bellona*, in June 1908. At 3,300 tons and armed with six 4-inch guns they were only superficially different from the last 'Scout' cruisers, except that they were turbine powered. The *Blanche* and *Blonde* of 1909 were very slightly larger and the armament increased to ten 4-inch guns. This was repeated with the *Active*, *Amphion* and *Fearless* of 1909–10.[37]

With the introduction of the 6-inch gun true light cruisers were built. The five ships of the Bristol class were laid down in 1909 and mounted two 6-inch guns in addition to ten 4-inch guns. There was a big increase in displacement to 4,800 tons and some protection was incorporated into the design. Successive classes increased the gun armament to eight or nine 6-inch guns. By 1912 the Royal Navy had 15 light cruisers armed with 6-inch guns and the size had crept up to 5,400 tons. In 1912 the displacement was dropped back to 3,500 tons with the eight-ship Arethusa class, armed with three 6-inch and four 4-inch guns. All the early light cruisers had a speed of 25–6 knots.[38]

The pre-war building programmes ensured that the Royal Navy had 26 light cruisers in 1914–15. This number was certainly not large. Germany also built light cruisers such as *Königsberg*, *Stuggart*, *Stettin*, *Nürnberg*, *Emden* and *Dresden*. They mounted ten 10.5-cm (4.1-inch) guns and were powered by triple expansion engines which gave a speed of 23–4 knots. The *Stettin* and *Dresden* were the first turbine-powered warships in the German Navy and their Parsons turbines gave them a speed of 24–5 knots.[39]

In the early destroyers sea-keeping qualities were poor, the machinery unreliable, the hulls constructionally weak and trials speeds were far above in-service speeds.[40] Three destroyers were fitted with turbines – *Viper*, *Cobra* and *Velox*. In 1901 the loss of *Viper* and *Cobra* condemned snake names in the Royal Navy and the loss of *Cobra* caused a committee to be formed on destroyer design. The result was a specification for a much larger ship in the 550–575 ton range. The forecastle was raised, which greatly improved the accommodation and sea-keeping qualities. A much stouter hull form was adopted with a design speed reduced to 26 knots. The result was a destroyer able to steam at considerably higher speeds in a seaway than the 30-knotter predecessors. A total of 34 River class destroyers were built, armed with one 12-pounder, five 6-pounder guns and two torpedo tubes. HMS *Eden* was turbine powered.[41]

The 1904 manoeuvres were a great success and showed clearly the superiority of the Rivers, which could steam at a reasonable speed in weather that forced the older, smaller, destroyers to seek shelter. When Fisher became First Sea Lord he defined the parameters for a new destroyer class, stipulating a speed of 33 knots, using oil fuel. The result was the first class of turbine powered destroyers, the famed Tribal or 'F' class (1905–8 programmes). A total of 12 were built, big for their day, between 850 and 1,050 tons and mounted two 4-inch guns and two 18-inch torpedoes.[42] All these boats were in some way different in appearance as the designs were left to the individual shipyards. These boats were often described as 'ocean-going' but they had a small radius of action – only 1,500 miles – so they were suitable for coastal work only.[43]

Fisher's next gambit was a 36-knot super-destroyer, really the first flotilla leader, HMS *Swift*. He wanted it based on the River class but this was over-ambitious. After several design revisions a 2,170 ton-design was used, with a speed of 35 knots. Armed with four 4-inch guns and two 18-inch torpedoes, she was an expensive ship (£236,000) and very heavy on fuel. In the destroyer programmes of pre-1914 it was originally intended that light cruisers would act as flotilla leaders. This concept was perfectly reasonable when destroyer speeds were in the region 27–8 knots. With the 'M' class destroyer speeds jumped to 35 knots and it was realised that no light cruiser could ever keep up in a fast destroyer action. The requirement for speed introduced the idea of flotilla leaders as a generic type. These leaders would be enlarged destroyers, carrying captain (D) and his staff. The first such boats were the Lightfoot class of 1913–15. There were five boats of 1,650 tons and all had a speed of 34.5 knots.[44]

Submersible Torpedo-Boats and Wireless

In the 1890s shipbuilding technology, changed radically by the steel and electricity revolution, had reached a point where submersible craft were possible. The *Jeune École* had emphasised the torpedo, carried by a torpedo-boat or perhaps a torpedo-cruiser, as the ultimate weapon of commerce destruction. The U-boats of both world wars performed the role of the torpedo-boat envisaged by Aube and effectively these first submarines were submersible torpedo-boats. If the submarine had been developed some 15 years earlier than was actually the case, it is quite possible that the *Jeune École* would have prevailed and the battleship in its Naval Defence Act form would not have established itself as the centrepiece of the world's navies.[45]

From the 1880s onwards the work of the early submarine pioneers was not lost on the French. The first attempt at building a French submersible was made by the French engineer Dupuy de Lôme. He died before his submersible could be built, but his colleague Gustave Zédé carried the idea forward. His vessel, the *Gymnote*, was 59 feet in length and powered by a 55 horsepower electric motor.[46] This vessel came immediately to the notice of British naval attachés. In March 1889, just at the moment the Naval Defence Act was being passed, Captain Cecil Domville commented:

> *Gymnote*: I was not allowed to see this vessel, the details of which are kept very secret. I was, however, informed that the dimensions given in the newspapers are correct. Length 56 feet 5 inches, Diameter 5 feet 11 inches, 30 tons, horsepower 55. The apparatus for rising or sinking appears to be satisfactory, as also the working of the horizontal rudders, but the question of steering, or rather reaching a desired point, has not been solved, and does not seem likely to be.[47]

In 1888, the United States Navy Department decided to hold a public competition for a submarine boat design. The early work of the Irish-American John Philip Holland resulted in his design *Holland III* being accepted, but after a good deal of argument the project was cancelled. In 1893, the scheme was resurrected and *Holland V* was accepted. The submarine was finally built and became known as the USS *Plunger*. As a result the United States Navy asked Holland to design a new submarine, *Holland VI*, arguably the first really successful submarine.[48] Built in 1896–7 she had most of the features of a modern submarine.

By the end of the 1890s, the Royal Navy had no submarine service or even a single experimental submarine. The fact that the French possessed a considerable number caused some foreboding in the Admiralty, but attaché reports at least gave them an accurate picture of what was going on. In 1901 Britain set up her submarine service against the background of pioneering submarine work performed abroad; there was an advantage in letting others pay for the initial research and development. Since *Holland VI* was demonstrably the best submarine in the world, Britain purchased the manufacturing rights from the Holland Torpedo Boat Company and Vickers at Barrow built the first five prototypes.

In assessing the Royal Navy's first submarines there were, of course, considerable technical advances to be made. The petrol engines used for running on the surface and charging batteries were not very reliable. The petrol was highly volatile and refuelling often produced scenes of hilarious intoxication for the crews.[49] In 1905 an experimental diesel engine was fitted to the A13, one of the last of the successor class to the Holland boats. Three years later in 1908, the D-class were the first boats to be fitted with twin screw diesel propulsion. The early Holland boats had no periscopes, but Bacon had primitive optical tubes fitted. This tube was erected and secured by stays. By 1910, retractable periscopes were available and were fitted to the 'D' class. These early periscopes had very unreliable optics that needed frequent disassembly for cleaning. The image was correct only when pointing ahead. It was upside-down astern and endwise when abeam. Early submarine commanders could judge relative target angles from the angle of skew on the target selected.[50] The early Holland boats carried one torpedo tube and one reload torpedo, by 1910–11 the 'D' class carried two bow and one stern tube.

By the end of the 1890s the early experimental years were over and submersibles were a very practical naval proposition, with France and the United States already experimenting with different types. Britain came late into the submarine business but bought the best designs and used her industrial strength to rapidly develop her own submarine force.

The final technical innovation of the 1890s to have a profound influence on the development of navies concerned the first experiments in naval radio. For a fleet of steam battleships at sea, manual signalling by flags was clumsy but necessary. It was more appropriate to wooden fighting ships moving at 4 knots than battleships steaming at 14 knots. The problem of communication at sea was exacerbated in the 1880s by the introduction of fast torpedo-boats. Accurate and fast identification was required by night as well as by day.[51] Searchlights and Morse signalling lamps were introduced and partially solved the problem provided the weather was clear. It became obvious to some of the less hidebound officers of the torpedo branch that a more radical approach was necessary. Amongst these officers was Commander Henry Jackson.

By the standards of the Victorian navy commander, Henry Jackson, was well versed in electricity and electrical matters. In 1881, he had completed an electricity course at HMS *Vernon* and became an Associate of the Society of Telegraph Engineers, the precursor of the Institution of Electrical Engineers.

As early as 1891, Jackson had suggested using Hertzian waves for signalling but did not pursue the idea. In January 1895, he was appointed in command of HMS *Defiance*, an old wooden battleship built in 1801 and now used as the torpedo school at Devonport. It was from the deck of the *Defiance* in 1896 that the early experiments in wireless telegraphy at sea were conducted. In his first experiments Jackson thought of Hertzian waves exactly as a searchlight or signalling beam. The Hertzian waves merely replaced the light beam. An induction coil was used to produce sparks between metal spheres, serving as a primitive generator and transmitter of radio waves. The receiver needed a rectifier or 'coherer' to detect the radio waves. A tube filled with metal filings performed this. Once this system was tested, Jackson's approach to radio development was entirely logical and he set about improving the performance of the various components that made up his radio installation. He obtained a much more powerful induction coil that gave a 2-inch as opposed to a 1-inch spark gap. Jackson carried out numerous experiments with different types of coherer, the coherer conducted electricity in one direction but not the other, essentially the diode principle of electrical rectification. These trials established that Jackson's metal filing tube was ideal for radio signal detection. Jackson also discovered that the handling wires for his apparatus greatly improved signal detection when connected to the coherer. With the discovery of the wireless aerial, Jackson moved away from the idea of radio wave searchlight beams and moved towards the idea of radio wave transmission in the sense that we understand it today.[52]

By July 1896, Jackson had a new receiver built, with a two-foot aerial and a coherer made up of tin and iron filings contained in an ebonite tube. The trembler from an electric bell was used as the de-coherer. On 20 August 1896, a Morse transmission was made across the deck of HMS *Defiance* and was received by an operator 25 yards away.

Marconi is usually considered the first radio pioneer and experimented a year earlier than Jackson at his parent's estate in Italy. Marconi filed his first British patents in June 1896 and met Jackson at the War Office in August 1896. Marconi demonstrated his equipment to Jackson, who was impressed by its more developed state. The range of the Marconi equipment was about 20 yards at this time. On 16 September 1896, Marconi demonstrated a radio system that worked at a range of two miles. As a result of the Marconi trials, Jackson increased his receiver aerial length to 8 feet and his range increased to 300 yards. By the spring of 1897, Jackson had increased his range to 1,200 yards and was using aerials 70 feet long. In March 1897, Marconi conducted his second series of trials. For the first time he used aerials of the Jackson type, up to 120 feet long. Results were spectacular, with ranges up to seven miles. In May 1897, Jackson obtained an induction coil with a 6-inch spark gap and his range increased to 1.75 miles. By October 1897, he was using a 10-inch spark gap and his ranges had increased to 6,000 yards.[53]

In 1898, Marconi increased his transmission ranges to 14.5 miles, using 120-foot aerials. For the first time a transformer was used to couple the aerial to the transmitter. There were considerable limitations to radio at this time. Friend and foe alike could receive radio signals. There were no tuned circuits, so every operator could receive all transmissions in range, though coding of messages overcame this. Radio jamming was particularly easy in the days before tuned circuits. The obvious advantage of radio was the ability to pass messages at night and in bad weather or fog.

The first 'in service' test for naval radio came during the summer manoeuvres of 1899. These exercises were designed to test the use of relatively fast armoured cruisers and slower battleships in different squadron deployments. On 14 July 1899, two ships were able to exchange Morse signals at ranges of 28 miles. Morse operating speeds were around 10 words per minute. Ships such as the armoured cruisers *Juno* and *Europa* had aerials elevated to 158 and 178 feet respectively. All these early radio systems had transmitters tuned to the aerials by transformers known as 'jiggers'. The transmitters all had 10-inch induction coils with a spark gap consisting of a pair of 1.5-inch diameter brass balls, spaced three-quarters of an inch apart. The receivers were Marconi type with coherers, tappers and relays.[54] These early sets worked reasonably well and by 1900, 32 radio stations were installed on board the larger battleships and armoured cruisers. Two trained signalmen manned each radio installation.

By 1901, the Royal Navy had a considerable amount of operating experience in wireless telegraphy. Both Jackson's and Marconi's equipment was in service. Ratings and officers alike were trained at HMS *Vernon* and wireless telegraphy was rapidly attaining respectability. Finally, it was Marconi who invented the tuned circuit. In the early days of naval radio all ships could hear the transmissions of all other ships. This lack of secure communication ensured the almost complete lack of interest by the United States Navy. The tuned circuit allowed a transmitter and receiver to work on a single frequency. This selectivity and the use of coded transmissions ensured security, and with security came effective radio networks. What cannot be in any doubt is that the role of the Royal Navy was critical in the development of wireless telegraphy.

In the first years of the twentieth century development was rapid. By 1909 157 British warships were fitted with radio telegraphy. This included all battleships and fleet cruisers but torpedo-boats, destroyers and submarines had to wait for the development of small installations.[55] Between 1909 and 1914 the number of ships equipped with wireless telegraphy increased from 157 to 435. In 1914 spark technology dominated the Royal Navy. Battleships were equipped with a 14 kw main spark set with a range of 500 miles and a 1 kw auxiliary spark set with a range of five miles. The battleships also carried a special 'war set' pre-tuned to service wavelengths, for use 'after-action' if the main and auxiliary sets were damaged. Cruisers were equipped with a $1^1/_2$ kw spark set with a range of 100 miles and an auxiliary $1^1/_4$ kw set with a range of 30 miles. Destroyers were fitted with a 1 kw spark set with a range of 30 miles and submarines with a similar set again with a range of 30 miles.[56] By 1914 radio was well on the way to becoming a developed, mature technology. Radio valves were under development and new modes of transmission, including telephony, were rapidly ceasing to be experimental.

Perspectives: A Rapidly Developing Arms Race

'We want eight, we wont wait', chanted the crowds in Trafalgar Square. The navy indeed got its eight dreadnoughts in one year and arguably the great naval arms race moved into its critical phase. Exactly how far the dreadnoughts represented a true arms race is open to question. Most historians would agree that Britain and Germany engaged in a naval arms race before World War I; others disagree. Choucri and North concluded that naval expenditures in both Britain and Germany were driven primarily by internal factors.[57] Fisher's wonder ships *Dreadnought* and *Invincible* can indeed be seen as driven by internal factors, particularly a fundamental strategic re-evaluation that made the battlecruiser the instrument of trade protection. Germany's response, including the building of battlecruisers was hardly driven by internal factors; it was a direct response to Britain's wonder ships. At the time of the 'we want eight' agitation the Kaiser wrote to Chancellor Bülow and described British naval policy as 'Dreadnoughtschweinerei'.[58] This extraordinary word may be taken as the epitaph to an age.

8

The Worldwide Dreadnought Arms Race

Prelude: Navies Outside Europe

The extraordinary development of dreadnought era navies inside and outside Europe emphasises the worldwide nature of dreadnought building in the years before World War I, best described as dreadnought mania. Nowhere was this more apparent than in the rapid development of the Japanese and United States navies. There was a forgotten subtext to these navies; they were building against each other. The South American ABC countries (Argentina, Brazil and Chile) produced their own dreadnought building race, as did the Mediterranean powers, Austria-Hungary, Italy, France, Russia, Spain and Turkey.

The Imperial Japanese Navy (Nihon Teikoku Kaigun)

Japan was the first Asian nation to become industrialised and reach the front rank of world powers. After 1905 Japan was unchallenged in the western Pacific and had acquired a colonial empire. This included Port Arthur, the Liaotung Peninsular and Russia's economic assets in South Manchuria.[1]

In terms of the evolution of doctrine in the Japanese Navy, the war with Russia helped shape doctrine in four crucial ways. The first was the idea of the decisive fleet engagement using battleships armed with the heaviest possible guns. The second was the value of attrition, particularly against a more powerful, more numerous enemy, followed by a preference for quality over quantity in terms of ships and finally the importance of night-time torpedo tactics.[2] The Japanese Naval Staff College had formulated the tactical principles that had led to the resounding victory at Tsushima and it now had to provide a strategic doctrine that justified a large expensive navy in the context of Japan's vital interests. The navy asserted that maintaining control over the seas surrounding Japan was far more effective than defending the home islands themselves. What was needed was carefully articulated strategic doctrine, rooted in history, which went far beyond the historical analysis provided by Mahan, John Laughton and the Colomb brothers.[3]

The man selected to provide this analysis was Satō Tetsutarō, a lieutenant-commander with an interest in naval history. In 1899 he was sent to London and read extensively on Western naval history. By 1902 he had completed his massive thesis, nearly 900 pages and none of it easy reading. His central theme was the advantage conferred from oceanic defence and an analysis of the problem of an attack on Japan by a superior enemy sea power. The United States had taken the Philippines in the Spanish-American War and was now a potential adversary, with a much more powerful fleet. Satō developed the idea that the Japanese battle fleet should have a minimum force strength defined by the United States as the hypothetical adversary. He pointed out that the United States had no option but to divide its navy between the Atlantic and Pacific oceans. The huge distances across the Pacific and the lack of coaling facilities on the way made American involvement in a naval war in the western Pacific very difficult and the Philippines were very vulnerable. Satō concluded that the Japanese Navy should be at least 70 per cent the strength of the United States Navy, a ratio worked out in 1907–9 by the Naval Staff College and adhered to for the next 30 years. This ratio was based on the fact that the new-age steel warships with breech-loaded guns had changed the dynamics of naval battle, greatly to the advantage of the side with the larger number of ships. This fact was given an algebraic form by an English engineer, Frederick William Lanchester, and is sometimes called the N^2 law. In the days of the sailing ship, all things being equal, which they never were, the larger fleet should defeat the smaller. A linear law applies, so ten sailing ships should defeat seven, with three remaining to the winning side. With the N^2 law if ten modern battleships meet seven, the margin of victory to the winning side would equal the square root of the difference between the square of the gun power of the two fleets. This is $\sqrt{(10^2 - 7^2)} \approx 7$. In a naval war with Japan, if the United States had ten battleships to Japan's seven the US would win but this assumed that all the American battleships could be deployed in the western Pacific. If five were deployed to seven Japanese the arithmetic changes in Japan's favour – $\sqrt{(7^2 - 5^2)} \approx 5$. If the remaining US battleships, say five, turn up, the odds are even.[4]

Japan's adherence to the N^2 law can only be described as one of the curiosities of the dreadnought era.

A colleague of Satō's at the Naval Staff College, Akiyama Saneyuki, worked on the problem of fleet size. For Akiyama the determining factor was firepower and flexibility. From his analysis of Tsushima, Akiyama concluded that the optimum force was eight battleships (a division), operating in line ahead to provide maximum broadside fire.[5] At Tsushima armoured cruisers had operated with the battle fleet so a second division was also conjectured. In due time this would be defined as a force of eight dreadnoughts and eight battlecruisers.

After Tsushima the two Satsuma class battleships were the first built in Japan and were armed with four 12-inch and twelve 10-inch guns, best described as an improved form of the British Lord Nelson class, with about 80 per cent of parts imported from Britain. It needs reiterating that these might have been the first all big gun ships to be laid down but for the financial strain imposed on Japanese government spending by the war with Russia.

The *Kurama* and *Ibuki* were 22-knot armoured cruiser versions of the *Satsuma*, armed with four 12-inch (30.5-cm) guns and eight 8-inch (20.3 cm) guns, re-rated as battlecruisers in 1912. There were two earlier armoured cruisers, sometimes described as battlecruisers, *Tsukuba* and *Ikoma*. Armed with four 12-inch (30.5-cm) and twelve 6-inch (15.2-cm) guns, they were 20.5 knot ships.[6] The battlecruiser type was close to fruition in the Japanese Navy and it again needs emphasising that Fisher's move to an *Invincible* type was the result of intelligence assessments of foreign design rather than technical innovation produced at home. The fact that Britain was in alliance with Japan and the two navies were freely exchanging information greatly aided the move towards a battlecruiser type.

The 1907 fleet expansion programme initiated the eight/eight fleet programme and the first Japanese dreadnoughts *Kawachi* and *Settsu* were laid down at Kure in January 1909, with about 20 per cent of parts imported from Britain. They were armed with twelve 12-inch (30.5-cm) guns disposed as in the German Nassaus. The problem was that the fore and aft turret guns were 50 calibres, while the four wing turret guns were 45 calibres. With different barrel lengths and consequently different ballistic characteristics they were not capable of salvo firing and from this viewpoint can be regarded as the last of the semi-dreadnoughts.

Then the Japanese decided to build a class of four super-dreadnought battlecruisers. The 27,500-ton name ship *Kongo* was built by Vickers, laid

Satsuma
Aki

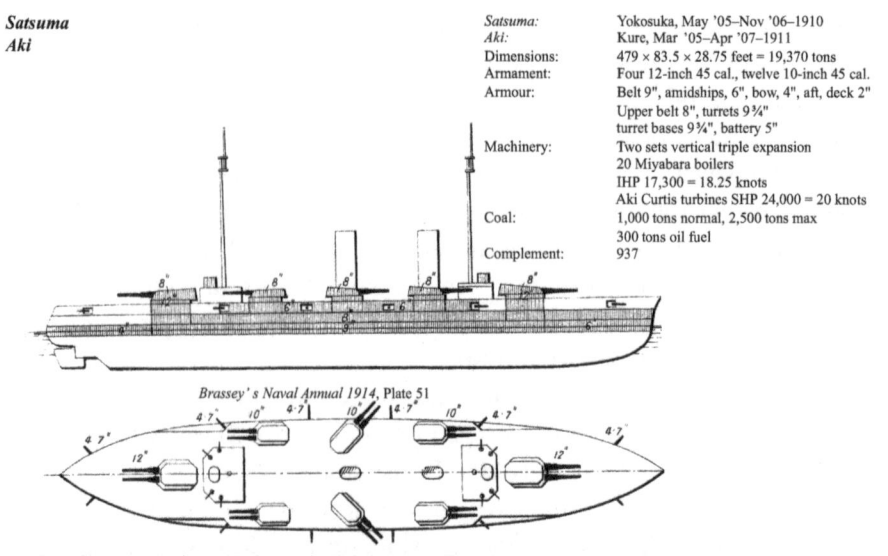

Satsuma: Yokosuka, May '05–Nov '06–1910
Aki: Kure, Mar '05–Apr '07–1911
Dimensions: 479 × 83.5 × 28.75 feet = 19,370 tons
Armament: Four 12-inch 45 cal., twelve 10-inch 45 cal.
Armour: Belt 9", amidships, 6", bow, 4", aft, deck 2"
Upper belt 8", turrets 9¾"
turret bases 9¾", battery 5"
Machinery: Two sets vertical triple expansion
20 Miyabara boilers
IHP 17,300 = 18.25 knots
Aki Curtis turbines SHP 24,000 = 20 knots
Coal: 1,000 tons normal, 2,500 tons max
300 tons oil fuel
Complement: 937

Brassey's Naval Annual 1914, Plate 51

These ships were built with considerable British technical assistance. The armament closely resembles the Lord Nelson class semi-dreadnoughts. It is almost certain that the Japanese constructors had access to the design papers for the *Lord Nelson*. Armstrong-Whitworth supplied the guns and gun mountings. *Aki* was powered by Curtis turbines, *Satsuma* by four cylinder triple expansion steam engines. *Aki* was a three-funnelled ship, *Satsuma* was two funnelled (ship illustrated). These ships took four and six years respectively to build.

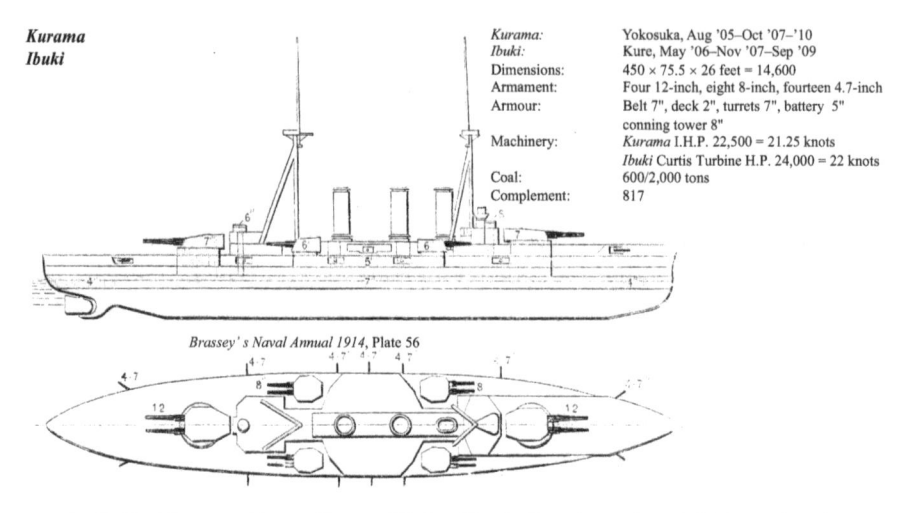

Kurama
Ibuki

Kurama: Yokosuka, Aug '05–Oct '07–'10
Ibuki: Kure, May '06–Nov '07–Sep '09
Dimensions: 450 × 75.5 × 26 feet = 14,600
Armament: Four 12-inch, eight 8-inch, fourteen 4.7-inch
Armour: Belt 7", deck 2", turrets 7", battery 5"
conning tower 8"
Machinery: *Kurama* I.H.P. 22,500 = 21.25 knots
Ibuki Curtis Turbine H.P. 24,000 = 22 knots
Coal: 600/2,000 tons
Complement: 817

Brassey's Naval Annual 1914, Plate 56

As with *Aki* and *Satsuma*, one ship was turbine powered (*Ibuki*), and the other (*Kurama*) powered by vertical triple expansion engines. The 1914 edition of *Jane's Fighting Ships* apparently had some difficulty categorising them. They are described as 'Japanese Armoured Ships' and in italics (*Battle Cruisers*). All four ships had a distinctly Japanese designed clipper bow and light pole masts.

Fig. 18 The Japanese 'Very Nearly' Dreadnoughts, Satsuma, Aki, Ibuki and Kurama

down in January 1911 and completed in August 1913. This was the last Japanese capital ship built in Britain. Designed by Sir George Thurston, the design was an improved Lion class ship with eight 14-inch (35.6-cm) guns. The turrets were disposed 'A', 'B', 'X', 'Y' as opposed to 'A', 'B', 'Q', 'Y' in the Lion class.[7] Exactly how far this ship influenced the design of the British battlecruiser *Tiger* is open to question. It can be argued that the *Tiger* benefited from the *Iron Duke* design and was the battlecruiser equivalent. Equally it can be argued that, unfettered by bureaucracy and design restrictions imposed by the Admiralty, Thurston came up with the best-ever battlecruiser design. In the opinion of David K. Brown there was no direct link between *Kongo* and *Tiger* but, in the era of the Anglo-Japanese alliance, the Japanese were allowed access to a great deal of British thinking, as were Vickers. The *Kongo* can then be seen as the independent end-product of similar lines of thinking.[8] Vickers were also building a Thurston designed battleship for Turkey, *Reshadieh*, destined to become HMS *Erin* in the Royal Navy. The *Kongo* can also be seen as the battlecruiser version of *Reshadieh*, which in turn owed a great deal to both the King George V and Iron Duke classes. The remaining three battlecruisers were built in Japan, *Hiei* at Yokosuka, *Haruna* at Kawasaki and *Kirishima* at Nagasaki. *Hiei* and *Haruna* were built in private yards with about 30 per cent of the materials imported from Britain, while *Kirishima* can be regarded as a home-grown product.[9] With the building of *Kirishima*, Japanese warship building capability finally came of age.

In 1912–13 the Japanese laid down the *Fuso* and *Yamashiro*, a pair of 30,000-ton ships armed with twelve 14-inch (35.6-cm) guns.[10] At the time of laying down, in 1912–13, they were potentially the largest battleships in the world. In fact, they were not completed until 1915 and 1917 respectively, when the British Queen Elizabeths and Royal Sovereigns were certainly their equal. A cycle of battleship design and development was brought to a close with the *Ise* and *Hiuga* of 31,000 tons. Again twelve 14-inch guns were mounted, but speed was increased to 23 knots.[11] These big 30,000-ton battleships show clearly a strand in Japanese strategic thinking – they could not afford the numbers of the other naval powers so they went for size and the heaviest gun armament. With the *Aki* and *Satsuma*, *Settsu* and *Kawachi*, *Fuso* and *Yamashiro* and *Ise* and *Hyuga* Japan now had its eight battleships. With the *Tsukuba* and *Ikoma*, *Ibuki* and *Kurama*, *Kongo*, *Hiei*, *Haruna* and *Kirishma*, Japan had eight battlecruisers. Not all of these ships were dreadnoughts but the first eight/eight programme had now been completed.

The United States Navy

Across the other side of the Pacific lay the United States, victorious in the war with Spain and the inheritor of the Spanish Empire. Puerto Rico now lay in American hands and Cuba was made independent, though this was hedged with numerous restrictions. In 1903 the USA took Guantanamo as a coaling station. Wake Island and Guam were annexed. The groundwork for the final takeover in Hawaii had already taken place and the archipelago was also annexed. The main problem for the US Navy was the requirement for effectively two navies, an Atlantic and a Pacific. The distance from New York to San Francisco, via Cape Horn, is over 13,000 miles, more than twice the distance from San Francisco to Yokohama. The prospect of German aggression in either the Atlantic or Pacific was fairly remote but fear of German interference in the Caribbean and South America was an obsession with President Theodore Roosevelt. He felt that Germany's search for colonies would almost inevitably bring her into conflict with the United States.[12]

In the case of the Philippines, the US Army was opposed to the construction of a fleet base at Subic Bay largely because they saw the defence of the Philippines in terms of a coast defence strategy, whereas the navy saw defence in terms of Mahan; possession of a battle fleet capable of taking the war to the enemy. Roosevelt was unable to resolve the impasse between the two services and in 1908 made the decision to develop Pearl Harbor at Hawaii as a main fleet base. American doctrine for a war against Japan was based on War Plan Orange. The battle fleet would be deployed in the Atlantic until the naval threat from Germany had disappeared. In the Pacific the army would hold Corregidor Island at the entrance to Manila Bay for at least 90 days, while the Atlantic Fleet was deployed to Pearl Harbor. An ocean offensive would then be launched to relieve Corregidor and the fleet would then be deployed directly against Japan. The use of the entire battle fleet in this way was based on Mahan's classic dictum, *never divide the fleet*. This led, in 1907, to the proposal that the entire battle fleet should be deployed to the Pacific as a form of test mobilisation for War Plan Orange.[13] This was developed into a plan for a round-the-world cruise by the American battle fleet.

In December 1907 the American Atlantic Fleet commenced its circumnavigation. Sixteen battleships set off from Hampton Roads, all painted white, giving the fleet the name of 'the Great White Fleet'. On the first leg of the voyage the fleet passed down the Atlantic coast of South America to the Magellan Straits and on to San Francisco. The second leg of the voyage was from San Francisco to Puget Sound and back. The third leg of the voyage, from San Francisco to Manila, took in Honolulu, Auckland, Sydney, Melbourne, Albany, Yokohama, Amoy and Manila (again), a distance of 16,336 nautical miles. The final leg of the voyage included Colombo, Suez, Gibraltar and finally back to Hampton Roads. It was an extraordinary *tour de force* and announced to the world that the United States was now a true world power with a navy to match. All over the world the fleet was greeted with enormous excitement. Much of strategic purpose of the cruise was aimed at Japan, making the point that America was quite capable of deploying a fleet in the Pacific. From Roosevelt's point of view this demonstrated the purpose of the new US Navy; it was the adjunct to diplomacy, able to project naval power into Asia, and anywhere else for that matter.

The voyage of the Great White Fleet coincided with the *Dreadnought* and the first American all big gun battleships were planned well before the British ship. From 1902 onwards discussions took place conjecturing an all big gun battleship. Progress was very slow and the first ship, *South Carolina*, was not laid down until December 1906, 14 months after the *Dreadnought*. *South Carolina* and *Michigan* mounted eight 12-inch guns with two turrets forward and two aft, with one turret superimposed over the other. A 12-inch gun turret weighed about 500 tons. On a ship in the 16,000–20,000-ton range, raising two turrets by 12 feet reduced the metacentric height by about 12 inches, depending on hull design. On a ship with a metacentric height of five to six feet, the superimposition of two turrets starts to become significant and the *South Carolina* and *Michigan* were rather beamier (80 ft) than their pre-dreadnought predecessors.[14] They were limited by Congress to 16,000 tons displacement and this severely restricted the design. Triple expansion machinery was used to give a speed of only 18 knots.

In their second pair of dreadnoughts, *Delaware* and *North Dakota*, an extra turret was worked in on the centre line. In contrast to British practice, 'Q' turret was at foredeck level, while the after two turrets were placed back to back at quarterdeck level. This was repeated in the *Utah* and *Florida*. In the next pair of dreadnoughts, *Arkansas* and *Wyoming*, six turrets were mounted, two forward two amidships and two aft with one turret superimposed over the other in each case. Six turrets were excessive as each turret represented a major hull opening that reduced hull strength. At some stage in the design process, probably at four or five turrets, either an increase in gun calibre is called for or the adoption of triple or quadruple mountings.

This argument produced the *New York* and *Texas*, which mounted ten 14-inch guns disposed exactly as the British Iron Dukes.[15]

In the next pair of American dreadnoughts, *Nevada* and *Oklahoma*, enormous armouring advances were made and 5,000 tons of armour in the first American dreadnoughts became 11,000 tons in the Nevadas.[16] The arguments about large deck openings were accepted and only four turrets were mounted. A triple 14-inch turret was adopted for the two lower turrets and a twin turret was superimposed over each. This four-turret arrangement was adhered to in the *Pennsylvania* and *Arizona*, except that all four turrets were triple mountings. The outbreak of war in 1914 increased American building programmes from two to three ships a year and the *New Mexico*, *Idaho* and *Mississippi* were all laid down in 1915. The three super-dreadnoughts of the 1914–15 programme were the best all-round battleship design of the period with the possible exception of the British Queen Elizabeth class. The ships described here gave the United States Navy a dreadnought fleet of 17 ships and represented a complete cycle of construction programmes, ended only by the 1916 'two ocean programme'.[17]

In engineering terms, *North Dakota* was turbine powered while *Delaware* was powered with triple expansion engines for comparison. *North Dakota* was not impressive and burnt 140 tons of fuel in 24 hours compared to 100 tons for *Delaware*. The next four dreadnoughts used four screw Parsons steam turbines. *Pennsylvania* had Curtis geared turbines and the *Arizona*, Parsons geared turbines, again for comparison.[18] Then the United States Navy took the most controversial step in warship engineering since Fisher put turbines in the *Dreadnought* and adopted General Electric turbines with electric reduction gearing, that is, turbo-electric drive. Economy is far greater in terms of fuel and cruising radius but there is a weight penalty to pay. Turbo-electric drive is usually half as heavy again as a turbine installation with mechanical reduction.[19]

In conclusion, in the pre-1914 era Japan built or was in the process of building eight dreadnoughts, battleships and battlecruisers to the 17 American dreadnoughts. As an arms race it was at a much lower level than the European building programmes. Nevertheless, the portents were ominous, and the pre-1914 naval competition clearly identified America and Japan as potential adversaries in some future war. With large colonial possessions in the Pacific basin, America needed an effective Pacific Fleet. They also needed a strong Atlantic Fleet. With the strongest Atlantic and Pacific navies in alliance, the development of a two-ocean school of American defence thinkers was probably inevitable.

The South American Republics

The first stirrings of South American naval rivalry went back a long way into the nineteenth century. The ABC countries, Argentina, Brazil and Chile, all built small, but in their own way, substantial navies. From notions of rivalry to outright megalomania, each country participated fully in the dreadnought era and this produced a South American naval arms race of considerable proportions.

At the dawn of the twentieth century the Brazilian Navy lagged seriously behind those of Argentina and Chile. Brazil was becoming a comparatively rich country, controlling the world's coffee and rubber markets. In 1904 the rather short-lived rubber boom tempted the Brazilian government in the direction of a large naval building programme aimed at remedying the defects and weaknesses in the navy. It took two years to order the first battleships and the announcement of their construction caused a considerable stir in naval and diplomatic circles – they were dreadnoughts.

The two dreadnoughts were ordered from British yards, *Minas Gerais* built by Armstrong's at Elswick and *Sao Paulo* by Vickers at Barrow. Laid down in April 1907 these were 20,000-ton ships armed with twelve 12-inch guns. Two twin turrets were superimposed forward and two aft, at a time when the British Admiralty was still arguing about blast effects from superimposed turrets. A further two twin turrets were worked in amidships in an *en echelon* arrangement. The superimposition of the gun turrets allowed a ship to be built that was only 15 feet longer than *Dreadnought*, with an extra twin turret. The unfortunate feature of the design was the use of steam reciprocating machinery. Brazil had only very limited dockyard resources and this was aimed at keeping maintenance costs down; nevertheless the ships had a speed of 21 knots. The first of these ships, *Minas Gerais*, arrived in Rio de Janeiro in April 1910, the largest and most powerful warship in the western hemisphere. Almost immediately prosperity began to wane and economic depression set in. The Brazilian armed forces were deeply racist and the result was a mutiny known as the 'revolt of the whip'. Inhumanely treated black sailors, led by the so-called black admiral João Cândido, on-board *Minas Gerais*, murdered several officers and the captain and held British engineers on board as hostages. The revolt petered out but did a huge amount of damage to the reputation of the Brazilian Navy.

There was much press speculation that these ships had been built for a foreign power with Brazil as the 'front' for perhaps Japan or Germany.

It was even rumoured that they were really destined for the Royal Navy.[20] Brazilian dreams of naval glory climaxed with the decision to build the battleship *Rio de Janeiro* at Armstrong's, potentially the largest and most powerful warship in the world. Four gun layouts were offered, fourteen 12-inch guns, twelve 14-inch guns, eight 16-inch guns or ten 15-inch guns.[21] At first the Brazilians decided in favour of twelve 14-inch guns. Then a new Minister of Marine was appointed who was friendly with the German Navy Minister. The Kaiser himself, that leading expert on all things naval, decided that fourteen 12-inch guns was a better option.[22] Eventually the Brazilians adopted the fourteen 12-inch gun design, perhaps logical enough when the standardisation of ammunition with the *Minas Gerais* and *San Paulo* is considered. In the wake of the naval mutiny and the economic depression, this 27,500-ton monster was sold to Turkey and became *Sultan Osman I*. Completing in August 1914, she was taken over by the Royal Navy and became HMS *Agincourt*.[23] *Agincourt* was the only dreadnought owned by three navies.

Brazilian dreadnoughts came as a shock to Argentina, a country in a state of financial exhaustion for much of the early twentieth century. Endemic border disputes with Brazil decided the issue and two dreadnoughts were ordered from abroad. In 1908 an Argentinean rear-admiral set up office in London and asked for dreadnought designs. No fewer than 15 proposals were submitted. The Argentineans then chose the best features from each design and gave the revised designs to the competing firms and repeated the process. Eventually the contract was awarded to the Fore River Shipbuilding Corporation of Quincy, Massachusetts, at a considerable saving of £224,000 per ship, compared to European shipyards. At 28,000 tons the *Rivadavia* and *Moreno* were much larger than *Minas Gerais* and *Sao Paulo*, but mounted the same armament in the same disposition. They took much longer to build than their Brazilian rivals, being laid down in 1910 and not completed until 1914 and 1915 respectively.[24] These were the only dreadnoughts built in the United States for a foreign power.

On the other side of the South American continent, Chile was in a difficult position. Then as now she had endless minor territorial disputes with Argentina over the southern territories and Tierra del Fuego. These disputes demanded a navy, as did her wars with Peru. Chile could not allow Argentine naval preponderance to remain too great in relation to its own naval strength and made the momentous decision to buy dreadnoughts. Never mind the crippling expenditure for a desperately poor country; in 1912 the *Almirante Latorre* and later the *Almirante Cochrane* were laid down by Armstrong's at Elswick, with the first due for completion in 1914. By 1912, the early dreadnoughts were rapidly being superseded by the super-dreadnoughts. Chile decided that 12-inch guns were not good enough and 14-inch calibre weapons were chosen. Ten 14-inch guns were mounted, using the same turret disposition as the British Iron Dukes. The hull size was a massive 28,000 tons, the same as the Argentine ships. Turbines were fitted and developed 37,000 horsepower, giving a service speed of 23 knots.[25] Only one of these ships, the *Almirante Latorre*, actually reached the Chilean Navy and then only after four years war service with the Royal Navy as HMS *Canada*. The other, the *Almirante Cochrane*, was purchased by Britain and became the aircraft carrier HMS *Eagle*, sunk in World War II.

The Austro-Hungarian Navy (Kaiserliche und Königliche Kriegsmarine)

There were two major Mediterranean naval powers, whose policies were at variance with Britain, Italy and Austria-Hungary, both members of the Bismarckian triple alliance or *triplice*. In spite of their nominal alliance both powers were naturally antagonistic to each other. Italy achieved unification in 1861, but there were numerous Italian populations in the Balkans and elsewhere, including Trieste, the main naval port and shipbuilding centre of the Austro-Hungarian Empire. In Italy the irredentist movement demanded the complete unification of all Italian-speaking people. In due time Italian irredentism provided a strong motive for Italy's entry into World War I and the 1919 Versailles Treaty addressed many of the irredentist claims, including Trieste, which was ceded to Italy.[26]

Austria-Hungary had a fairly short Adriatic coastline, just 370 miles in length, easily blockaded in wartime. The navy was part of a unified Ministry of War (or Ministry of Defence). Fleet headquarters were at Pola and a major arsenal was situated at Trieste. Austrian policy in the Balkans was one of territorial expansion in the direction of Greece, aimed at obtaining a port on the Aegean, specifically Salonica. In October 1908 Austria formally annexed Bosnia and Herzegovina. The declining power of the Ottoman Turks ensured that they were corralled into accepting the situation.

From 1866 to 1904 the Austro-Hungarian Navy received only between 7.7 and 15.7 per cent of the defence budget. The problem lay in the nature of the dualism between Austria and Hungary; the Hungarian side of the Dual Monarchy never really saw the need for a navy.[27] In spite of these difficulties, by the late 1890s Austria-Hungary was self-sufficient in armour plate manufacture (Witkowitz), gun manufacture (Skoda works) and shipbuilding (Stabilimento Tecnico Triestino, hereafter STT).[28] The commander-in-chief of the Austro-Hungarian Navy, Admiral Spaun, presented a fleet expansion programme to counter Italian plans. The budget of 50 million crowns (about £2.1 million) was cut by half, showing the real difficulties in getting a reasonable share of the defence budget. Spaun resigned and was replaced by Admiral Count Rudolf Montecuccoli.[29] Montecuccoli was a consummate politician in the manner of Fisher and Tirpitz and in less than a decade doubled the navy's share of the defence budget. In 1907 the first two Radetzky class battleships were laid down, with a third in 1909. The *Radetzky, Erzherzog Franz Ferdinand* and *Zrinyi* were all armed with four 30.5-cm (12-inch) guns and eight 24-cm (9.4-inch) guns.[30] With a speed of 20.5 knots these were proper pre-dreadnoughts and represented a move from the Austro-Hungarian Navy as an Adriatic coast defence force to a proper Mediterranean navy.

In early 1908 it became clear that Italy would shortly lay down her first dreadnought, so Austria-Hungary did the same. Four dreadnoughts were planned, three to be built by STT and one by Danubius at Fiume. The Fiume yard had no experience of big ship building, but was a notionally Hungarian yard and the Hungarians insisted that at least one dreadnought should be built in a Hungarian yard. When the first two dreadnoughts were laid down parliamentary approval had not been given, so STT proceeded at their own risk. A political crisis had caused the collapse of the government and arguments about a new coalition in Hungary left Budapest without a government for a full year. At this time the Radetzky class ships were nearing completion. Without new contracts Witkowitz, Skoda and STT would be without new orders and many skilled men would be laid off. This disruption to the work force would delay any new dreadnought construction. Commencing the new dreadnoughts without parliamentary approval was less risky than might be expected because STT, the Skoda Works and Witkowitz all obtained their finance from the Creditanstalt Bank and its founders, the Austrian branch of the Rothschild family.[31] It was also the case that Franz Ferdinand himself gave assurances to the Creditanstalt Bank that the crisis would be satisfactorily resolved. The result was four 20,000-ton dreadnoughts, *Viribus Unitis, Tegetthoff, Prinz Eugen* and *Szent Istvan*, all armed with twelve 30.5-cm (12-inch) guns and twelve 15-cm (5.9-inch) guns. The main armament was mounted in four triple turrets, two forward and two aft, one superimposed over the other. Parsons geared steam turbines gave a speed of just over 20 knots. Four turbine powered light cruisers were also built. These 3,500-ton ships had a speed of 27 knots and were armed with 10-cm (3.9-inch) guns.[32]

In 1910 Montecuccoli gave an interview to the *Magyar Figyeloe*, a Hungarian review magazine and stated the strategic purpose of the greatly expanded Austro-Hungarian Navy. He said that the country could not endure a blockade of the Adriatic by a hostile fleet, and that a strong fleet protecting the coast would relieve the military of some responsibilities for coast defence, hence the importance to Hungary. The navy would seek to exercise its influence in the Adriatic and eastern Mediterranean. Montecuccoli discounted the idea of acting on the defensive and said that the first principle in naval war was to damage the enemy. He concluded by saying that the Austro-Hungarian Navy should be compared with the fleets of the other Mediterranean naval powers. Nations with Atlantic coasts (obviously Britain and France) could not easily reinforce their Mediterranean fleets in wartime.[33]

Just before World War I a further four dreadnoughts were proposed, 24,500-ton ships armed with ten 35-cm (13.8-inch) guns. The war intervened and none were ever laid down.[34] Austria-Hungary entered the war with a relatively powerful striking force whose dreadnoughts had completely upset the Mediterranean balance of power so essential to British interests.

During World War I, Austro-Hungarian naval operations consisted mainly of coastal bombardments of Italy's Adriatic coastline. Coastal bombardments apart, the Italian and Austro-Hungarian navies kept their distance and it was only as the war drew to a close that two Austro-Hungarian dreadnoughts were actually sunk. On 10 June 1918 the SMS *Szent Istvan* was sunk by an Italian MAS boat, effectively a lightweight, fast motor launch, armed with two torpedoes. On 1 November 1918 the SMS *Viribus Unitis* was sunk in Pola harbour by a prototype human torpedo armed with a large mine. Dreadnoughts were very vulnerable to underwater attack.

The Italian Navy (Regia Marina Italiana)

In the era of the premiership of Francesco Crispi, Italy was very pro-German and based its foreign policy on the *Triplice* with Germany. In 1887 one of Crispi's first acts as premier was to visit Bismarck to discuss in some detail the working of the *Triplice*. Crispi's pro-German foreign policy was heavily supplemented by the status quo naval agreement with Britain, also in 1887. In 1902 the three *triplice* powers concluded an agreement that in a war with France and Russia, the defence of the western Mediterranean was assigned to Italy and the eastern Mediterranean to joint Austro-Italian control, while the Baltic and Atlantic were Germany's problem. The Triple Alliance was renewed in 1902, by which time Italy was playing a double game and had already come to a private agreement with France, which gave Italy a free hand in Libya in return for similar French arrangements in Morocco and Tunisia. It was the disputes with France over Tunisia that had driven Italy into the *triplice* in the first place, and now that the colonial disputes were settled the *triplice* became irrelevant. In 1901 the Italian Navy visited Toulon and by 1902 Italian naval leaders regarded the Austro-Hungarian Navy as its most likely adversary in wartime. For their part, the Austrians proceeded with a railway link from Prague to Trieste which would be invaluable for fast mobilisation in a war against Italy.[35]

The development of the Italian Navy and its strong English connections needs examination. In 1885 an Italian parliamentary enquiry concluded that the both the Italian mercantile marine and the navy were in a lamentable state. Benedetto Brin, the Italian Navy's former Chief Constructor, became the Minister for the Navy and more or less coerced Giovanni Ansaldo of Sampierdarena and Guppy of Naples to enter into partnership with the English firms of Maudsley and Hawthorn respectively. Sir William Armstrong was approached and persuaded to set up an ordnance factory at Pozzuoli, while an Italian firm set up a steel plant and armour plate factory at Terni. The German firm of Schwarzkopf were engaged to set up a torpedo production plant at Venice. To a large extent the Italian steel navy was the end-product of English capital and English industrial organisation. The 1885 act awarded a premium to Italian shipbuilders in proportion to both the shipping tonnage constructed and the engine power fitted to them. A second premium was paid to ship-owners in proportion to the tonnage and distance run by their ships. Italy now had the capital from subsidies to develop her private shipbuilding industries and her navy. By 1896 Italy was able to vie with Britain, France and Germany in building warships for foreign powers. Cruisers were built for Argentina and Spain, with two ending up in Japanese hands. In 1903 Ansaldo and Armstrong's merged, with all Italian Navy ordnance now effectively underwritten by English capital. The naval side of Italian industrial development can be seen in two stages; the first from 1885 to 1903, when various firms were effectively under state control through the medium of state subsidies, and the second from 1903 when two large naval combines were formed. Ansaldo-Armstrong has already been mentioned, while the second combine was defined by the shipyards of Sestri-Ponente and La Foce, owned by Odero and Co., and by the shipyard of Orlando at Leghorn.[36]

Italy built 11 pre-dreadnoughts, starting with the three 13,000-ton ships, *Re Umberto*, *Sicilia* and *Sardegna*, armed with four 13.5-inch (34-cm) guns and continuing with the rather smaller 10,000-ton *Ammiraglio Di Saint Bon* and *Emanuele Filiberto*, armed with four 10-inch (25-cm) guns. They were followed by the *Regina Margherita* and *Benedetto Brin*, 13,000-ton ships armed with four 12-inch, four 8-inch and twelve 6-inch guns. The final four Italian pre-dreadnoughts have already been mentioned because they attempted to combine the battleship and armoured cruiser type into a fast battleship that was something close to a battlecruiser. The *Regina Elena*, *Vittorio Emanuele*, *Roma* and *Napoli* mounted two 12-inch and twelve 8-inch guns on a displacement of just 12,500 tons, and had a speed of 21.5–22 knots.[37] Italian building times were notoriously slow and in the pre-dreadnought era averaged eight years and nine months, compared to just four years for their Austro-Hungarian counterparts. The Italian Navy also included seven armoured and 27 unarmoured cruisers.

In one sense the Austro-Hungarian Navy was better officered and manned than its Italian counterpart, but certainly until the Montecuccoli era was crippled by the lack of funds for new construction, whereas the Italian Navy was admired for the quality of its ships while observers of its operations were deeply critical of its personnel.[38] A British intelligence assessment of the Italian Navy from 1897 makes interesting reading:

> It is more than ever apparent that the value of Italy to one side or the other in a European war depends on her either having the command of the sea or being allied to another power which has it. Unless the security of her coastline is guaranteed [...] Italy, as a factor in a European war, may be practically neglected.[39]

Italy laid down her first dreadnought *Dante Alighieri* in June 1909. This ship mounted twelve 30.5-cm (12-inch) guns in four triple turrets. The first two Austro-Hungarian dreadnoughts were laid down 13 and 15 months later, in July and September 1910, completing in December 1912 and July 1913 respectively. By contrast the *Dante Alighieri* was completed in January 1913, having taken 43 months to build compared with 29 months and 34 months respectively for the Austro-Hungarian ships. The identical armament of the Italian and Austro-Hungarian ships should be noted. Italy built five more dreadnoughts, three laid down in 1911 and two in 1912. The *Conte di Cavour*, *Giulio Cesare* and *Leonardo da Vinci* mounted thirteen 30.5-cm (12-inch) guns in three triple and two twin turrets, the twins being superimposed fore and aft over the triples. These were 23,000-ton ships powered by Parsons steam turbines and had a speed of 22 knots. The final pair, *Andrea Doria* and *Duilio*, were very similar. In all Italy built six dreadnoughts to the Austro-Hungarian four. In common with her Adriatic rival, four additional dreadnoughts were laid down in 1914 and 1915 but only one of the Caracciolo class was launched and none were completed.[40] During the war the *Leonardo Da Vinci* blew up and sank on 2 August 1916. Austria was blamed but it is almost certainly the case that the cause of the explosion was faulty and decaying propellant charges.

The Royal Navy and the Mediterranean

Britain's Mediterranean policy changed steadily as the Triple Alliance navies expanded. The Moroccan crisis of 1905–6 increased the mutual dependence of Britain and France and initiated a series of Anglo-French naval conversations. At first these conversations were informal and no written record survives. In 1908 and again in 1911 the Bosnian and Agadir crises produced much more detailed discussions, with clearly defined roles for the British and French fleets in a war with Germany. With her dreadnought fleet concentrated in home waters, only pre-dreadnoughts were available for Mediterranean operations but as the Austro-Hungarian and Italian dreadnoughts took to the water so Britain's Mediterranean fleet was increasingly outclassed and obsolete.

Churchill argued that holding the Mediterranean permanently was not necessarily of supreme importance; what mattered was the ability to enter it with predominant strength when circumstances required. By August 1911 it had been decided that in a war with Germany the British Admiralty would have overall control of naval strategy, but that the British and French navies would have clearly defined zones in which each would act with complete independence. The French home fleets would be based in the Mediterranean to seek out and destroy the navies of Italy and Austria-Hungary.[41] These 1911 conversations took place when Arthur Wilson was First Sea Lord and Reginald McKenna First Lord. Wilson accepted the Fisher-era so-called 'conventions' but interestingly Fisher had wanted the

French to be responsible for the defence of the Straits of Dover. Wilson changed this and considered that the defence and blockade of the Straits should be left entirely to the British Navy. In the Mediterranean, Britain should maintain sufficient cruisers for trade protection.[42]

The Foreign Office and War Office were not in favour of any British withdrawal from the Mediterranean. In April 1912 the Committee of Imperial Defence met at Malta with the Prime Minister and First Lord of the Admiralty present. Also present were representatives of the War Staff, the General Officer Commanding-in-Chief Mediterranean, the Governor of Malta, the Naval Commander-in-Chief and Lord Kitchener, de facto Viceroy of Egypt.[43] In May 1912, Sir Eyre Crowe penned a lengthy memorandum on the effect of British withdrawal from the Mediterranean. He concluded that the abandonment of the Mediterranean would throw Italy completely into the arms of the Triple Alliance and solidify her hostility to Britain and France. He stated that any British withdrawal would weaken British influence at Constantinople and this would encourage Turkey to join forces with the Triple Alliance and perhaps attempt the reconquest of Egypt. At this time Spain had an understanding with France and England and any British withdrawal might encourage her towards the Triple Alliance in a war against France.[44] The result was a revised Mediterranean policy, in which Britain supported France and in due course deployed dreadnoughts in the Mediterranean.

The French Navy (Marine Français)

Any examination of the French Navy in this era reveals a navy in a state of chaos and decay. The great weakness of the French Navy lay in endless political interference. Each successive Navy Minister seemed bent on undoing the work of his predecessor. A series of ministers culminated in Charles Pelletan, labelled famously 'naufrageur de la marine', literally 'wrecker of the navy'. One consequence of this was a fleet that consisted of battleships each in some way completely different from nominally sister ships of supposedly the same class, quite literally a fleet of prototypes.[45] After 1906 things improved with the building of a class of six turbine powered semi-dreadnoughts. The *Danton, Condorcet, Diderot, Mirabeau, Vergniaud* and *Voltaire* were 18,000-ton ships armed with four 30.5-cm (12-inch) guns and twelve 24-cm (9.4-inch) guns. These ships were roughly comparable to the British Lord Nelsons. In addition, France possessed six effective pre-dreadnoughts, *République, Patrie, Démocratie, Justice, Libert,* and *Verité*.

These were 14,500-ton ships armed with four 30.5-cm (12-inch) guns and a secondary armament of 16.4-cm (6.4-inch) or 19.4-cm (7.6-inch) guns. *The Liberté* was sunk by an internal explosion on 25 September 1911. Spontaneous ignition of decomposing nitro-cellulose propellant, much of which was old and overdue for replacement, was the apparent cause. The ship might have been saved but the magazine flooding arrangements were inadequate. Four years earlier the battleship *Iéna* had also blown up for the same reason.[46] Against this background of incompetence and waste, a Parliamentary Commission investigated the French Navy and concluded that it needed expenditure of about £7.7 million to correct the deficiencies identified. In 1909 Admiral Boué de Lapeyrère was appointed Minister of Marine and proved a dynamic and effective administrator.[47]

British and French dispositions were reasonable until the first Mediterranean dreadnoughts appeared. Austria-Hungary was first with *Viribus Unitis*, completed in December 1912, and the other three in 1913, 1914 and 1915. Italy was next with *Dante Alighieri*, completed in January 1913, and the remainder after World War I had started. The first French dreadnoughts were *Jean Bart* and *Courbet*, laid down in 1911 and completed in June and November 1913 respectively. The second pair, *France* and *Paris*, were laid down in 1912 and were completed in July and August 1914. These were 22,000-ton ships, mounting twelve 30.5-cm (12-inch) guns. Three super-dreadnoughts – *Bretagne*, *Lorraine* and *Provence* – were laid down in 1912 and completed in 1915 and 1916. Armed with ten 34-cm (13.4-inch) guns, they corresponded to the British Iron Duke class.[48] By the 1912 period it was apparent that, in due course, seven Italian and four Austro-Hungarian dreadnoughts would face seven French dreadnoughts. At this point it became essential that Britain remain in the Mediterranean or Italy be extricated from the Triple Alliance.

By July 1912, in the wake of the Malta discussions, it was agreed in Cabinet that Britain should have dreadnoughts in the Mediterranean, equivalent to a one-power standard, excluding France.[49] In November 1912 Foreign Secretary Sir Edward Grey was writing to Paul Cambon, his French counterpart, to the effect that a strategic alignment existed between Britain and France in terms of fleets and their deployments, without necessarily a formal alliance. This was convenient for Grey and allowed him to claim that up to 1914 no alliance existed between Britain and France.[50] At the Admiralty it was agreed that the three Invincible class battlecruisers and *Indefatigable* should be transferred to the Mediterranean, when the ships of the 1909–10 and 1910–11 programmes had been completed. The battlecruiser *New Zealand* was completed in November 1912 and *Inflexible* was despatched to the Mediterranean in the same month. *Queen Mary* was completed in August 1913 and *Indomitable* went to the Mediterranean. *Invincible* and *Indefatigable* arrived in August and December 1913. In addition, four of the newer 23-knot armoured cruisers – *Defence, Black Prince, Duke of Edinburgh* and *Warrior* – were also sent to the Mediterranean.[51]

It is often forgotten that Britain obtained much of her food supply from the Mediterranean region. In May 1912 the Board of Trade pointed out that about one-sixth of Britain's wheat supply, five-sixths of barley, one-half of oats and two-ninths of maize imports came from the Black Sea region. One-sixth of Britain's raw cotton came from Egypt, one-seventh of manganiferous ore from Southern Russia and Greece and two-sevenths of other ores were shipped from Mediterranean ports. One-fifth of petroleum imports, both refined and lubricating, came from Russia and Roumania. About two-thirds of these commodities were carried in British ships. If the Mediterranean was abandoned, the huge volume of trade from the Far East and Australia would have to be diverted around the Cape, at enormous cost and inconvenience.[52]

Russia, Turkey, Greece and Spain

In the years before World War I the Russian Navy fell from third place in the world rankings to sixth. The humiliating defeats at the hands of the Japanese did permanent damage not only to her naval status but to society itself. One immediate effect was the formation of a Naval General Staff, and initially it was suggested that the Baltic and Far East fleets should be rebuilt. Russia now had a parliament (Duma) that would not vote funds for new ships. Then in 1908 the Bosnian crisis left Russia publicly humiliated by Germany and the Czar released 127 million roubles (about £13 million) for four Baltic dreadnoughts.[53] The *Gangut, Petropavlovsk, Poltava* and *Sevastopol* were 23,000-ton ships armed with twelve 30.5-cm (12-inch) guns mounted in four triple turrets. They were laid down in 1909 but not completed until 1914. The British John Brown shipyard gave a great deal of design assistance and the result was four ships capable of 23 knots. Three Black Sea dreadnoughts were built, *Imperatritsa Mariya, Volya* and *Imperatritsa Ekaterina Velikaya*. These were slightly smaller, slower versions of the Baltic ships, with the same armament.[54] The reality of Russia's permanently weakened Far East position ensured that no attempt was made to build a fleet to defeat Japan.

The Ottoman Empire was known throughout the nineteenth century as the 'sick man of Europe' and in 1908 the 'Young Turks' seized control. In the ensuing chaos other powers took the opportunity to appropriate Turkish territory. The Italian army seized Benghazi and Tripoli was annexed. In the two years of warfare that followed, the Turkish Navy played little part and proved powerless to prevent the capture of Turkey's Aegean islands, specifically Rhodes and the Dodecanese, by Greek and Italian forces. From the 1890s onwards Germany's influence at Constantinople steadily increased and in 1910 two old German Brandenburg class pre-dreadnoughts were purchased. The *Kurfürst Friedrich Wilhelm* and *Weissenburg* dated from 1891 and were renamed *Heireddin Barbarossa* and *Torgud Reis*. Wars with Greece pushed Turkey in the direction of dreadnoughts. In 1911 one was ordered from Vickers, the *Reshadieh*, a super-dreadnought armed with ten 13.5-inch guns. A second dreadnought building in Britain for Brazil, the *Rio de Janeiro*, was purchased on the stocks and renamed *Sultan Osman I*, but neither ship was ever delivered.[55] Both were completing in 1914 and were taken over by the Royal Navy.

The Greek Navy was sharply focused on the Turkish Navy, and her purchase of two pre-dreadnoughts from Germany prompted Greece to do the same. Two American pre-dreadnoughts were purchased, the *Mississippi* and *Idaho*, renamed *Kilkis* and *Limnos*. A Greek millionaire, Georgios Averof, left about £300,000 for improvements to the Greek Navy. The money went towards an armoured cruiser, purchased from the Italian shipyard; Orlando and Company of Leghorn. A single dreadnought was ordered from AG Vulkan of Hamburg, laid down in 1913 and launched in 1914. This ship, the *Salamis*, would have mounted eight 14-inch American guns which, owing to the outbreak of World War I, were never delivered. They went instead to Britain and armed some of the early monitors. It might be thought that a turbine-powered ship with a speed of 23 knots would have been of some use to the German Navy but this was not really the case. She would have been faster than any German dreadnought and slower than all German battlecruisers so just did not fit into the High Seas Fleet. Lengthy litigation ensued after the war, with the Greeks refusing to pay for an incomplete ship. *Salamis* was finally broken up in 1932.[56] A second dreadnought, *Vasilefs Konstantinos*, was proposed but never went beyond the planning stage.

The final Mediterranean navy was that of Spain. In the Spanish-American War the Spanish Navy had been heavily defeated and recovery was very slow. In 1908 a navy law was passed which ensured that a great deal of technical assistance was obtained from Armstrong's and John Brown. Three 15,000-ton dreadnought battleships, three destroyers and 24 torpedo-boats were planned, with Armstrong's heavily involved in the design. At 15,452 tons and only 435 feet in length, these battleships were the smallest, weakest dreadnoughts of any nation. They mounted eight 12-inch guns disposed as in the British Invincible class battlecruisers. When completed in 1913–15 they were completely outclassed by the super-dreadnoughts completing in Britain and Germany. Spain was the only European power to build dreadnoughts and remain neutral in World War I.

The Second Morocco Crisis: Agadir and the Anglo-French Response

The second Morocco crisis was in some respects the result of the 1906 Algeciras conference. In 1911 local opposition to French rule resulted in a full-scale Moroccan revolt. By April 1911 the Sultan was besieged in his palace at Fez and the French were prepared to send in troops to quell the rebellion. Technically this was against the terms of the Algeciras agreement and Germany would not allow any modification to the agreement without some form of compensation. In July 1911 the Germans ordered the gunboat *Panther* to Agadir, notionally to defend German nationals and interests. Since there were no German subjects at Agadir and the port was closed to Europeans, the real agenda was to reopen the whole Morocco question. Leaving aside the financial intrigue and the tangled web of deceit that constituted Moroccan affairs before 1914, Germany hoped to break the triple *entente* of Britain, France and Russia and they were quite prepared to use shock tactics to obtain their objectives.

By July 1911, realising that *entente* opinion was against them, the Germans informed the French government that they would accept the French protectorate in Morocco in return for further territorial concessions in the French Congo. Britain was pledged to support France and her policy in Morocco but would not interfere in any reasonable accommodation between France and Germany over African colonial boundaries. Britain's reply came on 21 July 1911 in the form of David Lloyd George's Mansion House speech. He delivered a stern warning:

> I believe it is essential in the highest interests, not merely of this country, but of the world, that Britain should at all hazards maintain her place and her

prestige amongst the Great Powers of the world [...] I would make great sacrifices to preserve peace [...] But if a situation were to be forced upon us in which peace could only be preserved by the surrender of the great and beneficent position Britain has won by centuries of heroism and achievement [...] then I say emphatically that peace at that price would be a humiliation intolerable for a great country like ours to endure.[57]

Negotiations started on 9 July and by 4 November an agreement known as the treaty of Fez had been hammered out. Germany accepted France's position in Morocco in return for territory in the French Congo. About 275,000 km² of formally French territory were joined to the German Cameroons. British backing for France during the crisis reinforced the *entente* between the two countries and also relations with Russia. The problem was that the divisions between the two power blocs, the now *triple entente* and the German *triplice*, deepened perceptibly. Another step down the road to war had been taken.

The British Attempts at a Naval Settlement with Germany

Not all Germans in high places supported fleet building. One such man was Count Paul Von Wolff-Metternich who became ambassador in London in 1901 and remained until dismissed in 1912. After the Tweedmouth affair and the *Daily Telegraph* letter, it was obvious that any attempt at dealing directly with the Kaiser was fraught with difficulty. Indirect methods were tried and Metternich was the central figure in the attempts at a diplomatic approach. It was carefully explained to him by a succession of British ministers that continued expansion of the German Fleet would meet with a large increase in the British naval estimates. Transcripts of these conversations were all relayed to Berlin, read by the Kaiser, heavily annotated by him and the contents ignored.

Sir Edward Grey then tried another approach. Perhaps an informal discussion between two leading businessmen might open up lines of communication. In contemporary parlance these would be 'talks about talks'. Sir Ernest Cassal was chosen, as a close personal friend of Albert Ballin, the Managing Director of the Hamburg-Amerika shipping line. Ballin knew the Kaiser well and was approached and asked if information on German fleet building might be forthcoming. The German view was that any suggestion of limitation on her armaments was an insult to her sovereignty and a *casus belli* in itself. For his part Ballin wanted discussions between naval experts without reference to the 'political sphere', but the German Foreign Office would not separate the naval issues from the political. A tentative proposal was made for new dreadnought construction at 3:4 in Britain's favour.[58] This was greatly to Germany's advantage; she kept her 1909–10 programme and the British 'eight' of 1909–10 would be cut to four. These proposals were abandoned during the two British general elections of 1910.

Tirpitz was badly shaken by the huge British programme of 1909–10 and was more open to suggestion than before. He seemed ready to accept a simultaneous exchange of information and a one-year limitation on new construction based on information exchanged.[59] This information would all be technical; ship dimensions, armament etc. The idea of informal conversations concerning naval programmes was revived and again it was Cassel and Ballin who acted as intermediaries. Eventually a meeting was arranged between the British War Minister, Viscount Haldane and the German Chancellor. Haldane arrived in Berlin in January 1912 and it became clear from his first conversation with Bethmann-Hollweg that the price of an agreement on naval matters was British neutrality in any future European war. This was too high a price to pay for a naval agreement but it did illustrate the different thinking of the British and German governments. For the Germans, a political agreement was a pre-condition of any naval agreement, while for the British a naval agreement was a pre-condition for any political settlement.[60]

The result of the failed diplomacy with Germany came down to the fact that Germany did not want an agreement. Every diplomatic overture was met with rebuff. Metternich, increasingly isolated by his warnings to Berlin, was eventually dismissed. If Metternich objected to any of the naval attaché's reports of Korvettenkapitän Widenmann, he complained to Tirpitz and Tirpitz took the complaints to the Kaiser. Even rejected reports would then be called forth and presented to the Kaiser, who always supported them. The diplomacy of the German embassy in London became subverted by a naval attaché who was at variance with the ambassador. The military and naval commanders had direct access to the Kaiser; civilians, even those who held the great offices of state, had no such easy access. When Metternich fell out with the Kaiser, he was described as a 'civilian', much affected by the 'dear English' and 'absolutely unteachable on naval questions'.[61] The British tried other avenues of approach. Exchanges of information were proposed, as were offers of a naval building holiday, but both were taken as signs of British exhaustion in the face of German expansionism.

Much of the problem lay with the Kaiser himself. After the *Daily Telegraph* affair his behaviour became, in the words of a distinguished historian of this period, 'autistic', with increasingly irrational outbursts.[62] In 1912 Sir Edward Grey remarked: 'The German Kaiser is aging me; he is like a battleship with steam up and screws going, but with no rudder, and he will run into something some day and cause a catastrophe.'[63] Lord Haldane recorded that in attempting to arrive at a naval settlement he had experienced nothing but chaos at the top of the German government.[64] Haldane was not helped when, during his time in Berlin, the young Winston Churchill, in a major speech, said that 'from some points of view the German Navy is to them more in the nature of a luxury'.[65] The German word *Luxus* has unfortunate connotations. Then came the third *novelle* which added an extra battleship to each second year's building programme.

Churchill introduced the naval estimates on 18 March 1912 and answered the 1911 supplement to German Navy Law. If Germany laid down two battleships a year, then Britain would add four ships and three ships each alternate year. This would give Britain 60 per cent superiority in capital ships. If the supplement to German Navy Law meant two additional ships, Britain would lay down another four; three additional ships and Britain would lay down six. Churchill then proposed a 'naval holiday'. If Germany gave up her three ships for 1912, Britain would give up her proposed five for 1912, more than the German Navy could ever hope to sink in battle with their three. This idea was greeted with scorn in Germany – 'only possible between allies', commented the Kaiser.[66] In other words, the price of a naval agreement was no longer neutrality but actual alliance with Germany. As for the five British ships on offer, they were the Queen Elizabeth class, the most successful tactical group of battleships built by any nation. They served through both world wars, were the backbone of the British Fleet between the wars and on one of these ships, the *Queen Elizabeth*, David Beatty took the surrender of Germany's High Seas Fleet in 1918.

The two-power standard was discussed in Chapter 1 and apparently laid to rest by Winston Churchill in March 1914 and with it Tory insistence that naval strength should always be related to the two next strongest naval powers, regardless of relations with those powers. Churchill summarised the history of the two-power standard from 1889 onwards, then continued:

Formerly we have followed the two-power standard. The next two strongest powers, if you take the whole world, would be Germany and the United States, and if you left out the United States, as common sense would dictate, the next two strongest powers would be Germany and France, which is not a very helpful and reasonable standard to adopt [. . .] the 60 per cent standard (60% over Germany) was adopted by the Admiralty in 1908 or 1909.[67]

Exactly how far the 60 per cent rule moved from the two-power standard is difficult to assess. In December 1914 Britain had completed 32 dreadnought battleships and battlecruisers, Germany 22 and the United States ten, placing Britain exactly on a two-power standard. It is also the case that 32 British dreadnoughts to 22 German is close to the 60 per cent over Germany ratio of naval strength.

The Balkan Wars 1912–14

It is unnecessary to detail the exact sequence of events in the three Balkan wars. The central problem for the Great Powers was how to prevent the spread of the fighting and to hold the ring containing the battlefield. German influence in Vienna and Franco-British influence in Moscow could help to hold the ring. Co-operation between Germany, Britain and France was good. A peace conference was held in London, chaired by the Foreign Secretary, Sir Edward Grey. The German chancellor Bethmann-Hollweg thought that an Anglo-German agreement on the Balkans was worth any amount of naval agreements. The real truth is that relations between Russia and Austria were strained to breaking point over Bulgarian defeats and Germany became convinced that in the coming 'world historical decision' Britain would support the Gallic and Slav peoples against Germany.[68]

The Balkan wars again showed just how autocratic the Kaiser had become and the extent to which he distrusted civilians. A good example of this was the notorious meeting of December 1912, held against the deepening crisis in the Balkans. Initially the Kaiser's reaction was surprisingly peaceful but news from London suggested that Britain would not stay out of a European conflict involving France. In the view of the Kaiser, Britain's anti-German stance demanded action. He invited his military and naval advisors to a meeting and the Chief of the General Staff Helmuth von Moltke argued that war was inevitable, and advocated it as soon as possible. Admiral Tirpitz argued that war should be postponed for about 18 months until the navy was more fully prepared. Very reluctantly, the more bellicose participants at the meeting agreed to the delay. This meeting is a good example of how civilian input was excluded from military and political decision making in Imperial Germany. The responsible politicians, including the Chancellor, were merely informed that this war council meeting had taken place.[69]

The Balkan wars had a hidden influence on German defence policy. These wars showed very clearly that Germany needed a strong army and re-established the army as the dominant force in German defence spending. In 1911 the German Navy received 54.8 per cent of the army outlay; in 1912 it fell to 49.4 per cent and 32.7 per cent in 1913. Tirpitz paid a heavy price for the third *novelle* and Reich support for fleet building fell away rapidly. For Germany, the cost of a navy had become financially crippling. In 1905–6 German spent 233.4 million Goldmarks (£11.404 million) on her navy, up to 478.963 million Goldmarks (£23.44 million), by 1914, a rise of 105 per cent in nine years. Over the same period the British naval estimates increased by only 39 per cent.[70] It was the same story with unit costs per ship. The *Dreadnought* cost £1.783 million, *Bellerophon* £1.765 million and *St Vincent* £1.754 million, a net reduction of 1.6 per cent. By contrast the Nassaus cost 38.399 million Goldmarks (£1.86 million), Helgolands 46.196 million Goldmarks (£2.26 million) and Kaisers 44.997 million Goldmarks (£2.2 million), a 17.2 per cent rise in three years. The situation was worse for the battlecruisers, which saw a huge increase from 36.523 million Goldmarks (£1.78 million) for *Von der Tann* to 56 million Goldmarks (£2.74 million) for *Derfflinger*, an increase of 53.3 per cent in four years. The similar British figures show a cost of £1.67 million for *Invincible* to £2.08 million for *Lion*, a much smaller increase of 24.6 per cent over five years.[71]

Perspectives: Tirpitz Admits Defeat

By 1912, the cost of German naval building programmes had become ruinous, hence the Reichstag's reluctance to continue with large building programmes. In 1913 Tirpitz at last agreed that the German Admiralty would accept a relationship of 16:10 in dreadnoughts between Britain and Germany. Tirpitz put this in terms of squadrons at 8:5. Churchill pointed out that as the pre-dreadnoughts became obsolete, to maintain this ratio in dreadnoughts Britain must lay down two hulls to one for each German supplementary law ship. The naval estimates for 1913–14 were brought before the House of Commons on 26 March 1913. They provided for five battleships, eight light cruisers, 16 destroyers and 7,000 extra men. There was an overall increase in naval expenditure of £1.3 million and it was decided that the 60 per cent rule did not apply to the Australian and New Zealand battlecruisers.[72] The option was left open that in the years ahead Britain might increase her programme still further as the pre-dreadnoughts became obsolete. Churchill again suggested a 'naval holiday' with no ships laid down by either party for an entire fiscal year. The French did not like the idea of a naval holiday; they thought, probably correctly, that Germany would devote the saved money to her army.

From 1912 Britain's dreadnought and super-dreadnought navy was concentrated in the North Sea and it was here that the fate of Britain and its dominions and colonies would be decided. In March 1914 the naval estimates were discussed and four new battleships were projected. With the big programmes of 1910–14 the 60 per cent rule was firmly established. In the 14 years since 1900 the Tirpitz-defined 'danger zone' had not yet been passed. The notorious 'Risk Theory' had failed. Tirpitz had counted on French and Russian hostility to Britain to keep the British Fleet weak at home. This had not happened, and Britain had actually joined with France and Russia to defeat German intentions.

9

World War I to Jutland

Prelude: 1914

On 24 June 1914 Germany's High Seas Fleet gathered in review order in the roadstead of Kiel. In his yacht *Hohenzollern*, the Kaiser made a stately progress through the cheering crowds on the banks of the newly modernised Kiel Canal, *Hohenzollern* becoming the first ship to enter the newly completed locks at the eastern end. The last obstacle to the full deployment of Germany's naval might between the North Sea and the Baltic was swept away and she was ready to challenge Britain in her own element. Also present were four British super-dreadnoughts, looking menacing in their dark grey paint, to remind him that the Royal Navy stood between him and his goal. Into the frenetic round of yacht racing by day and banqueting by night there came news of the assassination of Franz Ferdinand. Public entertainments were cancelled and the Kaiser departed for Vienna. As the British squadron sailed away on 30 June, Admiral Sir George Warrender signalled, 'Friends in the past; friends for ever'.[1]

After the display of Germany's naval might at Kiel it was Britain's turn. On 15 July Britain's three fleets gathered at Spithead. This was much more than a mere review; it was a full test mobilisation. Including the pre-dreadnoughts still in commission, there were 57 battleships and battle-cruisers present. The First Fleet contained all the first-line vessels; the dreadnought battleships and battlecruisers. This was the main naval force kept fully crewed and trained in time of peace. The Second Fleet consisted of ships staffed by a proportion of their crews, sufficient to keep the machinery and armament in good order. It was capable of going to sea for short periods and exercising a proportion of its armament at a time. Then there was the Third or Reserve Fleet, looked after by small care and maintenance parties who kept the machinery and armament in a state of preservation. For the review a test mobilisation had been ordered and the Second and Third Fleets were fully manned. On 20 July, the King arrived onboard the Royal Yacht *Victoria and Albert*. He received the usual homage of the fleet to royalty, the inevitable gun salutes and cheers. The *Victoria and Albert* then steamed seawards and dropped anchor near the Nab lighthouse. There, the King stood and watched as the great armada put to sea. Squadron after squadron steamed past in stately array and faded out of sight into the Channel haze. The three fleets began their four-day programme of manoeuvres and battle practice, at the end of which they were to disperse, the First Fleet for 'flag showing' cruises, the Second and Third to their home ports to release their reservists and revert to second line status.

In Whitehall the atmosphere of crisis deepened as the month of July passed. Asquith's Liberal government hoped for peace and that Britain would not be drawn into the war. The test mobilisation of the three fleets gave Britain an opportunity for war readiness not to be lightly thrown away. On 27 July orders went out to Admiral Sir George Callaghan, commanding the First Fleet, to keep all his ships concentrated at Portland until further notice. On 29 July, with the European situation worsening by the hour, the First Fleet sailed from Portland for a destination unknown outside a small circle of naval officers and Admiralty officials. The unknown destination lay in the Orkneys. The First Fleet, now given the more glamorous title of the Grand Fleet, soon reached its war base: Scapa Flow.[2]

On 27 July, after four weeks of threats, counter-threats, entreaties, offers, negotiations, denials, warnings and ultimatums, Austria declared war on Serbia. On 30 July Russia ordered general mobilisation. On 31 July Austria and Germany followed suit. On 1 August Germany declared war on Russia and demanded to know what France's attitude would be in the event of a Russo-German war. France replied that she would act in her best interests and ordered general mobilisation. On 3 August Germany declared war on France and demanded passage through Belgium for her armies; Belgium refused the demand. Germany declared war on France and her armies entered Belgium. Britain, as a guarantor of Belgian neutrality, required that Germany withdrew her armies from Belgium at once. An ultimatum was delivered to Germany, due to expire at 2300 hours on 4 August. It was 60 years since Britain had taken part in a European war – the Crimean War against Russia. It was 99 years since Britain had contemplated the deployment of her armies in north-western Europe.

Strategic Realities in 1914

The Royal Navy that developed after 1889 was indeed a battle-fleet navy, but designed for blockade warfare in an age without convoy. The rejection of convoy as the primary means of trade defence in wartime was the hidden influence that drove the Royal Navy in the direction of a large battle fleet able to defend trade by locking up an adversary's warships in their home ports at the start of a naval war. The fighting of big battles was not the primary function of the battle-fleet navy; the primary function was blockade.

The establishment of the Naval War Staff in 1912 ensured that any idea of close blockade was finally abandoned and an intermediate blockade substituted. Naval exercises showed the weakness of an intermediate blockade and in 1913 Captain Ballard suggested a distant blockade across the Orkney–Norway gap, with light (flotilla) forces guarding the Straits of Dover. The northern blockade would be upheld by the main British fleet in a Scottish base. As a blockade strategy this was perfectly reasonable in the context of 1914, though it took time to make it work effectively.[3] Britain can be considered a gigantic breakwater across the approaches to Germany. With their battle fleet based in the Orkney Islands, well to the north of Scotland, and sufficient naval forces to hold the Straits of Dover, the British held the keys to the North Sea gates.[4]

By contrast, if the German geographic position was offensively weak it was an ideal defensive position. Their determined mining activities soon made the Heligoland and Fresian coasts inaccessible to the British. Indeed, on the grounds of geography and mining it is easy to see why the battle-fleet war of 1914–18 was so defensive. Nevertheless, in the autumn of 1914 the British position of geographical advantage was severely compromised by the lack of a fortified North Sea base or even a defended anchorage. The Rosyth dockyard was not useable until 1916 and the fleet anchorages at Scapa Flow and Cromarty were not in any sense protected until November 1914. As a result, the Grand Fleet was forced to withdraw to Loch Ewe and then to Loch Swilly. This withdrawal to north-west Scotland and Northern Ireland gave the Germans an unexpected bonus. On 27 October 1914 the super-dreadnought *Audacious* struck a mine 28 miles from Lough Swilly and sank. Not surprisingly the dangers of mines and submarines weighed heavily on Admiral Sir John Jellicoe, the Grand Fleet's Commander-in-Chief.

Three days later Jellicoe wrote to the Admiralty and stated clearly his preferred method of defeating the High Seas Fleet. In view of what he considered to be Germany's reliance on submarines, mines and torpedoes, he felt it was only safe to fight in the northern reaches of the North Sea, the southern parts being far too dangerous. He also felt that a retreating German Fleet would lead him over mines and submarines so he would not follow.[5] The prospect of mines, submarines and torpedoes had forced Jellicoe onto the defensive.

If Jellicoe's tactics were defensive, it is equally the case that Germany's High Seas Fleet was not inclined to put in an appearance. It is surprising that they made no attempt to interfere with the deployment of the British Army in north-western France. Breaking the *entente* between Britain and France had been a primary objective of German foreign policy since the first Morocco crisis in 1905. With the policy of distant blockade established there were a number of minor naval actions in the period 1914–15.

British and German Stratagems 1914–15

In 1914 both the Foreign Office and the Admiralty were deeply concerned about Turkey and her attitude towards Britain and Germany. With the building of the Berlin to Bhagdad railway and direct communications between Berlin and Constantinople, Turkey was gradually drawn into the German sphere of influence.

The Turks were outraged by the British seizure of two battleships building for Turkey and Germany stepped into the breach with the offer of the battlecruiser *Goeben* and the light cruiser *Breslau*. The escape of the *Goeben* to Turkey, arguably due to British cack-handedness, caused the Royal Navy a major headache in the eastern Mediterranean that lasted throughout World War I. It was an inauspicious start to the war. Then the action switched to the North Sea.

In August 1914 Commodore Tyrwhitt's Harwich Force of light cruisers sortied into the Heligoland Bight but were badly mauled by German light cruisers. Admiral Beatty took his battlecruisers deep into the Bight and the Germans suffered a defeat with three light cruisers sunk – *Koln*, *Mainz* and *Ariadne* – and three heavily damaged. Just over 1,000 Germans were killed, and this included the flotilla admiral and the destroyer commodore.[6] The British press hailed the action as a great victory, while in Berlin the Kaiser was furious at the loss of his precious ships.

Less than a month later, on 20 September, the sinking of the German light cruisers was avenged in the Broad Fourteens with the sinking of three British armoured cruisers by one small submarine. The three old armoured cruisers were *Aboukir, Cressy* and *Hogue*; all dating from the 1899 period and nicknamed the 'live-bait' squadron by the Grand Fleet. Their intended purpose was to provide early warning in case of a German attack on the Channel transports.[7] As patrol cruisers they were of little use and had failed even to zig-zag, hence the ease with which they were sunk. The loss of life, which stood at some 1,400, was terrible.

The escape of the *Goeben* and the loss of these three cruisers and various other patrol cruisers, combined with the apparent stalemate between the British and German navies, appeared unsatisfactory in the extreme and much of the blame fell quite unfairly on the First Sea Lord, Prince Louis of Battenberg. His German ancestry was blamed for a lackadaisical approach to resolving the problems of the naval war. He resigned and Churchill decided to bring Fisher back as First Sea Lord even through he was 73 years old.

Fisher resumed his old position on 30 October. The battle of Coronel was fought and lost on 1 November. Fisher reacted with commendable speed and the battlecruiser *Princess Royal* was despatched to the West Indies in case Von Spee decided to attempt a run for home through the newly completed Panama Canal. Two of the older battlecruisers, *Invincible* and *Inflexible*, were dispatched south to the Falkland Islands.

The battles at Coronel and the Falklands were one-sided gunnery duels, the first with overwhelming gunnery advantage to the Germans and the second overwhelmingly to the British. The casemate mounted 6-inch guns of *Good Hope* and *Monmouth* could not be worked easily in a seaway, which ensured that the British had just two 9.2-inch guns and four 6-inch guns against sixteen 21-cm (8.2-inch) guns on *Scharnhorst* and *Gneisnau*. Not surprisingly, the British ships were hammered into oblivion, though the German ships used above 50 per cent of their ammunition. The presence of the pre-dreadnought battleship *Canopus* would hardly have made a difference; her 1897 vintage guns had a range only minimally greater than the guns of *Scharnhorst* and *Gneisnau* (14,000 yards as opposed to 13,500 for the German ships). If anything her armour was inferior to that of the German ships.[8] The Falkland Islands battle, fought on 8 December 1914, was a substantial success for the British, with the *Scharnhorst* and *Gneisnau* dispatched in much the same way as the British cruisers at Coronel. The important lesson of the battle was the comparatively enormous number of 12-inch calibre shells needed to achieve this result – 1,174 rounds, of which 285 were armour piercing. British fire control was inadequate and someone might have surmised that the shells in use were not up to the mark, particularly against the lightly armoured German cruisers.[9]

For the Germans in the North Sea the problem was finding a method of bringing a portion of the British Fleet to action under conditions of local German superiority. The British must be persuaded to split their forces and hopefully an isolated portion of the Grand Fleet would meet the German Fleet and be destroyed. After two or three such encounters, with near parity or perhaps actual supremacy, the High Seas Fleet could win a decisive naval battle against the British.

In November 1914 the strategy designed to split the British Fleet was initiated and three German battlecruisers arrived off Great Yarmouth bombarding the town with 11- and 12-inch shells. In December the Germans tried again and on this occasion bombarded Scarborough, Hartlepool and Whitby. Almost at the start of the war the German light cruiser *Magdeburg* had been sunk in the Baltic. The Russians had salvaged the code books and given them to the British. As a result, for the first time wireless signal intelligence derived from the work of Room 40 at the Admiralty was able to give warning of the next raid, though not of its composition. In fact it consisted of *Seydlitz, Moltke, Von der Tann, Derfflinger* and *Blücher*.[10] What Room 40 did not know was that the entire High Seas Fleet was to be at sea in support of the battlecruisers. The Admiralty ordered the Second Battle Squadron to support the battlecruisers. At dawn on 16 December the two forces met off the Dogger Bank. The Germans had apparently achieved their ultimate goal, the High Seas Fleet had caught an isolated British squadron but, believing the force to be the entire Grand Fleet, turned for home. The position was now reversed, with the British within striking distance of catching the German battlecruisers at a massive disadvantage. The German battlecruisers bombarded Scarborough, Hartlepool and Whitby but in wild December weather the British failed to catch the German battlecruisers.

The 'tip and run' raids on the east coast produced a predictable outcry on the lines of 'What is the Navy doing about it?', calculated to pressurise Jellicoe into splitting his forces, and it worked. On 20 December the battlecruiser force was moved from Cromarty to Rosyth. It can be argued that the establishment of the battlecruisers as an independent fleet command was a mistake.

On 23 January Room 40 picked up a cipher signal authorising Vice-Admiral Von Hipper to reconnoitre the Dogger Bank area. There was just time to get Beatty's battlecruisers to sea and in a position to intercept at dawn the next day. This force, with accompanying light cruisers, would be positioned only 10 miles East of Hipper's expected position at dawn and would hopefully interpose the British forces between Hipper and his route home.

In the ensuing battle the armoured cruiser *Blücher* was sunk and the picture of her upside down and sinking was published in the *Daily Mail*, laying claim to a British victory but signalling errors on the British side that had allowed the German battlecruisers to escape. This was the first naval action of the 1914–18 war in which both sides had their capital ships in action against each other and it is worth analysis, particularly in view of subsequent events at Jutland. The *Blücher*, an armoured cruiser, was completely out-classed by the battlecruisers but she withstood severe punishment for three hours, sustaining 50 hits from heavy guns and two torpedo hits. This was not so much a tribute to her builders as a comment on the defective nature of British shells, which tended to break up on impact.

The German battlecruiser *Seydlitz* was very badly damaged in the Dogger Bank action and 62 complete 28-cm (11-inch) charges ignited and burnt. The same thing happened to the *Derfflinger* at Jutland and in both cases the aft turrets were burnt out but the ships were saved. There can be no question that had the German Navy used British-style Vaseline stabilised cordite, *Seydlitz* and *Derfflinger* would have blown up in the manner of the three British battlecruisers at Jutland. As it was, the cordite fire onboard *Seydlitz* spread to the turret ammunition handling rooms and only prompt flooding of the magazines saved her from blowing up. It has been wrongly stated time and time again that as a result of the fire in the after turrets of the *Seydlitz*, the German's introduced new flash precautions before Jutland. This is not in fact the case; no constructional changes were made to their ships but the number of charges out of their magazine cases at a moment in time was drastically curtailed.[11] Finally, mention must be made of the relative gunnery performance at the Dogger Bank. Leaving aside the *Blücher*, British battlecruisers received 22 hits and scored only six on comparable German ships.[12] It was an ominous note that presaged ill for the future.

In Berlin the Kaiser was furious; the *Blücher* had been sunk and *Seydlitz* was very badly damaged. The German Commander-in-Chief Admiral Von

Ingenohl was replaced by Admiral Von Pohl, the former Chief of Naval Staff. If anything, Von Pohl was more defensive than Von Ingenohl.

The Great Strategic Flanking Options: The Baltic and the Dardanelles

By a long measure, the proposed Baltic operations were the most controversial part of Fisher's plan to end the war with a strategic flanking operation. His thinking was by no means as unique or as mad as some have suggested. Sir Julian Corbett, drawing on historical examples from the eighteenth century, believed in amphibious flank operations, effectively exploiting the mobility given by sea power. In November 1914 Fisher submitted a four-page paper, prepared in collaboration with Corbett, which made the general case for the Baltic enterprise.[13] Churchill supported the idea but by 29 December War Council opinion was shifting in favour of a strategic flanking operation not in the north but in the south: the Dardanelles.

On 3 January 1915 Fisher and Maurice Hankey submitted a plan to use pre-dreadnought battleships for bombardment purposes against the Dardanelles forts. Allied forces including Greece, Bulgaria and Russia would go for Gallipoli and Constantinople. The plan had one huge defect; it assumed that these neutral countries would come in on the allied side. Churchill did not reject the plan in its entirety; rather he seized on the idea of a navy-only operation using old battleships and sold the idea to the War Council. This proposal was fatally flawed but Fisher initially backed it, and so was born the Gallipoli tragedy.[14]

At this time Vice-Admiral Oliver had taken over as Director of the Operations Division. Oliver recorded the arguments concerning strategy that took place at this time.

> Wilson wanted to bombard Heligoland with the old pre-Dreadnought battleships and land and capture it; our old ships with their short 12-inch guns would have stood little chance against the modern guns of shore batteries. If captured, every time supplies were required would involve a major operation for the Grand Fleet in the minefields, and the island was within gun range of the mainland. 'I hated all these projects but had to be careful what I said. The saving clause was that two of the three were always violently opposed to the plan of the third under discussion. I was glad when the Dardanelles project came along as it took the old battleships out of the North Sea picture'.[15]

Rarely can such specious arguments have past muster as strategic planning. Fisher seems to have gone cold on the Dardanelles project between 13 and 28 January and realised the strategic flaws in the plan with the inevitable draining away of resources from the North Sea, which was, after all, the decisive theatre.[16] Before the War Council meeting on 28 January Fisher stated his objections to the prime minister, Asquith. At this point old age and strain set in. At the age of 74 he was not really capable of a 14-hour day and flagged by the evening when his political head, Churchill, was just getting his second wind. It was against this background of physical and mental exhaustion that Fisher surrendered to Churchill and Asquith.

The resultant Dardanelles campaign and Gallipoli ended the career of Jacky Fisher and came within a whisker of destroying Churchill's. In the case of Fisher, back in 1906 he was writing to the then First Lord of the Admiralty, Lord Tweedmouth and arguing against any sort of Dardanelles operation.

> The forcing of the Dardanelles is in the first place, a military operation [...] with the altered conditions of German supervision and German handling of the Dardanelles defences, and German mines and German torpedoes, I agree with Sir John French that we cannot now repeat [Admiral] Sir Geoffrey Hornby's passage of the Dardanelles [1878], and even if we get passage, there is the getting back, as [Admiral] Sir John Duckworth found to his cost [1807].[17]

In 1907 the Army General Staff had considered Dardanelles and Gallipoli operations and concluded that they were fraught with difficulty. The failure of the Dardanelles was the price paid for the late acceptance of the idea of a Naval Staff, only established in 1912. In arguments about ships versus forts the advantage is always with the fort. A gun emplacement needs a direct hit to knock it out and this represents a very small target for a ship to hit. The shore gun has a large ship target, some hundreds of feet in length to aim at. On shore the gunners have a fixed platform for observation and spotting the fall of shot is easy. Ships either cannot spot the fall of shot or require flank spotters to assist. Battleship guns are large-calibre flat-trajectory weapons unsuited to bombard forts. Most had a gun elevation of 13.5 degrees with the maximum in any ship at 20 degrees. In the guns versus forts argument, Churchill and the Dardanelles enthusiasts assumed that, because large German guns had reduced the Belgium forts at Namur and

Liege, the same thing would happen at the Dardanelles, but the German guns used for bombardment were Howitzers, high elevation weapons, not flat trajectory naval guns.[18] Then there were the minefields; these proved impossible to sweep when the minesweepers were under fire and a small minefield went undetected, which accounted for three battleships in one day. The pre-dreadnoughts were expendable, but the loss of a total of six in the Dardanelles operations was a heavy price to pay.

Fisher proved to be a better strategist than Churchill and the other Dardanelles enthusiasts, yet his contempt for the Naval War Staff and his own advocacy of Baltic and other amphibious enterprises laid much of the ground for the Dardanelles disaster.[19] It is unnecessary to give a blow-by-blow account of the disastrous end of the Churchill–Fisher Board of the Admiralty. By 20 May Fisher's resignation had been accepted and he had been replaced by Sir Henry Jackson. Churchill lingered in government as Chancellor of the Duchy of Lancaster, a non-Cabinet post accurately described by Anthony Trollope as a fainéant office.[20]

In retrospect, Fisher was far too old for the position of First Sea Lord. He was the only man of any nation to fight in both the Crimean War and World War I. Fisher, like Churchill, also lingered in Whitehall, as Chairman of the Board of Invention and Research, aptly nicknamed the Board of Intrigue and Revenge. He attempted in vain to get back into high office but this never happened. He died in 1920 and thus passed John 'Jacky' Fisher, 'Radical' Jack Fisher, Admiral of the Fleet Sir John Fisher, First Earl of Kilverstone, the Dark Angel of the Navy.

The First and Second U-boat Campaigns, 1914–16

In October 1914 a British merchant vessel, the 866-ton steamer *Glitra*, was boarded and sunk by the German submarine U-17, commanded by Lieutenant-Commander Feldkircher. The crew were given time to escape in small boats before the boarding party opened the sea-cocks.[21]

Under international law decided at the Hague Conferences of 1899 and 1907 a belligerent warship was supposed to ascertain the identity of the vessel under attack and make adequate provision for the safety of the crew and passengers, and indeed this is what happened to *Glitra*.[22] At the outbreak of war both Britain and Germany stated that the rules of naval warfare as laid down in the 1909 Declaration of London applied to the conflict but subsequent modifications eventually rendered the Declaration worthless. The Declaration had established comprehensive classifications of absolute and conditional contraband. Absolute contraband included arms, munitions, chemicals and certain types of machinery, all of which could be used for war purposes. Provisional contraband included foodstuffs and livestock feed. It could also include soap, paper, clocks and agricultural machinery. The British blockade of Germany was unusually restrictive and by 1916 conditional and provisional contraband included nearly all waterborne cargo bound for Germany.[23]

In early November 1914 Britain declared the North Sea to be a war zone, with merchant ships entering it entirely at their own risk. The only way Germany could blockade Britain was by use of U-boats. In the first weeks of the war it was apparent that the submarine was now a very serious factor in naval warfare.

On 2 February 1915 Germany published a notice warning against neutral shipping approaching the British coast. Two days later, on 4 February, Admiral Hugo Von Pohl, commander of the German High Seas Fleet, published a warning in the *Deutscher Reichsanzeiger* (*Imperial German Gazette*):

1. The waters around Great Britain and Ireland, including the whole of the English Channel, are hereby declared to be a war zone. From February 18 onwards every enemy merchant vessel encountered in this zone will be destroyed, nor will it always be possible to avert the danger thereby threatened to the crew and passengers.
2. Neutral vessels will also run a risk in the War Zone, because in view of the hazards of sea warfare and the British authorisation of January 31 of the misuse of neutral flags, it may not always be possible to prevent attacks on enemy ships from harming neutral ships.[24]

The British blockade resulted in a vast disruption of neutral rights of trade and this caused increasingly fraught relations with the United States. Between August and December 1914, 312,672 tons of merchant shipping was destroyed by U-boats. This increased markedly in 1915, with 47,981 tons destroyed in January, 59,921 in February and 80,775 in March.[25] On 28 March 1915, the passenger ship *Falaba* was torpedoed and sunk by U-28, close to the Coningbeg Light Vessel, at the entrance to the St Georges Channel.[26] One hundred and four people were killed, including an American engineer, Leon Chester Thrasher. The Americans protested and the *Falaba* sinking became known in America as the 'Thrasher' incident. Exactly 40 days later, on 7 May 1915, the Cunard liner *Lusitania* was torpedoed off the Irish coast, close to the Old Head of Kinsale, by U-20, commanded by Kapitanleutnant Walther Schweiger. There were 1,600 passengers onboard, of whom 1,198 died as a result of the attack. Of the crew of 1,100 only 28 lost their lives, but 128 American citizens were killed. The Germans tried to justify the sinking with a range of arguments, but the sense of outrage in both Britain and America was massive. Prior to the sinking, on 23 April, the German Embassy published an advertisement in the New York papers stating that the waters around Britain were a war zone, that vessels flying the British flag were liable to be attacked and that passengers on British flag vessels travelled at their own risk.[27] Schweiger claimed that he had seen two twin-funnelled steamers but this is contradicted by his log which stated that at 1430 hours, 'Sight dead ahead four funnels and two masts of a steamer steering straight for us [...] Ship identified as a large passenger steamer'.[28] *Lusitania* was torpedoed from a range of just 700 metres.

At the start of Germany's U-boat campaign US President Woodrow Wilson had warned the German government that they would be held responsible for any violation of American neutral rights. Six days after the sinking Wilson affirmed the right of Americans to travel on passenger vessels and called for the abandonment of submarine warfare against merchant vessels. In a second diplomatic note of 9 June Wilson rejected the German arguments that the British blockade was illegal and stated that the German attack on *Lusitania* was a cruel and deadly attack on innocent civilians. In a third note of 21 July Wilson issued an ultimatum to the effect that any subsequent sinking was 'deliberately unfriendly'. America was not yet ready for war but was set on the course for war by the *Lusitania* sinking.[29] A great deal has been written about the *Lusitania* and her untimely demise. It has even been suggested that the ship was deliberately put into harm's way in order to ensure the entry of America into the war. Much of this information originated from Commander Kenworthy, briefly a Naval Staff officer, but a modern interpretation of the naval staff in World War I suggests that 'Kenworthy's opinions and memories need to be treated with a degree of circumspection'.[30]

Then, on 19 August, the White Star liner *Arabic* was sunk. On 28 August the German Chancellor issued new orders to submarine commanders and relayed them to Washington. In future passenger ships could only be sunk after warning and the saving of the lives of both passengers and crew. The German Naval High Command considered this unworkable, and on 18 September the U-boats were withdrawn from the war against merchant ships. Almost entirely as a result of protests from the United States, the first U-boat campaign came to an end.

By June 1915 U-boats had entered the Mediterranean and, working from Austrian Adriatic ports, had become a serious menace to the Dardanelles and Salonika operations. The British used submarines in the Sea of Marmora and their Dardanelles submarine operations represented the first-ever sustained British submarine campaign. During the winter of 1915–16 Germany greatly enhanced their U-boat fleet and decided to attack defensively-armed merchant ships without warning, though passenger ships were to be spared. By this stage in the war the allied blockade was doing a great deal of damage to American trade and American feelings towards Britain and France were becoming rather bitter. This encouraged Germany to renew the war against merchant ships.

On 1 March 1916 unrestricted submarine warfare was again initiated and on 24 March the cross-channel passenger ferry *Sussex* was torpedoed and seriously damaged off Dieppe. Some 50 lives were lost; the US president protested strongly and threatened to break off diplomatic relations with Germany. Again Germany gave way and on 4 May issued the *Sussex* pledge, which promised a change in Germany's submarine policy. In future, passenger ships were not to be targeted; merchant ships would not be torpedoed unless the presence of weapons had been established; merchant ships would not be sunk until arrangements had been made for the safety of passengers and crew.[31] In future all U-boat activities would be focused on the Grand Fleet, and it was out of this more focused campaign on the Grand Fleet that the battle of Jutland took place.

Jutland: The Battlecruisers in Action

Scheer appeared to be achieving his aim; the east coast bombardments had resulted in the battlecruisers being moved to Rosyth and the Second Battle Squadron was now based on Cromarty, a major force realignment. By 1916 Beatty had ten battlecruisers available. His now considerable force was split into three squadrons, each commanded by a rear-admiral. Beatty's command was now known as the Battlecruiser Fleet and Beatty himself elevated to the status of Fleet Commander. In May 1916 the British possessed 28 battleships to Germany's 16 and ten battlecruisers to Germany's five.[32]

In the second week of May 1916, U-boats took up their positions off Scapa Flow, the Moray Firth, the Humber, the Thames estuary and to the north of Terschelling. Using Hipper's battlecruisers, Scheer intended to bombard Sunderland and entice Beatty's battlecruisers out, perhaps with a battle squadron in support. As the British ships left port, as many as possible would be torpedoed.[33] The High Seas Fleet would then engage the Grand Fleet on conditions of near parity. In the event the weather was too poor for zeppelin reconnaissance and the U-boats gave very little useful intelligence.[34]

At precisely the moment that Scheer intended to bombard Sunderland and catch Beatty's battlecruisers, or better still an isolated portion of the Grand Fleet, Jellicoe planned his most ambitious operation to date. Two light cruiser squadrons were to enter the Kattegat. A full battle squadron would be in support with the entire Grand Fleet behind. If the High Seas Fleet put to sea then they would be well and truly caught on terms and conditions of British choosing. On 30 May a German radio signal 31Gg.2490 was intercepted. The message could not be deciphered but it was concluded that a German operation was imminent.[35]

Jellicoe and Beatty were immediately ordered to sea, sailing many hours before the High Seas Fleet. The Third Battlecruiser Squadron had been temporarily assigned to Jellicoe's forces for gunnery training purposes and in return Beatty had received the four very powerful units of the Fifth Battle Squadron, the new ships of the Queen Elizabeth class. Beatty was instructed to sweep in towards the Danish coast and if nothing was sighted by 1400 hours he was to turn northwards and rendezvous with Jellicoe's forces. Beatty did not reach his planned turning point until 1415 hours and as he did so a light cruiser, *Galatea*, on the extreme left of Beatty's screen, sighted a Danish steamer, *N.J.Fjord*. Simultaneously Hipper's outer screen sighted the *N.J.Fjord* and the light cruiser *Elbing* went to investigate. At 1418 hours the *Galatea* signalled 'Enemy in sight', and ten minutes later opened fire, accompanied by her sister ship *Phaeton*.[36]

Jellicoe and Beatty were too far apart to spring an effective trap on Scheer and Hipper. The inadvertent presence of the *N.J.Fjord* ensured that the light forces had come into contact prematurely. Without the presence of the *N.J.Fjord* the first contact might have been delayed until Jellicoe was in a position to back up Beatty directly.[37]

Beatty's force was not well deployed and the Fifth Battle Squadron was some five miles away from the battlecruisers. In the years that followed endless excuses were made for the dispersion of Beatty's forces but none really work. A Nelson or a Collingwood would automatically have concentrated their forces. Between 1520 hours and 1525 hours the two battlecruiser forces actually sighted each other. Beatty had six battlecruisers to Hipper's five and was not much concerned that the Fifth Battle Squadron was now seven miles behind.

The first phase of the action is often referred to as the 'run to the south'. More properly it should be called the battlecruiser action. With an advantage of six ships to five, the *Lion* and *Princess Royal* engaged *Lutzow* at the head of the German line. *Queen Mary* missed out *Derfflinger* and fired at *Seydlitz* while *Tiger* and *New Zealand* engaged *Moltke*. At the rear of the line *Indefatigable* and *Von der Tann* fought it out, leaving the *Derfflinger* to make undisturbed target practise on the *Queen Mary*. In this phase of the action the British did badly; the battlecruisers *Indefatigable* and *Queen Mary* blew up with an almost total loss of life and *Lion* suffered near fatal damage. One thousand and seventeen men perished aboard the *Indefatigable* and 1,266 aboard the *Queen Mary*. For Hipper's battlecruisers it was a notable success on which their claim to victory at Jutland rests. They scored 44 hits on British ships and destroyed two of them. In return they received 11 hits from Beatty's ships and six from the Fifth Battle Squadron.[38] Jellicoe was to remark later that the 'result cannot be other than unpalatable'.

> What is indisputable is that in the first phase of the battle, a British squadron, greatly superior in numbers and gun-power, not only failed to defeat a weaker enemy who made no effort to avoid action, but, in the space of 50 minutes, suffered what can only be described as a partial defeat.[39]

The sad truth about the battlecruiser losses was not so much the poor armour protection but appalling magazine and handing room practices, particularly stacking cordite charges in their silk bags at the bottom of ammunition hoists. After the battle on 20 June 1916 Jellicoe stated the truth to the Admiralty.

> The amount of exposed cordite about the ship was enormous and that as regards turrets, if bare charges were permitted to remain in the handing rooms, as there is every reason to believe was the case, these must have furnished trains of explosives to the magazines [...] Flame reached the turret magazines causing them to explode. It is now generally accepted opinion that the fault lay in the method adopted in the transportation of charges to the guns, whereby these charges which are not in non-inflammable cases had an open course from the magazine to the gun, and this in association with the number of charges that were usually in the handing room revolving trunk,

working chamber and gun house, gave a direct train from the turret to the magazine [...] There would seem to be an impression in the Fleet that these ships were lost because German shells penetrated the vitals, and there exploded, vide reports of the Rear-Admiral 1st Battlecruiser Squadron, where it is stated that the Queen Mary was hit by a plunging salvo which apparently penetrated the armoured deck, and ignited the magazine. Such a statement is not substantiated by a detailed examination of all the reports that have been received.[40]

The light cruiser squadrons had pushed ahead of the battlecruisers led by Commodore Goodenough's Second Light Cruiser Squadron. From the bridge of *Southampton* he saw the topmasts of battleships that could only be the battleships of the High Seas Fleet. Goodenough immediately radioed Jellicoe and Beatty the momentous news, 'Have sighted enemy Battlefleet'.

Beatty turned towards Goodenough and within minutes sighted the masts and funnels of Scheer's High Seas Fleet. Beatty's intention was to lead Hipper and Scheer towards the battleships of the Grand Fleet. As Beatty turned north, so the first phase of the action, the so-called 'run to the south', ended. The remaining controversy concerns the Fifth Battle Squadron. Most accounts of Jutland state that the Fifth Battle Squadron turned and were positioned on Beatty's disengaged side. This now appears unlikely; they turned and came around on Beatty's engaged side.[41] In this second phase of the action, the so-called 'run to the north', the British did rather better and hit after hit was scored on Hipper's battlecruisers.

Jutland: The Main Fleets Engage and Disengage as Rapidly as Possible

As the battlecruisers approached the Grand Fleet Jellicoe was still in his tight steaming formation, six columns of four battleships, 24 dreadnoughts and super-dreadnoughts, Britain's entire battle-fleet strength. Jellicoe could not deploy his fleet into line ahead until he knew the position of the German fleet.

Jellicoe was starved of information and it took time to extract basic information from Beatty. At last Beatty gave the vital piece of information that the entire battle depended on: 'Have sighted enemy battlefleet bearing southwest.'[42] This gave Jellicoe the information he needed and he gave the deployment order, 'hoist equal speed pendant south-east'. The order was given to Commander Woods, the Fleet Signal Officer. Woods said, 'would you make it a point to port, sir, so that they will know it is on the port wing column'. Jellicoe replied, 'very well, hoist equal speed pendant south-east-by-east'. Woods called to the signals boatswain; 'hoist equal speed Charlie London'. The message was repeated by wireless and at 1815 hours the Grand Fleet deployed.[43]

By placing his fleet across the High Seas Fleet line of advance, Jellicoe would cross Scheer's 'T', always the strongest opening gambit in a fleet deployment. The disadvantage of Jellicoe's deployment was that it was already early evening and as dusk approached there was now scarcely time for a full fleet action to be fought through to its conclusion.[44] By 1837 hours all 24 ships had rounded the turning point, often referred to as 'Windy Corner' and Beatty's ships had crossed ahead of the Grand Fleet, to take up a position ahead.

The Third Battlecruiser Squadron was ahead of Jellicoe and from 1820 hours onwards was firing steadily at Hipper's ships. The range was down to 8,000–10,000 yards and a total of eight hits were scored by *Invincible* and *Inflexible* on *Lutzow* and *Derfflinger*, then at 1832 disaster struck and the *Invincible* was hit on 'Q' turret. The hit burst inside the turret and the flash reached the magazines. The *Invincible* blew up in exactly the same manner as had the *Indefatigable* and *Queen Mary*. One thousand and twenty-six officers and men were killed instantly; there were six survivors.[45] Out ahead of Jellicoe's forces the old armoured cruisers of Sir Robert Arbuthnot's First Cruiser Squadron came into action; *Defence, Black Prince* and *Warrior*. The *Defence* was hit and almost at once her magazines were penetrated. She blew up in a single vast explosion, taking her entire crew of 900 officers and men with her. *Warrior* only just escaped the same fate and *Black Prince* was sunk later in the action.

The Grand Fleet, having deployed in line ahead, had turned through 090 degrees across the head of Scheer's line of advance and presented an inverted 'V' to the High Seas Fleet. At this juncture Scheer still thought he was up against a detached squadron of the Grand Fleet and in any event he did not want to risk an action with even a large detached squadron so at 1835 hours he ordered the manoeuvre known as *Gefechtskehrtwendung*, or about-turn.[46] This was not the battle turn-away described in so many accounts of Jutland but a progressive turn started by the rearward ship and continued down the line. The pre-dreadnoughts were well astern of Scheer's force so *Westfalen*, the last dreadnought in line, started the manoeuvre.

From the British side, the High Seas Fleet faded out of view and it was some minutes before Jellicoe realised that Scheer had turned away.

At 1855 hours Scheer executed his second turn through 180 degrees in an attempt to get to the east of the British fleet before nightfall, only an hour away.[47] Scheer ran up against the Grand Fleet almost at once and across an arc of 120 degrees across his front he could see nothing at all except the rippling orange cordite flashes as ship after ship of the Grand Fleet opened fire. For Scheer this was the ultimate moment of truth and the realisation that he was up against the entire Grand Fleet. His actions during the remainder of the action were hardly those of an admiral intent on the destruction of the Grand Fleet.

At 1913 hours Scheer realised his position was hopeless and he had no choice but to make his third *Gefechtskehrtwendung*. His battle line was now close to chaos and barely retaining its coherent unity after two about turns in 18 minutes.[48] At this juncture German claims to victory at Jutland are at their least credible. For Scheer the only way to cover the third and final turn, to cloak what was now a precipitate retreat, was a blow at the centre of the British line. Scheer issued his famous signal, which should have resulted in the death ride of the German battlecruisers: 'Schlachtkreuzer ran an den Fiend, voll einsetzen' ('Battlecruisers at the enemy! Give it everything!'). Onboard *Seydlitz* Captain von Egidy took in Scheer's signal and ordered the ratings manning the telephones to pass the message to the crew: *Schlachtkreuzer ran*. As the stations received the message there was a momentary awed hush. Then, through the voice pipes, ventilation shafts and armoured passageways came the sound of cheering and the strains of *Wacht am Rhein*. The stokers hammered their shovels against the bulkheads, shouting *Drauf Seydlitz* (attack *Seydlitz*), the war cry of Frederick the Great's Seydlitz cuirassiers.[49]

At this stage of the action the *Lutzow* was limping away to the south, to sink in the early hours of the next morning. The *Derfflinger* was down by the head, heavily flooded forward. The *Seydlitz* and *Von der Tann* were hardly in better shape and only the *Moltke* was in anything resembling a reasonable fighting condition. From 1900 hours to 1930 hours Hipper's battlecruisers and the leading German battleships came under very heavy fire indeed. Of the battleships, *Grosser Kurfurst* was hit seven times and *Markgraf* and *König* once each. Having ordered his battlecruisers into a death ride, Scheer cancelled the order three minutes later and substituted a destroyer attack instead.[50] Four destroyers of the Third Flotilla fired their torpedoes at a range of 6,000–8,000 yards. This was followed with an attack by the Sixth and Ninth Destroyer Flotillas. The Sixth Flotilla fired 11 torpedoes and the Ninth fired 17.[51]

As the High Seas Fleet retreated it would appear that Jellicoe had established a position of considerable tactical superiority, but in the face of a concerted torpedo attack Jellicoe turned away, first by 22.5 degrees, then by a further 22.5 degrees.[52] Turning away from torpedoes gave a component of velocity in the direction of the torpedo and if the turn was made sufficiently early the torpedo could easily be avoided at the end of its run when it was going slowly.[53] While it must be admitted that there is a certain logic behind a turn away from torpedoes, if ever there was an argument for abandoning the rule book this was it.[54] The trouble was that Jellicoe had no information that could justify such a high risk decision, so he turned away and Jutland became an inconclusive stalemate. Both Scheer and Jellicoe had turned away and by declining action both brought the third stage of Jutland, the main fleet action, to an unsatisfactory conclusion.

Night Action/Inaction

Jellicoe and Scheer were now faced with the hours of darkness. Jellicoe was determined under no account to risk a night action and ordered his fleet into three columns of eight ships. Scheer was in a much more difficult position. He was west of the Grand Fleet and was faced with a fleet action the next day unless he could work his way to the east and get inside his minefields by daybreak. Scheer took the easiest option open to him and at 2114 hours he decided to head for Horns Reef, his shortest route home. To avoid a fleet action Scheer had to be at Horns Reef, 90 miles away, by dawn on 1 June. As Jellicoe and Scheer took up their night formations they were on a converging course and at 2330 hours the Grand Fleet passed ahead of the High Seas Fleet by only a matter of minutes.[55]

Scheer passed steadily astern of Jellicoe in the period 2330 to 0100 hours on 1 June.[56] If Jellicoe had noted the movement of gun flashes from west to east and combined this with the Admiralty intelligence reports; again he might have deduced that Scheer was heading for Horns Reef.[57]

At 0239 hours Jellicoe formed his fleet into a long line, and turned to 324 degrees at 0300 hours.[58] The Germans were obviously not ahead and a search to the north was called for. Then at 0410 hours an Admiralty signal was received, timed at 0329 hours. This gave Scheer's 0230 hours position and Jellicoe now knew that Scheer had escaped. The High Seas Fleet reached the Lister Deep at 0600 and the battlecruisers were ordered to return to port. *Ostfriesland* struck a British mine at 0520 hours and this caused a good deal of panic and false periscope sightings.[59] On the British side, having searched the area of the battle for stragglers, Jellicoe turned for home.[60] Jutland, the greatest naval battle in history, had come to a bloody and inconclusive end.

Perspectives on the Jutland Conundrum

Over the decades since Jutland, both sides have claimed victory on various grounds. The High Seas Fleet arrived back in port first and the evening papers of 1 June 1916 screamed their banner headlines, 'Great Victory at Sea'; 'A crushing defeat' boasted the *Neues Wiener Journal*. The *Leipziger Neueste Nachrichten* proclaimed that 'England's invincibility on the seas is broken. The German fleet has torn the venerable Trafalgar legend into shreds.'[61] It was not until the next day that the first tentative communiqué was issued by the British Admiralty. Rumours of defeat ran rife and the crew of the *Lion* were jeered and booed by dockyard workers as Beatty's terribly battered flagship struggled into port. The Admiralty's first report was uninspired to say the least.

> On the afternoon of Wednesday May 31st, a naval engagement took place off the coast of Jutland. The British ships on which the brunt of the fighting fell were the battlecruiser fleet and some cruisers and light cruisers supported by four fast battleships. Among these losses were heavy. The German Battlefleet, aided by low visibility, avoided prolonged action with our main forces and soon after these appeared on the scene the enemy returned to port, though not before receiving severe damage from our battleships. The battlecruisers *Queen Mary*, *Indefatigable*, *Invincible* and the cruisers *Defence* and *Black Prince* were sunk. The *Warrior* was disabled and after being towed for some time, had to be abandoned by her crew. It is also known that the destroyers *Tipperary*, *Turbulent*, *Fortune*, *Sparrowhawk* and *Ardent* were lost and six others are not yet accounted for. No British battleships or light cruisers were sunk. The enemy losses are serious. At least one battlecruiser was destroyed; one battleship reported sunk by our destroyers during a night attack; ten light cruisers were disabled and probably sunk. The exact number of enemy destroyers disposed of during the action cannot be ascertained with any certainty, but it must have been large.[62]

As a bald statement of fact the communiqué was true enough. The loss of three battlecruisers and three armoured cruisers could not be concealed. Apart from anything else, more than 6,000 officers and men were killed. The casualty lists fell like a thunderclap in Portsmouth, the home port of

Invincible and *Queen Mary*.⁶³ To a public brought up in the belief that the British Navy always won great victories it all looked suspiciously like defeat and an attempt at Admiralty cover up. A second communiqué was issued that attempted to magnify German losses, then the German communiqué was issued in full. The public was left in no doubt that the Germans had sunk considerably more ships than they had lost and this still looked like a British defeat. The Germans had sunk 14 British ships, totalling 112,450 tons, whereas the British had sunk 11 German ships, totalling 59,610 tons. The British lost over 6,000 men, some 11 per cent of their personnel. By contrast Germany lost fewer than 3,000 men, 6.8 per cent of their personnel.⁶⁴ The fact that Scheer had been stopped dead in his tracks and had turned and run for home under the cover of darkness was ignored. The truth about the loss of the *Lutzow* could not be concealed for long, or the truth about the German cruiser losses, *Weisbaden, Elbing, Rostock* and *Frauenlob*. There was also the inconvenient fact of the loss of the pre-dreadnought battleship *Pommern* and five destroyers.⁶⁵ As time went by the realisation that Jutland was a stalemate became more and more apparent. By 1917 the *Spectator* was writing.

> When the German's call the sea fight off the Skaggerak a victory they do not mean that the English Fleet was defeated in the military sense, they mean that it was baffled of its purpose to destroy themselves. They had been in the Lion's jaws but they had managed to wriggle out before those terrible jaws could close. That is what the German's mean when they celebrate Skagerrak (Jutland) as a 'Victory' [...] Their claim, critically examined, is simply that, in the circumstances, it was a very successful escape for the German ships. And so indeed it was.⁶⁶

A New York newspaper summed up the situation rather more succinctly: 'The German Fleet has assaulted its jailer, but it is still in jail.'⁶⁷ It was out of this sort of analysis that British claims of an overall strategic victory were made. The British, by reasons of geography, held the keys to the North Sea gates. Indeed, German claims to victory seem to have rested on a profound sense of relief that they had escaped intact. That this was a considerable achievement cannot be denied, but victory can hardly be numbered among German accomplishments.

Jutland did not alter the fact that the British position of strategic advantage was maintained. The position of relative German inferiority remained to the war's end. By turning away Jellicoe preserved Britain's naval strength.

Why, ran this particular argument, should Britain risk a naval battle to fight for what she already possessed, a situation of considerable strategic advantage? These arguments engendered bitter rivalry between the supporters of Jellicoe and Beatty.

The best, or perhaps worst, of the pro-Beatty propaganda was the stance adopted by Carlyon Bellairs, who suggested that 'Jellicoe came, he saw, he turned away'. The same author asserted that Jellicoe's turn away from torpedo attack was in reality a situation where 11 destroyers dismissed 37 battleships.[68] The Jellicoe supporters suggested that Beatty, with his 'up boys and at them' attitude, would have risked Britain's naval supremacy on the throw of a dice and that he never understood the strategy of the higher command, a view amply represented by the published works of Sir Reginald Bacon and Rear-Admiral Harper.[69]

Just how good the respective admirals were and indeed what was the quality of leadership at Jutland, needs closer examination. The relative failure of Beatty's signalling and staff organisation has not been covered here and has been the focus of a considerable number of studies.[70] His poor deployment of the Fifth Battle Squadron is usually justified by stating that the Germans would have been scared off, outnumbered ten to five, assuming that the battleships of the Fifth Battle Squadron were the vanguard of the Grand Fleet. This is not really justified from the German side. The Fifth Battle Squadron was sighted soon after the battlecruisers and Hipper deduced correctly that the Fifth were fast battleships acting in support of battlecruisers. On this basis, the Fifth Battle Squadron should have been two miles distant at the start of the action, not five miles.

If Beatty's signalling and tactical dispositions were poor he did what he was supposed to and effected the junction of the main battle fleets. He has been much criticised over the years for not keeping Jellicoe properly informed but his radio was shot away and his flagship was badly damaged. A surviving account of conditions onboard *Lion* at Jutland makes interesting reading.

> The state of the ship during and after the battle was indescribable. The sheets of water which came onboard her when the German salvoes dropped nearby, the streams of water pouring from the fire hoses, the inrush of the sea through her terrible injuries left her decks awash, so that the wounded could not be placed on them without grave risk of being drowned. Everywhere were fires, dense choking smoke, steel splinters and torn plates with edges so sharp they cut like razors.

Beatty and a small group of officers forming his personal staff directed the battle from the high upper bridge, just below the foretop. They were quite in the open, unprotected from the smallest splinter, while about them whizzed fragments of German shells. At one point huge masses of steel were hurled from the *Lion*'s bows by German fire. A great fragment of capstan went past, turning over and over in the air and there were constant narrow escapes. In this inferno Beatty gave his orders, made his tactical dispositions, worked out his strategy and effected the junction of the main fleets.[71]

The final argument relating to Beatty and the battlecruiser fleet concerns gunnery. During the course of the battle the First and Second Battlecruiser Squadrons expended 1,469 heavy shells and scored 21 hits (1.43 per cent). By contrast the Fifth Battle Squadron expended 1,099 heavy shells and scored 29 hits (2.64 per cent). Jellicoe's battleships scored 57 hits out of 1,593 heavy shells fired (3.70 per cent). Hood's Third Battlecruiser Squadron scored 16 hits out of 373 shells (4.29 per cent). By contrast Hipper's ships scored 65 hits out of 1,670 shells fired (3.89 per cent) and Scheer's ships 57 hits out of 1,927 shells (2.96 per cent).[72] From the foregoing it is apparent that the British battlecruiser gunnery performance, the Third Battlecruiser Squadron excepted, was very poor.

As a fleet commander Jellicoe brought the Grand Fleet to a pitch of fighting efficiency that was probably unobtainable by anyone else.[73] His deployment of the fleet cannot be faulted but it has long been argued that his actions after 1830 on 31 May show a commander far short of the Nelson touch. Such arguments ignore the reality of a situation where the fleet commander was so starved of information that it was virtually impossible to have made a decision, which involved a high degree of risk. The four fleet commanders – Jellicoe, Scheer, Beatty and Hipper – were able men but the weapons system they commanded in the form of dreadnoughts was singularly ill-suited to any display of the Nelson touch.[74] Arthur Marder's assessment of Scheer is probably correct.

> Scheer may have been a great tactician. But if so, he had a very bad off-day at Jutland, since every time he came within sight of the British Fleet, he did so by accident and was so completely taken by surprise that on each occasion he found the British battle line across his 'T'. Of course he did brilliantly in extricating himself; but an exceptionally able tactician would never have twice got his fleet into such suicidal situations.[75]

Hipper was better served on the materiel side and his battlecruisers were superb fighting machines with a much better balance of qualities than the comparable British ships, made possible by the adoption of British technology in the form of Parsons steam turbines and Thorneycroft small tube boilers. Apart from Dogger Bank and Jutland, Hipper's main claim to fame was an ability to bombard the east coast of Britain, which earned him the deserved epithet of 'babykiller'.

In reading Scheer's memoirs, *Germany's High Seas Fleet in the World War*, it is eerily similar to Jellicoe's apologia *The Grand Fleet 1914–16, its Creation, Development and Work*, and about as pedestrian. Jellicoe and Scheer, Beatty and Hipper somehow become each the mirror image of the other.

10

From Jutland to Washington

Germany's Last Throw of the Dice: The Third U-boat Campaign

In spite of the braggadocio, the realisation that Jutland was a stalemate battle was quickly appreciated in Germany. The unpalatable truth was that the Grand Fleet had stopped them dead in its tracks. They had lost the battlecruiser *Lutzow* and come within a hair's breadth of losing both *Seydlitz* and *Derfflinger*. It is often forgotten just how badly *Derfflinger* was damaged. She was hit by 21 heavy shells and the two rear turrets were completely burnt out, with the loss of over 150 men. If *Seydlitz* and *Derfflinger* had been sunk the story of Jutland would have been very different. With three of their five battlecruisers sunk and three of the British ten, German proportionate losses would have been twice those of Britain. With claims of a victory for the British Navy, much of the criticism of John Jellicoe might never have surfaced. The German battlecruisers survived because British shells tended to break up on impact; they were just not lethal enough. Scheer's report to the Kaiser on 7 July 1916, just six weeks after Jutland, needs to be quoted.

> With a favourable succession of operations the enemy may be made to suffer severely, although there can be no doubt that even the most successful result from a high sea battle will not compel England to make peace [...] A victorious end to the war at not too distant a date can only be looked for by the crushing of English economic life through U-boat action against English commerce.[1]

Scheer and the German Naval Staff were concluding that unrestricted submarine warfare was the only way to break England's power. The other type of naval warfare, *guerre de course*, waged by U-boats against England's mercantile trade, was becoming a more and more attractive proposition. For Germany, breaking the British blockade became a matter of supreme importance and this could only be attained by unrestricted submarine warfare. Admiral Scheer knew this, hence his letter to the Kaiser just six weeks after Jutland that stated unequivocally the arguments in favour of defeating Britain by means of U-boat warfare.

After Jutland the blockade of Germany continued unabated. As far back as 1914 the German civilian population started eating a product known as K-bread (*Kriegsbrot* – war bread). This type of bread used potatoes instead of wheat. The winter of 1916–17 was known in Germany as the 'turnip winter'. The extreme distress, bordering on starvation, was not entirely the doing of the blockade. Early frosts killed off much of the German potato crop and only the last-minute planting of turnips, usually used as cattle fodder, averted famine.

By December 1916 Britain had lost 2,400,000 tons of merchant shipping. Of course German merchant ships seized by Britain helped replace the tonnage lost, as did new construction. Nevertheless, the total tonnage available had fallen by 750,000 tons.[2] In December 1916 Admiral Von Holtzendorff prepared a memorandum on unrestricted submarine warfare. As 1917 dawned Germany's situation was increasingly grim. On the Western Front 190 allied divisions faced 150 German divisions. The Kaiser and his Chancellor, Bethmann-Hollweg, urged on by the naval and military leadership, decided to resume unrestricted submarine warfare. At the beginning of February Germany had 105 U-boats ready for action. The initial campaign was a great success with nearly 500,000 tons of merchant shipping sunk in February and again in March. The April figure topped 860,000 tons.

Jellicoe was appointed First Sea Lord in December 1916 and the vexed issue of convoy, rejected from the 1880s onwards as a viable means of trade protection in wartime, reared its ugly head again. Jellicoe was opposed to the idea of convoy, believing that merchant ships would never be able to keep station and many merchant ship captains agreed with him. It was also felt that convoy was likely to cause severe delays to shipping and the loss of carrying capacity amounted to a massive 'own goal'. Paradoxically, convoy was tried with success early in the war for troop transportation, as were Channel convoys for the coal trade between Britain and France. It was also tried on the Dutch, French and Scandinavian trade routes. The problem lay in the trans-Atlantic routes; there would never be enough escorts to provide an effective convoy system. It was then discovered that the figures for vessels leaving and entering British ports were totally misleading. These statistics showed about 5,000 vessels clearing British ports per week and included small coastal craft, some as small as 100 tons, with perhaps two or even three clearances per week. The number of trans-Atlantic crossings of vessels over 1,600 gross registered tons was much less, at 120–40 per week. At between 20 arrivals and departures per day there would indeed be adequate numbers of ocean escorts for convoy work.[3]

Despite pessimism concerning its effectiveness the Admiralty came to accept the idea of convoy. By the end of April 1917 the general idea of ocean convoy was adopted, with an experimental convoy from Gibraltar in May. Transatlantic convoys were adopted in May and June and after July monthly losses never went above 500,000 tons.

In the first year of unrestricted submarine warfare some 6.2 million tons of shipping was sunk. As convoy was adopted on a more and more widespread basis, so the level of mercantile losses reduced. Between January and June 1918 the average tonnage sunk was 298,000 tons, falling to a monthly average of 172,000 tons in the last five months of the war.[4] By the autumn of 1918 nearly 90 per cent of shipping was sailing in convoy; indeed, throughout the war the U-boats sank only 96 ships in convoy.[5] In all, Britain lost seven and three-quarters of a million tons of shipping, some 28 per cent of her pre-war tonnage.[6]

By the end of the Great War the allies had 300 anti-submarine destroyers of which about 50 were American. There were patrol (P-boats), sloops and about 4,000 auxiliary vessels, mostly trawlers and drifters used for anti-submarine patrols. Some 500 of these were fast motor launches, 77 were Q-ships, 24 were paddle steamers and 49 were yachts. Support was given by 65 submarines, 550 aircraft and 75 airships. These ships were manned by 140,000 men and it needed a further half a million men to build, refit and support them.[7] By the end of 1918 Britain had an effective sonar device for submarine detection and, had the war continued into 1919, sonar, then known as ASDIC (Admiralty Submarine Detection Investigation Committee), would have been operational. During the course of the war nearly 5,000 merchant ships were sunk with the loss of 15,000 seamen.

Blockade Made Effective: America Enters the War

At the start of the war blockade was maintained by elderly cruisers, many dating from the Naval Defence Act era. The Edgar class were typical and with their casemate mounted armament close to the waterline, were unsuited to the atrocious weather of the northern North Sea. In the winter of 1914–15 they were replaced with armed merchant cruisers. High-sided merchant ships armed with a few light guns proved far more suitable for blockade work. The tenth cruiser squadron grew rapidly from eight to over 40 vessels and asserted an increasingly tight control over vessels bound for the continent of Europe.[8]

As the war progressed, so the system of blockade became more and more sophisticated. The idea of a 'Letter of Assurance' or Navicert came into being. A neutral ship bound for Europe would be inspected by British Consular officials before leaving the loading port, usually in the United States. Each item on a cargo manifest required its own Navicert but despite the vast complication of the scheme, the cargo manifest could be telegraphed to the blockade authorities.[9] There were various agreements with shipping lines of neutral countries and with Scandinavian governments.[10] The blockade's effectiveness increased steadily with time and became total with the entry of America into the war. The effectiveness of the blockade was multiplied by poor German government organisation, particularly in regard to food distribution. The armed merchant cruisers used for the blockade were technically warships, and it is a surprise that the German Navy did not use its U-boats more effectively against the armed merchant cruisers.

As the control of shipping at neutral ports and in the United States became complete the northern patrol usefulness on the high seas steadily lessened. The entry of the United States into the war in April 1917 effectively rendered the patrol obsolete, though it took time for this to become obvious. Nevertheless, in January 1918 the patrol was discontinued. The laying of the vast northern minefield barrage contributed to the ending of the northern patrol. Paradoxically the minefield barrage was rather ineffective.[11]

The End of World War I

World War I was a prolonged and bloody conflict of mass armies in which sea power and the possession of a battlefleet was subsidiary to the role of armies. If the U-boats had won the battle for the Atlantic sea routes then Britain would have been defeated in both world wars. The grim reality of sea power in the twentieth century shows the extent to which it had become essentially negative. The navy could lose the war but never win it. The battle against the U-boats, the ultimate expression of that other type of naval warfare, *guerre de course*, the long-drawn-out war of attrition against Britain's trade and commerce, was solved by the adoption of convoy. The war against the U-boats was absolutely critical to Britain's survival but the huge fleet of battleships, the Grand Fleet, played no part in this crucial battle. Indeed, the battleships appeared somewhat discredited in 1918.[12]

The surrender of the High Seas Fleet was hardly a surrender at all. The High Seas Fleet had nowhere else to go. No neutral country would take it so it went to the Firth of Forth. Under the terms of the armistice in 1918 the British could not inspect the ships, merely ask that the German flag not be flown in a British port. The High Seas Fleet was interned – it did not surrender and chose to scuttle rather than face prolonged internment. When it scuttled at Scapa Flow in 1919, the German Navy effectively committed suicide. It was an unsatisfactory end to Germany's bid for naval dominion. It was equally unsatisfactory for the Grand Fleet, which never had the decisive battle it felt it deserved.

Added to this were the politics and diplomacy of the United States. The warm relations between Britain and the United States associated with the Teddy Roosevelt era gave way to a feeling that all European powers were tainted by secret diplomacy and while Britain was an ally, her diplomacy had about it many of the characteristics of Wilhelmine Germany. The British blockade was felt to have violated neutralist American principles of open seas for open trade. Indeed, in 1917 American indignation concerning blockade caused a substantial modification in British blockading policies.[13]

The Dreadnought as a Weapons System

The dreadnoughts as a weapons system need careful analysis. In the case of the battleships their deployment and usage was heavily proscribed by covert weapons such as mines, torpedoes and submarines. There were other factors that forced battleships onto the defensive. In 1815 there were 214 line-of-battleships and 792 frigates (cruisers). The dreadnought era produced 48 battleships and battlecruisers, the battlecruiser *Hood* being the last World War I ship. The cost of warships rose staggeringly. The £1 million battleships of the late Victorian period became the £2 million dreadnoughts and the £6 million *Hood*. The relative costs of each successive class of ships were always greater than their predecessors', and in turn this meant there were fewer, ever more expensive ships. Each dreadnought lost, as one of the 48, was a far greater calamity than the loss of one of the 214 line-of-battleships of the Napoleonic era. The relative value of each dreadnought, proportionally so much greater than a single line-of-battleship, was a further proscription on their deployment and usage.

When these broader strategic and philosophical arguments are reviewed, the pressures on Jellicoe to fight a defensive war become very clear indeed. Both Jellicoe and Beatty realised that the dreadnoughts were too valuable to be risked and as Grand Fleet commanders both men acted accordingly. These comparisons between the dreadnoughts and the age of Nelson indicate clearly that the big battleships of World War I cannot really be compared with the wooden line-of-battleships of the Napoleonic era. A twentieth-century Nelson might well have been forced into the same strategy as Jellicoe and Beatty. The German Navy was in exactly the same position.

In an age of deterrent weapons their deployment is based on the possession and preservation of the weapon rather than its use. In this sense the dreadnoughts were yesterday's deterrent and it was more important to preserve the deterrent than to risk it fighting for something already possessed – command of the seas. That the dreadnoughts were not a very effective deterrent is beyond doubt, which leads again to the conclusion that the effectiveness of a deterrent is directly related to the available counter-measures deployed against it. A corollary to this argument again shows that the wooden line-of-battleships of Nelson's age were not proscribed by any weapons of covert subversion. Nelson's ships operated in a 'classical' role and fought 'classical' battles as defined by Mahan and others. Strategic deterrents in our own age have yet to be subverted by effective counter-measures and for the moment in some sense remain 'classical' weapons. The dreadnoughts were caught in a terrible dilemma. They were designed as 'classical' weapons to emulate the role of the eighteenth-century wooden line-of-battleships, yet were compromised by covert weapons that proscribed their role to an extraordinary degree. The result was relatively few big expensive ships that were unsuccessful in the eighteenth-century 'classical' context and bad deterrents in the late twentieth-century context. Howbeit, the disinclination of the fleet commanders to seek action places the dreadnoughts much closer to the strategic deterrents of the late twentieth century than to the wooden battleships of the age of Nelson.

Perspectives: At the End of the Day

In the centuries of Britain's rise as a maritime empire the exercise of naval command had a huge positive influence on Britain's growth. Colonies and commerce were linked by sea power. By 1914 the nature of sea power had changed radically compared to those earlier centuries. A population of nine million in 1815 had become a population of over 40 million in 1914.[14] Britain was no longer able to feed such a population and was heavily reliant on food imports. Industrial raw materials were also imported and the finished manufactured products were then exported – all by sea. Approximately 27 per cent of all Britain's' national wealth was invested overseas and this made British trade dangerously vulnerable to outside pressure or attack.[15] This large volume of imports and exports turned the role of sea power from a positive factor in Britain's growth as a maritime trading nation to a negative factor in the world wars. In both world wars Britain had to hold on to seapower or lose the greatest wars in history.

From 1902 Britain was in alliance with Japan and a considerable element of American opinion interpreted this as a possibility of a two-ocean war between America on the one hand and the combined navies of Britain and Japan on the other. Against this background of disillusionment with European politics and diplomacy, the United States Navy lobbied for a big two-ocean battleship-building programme. By 1918 America had 16 dreadnoughts, a total equal to the combined fleets of France, Italy and Japan. The Navy Department wanted a total of 39 battleships and 12 battlecruisers. It was a fleet that would have dwarfed the Grand Fleet itself. America proposed six battleships of the Indiana class, 43,200 tons and armed with twelve 16-inch guns and also six Constellation class battlecruisers, 43,000 tons and armed with eight 16-inch guns. The Japanese Navy planned two 33,800-ton battleships, *Nagato* and *Mutsu*, armed with eight 16-inch guns, while the *Kaga* and *Tosa* would displace 39,900 tons and were to be armed with ten 16-inch guns. In 1919 Britain possessed only one post-Jutland ship, the *Hood*, with no new ships planned. Two lightly armoured battlecruisers, *Repulse* and *Renown*, had been completed in 1916 but were hopelessly ill-protected in the post-Jutland world. Within a very few years the Americans would possess 12 and the Japanese eight battleships and battlecruisers armed with 16-inch guns. Britain planned two new classes of capital ships, four battleships and four battlecruisers, all armed with 16-inch guns. In the event they were never built.

In 1921 Britain intended to call a conference on Pacific and Far Eastern affairs. In America President Harding seized the initiative and stole a diplomatic march on Britain by calling a Pacific powers conference. Charles Evans Hughes, the American Secretary of State, then suggested that the conference should be widened to include all the principal naval powers – Britain, America, France, Italy and Japan. Since the five principal naval powers had all been in alliance during the Great War, the Washington Treaty that emerged was a treaty between allies. It is surprising how often it is forgotten that Italy and Japan were on the allied winning side in World War I. By the time of the Washington Conference, American economic power was considerably greater than its potential rivals. American gross domestic product (GDP) was three times that of Britain and six times that of Japan.

America and Japan were in a much stronger negotiating position than Britain. By 1921 America had already commissioned the first of the new battleships, the *Maryland*, 32,600 tons and armed with eight 16-inch guns. Two others, the *West Virginia* and *Colorado*, were nearly completed and only one, the *Washington*, was scrapped under the terms of the treaty. The remaining six American ships were only about 25 per cent complete so scrapping them was no great loss. The Japanese had just completed the *Nagato* and *Mutsu*, 33,800 tons, also armed with eight 16-inch guns.

The opening session of the conference took place on 12 November 1921. Hughes proposed that all capital ship building programmes whether approved or projected should be scrapped. He went on to propose a massive scrapping policy that deposed of about 846,000 tons of American warships. Britain and Japan were to take commensurate action. This involved the scrapping of around 583,000 tons of British warships and 449,000 tons of Japanese warships. Britain would retain 22 capital ships against 18 American and ten Japanese. The greater number of British ships was accounted for by the relatively greater age and technical inferiority of the British ships. Hughes further proposed that there should be a ten year moratorium on battleship building, with a displacement limit of 35,000 tons on any future construction after the ten years had elapsed. When initiated this programme would put in place a 5:5:3:1.75:1.75 ratio of capital ship tonnage for America, Britain, Japan, France and Italy. The effect of these proposals was dramatic, and around the world popular opinion was very much on the side of the Americans.

What was unknown to the nations represented at the conference was that the Americans under Herbert Yardley were eavesdropping on the delegates and monitoring their communications with their home countries. It was particularly the case that Japanese communications were laid bare to the Americans, who knew to an exactitude, the minimum deal acceptable to the Japanese.

Punch Magazine January 4th, 1922
It was recognised at the Washington Treaty Conference that Britain's Naval supremacy was a thing of the past. Note Uncle Sam, the chief beneficiary, applauding in the background.

Fig. 19 Punch cartoon

The British were not against these proposals but wanted the 5:5:3 ratio expressed directly in ships and not tonnage. They also wanted to build at least two post-Jutland ships in which the hard lessons of experience were finally learned. After much argument, limitations of size were imposed on battleships and cruisers, 35,000 tons for battleships and 10,000 tons for cruisers. Britain was allowed two new ships but agreed that when each was completed two super-dreadnoughts of the King George V and Orion classes would be scrapped. Each post-Jutland ship was therefore considered equal to two pre-war ships. The initial British designs were battlecruisers of 48,000 tons. The 'Washington Treaty' battleships that emerged, *Nelson* and *Rodney*, were limited to 35,000 ton and armed with nine 16-inch guns. By the end of the 1920s the Royal Navy's capital ship strength fell to 15 battleships and battlecruisers, with a similar number of American ships. The 5:5 ratio of capital ships was finally met.

For the Royal Navy it was the end of a naval mastery that stretched back to the middle of the eighteenth century. In 1922 Britain accepted naval parity with an emerging continental superpower, a country that was, by the nature of its continental status, not subject to the workings of sea power. The battleships themselves were no longer considered supreme at sea. A new type of capital ship was entering the lists, the aircraft carrier. Submarines were not banned by Washington and in the 1920s France in particular built a number of super-submarines exceeding 2,000 tons. The age of the battleship was effectively over, though a few more were built before and during World War II. World War I was the dreadnoughts war and it was inconclusive and unsatisfactory. Sea power was the muscle and sinew of the old British Empire but in the twentieth century the nature of sea power changed and with it the hugely favourable geo-strategic position occupied by Britain and her Empire. It was indeed the end of the day and eventide for the British Empire and its dreadnought-era navy.

Appendix

British Dreadnoughts and Super-Dreadnoughts: Building Times, Costs and Fate

Name	Builder	Tons	Armament	Estimates	Cost (£)	Building Dates	Time	Fate
Dreadnought	Portsmouth Dyd.	18,110	10 12-inch, 28 12pdrs	1905–06	1,783,883	2.10.05–10.2.06–12.06	14 months	Sold for breaking up 9.5.21
Invincible	Elswick	17,373	8 12-inch, 16 4-inch	1905–06	1,752,739	2.4.06–13.4.07–3.08	23 months	Blew up and sunk 31.5.16
Indomitable	Fairfield	"	"	"	1,752,337	1.3.06–16.3.07–6.08	27 months	Sold for breaking up 1922
Inflexible	Clydebank	"	"	"	1,757,515	5.2.06–26.6.07–10.08	32 months	Sold for breaking up 1922
Bellerophon	Portsmouth Dyd.	18,800	10 12-inch, 16 4-inch	1906–07	1,765,342	3.12.06–22.7.07–2.09	26 months	Sold for breaking up 8.11.21
Temeraire	Devonport Dyd.	"	"	"	1,751,144	1.1.07–24.8.07–5.09	28 months	Sold for breaking up 7.12.21
Superb	Elswick	"	"	"	1,676,529	6.2.07–7.11.07–5.09	27 months	Sold for breaking up 12.12.23
Collingwood	Devonport Dyd.	19,560	10 12-inch, 20 4-inch	1907–08	1,731,640	3.2.08–7.11.08–4.10	26 months	Sold for breaking up 12.12.22
St Vincent	Portsmouth Dyd.	"	"	"	1,754,615	30.12.07–10.9.08–5.10	30 months	Sold for breaking up 1.12.21
Vanguard	Vickers, Barrow	"	"	"	1,607,780	2.4.08–22.2.09–2.10	23 months	Blew up and sunk 9.7.17
Neptune	Portsmouth Dyd.	19,680	10 12-inch, 16 4-inch	1908–09	1,668,916	19.1.09–30.9.09–1.11	33 months	Sold for breaking up 1922
Indefatigable	Devonport Dyd.	18,470	8 12-inch, 16 4-inch	1908–09	1,641,700	23.2.09–28.10.09–4.11	24 months	Blew up and sunk 31.5.16
Australia	John Brown	18,500	"	Dominion	1,779,190	23.6.10–25.10.11–6.13	36 months	Scuttled 12.4.24
New Zealand	Fairfield	"	"	"	1,779,190	20.6.10–17.11–11.12	27 months	Sold for breaking up 19.12.22
Colossus	Scotts	20,225	10 12-inch, 16 4-inch	1909–10	1,672,102	8.7.09–9.4.10–7.11	23 months	Sold for breaking up 7.28
Hercules	Palmers	"	"	"	1,661,240	30.7.09–10.5.10–8.11	23 months	Sold for breaking up 11.21
Orion	Portsmouth Dyd.	22,200	10 13.5-inch, 16 4-inch	1909–10	1,918,773	29.11.09–20.8.10–1.12	34 months	Sold for breaking up 12.22
Monarch	Armstrong	"	"	"	1,886,912	1.4.10–30.3.11–3.12	34 months	Sunk as a target 1925
Conqueror	Beardmore	"	"	"	1,860,648	5.4.10–1.5.11–11.12	34 months	Sold for breaking up 12.22
Thunderer	Thames I W	"	"	"	1,885,145	13.4.10–1.2.11–6.12	26 months	Sold for breaking up 12.26
Lion	Devonport Dyd.	26,270	8 13.5-inch, 16 4-inch	1909–10	2,086,458	29.9.09–6.8.10–5.12	31 months	Sold for breaking up 1.24
Princess Royal	Vickers	"	"	"	2,089,178	2.5.10–24.4.11–11.12	30 months	Sold for breaking up 12.22
King George V	Portsmouth Dyd.	23,000	10 13.5-inch, 16 4-inch	1910–11	1,961,096	16.1.11–9.10.11–11.12	22 months	Sold for breaking up 12.26
Centurion	Devonport Dyd.	"	"	"	1,950,671	16.1.11–18.11.11–5.13	28 months	Scuttled 1944
Ajax	Scotts	"	"	"	1,889,387	27.2.11–21.3.12–3.13	32 months	Sold for breaking up 11.26
Audacious	Cammell Laird	"	"	"	1,918,813	2.11–14.9.12–10.13	31 months	Mined and sunk 27.10.14
Queen Mary	Palmers, Jarrow	26,770	8 13.5-inch, 16 4-inch	1910–11	2,078,491	6.3.11–20.3.12–8.13	29 months	Blew up and sunk 31.5.16

British Dreadnoughts and Super-Dreadnoughts (2)

Name	Builder	Tons	Armament	Cost (£)	Building Dates	Time	Fate
Iron Duke	Portsmouth Dyd.	25,000	10 13.5-inch, 16 4-inch	1911–12	12.1.12–12.10.12–3.14	26 months	Sold for breaking up 3.46
Marlborough	Devonport Dyd.	"	"	"	25.1.12–24.10.12–6.14	29 months	Sold for breaking up 6.32
Benbow	Beardmore	"	"	"	30.5.12–12.11.13–10.14	29 months	Sold for breaking up 3.31
Emperor of India	Vickers	"	"	1,891,122	31.5.12–27.11.13–11.14	29 months	Sunk as target 1.9.31
Tiger	John Brown	28,430	8 13.5-inch, 12 6-inch	2,593,100	20.6.12–15.12.13–10.14	28 months	Sold for breaking up 2.32
Agincourt	Armstrong	27,500	14 12-inch, 20 6-inch	2,900,000	9.11–22.1.13–8.14	35 months	Sold for breaking up 12.22
Erin	Vickers	22,780	10 13.5-inch, 16 6-inch	2,500,000	1.8.11–3.9.13–8.14	32 months	Sold for breaking up 12.22
Canada	Armstrong	28,600	10 14-inch, 16 6-inch	2,500,000	12.11–27.11.13–9.15	46 months	Returned to Chile 4.20
Queen Elizabeth	Portsmouth Dyd.	27,500	8 15-inch, 14 6-inch	3,014,103	21.10.12–16.10.13–1.15	27 months	Sold for breaking up 4.48
Warspite	Devonport Dyd.	"	"	2,524,148	31.10.12–26.11.13–3.15	29 months	Sold for breaking up 7.46
Barham	John Brown	"	"	2,470,113	24.2.13–31.10.14–10.15	32 months	Sunk 25.11.41
Valiant	Fairfield	"	"	2,537,037	31.1.13–4.11.14–2.16	37 months	Sold for breaking up 3.48
Malaya	Armstrong	"	"	2,945,709	20.10.13–18.3.15–2.16	28 months	Sold for breaking up 2.48
Revenge	Vickers	28,000	8 15-inch, 14 6-inch	2,406,368	12.11.13–29.16–9.17	27 months	Sold for breaking up 9.48
Ramilles	Beardmore	"	"	3,295,810	12.11.13–12.9.16–9.17	46 months	Sold for breaking up 2.48
Royal Oak	Devonport Dyd.	"	"	2,468,269	15.1.14–17.11.14–5.16	28 months	Torpedoed and sunk 14.10.39
Royal Sovereign	Portsmouth Dyd.	"	"	2,570,504	15.1.14–29.4.15–5.16	28 months	Sold for breaking up 2.49
Resolution	Palmers	"	"	2,449,680	29.11.13–14.1.15–12.16	36 months	Sold for breaking up 5.48
Renown	Fairfield	27,650	6 15-inch, 17 4-inch	3,117,204	25.1.15–4.3.16–9.16	20 months	Sold for breaking up 3.48
Repulse	John Brown	"	"	War Programme	2,829,087	25.1.15–8.1.16–8.16	19 months	Sunk 10.12.41
Courageous	Elswick	19,230	4 15-inch, 18 4-inch	2,038,225	28.3.15–5.2.16–1.17	22 months	Sunk 17.9.39
Glorious	Harland & Wolff	"	"	War Programme	1,967,223	1.5.15–20.4.16–1.17	19 months	Sunk 8.6.40
Furious	Armstrong	19,513	2 18-inch, 11 5.5-inch	War Programme	1,050,000	8.6.15–15.8.16–7.17	25 months	Sold for breaking up 1946
Hood	John Brown	42,670	8 15-inch, 12 5.5-inch	War Programme	6,025,000	1.9.16–22.8.18–5.20	44 months	Sunk 24.5.41

In the pre-dreadnought era 36 battleships were built in the Royal Dockyards and 26 were contract built.
In the dreadnought era, 17 dreadnoughts were built in the Royal Dockyards and 26 were contract built. Average building time 28.74 months.
In the case of armoured cruisers only 11 were built in the Royal Dockyards and 24 were contract built.

German Dreadnoughts and Super-Dreadnoughts: Building Times, Costs and Fate

Name	Builder	Tons	Armament	Estimates	Cost (GM.)	Building Dates	Ersatz	Time (Bldg.)	Fate
Nassau	Wilhelmshaven N.Yd.	18,570	12 28cm, 12 15cm	1906–07	37.399	22.7.07–7.3.08–3.5.10	Bayern	34 months	Broken up 1921
Westfalen	Weser, Bremen	"	"	1906–07	37.615	12.8.07–1.7.08–3.5.10	Sachsen	33 months	Broken up 1924
Rheinland	Vulcan, Stettin	"	"	1907–08	36.916	1.6.07–26.9.08–21.9.10	Württemberg	39 months	Broken up 1921
Posen	Germaniawerft, Kiel	"	"	1907–08	36.92	11.6.07–12.12.08–21.9.10	Baden	39 months	Broken up 1922
Helgoland	Howaldswerke, Kiel	22,440	12 30.5cm, 14 15cm	1908–09	46.196	24.12.08–25.9.09–19.12.11	Siegfried	36 months	Broken up 1924
Oldenburg	Schichau, Danzig	"	"	1909–10	45.801	1.3.09–30.6.10–1.7.12	Fritjof	40 months	Broken up 1921
Ostfriesland	Wilhelmshaven N.Yd.	"	"	1908–09	43.597	19.10.08–30.9.09–15.9.11	Oldenburg	35 months	Target, sunk 21.7.21
Thüringen	Weser, Bremen	"	"	1908–09	46.314	7.11.08–27.11.09–10.9.11	Beowulf	34 months	Broken up 1923
Kaiser	Kiel N.Yd.	24,330	10 30.5cm, 14 15cm	1909–10	44.997	12.09–22.3.11–7.12.12	Hildebrand	36 months	Scuttled 21.6.19
Friedrich der Grosse	Vulcan, Hamburg	"	"	1909–10	45.802	26.1.10–10.6.11–22.1.13	Heimdall	36 months	Scuttled 21.6.19
Kaiserin	Howaldswerke, Kiel	"	"	1910–11	45.173	11.10–11.11.11–13.12.13	Hagen	37 months	Scuttled 21.6.19
König Albert	Schichau, Danzig	"	"	1910–11	45.761	17.7.10–27.4.12–8.11.13	Ägir	40 months	Scuttled 21.6.19
Prinzregent Luitpold	Germaniawerft, Kiel	"	"	1910–11	46.374	1.11–17.2.12–6.12.13	Odin	35 months	Scuttled 21.6.19
König	Wilhelmshaven N.Yd.	25,390	10 30.5, 14 15cm	1911–12	45.0 (Av.)	10.11–1.3.13–1.15	'S'	39 months	Scuttled 21.6.19
Grosser Kurfürst	Vulcan, Hamburg	"	"	1911–12	"	10.11–5.5.13–9.14	K.F. Wilhelm	35 months	Scuttled 21.6.19
Markgraf	Weser, Bremen	"	"	1911–12	"	11.11–4.6.13–1.15	Weissenburg	39 months	Scuttled 21.6.19
Kronprinz	Germaniawerft, Kiel	"	"	1912–13	"	5.12–21.2.14–2.15	Brandenburg	33 months	Scuttled 21.6.19
Bayern	Howaldswerke, Kiel	28,074	8 38cm, 16 15cm	1913–14	48.5 (Av.)	1.14–18.2.15–30.6.16	'T'	29 months	Scuttled 21.6.19
Baden	Schichau. Danzig	"	"	1913–14	"	20.12.13–30.10.15–2.17	Wörth	39 months	Target, sunk 16.8.21
Sachsen	Germaniawerft, Kiel	"	"	1914–15	"	7.4.14–21.11.16–n/c.	K. Freidrich III		Broken up 1921
Württemberg	Vulcan, Hamburg	"	"	1914–15	"	4.15–20.6.17–n/c.	K. Wilhelm II		Broken up 1921
Blücher	Kiel N.Yd	15,590	12 21cm, 8 15cm	1906–07	28.5	21.2.07–11.4.08–24.3.10	'E'	37 months	Sunk 24.1.15
Von der Tann	Blohm & Voss, Hamburg	19,064	8 28cm, 10 15cm	1907–08	36.523	25.3.09–20.3.09–20.2.11	'F'	35 months	Scuttled 21.6.19
Moltke	Blohm & Voss, Hamburg	22,616	10 28cm, 12 15cm	1908–09	42.603	7.12.08–7.4.10–31.3.12	'G'	39 months	Scuttled 21.6.19
Goeben	Blohm & Voss, Hamburg	"	"	1909–10	41.564	28.8.09–28.3.11–28.8.12	'H'	36 months	Broken up 1971
Seydlitz	Blohm & Voss, Hamburg	24,594	10 28cm, 12 15cm	1910–11	44.685	4.2.11–30.3.12–17.8.13	'J'	30 months	Scuttled 21.6.19
Derfflinger	Blohm & Voss, Hamburg	26,180	8 30.5cm, 12 15cm	1911–12	56.0	1.12–1.7.13–11.14	'K'	34 months	Scuttled 21.6.19
Lützow	Schichau, Danzig	"	"	1912–13	58.0	5.12–29.11.13–3.16	K. Augusta	46 months	Sunk, Jutland 1.6.16
Hindenburg	Wilhelmshaven N.Yd.	26,513	8 30.5cm, 14 15cm	1913–14	59.0	30.6.13–1.8.15–25.10.17	Hertha	52 months	Scuttled 21.6.19

For currency conversion £1 = 20.43 Goldmark. Costs given in million Goldmark. Average Building Time 35.14 months

251

American Dreadnoughts and Super-Dreadnoughts

Name	Builder	Tons	Armament	Authorised	Cost (£)	Building Dates	Time	Fate
South Carolina	New York SB	16,000	8 12in, 22 3in	1905	700,000	18.12.06–11.7.08–1.3.10	39 months	Stricken 1924
Michigan	Cramp	"	"	"	"	17.12.06–26.5.08–4.1.10	39 months	Stricken 1924
Delaware	Newport News	20,380	10 12in, 14 5in	1906	817,300	11.11.07–6.2.09–4.4.10	28 months	Stricken 1924
North Dakota	Fore River	"	"	1907	899,500	16.12.07–10.11.09–11.4.10	28 months	Stricken 1931
Florida	New York N Yd.	21,825	10 12in, 16 5in	1908	1,280,000	9.3.09–12.5.10–15.9.11	30 months	Stricken 1931
Utah	New York SB	"	"	"	813,500	15.3.09–23.12.09–31.8.11	29 months	Sunk 7.12.41
Wyoming	Cramp	26,000	12 12in, 21 5in	1909	963,800	9.2.10–25.5.11–25.9.12	31 months	Stricken 1947
Arkansas	New York SB	"	"	"	964,000	25.1.10–14.1.11–17.9.12	32 months	Target 26.7.46
New York	New York N Yd	27,000	10 14in, 21 5in	1910	1,315,114	11.9.11–30.10.12–15.4.14	31 months	Sunk 8.7.48
Texas	Newport News	"	"	"	1,166,000	17.4.11–18.5.12–12.3.14	35 months	Memorial ship 1948
Nevada	Fore River	27,500	10 14in, 21 5in	1911	1,211,342	4.11.12–11.7.14–11.3.16	40 months	Sunk 31.7.48
Oklahoma	New York SB	"	"	"	2,200,000	26.10.12–23.3.14–2.5.16	43 months	Sunk 7.12.41
Pennsylvania	Newport News	31,400	12 14in, 22 5in	1912	1,485,000	27.10.13–16.3.15–12.6.16	32 months	Scuttled 10.2.48
Arizona	New York N Yd	"	"	1913	1,485,000	16.3.14–19.6.15–17.10.16	31 months	Sunk 7.12.41
New Mexico	New York N Yd	32,000	12 14in, 14 5in	1914	1,485,000	14.10.15–23.4.17–20.5.18	31 months	Stricken 1947
Mississippi	Newport News	"	"	"	1,485,000	5.4.15–25.1.17–18.12.17	32 months	Stricken 1956
Idaho	New York SB	"	"	"		20.1.15–30.6.17–24.3.19	50 months	Stricken 1947
Tennessee	New York N Yd	32,300	12 14in, 14 5in	1915		14.5.17–30.4.19–3.6.20	37 months	Stricken 1959
California	Mare Island N Yd	"	"	"		25.10.16–20.11.19–10.8.21	58 months	Stricken 1959
Colorado	New York SB	32,600	8 16in, 14 5in	1916		25.5.19–22.3.21–20.8.23	51 months	Stricken 1959
Maryland	Newport News	"	"	"		24.4.17–20.3.20–21.7.21	51 months	Stricken 1959
Washington	New York SB	"	"	"		30.6.19–1.9.21		Cancelled, Washington and sunk
West Virginia	Newport News	"	"	"		12.4.20–19.11.21–1.12.23	44 months	Stricken 1959

American Dreadnoughts and Super-Dreadnoughts (2)

Name	Builder	Tons	Armament	Authorised	Cost (£)	Building Dates	Time	Fate
South Dakota	New York N Yd	43,200	12 16in, 16 6in	1917	unknown	15.3.20	N/A	Cancelled 8.2.22
Indiana	New York N Yd	"	"	"	"	1.11.20	N/A	"
Montana	Mare Island N Yd	"	"	"	"	1.9.20	N/A	"
North Carolina	Norfolk N Yd	"	"	1918	"	121.1.20	N/A	"
Iowa	Newport News	"	"	"	"	17.5.20	N/A	"
Massachusetts	Fore River	"	"	"	"	4.4.21	N/A	"
Lexington	Fore River	43,500	8 16in, 16 6in	1916	unknown	8.1.21		Became carrier CV2
Constellation	Newport News	"	"	"	"	18.8.20	N/A	Cancelled 17.8.23
Saratoga	New York SB	"	"	"	"	25.9.20		Became carrier CV3
Ranger	Newport News	"	"	"	"	23.6.21	N/A	Cancelled 17.8.23
Constitution	Philadelphia N Yd	"	"	1917	"	25.9.20	N/A	"
United States	Philadelphia N Yd	"	"	1918	"	25.9.20	N/A	"

Note: Brassey's Naval Annuals of 1914 and 1919 were used for the costs, which exclude the cost of guns and armour.
Costs are given in Sterling, assuming an exchange rate of £1 = 4.8665

Japanese Dreadnoughts and Super-Dreadnoughts

Name	Builder	Tons	Armament	Cost (£)	Building Dates	Time	Fate
Satsuma	Kure N Yd	19,372	4 12in, 12 10in	1,750,000	15.5.05–15.11.06–25.3.10	58 months	Sunk as target 7.9.24
Aki	Yokosuka N Yd	20,100	"	"	15.3.06–15.4.07–11.3.11	60 months	Sunk as target 2.9.24
Settsu	Kure N Yd	21,443	12 12in, 10 6in	1,750,000	18.1.09–30.3.11–1.7.12	42 months	Sunk 24.7.45
Kawachi	Yokosuka N Yd	20,823	"	"	1.4.09–15.10.10–31.3.12	35 months	Sunk 12.7.18
Fuso	Kure N Yd	30,600	12 14in, 16 6in	2,500,000	11.3.12–28.3.14–18.11.15	44 months	Sunk 25.10.44
Yamashiro	Yokosuka N Yd	39,154	"	"	20.11.13–3.11.15–31.3.17	40 months	Sunk 25.10.44
Ise	Kawasaki, Kobe	31,260	12 14in, 20 5.5in	3,000,000	10.5.15–12.11.16–15.12.17	31 months	Sunk 28.7.45
Hyuga	Mitsubishi, Nagasaki	"	"	"	6.5.15–27.1.17–30.4.18	35 months	Sunk 24.7.45
Nagato	Kure N Yd	33,800	8 16in, 20 5.5in	5,000,000	28.8.17–9.11.19–25.11.20	39 months	Sunk 19.7.46
Mutsu	Yokosuka N Yd	"	"	"	1.6.18–31.5.20–22.11.21	41 months	Sunk 8.6.43
Kaga	Kawasaki, Kobe	39,900	10 16in, 20 5.5in	Not known	19.7.20–17.11.21–(25.12.22)	29 months	Completer as carrier
Tosa	Mitsubishi, Nagasaki	"	"	"	16.2.20–18.12.21–(3.23)	37 months	Sunk 9.2.25
KII	Kure N Yd	42,600	10 16in, 16 5.5in	Not known	N/A	N/A	Never laid down
Owari	Yokosuka N Yd	"	"	"	N/A	N/A	"
No.11	Kawasaki, Kobe	"	"	"	N/A	N/A	"
No.12	Mitsubishi, Nagasaki	"	"	"	N/A	N/A	"
Tsukuba	Yokosuka N Yd	13,750	4 12in, 12 6in	Not known	14.1.05–26.12.05–14.1.07	24 months	Sunk 14.1.17
Ikoma	Kure N Yd	"	"	"	15.3.05–9.4.06–24.3.08	36 months	Broken up 13.11.24
Ibuki	Kure N Yd	14,636	4 12in, 8 8in	Not known	22.5.07–21.11.07–1.11.09	30 months	Broken up by 9.12.24
Kurama	Yokosuka N Yd	"	"	"	23.8.05–21.10.07–28.2.11	66 months	Broken up 1924-25
Kongo	Vickers	27,500	8 14in, 16 6in	2,500,000	17.1.11–18.5.12–16.8.13	31 months	Sunk 21.11.24
Hiei	Yokosuka N Yd	"	"	"	4.11.11–21.11.12–4.8.14	33 months	Sunk 13.11.42
Haruna	Kawasaki, Kobe	"	"	"	16.3.12–14.12.13–19.4.15	37 months	Sunk 28.7.45
Kirishima	Mitsubishi, Nagasaki	"	"	"	17.3.12–1.12.13–19.4.15	37 months	Sunk 15.11.42
Amagi	Yokosuka N Yd	41,217	10 16in, 16 5.5in	Not known	16.12.20	N/A	Wrecked 1.9.23
Akagi	Kure N Yd	"	"	"	6.12.20	N/A	Completed as carrier
Atago	Kawasaki, Kobe	"	"	"	22.11.21	N/A	Broken up 1924
Takao	Mitsubishi, Nagasaki	"	"	"	19.12.21	N/A	"
No.13	Yokosuka N Yd	47,500	8 18in, 16 5.5in	Not known	N/A	N/A	Cancelled 19.11.23
No.14	Kure N Yd	"	"	"	N/A	N/A	"
No.15	Mitsubishi, Nagasaki	"	"	"	N/A	N/A	"
No.16	Kawasaki, Kobe	"	"	"	N/A	N/A	"

Where possible building costs have been given in Sterling, assuming an exchange rate of 9.8 Yen to one pound.

French Semi-Dreadnoughts, Dreadnoughts and Super-Dreadnoughts

Name	Builder	Tons	Armament	Cost	Building Dates	Time	Fate
Condorcet	A C de la Loire, St Nazaire	18,318	4 30.5cm (12in), 12 24cm (9.4in)	2,165,200	23.8.07–20.8.09–25.7.11	47 months	Deleted 1931
Danton	Arsenal de Brest	"	"	2,068,000	2.06–4.7.09–1.6.11	59 months	Sunk by U-boat 19.3.17
Diderot	A C de la Loire, St Nazaire	"	"	2,167,000	20.10.07–19.4.09–1.8.11	46 months	Condemned 1936, broken up
Mirabeau	Arsenal de Lorient	"	"	2,032,000	4.5.08–28.10.09–1.8.11	39 months	Target 1922, broken up 1928
Vergniaud	C de la Gironde, Bordeaux	"	"	2,165,200	7.08–12.4.10–22.9.11	38 months	Deleted 1921, aircraft target
Voltaire	F C de la Méditerranée La Seyne	"	"	2,169,200	30.7.07–16.1.09–1.8.11	49 months	Condemned 1935, broken up
Courbet	Arsenal de Brest	22,189	12 30.5cm (12in), 22 13.86cm (5.4in)	2,508,388	1.9.10–23.9.11–19.11.13	38 months	Scuttled 1944 (Mulberry)
France	A C de la Loire, St Nazaire	"	"	2,603,920	30.11.11–7.11.121–8.14	33 months	Foundered 26.8.22
Jean Bart	Arsenal de Brest	"	"	2,528,888	15.11.10–22.9.11–5.6.13	31 months	Sold for breaking up 14.12.45
Paris	F C de la Méditerranée La Seyne	"	"	2,603,920	10.1.11–28.9.12–1.8.14	33 months	Broken up 1955
Bretagne	Arsenal de Brest	23,230	12 34cm (13.4in), 24 13.86cm (5.4in)	2,589,439	1.7.12–21.4.13–9.15	38 months	Sunk by British 3.7.40
Lorraine	A C de St Nazaire-Penhoët	"	"	2,642,439	1.8.12–30.9.13–7.16	35 months	Broken up 1954
Provence	Arsenal de Brest	"	"	2,600,195	1.5.12–20.4.13–6.15	37 months	Broken up 1953
Béarn	F C de la Méditerranée La Seyne	25,230	12 34cm (13.4in), 24 13.86cm (5.4in)	Not Known	10.1.14–4.20	N/A	Converted to aircraft carrier
Flandre	Arsenal de Brest	"	"	"	1.10.13–20.10.14	"	Broken up from 10.24
Gascoigne	Arsenal de Lorient	"	"	"	1.10.13–20.9.14	"	Broken up 1923–24
Languedoc	F C de la Gironde, Bordeaux	"	"	"	18.4.13–19.10.14	"	Broken up from 6.29
Normandie	A C de la Loire, St Nazaire	"	"	"	18.4.13–19.10.14	"	Broken up 1924–25
Duquesne	Arsenal de Brest	29,000	16 34cm (13.4in), 24 13.86cm (5.4in)	Not Known	Never started	N/A	Never started
Lille	F C de la Méditerranée La Seyne	"	"	"		"	"
Lyon	A C de la Loire et Penhoët, St Nazaire	"	"	"		"	"
Tourville	Arsenal de Lorient	"	"	"		"	"

Costs taken from *Brassey's Naval Annual 1919* and given in sterling at a conversion rate of £1 = 25 Francs

Italian Dreadnoughts and Super-Dreadnoughts

Name	Builder	Tons	Armament	Cost	Building Dates	Time	Fate
Dante Alighieri	Castellammare RN Yd	19,552	12 30.5cm (12in), 20 12cm (4.7in)	Not Known	6.6.09–20.8.10–15.1.13	43 months	Stricken 1.7.28
Conte Di Cavour	La Spezia RN Yd	22,992	13 30.5cm (12in), 18 12cm (4.7in)	Not Known	10.8.10–10.8.11–1.4.15	44 months	Sunk 12.11.40, broken up
Giulio Cesare	Ansaldo, Genoa	23,193	"	"	24.6.10–15.10.11–14.5.14	47 months	Handed to USSR 1948
Leonardo Da Vinci	Odero, Sestri Ponente	23,087	"	"	18.7.10–14.10.11–17.5.14	46 months	Sunk 2.8.16
Andrea Doria	La Spezia RN Yd	22,956	13 30.5cm (12in), 16 15.2cm (6in)	Not Known	24.3.12–30.3.13–13.3.16	48 months	Stricken 1.11.56
Duilio	Castellammare RN Yd	22,994	"	"	24.2.12–24.4.13–10.5.15	51 months	Stricken 15.9.56
Francesco Caracciolo	"	31,400	8 38.1cm (15in), 12 15.2cm (6in)	Not Known	16.10.14–12.5.20	N/A	Stricken 2.1.21
Cristoforo Colombo	Ansaldo, Genoa	"	"	"	14.3.15	"	"
Marcantonio Colonna	Odero, Sestri Ponente	"	"	"	3.3.15	"	"
Francesco Morosini	Orlando, Leghorn	"	"	"	27.6.15	"	"

Russian Dreadnoughts and Super-Dreadnoughts

Name	Builder	Tons	Armament	Cost	Building Dates	Time	Fate
Gangut	Admiralty Yd, St. Petersburg	23,360	12 12in (30.5cm), 16 4.7in (12cm)	Not Known	16.6.09–7.10.11–12.14	66 months	Broken up 1959
Petropavlovsk	Baltic Yd, St Petersburg	"	"	"	16.6.09–9.9.11–12.14	66 months	Total loss 23.9.1941
Poltava	Admiralty Yd, St. Petersburg	"	"	"	16.6.09–10.7.11–17.12.14	66 months	Stricken 1925
Sevastopol	Baltic Yd, St Petersburg	"	"	"	16.6.09–27.6.11–17.11.14	65 months	Broken up 1957
Imperatritsa Maria	Russud Yd, Nikolayev	22,600	12 12in (30.5cm), 20 5.1in (13cm)	Not Known	30.10.11–1.11.13–6.7.15	44 months	Lost 20.10.16
Imperatritsa Ekaterina	Russud Yd, Nikolayev	23,783	"	"	30.10.11–15.4.14–28.6.17	68 months	Sold 1924
Imperator Alexandr III	Naval Yd, Nikolayev	22,600	"	"	30.10.11–6.6.14–18.10.15	48 months	Sunk 18.6.18
Imperator Nikolai II	Russud Yd, Nikolayev	27,300	12 12in (30.5cm), 20 5.1in (13cm)	Not Known	28.1.15–18.10.16	N/A	Incomplete, broken up 1924
Borodino	Admiralty Yd, St. Petersburg	32,500	12 12in (30.5cm), 20 5.1in (13cm).	Not Known	19.12.13–1.7.15	N/A	Incomplete, broken up 1923
Izmail	Baltic Yd, St Petersburg	"	"	"	19.12.13–27.6.15	"	"
Kinburn	Baltic Yd, St Petersburg	"	"	"	19.12.13–30.10.15	"	"
Navarin	21	"	"	"	19.12.13–9.11.16	"	"

Austro-Hungarian Semi-Dreadnoughts, Dreadnoughts and Super-Dreadnoughts

Name	Builder	Tons	Armament	Cost	Building Dates	Time	Fate
E. Franz Ferdinand	Stabilimento Tecnico, Trieste	14,508	4 30.5cm (12in), 8 24cm (9.4in)	Not Known	12.9.07–30.9.08–5.6.10	33 months	Broken up 1920
Radetzky	"	"	"	"	26.11.07–3.7.09–15.1.11	38 months	Broken up 1920
Zrinyi	"	"	"	"	20.1.09–12.4.10–15.9.11	32 months	Broken up 1920
Viribus Unitis	Stabilimento Tecnico, Trieste	20,013	12 30.5cm (12in), 12 15cm (5.9in)	Not Known	24.7.10–24.6.11–5.12.12	29 months	Sunk 1.11.18
Tegetthoff	"	"	"	"	24.9.10–21.3.12–21.7.13	34 months	Broken up 1924/25
Prinz Eugen	Danubius, Fiume	"	"	"	16.1.12–30.11.12–17.7.14	30 months	Sunk 28.6.22
Szent Istvan	Stabilimento Tecnico, Trieste	20,008	"	"	29.1.12–17.1.14–13.12.15	47 months	Sunk 10.6.18
Ersatz Monarch		24,500	10 35cm (13.8in), 15 15cm (5.9in)	Not Known	N/A	N/A	Never laid down
Ersatz Budapest	Danubius, Fiume	"	"	"	"	"	"
Ersatz Wein	Stabilimento Tecnico, Trieste	"	"	"	"	"	"
Ersatz Habsburg	Danubius, Fiume	"	"	"	"	"	"

Spanish Dreadnoughts

Name	Builder	Tons	Armament	Cost	Building Dates	Time	Fate
España	Ferrol Dyd	15,452	8 12in (30.5cm), 20 4in (10.2cm)	Not Known	6.12.09–5.2.12–28.10.13	46 months	Wrecked 26.8.23
Alfonso XIII	"	"	"	"	23.2.10–7.5.13–16.8.15	56 months	Mined 30.4.37
Jaime I	"	"	"	"	5.2.12–21.9.14–20.12.21	117 months	Lost 17.6.37

Turkish Dreadnoughts

Two Turkish Dreadnoughts were built in Britain, neither saw service in the Turkish Navy. *Reshadieh* became HMS *Erin*, *Sultan Osman I* became HMS *Agincourt*

Greek Dreadnoughts

Name	Builder	Tons	Armament	Cost	Building Dates	Time	Fate
Salamis	AG Vulkan, Hamburg	19,500	8 14in (35.6cm), 12 6in (15.2cm)	Not Known	23.7.13–11.11.14	N/A	Unfinished, broken up 1932

South American Dreadnoughts

Brazil

Name	Builder	Tons	Armament	Cost	Building Dates	Time	Fate
Minas Gerais	Armstrong, Elswick	19,281	12 12in (30.5cm), 22 4.7in (12cm)	1,821,400	17.4.07–10.9.08–6.1.10	33 months	Sold 1953
Sao Paulo	Vickers, Barrow	"	"	"	30.4.07–19.4.09–7.10	39 months	Sold 1951
Rio de Janeiro	Armstrong, Elswick	27,500	14 12in (30.5cm), 20 6in (15.2cm)	2,725,000	9.11–22.1.13–8.14	35 months	Appropriated by Britain

One further dreadnought was planned but was cancelled in the planning stage

Argentina

Name	Builder	Tons	Armament	Cost	Building Dates	Time	Fate
Rivadavia	Fore River	27,940	12 12in (30.5cm), 12 6in (15.2cm)	2,200,000	25.5.10–26.8.11–12.14	55 months	Sold 8.2.56
Moreno	New York SB	"	"	"	9.7.10–23.9.11–3.15	55 months	"

Chile

Name	Builder	Tons	Armament	Cost (£)	Building Dates	Time	Fate
Almirante Latorre	Armstrong, Newcastle	28,600	10 14in (35.6cm), 16 6in (15.2cm)	2,000,000	12.11–17.11.13–30.9.15	33 months	Returned to Chile
Almirante Cochrane	"	N/A	N/A	N/A	N/A		Converted to carrier *Eagle*.

Notes

Preface

1. E.L. Woodward, *Great Britain and the German Navy* (Oxford, 1935), p. 238.
2. Arthur Marder, *From the Dreadnought to Scapa Flow*, Vol. 1: *The Road to War 1904–1914* (Oxford, 1961), p. 6.
3. Paul M. Kennedy, *The Rise and Fall of British Naval Mastery* (London, 1976), pp. 239–98.

1 The Origins of the Pre-Dreadnought Era

1. Arthur Marder, *From the Dreadnought to Scapa Flow*, Vol. 1: *The Road to War 1904–1914* (Oxford, 1961), p. 6.
2. Andrew Lambert, 'Preparing for the long peace: the reconstruction of the Royal Navy 1815–1830', *The Mariner's Mirror* 82/1 (February 1996), pp. 41–2.
3. Arthur Marder, *British Naval Policy, 1880–1905: The Anatomy of British Sea-Power* (London, 1940), pp. 119–43. Marder argued that there was a gradual weakening of the navy after 1868, but his argument only works if all the French wooden-hulled ironclads without watertight compartments are counted as the equal of the iron-hulled ironclads with watertight compartments. Ten years later, in 1878, France still had only three iron-hulled ironclads. Britain by contrast had 26.
4. Eric J. Grove, *The Royal Navy since 1815: A New Short History* (London, 2005), p. 77.
5. *The Times*, 22 January 1877, p. 6 (arrival), 19 May 1877, p. 7 (departure). See also NMM MLN163/12 Second Report, Carnarvon Commission 1880, p. 1, para. 3.
6. Donald M. Schurman, *Imperial Defence 1868–1887* (London, 2000), pp. 83–4.
7. National Maritime Museum (hereafter NMM) MLN 163/10, First Report Carnarvon Commission 1879, evidence of George Duncan, head of Statistical Section, Board of Trade, para. 1442.

8. Ibid., First Report Carnarvon Commission, 1879, evidence of Alfred Holt, para. 390.
9. Ibid., evidence of Charles Maciver, paras 438, 525.
10. Ibid., evidence of Thomas Ismay, para. 717.
11. Ibid., evidence of William Young, para. 1893.
12. Geoffrey Bennett, *Charlie B* (London, 1968), p. 156fn. See also Julian Corbett, *Some Principles of Maritime Strategy* (London, 1911), pp. 263–84.
13. NMM MLN 163/12 Second Report, Carnarvon Commission 1880, p. 4, para. 15.
14. Oscar Parkes, *British Battleships* (London, 1957), p. 328.
15. N.A.M. Rodger, 'The dark ages of the Admiralty, 1869–85, Part III: Peace, retrenchment and reform', *The Mariner's Mirror* 6/2 (May 1976), p. 125.
16. The National Archives (hereafter TNA) ADM231/5 Remarks on a Naval Campaign, 24 September 1884, p. 4 and TNA ADM231/6 General Outline of Possible Naval Operations against Russia, 14 March 1885, p. 2.
17. Parkes, *British Battleships*, p. 350.
18. Bennett, *Charlie B*, pp. 136–7.
19. Donald M. Schurman, *The Education of a Navy* (London, 1965), p. 16.
20. Ibid., p. 46.
21. Ibid., pp. 84–7.
22. TNA ADM231/5 FIC No. 51, pp. 4–5.
23. Richard Hill, *War at Sea in the Ironclad Age* (London, 2000), p. 91.
24. Theodore Ropp, *The Development of a Modern Navy* (Annapolis, MD, 1987), pp. 159–60.
25. Ibid., p. 171.
26. Marder, *British Naval Policy 1880–1905*, p. 131.
27. TNA CAB37/22 No. 36, 14 November 1888, No. 28 1888 and No. 40 December 1888.
28. Richard Hough, *Admirals in Collision* (London, 1959), pp. 11–22.
29. George Clarke and James Thursfield, *The Navy and the Nation* (London, 1897), pp. 77–8.
30. *Brassey's Naval Annual 1889*, p. 416, see also House of Commons Parliamentary Papers C.5632, Extracts from Report of the Committee on Naval Manoeuvres, of Operations, and Rules, 1889, pp. 5–6.
31. Ibid., p. 33.
32. Parkes, *British Battleships*, p. 352.
33. Hansard 3rd Ser. CCCXXIII, 1171: 7 March 1889 and *Brassey's Naval Annual 1889*, p. 137.
34. Hansard 3rd Ser. CCCXXIII, 1171: 7 March 1889.
35. *Conway's All The Worlds Fighting Ships 1860–1905* (London, 1979), pp. 33, 66, 76–7.
36. Robert Blake, *The Conservative Party from Peel to Churchill* (London, 1970), pp. 281–4.

37. Ropp, *The Development of a Modern Navy*, p. 198.
38. Ibid., p. 185.
39. Clive Parry (ed.), *The Consolidated Treaty Series*, Vol. 169 [1887] (Dobbs Ferry, NY, 1978), pp. 119–29.
40. A.J.P. Taylor, *The Struggle for Mastery in Europe, 1848–1918* (Oxford, 1960), p. 311.
41. *Chambers Encyclopaedia* 1927, Vol. 9, pp. 346–7.
42. W.H. White, *A Manual of Naval Architecture* (London, 1877), p. 424 and Lloyds 'Register of British and Foreign Shipbuilding – Extended Report on Steel for Shipbuilding Transactions of the Institute of Naval Architects XVIII' (1877), p. 393.
43. Andrew Tylcote, *The Long Wave in the World Economy* (London, 1992), p. 49.
44. *Conway's 1860–1905*, p. 52.
45. Parkes, *British Battleships*, pp. 288–92.
46. Sydney Eardley-Wilmot, *The Development of Navies* (London, 1892), p. 179.
47. William Hovgaard, *Modern History of Warships* (London, 1978), p. 364. See also, David K. Brown, 'Marine engineering in the RN 1860–1905 Part II. The ship is a steam being', *Journal of Naval Engineering* 34/3 (1993), p. 653.
48. N.J.M. Campbell, 'The development of naval guns 1850–1900', in Robert D. Smith (ed.), *British Naval Armaments*, Royal Armouries Conference Proceedings (London, 1989), pp. 56–61 and D.K. Brown, *Warrior to Dreadnought* (London, 1997), p. 78.
49. Ropp, *The Development of a Modern Navy*, pp. 216–17.
50. W.H. Simmons, 'A short history of the royal gunpowder factory at Waltham Abbey', monograph produced by the Controllerate of Royal Ordnance Factories (1963), pp. 53–4.
51. Campbell, 'The development of naval guns 1850–1900', p. 53.
52. Hovgaard, *Modern History of Warships*, pp. 396–7.
53. *Chambers Encyclopaedia* 1927, Vol. 2, pp. 422–3.
54. Ruddock F. Mackay, *Fisher of Kilverstone* (London, 1973), p. 187.
55. Ibid., p. 145.
56. TNA ADM116/267 Naval Armaments: November 1886, Question of transfer of responsibility for provision from Army to Navy votes.
57. Campbell, 'The development of naval guns 1850–1900', p. 62.
58. Robert Gardiner, *Steam Steel and Shellfire: The Steam Warship 1815–1905* (London, 1992), pp. 84–5.
59. Lawrence Sondhaus, *Naval Warfare 1815–1914* (London, 2001), p. 112.
60. Parkes, *British Battleships*, p. 252.
61. 'Estimates for the Italian Navy for 1878 and account of the new Ironclad Italia building at Castellamare', *Journal of the Royal United Services Institution* 22 (1878), pp. 260–2. See also Major Nabor Soliani, 'Steam trials of the Royal

Italian Ironclad Lepanto', *Transactions of the Institute of Naval Architects* 33 (1889), pp. 113–29.
62. Parkes, *British Battleships*, pp. 262–6, 288–92.
63. *Conway's 1860–1905*, p. 178 (*Ekaterina*), pp. 290–1 (*Duperre* and *Terribles*).
64. Parkes, *British Battleships*, p. 299 and P.H. Colomb, *Some Memoirs of Sir Astley Cooper-Key* (London, 1898), pp. 424–6 (Parkes evidently used this passage as his primary source material).
65. Parkes, *British Battleships*, pp. 317–46.
66. W.H. White, 'On the designs for the new battleships', *Transactions of the Institute of Naval Architects* XXX (1889), pp. 150–80.
67. N.A.M. Rodger, 'The design of the *Inconstant*', *The Mariner's Mirror* 61/1 (February 1975), pp. 9–22.
68. Admiral G.A. Ballard, 'British frigates of 1875, the *Inconstant* and *Raleigh*', *The Mariner's Mirror* 22/1 (February 1936), pp. 42–53, p. 46. See also *Brassey's Naval Annual 1887*, p. 289.
69. Rodger, 'The design of the *Inconstant*', pp. 21–2. See also, Admiral G.A. Ballard, 'British frigates of 1875, the *Shah*', *The Mariner's Mirror* 22/3 (August 1936), pp. 305–15 and 'British corvettes of 1875, the *Volage, Active* and *Rover*', *The Mariner's Mirror* 23/1 (February 1937), pp. 53–67.
70. Eardley-Wilmot, *The Development of Navies*, pp. 229–36.
71. *Conway's 1860–1905*, p. 76.
72. Antony Preston, 'Corps of Constructors', *Navy International* (August 1980), p. 497.
73. Parkes, *British Battleships*, p. 347.
74. Frederic Manning, *The Life of Sir William White* (London, 1923), pp. 89–95.
75. TNA ADM116/31 Royal Corps of Naval Constructors. The order in council establishing the Royal Corps is dated 23 August 1883. This paper gives the pay rates and duties of Constructors.
76. Preston, 'Corps of Constructors', p. 497.
77. Parkes, *British Battleships*, p. 347.
78. Antony Preston, 'The end of the Victorian Navy', *The Mariner's Mirror* 60/4 (November 1974), pp. 363–81, p. 373.
79. *Conway's 1860–1905*, p. 64.
80. J.M. Haas, *A Management Odyssey: Royal Dockyards 1714–1914* (Lanham, MD, 1994), pp. 147–8.
81. Ibid., pp. 148–9.

2 The Pre-Dreadnought Era in the 1890s

1. Lawrence Sondhaus, *Naval Warfare 1815–1914* (London, 2001), pp. 156, 166.
2. Arthur Marder, *British Naval Policy 1880–1905* (London, 1940), p. 162.

3. Ibid. and David Steele, *Lord Salisbury: A Political Biography* (London, 1999), p. 252.
4. *Conway's All the World's Fighting Ships 1860–1905* (London, 1979), p. 178.
5. Ibid., pp. 179–84.
6. Sondhaus, *Naval Warfare 1815–1914*, p. 148. *Brassey's Naval Annual 1891* gives the exchange rate as £1 = 9 roubles, p. 456.
7. Theodore Ropp, *The Development of a Modern Navy* (Annapolis, MD, 1987), pp. 181–2.
8. Sondhaus, *Naval Warfare 1815–1914*, pp. 184–5.
9. John B. Hattendorf, R.J.B. Knight, A.W.H. Pearsall, N.A.M. Rodger and Geoffrey Till (eds), *British Naval Documents 1204–1960* (Leicester, 1993), Minute for the Board of Admiralty by Admiral Sir Frederick Richards, First Naval Lord, August 1893, pp. 620–1.
10. TNA ADM116/878 Shipbuilding Papers 1893–1899, Programme of new construction 22 November 1893, p. 1.
11. Ibid., Memorandum by Senior Naval Lord explanatory of Memorandum of 22 November 1893, p. 15.
12. Peter Gordon, *The Red Earl, The Papers of the Fifth Earl Spencer 1835–1900*, Vol. II: *1885–1910* (London, 1986), pp. 207–43.
13. *Encyclopaedia Britannica 1960*, Vol. 2, p. 390.
14. C.E. Ellis, 'Recent experiments in armour', *Transactions of the Institute of Naval Architects* XXXV/215–41 (1894), pp. 220–1.
15. William Hovgaard, *Modern History of Warships* (London, 1978), p. 81.
16. Ian Buxton, *Big Gun Monitors* (London, 1978), p. 181.
17. Oscar Parkes, *British Battleships 1860–1957* (London, 1957), pp. 384, 395–6, 404–5.
18. Frederic Manning, *The Life of Sir William White* (London, 1923), p. 344.
19. *Encyclopaedia Britannica 1960*, Vol. 2, p. 390.
20. The 47 British battleships were six Admirals, one Sans Pareil, two Trafalgars, seven Royal Sovereigns, one Hood, one Renown, nine Majestics, six Canopus, three Formidables, five Londons and six Duncans. The 25 Russian battleships were four Ekaterinas, two Imperator Alexander II, one Dvienadsat Apostolov, one Gangut, one Navarin, one Tri Svititelia, one Sissoi Veliki, four Amiral Ushakov, three Petropavlovsk, one Rostislav, three Peresviet, one Pantelimon, one Retvisan and one Tsessarevitch. The 22 French battleships were four Terrible, two Amiral Baudin, one Hoche, 3 Marceau, one Brennus, one Charles Martel, one Carnot, one Jauréguiberry, one Masséna, one Bouvet, 3 Charlemagne, one Henri IV, one Iena and one Suffren.
21. Marder, *British Naval Policy*, pp. 174–5.
22. *Brassey's Naval Annual 1894*, p. 36.
23. *The Times*, 11 October 1893, p. 3 Issue 34079, col. B, 'The visit of the Russian Fleet to France'. There are numerous articles in *The Times* concerning France and Russia over the next three months.

24. TNA ADM 116/3089 Mediterranean Station, Naval Strategy and Policy, 1887–94.
25. J.A.S. Grenville, 'Goluchowski, Salisbury, and the Mediterranean agreements, 1895–1897', *The Slavonic and East European Revue* 36 (1957–8), pp. 340–69, at p. 340.
26. *Jane's Fighting Ships 1906–7*, pp. 294–7 (Italian *en echelons* and Sardegna class).
27. Marder, *British Naval Policy*, pp. 243–4.
28. Ibid., pp. 244–5.
29. Eric Grove, *The Royal Navy since 1815: A New Short History* (London, 2005), p. 77.
30. Eric Grove, 'The battleship *Dreadnought*: technological, economic and strategic contexts', in Robert J. Blyth, Andrew Lambert and Jan Rüger (eds), *The Dreadnought and the Edwardian Age* (London, 2011), p. 167.
31. For battleship costs and tonnage see Parkes, *British Battleships*. For cruiser costs and tonnages see *Jane's Fighting Ships 1906–7* and *Brassey's Naval Annuals 1889–1908*.
32. *Brassey's Naval Annual 1894*, p. 163.
33. *Brassey's Naval Annuals 1889–1908*; *Jane's Fighting Ships 1907*.
34. *Conway's 1860–1905*, pp. 186–90.
35. *Jane's Fighting Ships 1906–7*, p. 65.
36. Rear-Admiral Samuel Long, 'On the present position of cruisers in naval warfare', *Transactions of the Institute of Naval Architects* XXXIV (1893), p. 3.
37. *Brassey's Naval Annual 1893*, pp. 8–9.
38. Parkes, *British Battleships*, p. 441.
39. *Conway's 1860–1905*, p. 304.
40. *Brassey's Naval Annual 1900*, pp. 27–8.
41. *Brassey's Naval Annual 1899*, p. 8.
42. TNA ADM116/446 *Cressy* class twin-screw armoured cruisers, *Dupuy du Lome* and *Edgar* compared.
43. *Conway's 1860–1905*, pp. 68–9. See also *Jane's Fighting Ships 1906–7*, pp. 61–2.
44. Hovgaard, *Modern History of Warships*, p. 468.
45. *Brassey's Naval Annual 1898*, p. 4.
46. *Brassey's Naval Annual 1906*, p. 190.
47. Ruddock F. Mackay, *Fisher of Kilverstone* (Oxford, 1973), p. 1.
48. Ibid., pp. 2–7.
49. Richard Hough, *First Sea Lord* (London, 1969), pp. 25–7.
50. Arthur J. Marder (ed.), *Fear God and Dread Nought: The Correspondence of Admiral of the Fleet Lord Fisher of Kilverstone*, Vol. I: *The Making of an Admiral 1854–1904* (London, 1952), p. 72.

51. Mackay, *Fisher of Kilverstone*, pp. 52–8.
52. Admiral Sir R.H. Bacon, *The Life of Lord Fisher of Kilverstone*, Vol. I (London, 1929), p. 64.
53. Parkes, *British Battleships*, p. 239.
54. Mackay, *Fisher of Kilverstone*, pp. 148–9.
55. Parkes, *British Battleships*, pp. 252–7.
56. Mackay, *Fisher of Kilverstone*, p. 165.
57. Ibid., p. 187.
58. Ibid., p. 203. See also Bacon, *Lord Fisher of Kilverstone*, Vol. I, p. 104 and Hough, *First Sea Lord*, p. 90.
59. Edgar J. March, *British Destroyers 1892–1953* (London, 1966), pp. 24–6.
60. Nathaniel Barnaby, *Naval Developments of the Century* (London, 1904), pp. 124–5.
61. *Conway's 1860–1905*, pp. 292–3.
62. See for example, Fortescue Flannery, 'On water-tube boilers', *Transactions of the Institute of Naval Architects* XVII (1876), pp. 259–82 and William Parker, 'On the progress and development of marine engineering', *Transactions of the Institute of Naval Architects* XVII (1886), pp. 125–46. There are at least nine other major articles in the *Transactions*. Most are dated between 1889 and 1895.
63. Fred T. Jane, *The British Battlefleet*, Vol. 2 (London, 1912), p. 93.
64. Mackay, *Fisher of Kilverstone*, p. 207.
65. Parkes, *British Battleships*, p. 393.
66. Jane, *The British Battle Fleet*, Vol. 2, p. 94.
67. Keith McBride, 'Queen Victoria's battlecruisers: the Canopus and Duncan class battleships', *The Mariner's Mirror* 80/4 (November 1994), pp. 431–49.
68. Ibid., pp. 434–5.
69. Parkes, *British Battleships*, pp. 391–9.
70. Bacon, *Lord Fisher of Kilverstone*, Vol. 1, p. 144 and Hough, *First Sea Lord*, p. 108.
71. Mackay, *Fisher of Kilverstone*, pp. 232–3; see also Hough, *First Sea Lord*, p. 135.
72. Geoffrey Penn, *Infighting Admirals: Fisher's Feud with Beresford and the Reactionaries* (London, 2000), p. 76.
73. Nicholas Lambert, *Sir John Fisher's Naval Revolution* (Columbia, SC, 1999), pp. 77–8.
74. J.K. Laughton, 'On the several European systems of naval education', *Journal of the Royal United Services Institution* XXIV (1880–81), pp. 849–69. There are numerous RUSI journal articles on the subject.
75. Penn, *Infighting Admirals*, p. 85.
76. Commander P.M. Rippon, *Evolution of Engineering in the Royal Navy*, Vol. 1: *1827–1939* (London, 1988), p. 110.

77. Rupert Nichol and Alan York, *RNEC 1880–1980* (Plymouth, 1980) (publicity booklet celebrating 100 years of Keyham), p. 16.
78. *Brassey's Naval Annual 1906*, pp. 118–31.
79. Mackay, *Fisher of Kilverstone*, pp. 278–82.
80. *Brassey's Naval Annual 1906*, p. 137.
81. Nichol and York, *RNEC 1880–1980*, p. 19.
82. Rippon, *Evolution of Engineering in the Royal Navy*, p. 112.
83. Mackay, *Fisher of Kilverstone*, pp. 379–80.
84. Ibid., p. 285.
85. Ibid., p. 129.
86. Lambert, *Sir John Fisher's Naval Revolution*, pp. 80–1.
87. Ropp, *The Development of a Modern Navy*, p. 292, See also, Parkes, *British Battleships*, p. 376.
88. H.P. Willmott, *Battleship* (London, 2002), pp. 14–15.

3 The New Navies of the 1890s

1. William Thiesen, 'Construction of America's "new navy" and the transfer of British naval technology to the United States 1870–1900', *The Mariner's Mirror* 85/4 (November 1999), pp. 428–45, at p. 428.
2. *Conway's All the Worlds Fighting Ships 1860–1905* (London, 1979), p. 115.
3. Admiralty Library: Pamphlets Vols 825 for 1881 Reports of Naval Attachés: Report by Captain William Arthur C.B. dated 6 August 1881, pp. 3–4.
4. Thiesen, 'Construction of America's "new navy"', p. 434.
5. *Conway's 1860–1905*, p. 150.
6. George W. Baer, *One Hundred Years of American Sea-power* (Stanford, CA, 1993), pp. 9–10.
7. *Brassey's Naval Annual 1890*, pp. 128–9.
8. TNA ADM231/24 NID No. 381 US Navy, Ship Construction etc. Report by Captain R.N. Custance RN, Naval Attaché, p. 10.
9. Thiesen, 'Construction of America's "new navy"', pp. 431–9.
10. Donald Mitchell, *History of the Modern American Navy* (London, 1947), pp. 28–9.
11. Baer, *One Hundred Years of American Sea-power*, pp. 14–16.
12. A.T. Mahan, *The Influence of Sea Power upon History 1660–1783* (Boston, 1890), p. 88.
13. Ibid., p. 25.
14. Paul M. Kennedy, *The Rise and Fall of British Naval Mastery* (London, 1976), p. 2.
15. Jon Tetsuro Sumida, 'Geography, technology, and British naval strategy in the *Dreadnought* era', *Naval War College Review* 59/3 (Summer 2006), pp, 89–102, at p. 89.

16. Alfred T. Mahan, 'Retrospect and prospect', *The World's Work* (February 1902), also quoted in Jon Tetsuro Sumida, *Inventing Grand Strategy and Teaching Command: The Classic Works of Alfred Thayer Mahan Reconsidered* (Annapolis, MD, 1997), p. 90.
17. Mahan, *The Influence of Sea Power upon History 1660–1783*, p. 138. See also Sumida, *Inventing Grand Strategy and Teaching Command*, p. 46.
18. Sumida, *Inventing Grand Strategy and Teaching Command*, p. 46.
19. J. D'A. Samuda, 'The Riachuelo, Brazilian armour-clad turret-ship; its construction and performances', *Transactions of the Institute of Naval Architects* 25 (1884), pp. 1–16.
20. *Conway's 1860–1905* (London, 1979), pp. 406–7.
21. Ibid., p. 139.
22. *Jane's Fighting Ships 1905–6*, p. 107.
23. Mitchell, *History of the Modern American Navy*, p. 20.
24. *Conway's 1860–1905*, p. 140.
25. H.W. Wilson, *Battleships in Action*, Vol. I (London, 1927), pp. 82–6.
26. *Conway's 1860–1905*, p. 141.
27. Mitchell, *History of the Modern American Navy*, p. 49.
28. Wilson, *Battleships in Action*, p. 120.
29. J. Saxon Mills, *The Panama Canal* (London, 1913), p. 66.
30. Wilson, *Battleships in Action*, p. 154.
31. Mitchell, *History of the Modern American Navy*, p. 65.
32. Wilson, *Battleships in Action*, pp. 156–7.
33. Baer, *One Hundred Years of Sea-power*, pp. 28–9.
34. Ibid., p. 28.
35. Hugh Brogan, *The Penguin History of the United States of America* (London, 1985), pp. 389–90.
36. *Encyclopedia Britannica 1960*, Vol. 19, p. 921.
37. Rear-Admiral P.W. Brock and Basil Greenhill, *Sail and Steam in Britain and North America* (London, 1973), pp. 65–6.
38. *Britannica 1960*, Vol. 19, p. 921.
39. *Chambers Encyclopedia 1927*, Vol. 1, p. 118.
40. Wilson, *Battleships in Action*, pp. 39–40.
41. *Chambers Encyclopedia 1927*, Vol. 1, p. 118.
42. Andrew Roberts, *Salisbury: Victorian Titan* (London, 1999), pp. 616–17.
43. *Britannica 1960*, Vol. 1, pp. 502–3.
44. Mills, *The Panama Canal*, pp. 38–43.
45. Ibid., pp. 60–70.
46. TNA ADM 231/21 NID No. 297 February 1892, p. 3.
47. Ibid., pp. 4–5.
48. Ibid., p. 6.
49. Ibid., p. 11.

50. Sumida, 'Geography, technology, and British naval strategy', p. 89.
51. Kennedy, *The Rise and Fall of British Naval Mastery*, p. 211.
52. See TNA 231/22 NID No. 351 United States Navy, Dockyards, Materials etc. See also TNA 231/24 NID No. 381 United States, Navy, Ship Construction etc. 1894.
53. Fred T. Jane, *The Imperial Japanese Navy* (London, 1904), pp. 7–15.
54. Brian Reading, *Japan the Coming Collapse* (London, 1992), pp. 14–16.
55. *Conway's 1860–1905*, p. 216.
56. Reading, *Japan the Coming Collapse*, p. 13.
57. Bernard Edwards, *Salvo! Classic Naval Gun Actions* (London, 1999), p. 9.
58. Nicholas Rodger, 'British belted cruisers', *The Mariner's Mirror* 64/1 (February 1978), pp. 23–36, at p. 28.
59. FIC No. 9: Admiralty Library Pamphlets Vol. 842 (1883).
60. *Conway's, 1860–1905*, pp. 216–27.
61. David C. Evans and Mark R. Peattie, *Kaigun, Strategy, Tactics and Technology in the Imperial Japanese Navy 1887–1941* (Annapolis, MD, 1997), pp. 12–13.
62. Ibid., pp. 36–7.
63. Sydney Eardley-Wilmot, *Our Fleet Today* (London, 1902), pp. 280–1.
64. *Conway's 1860–1905*, p. 395.
65. Ibid., pp. 396–7.
66. Jane, *The Imperial Japanese Navy*, pp. 101–3.
67. *Conway's 1860–1905*, pp. 396–9.
68. Edwards, *Classic Naval Gun Actions*, p. 10.
69. Jane, *The Imperial Japanese Navy*, p. 104.
70. Edwards, *Classic Naval Gun Actions*, pp. 10–11.
71. Jane, *The Imperial Japanese Navy*, pp. 106–9.
72. Edwards, *Classic Naval Gun Actions*, p. 11.
73. Jane, *The Imperial Japanese Navy*, pp. 110–15.
74. Edwards, *Classic Naval Gun Actions*, p. 13.
75. *Conway's 1860–1905*, pp. 219–20.
76. Jane, *The Imperial Japanese Navy*, p. 116.
77. Ibid., pp. 123–4.
78. Edwards, *Classic Naval Gun Actions*, p. 16.
79. Wilson, *Battleships in Action*, Vol. I, p. 103.
80. Ibid., p. 102.
81. Evans and Peattie, *Kaigun*, p. 46.
82. Martin H. Brice, *The Royal Navy and the Sino-Japanese Incident 1937–41* (London, 1973), p. 19.
83. Wilson, *Battleships in Action*, Vol. I, pp. 163–4.
84. Jonathan Steinberg, *Tirpitz and the Birth of the German Battlefleet* (London, 1965), pp. 154–5.

85. I.H. Nish, 'The Royal Navy and the taking of Weihaiwei 1898–1905', *The Mariner's Mirror* 54/1 (February 1968), pp. 39–54, p. 39.
86. Ibid., pp. 39–54.
87. Evans and Peattie, *Kaigun*, p. 58.
88. *Jane's Fighting Ships 1906–7*, p. 194 states that this ship was built and engined by Vickers at Barrow. *Conway's 1860–1905*, pp. 221–2, states that *Mikasa* was built by Armstrong's at Elswick. *Jane's* appears to be correct.
89. *Jane's Fighting Ships 1906–7*, p. 193.
90. Evans and Peattie, *Kaigun*, p. 58.
91. George D. Boyce (ed.), *The Crisis of British Power, The Imperial and Naval Papers of the Second Earl of Selborne, 1895–1910* (London, 1990), p. 125.
92. Roberts, *Salisbury*, p. 813.
93. TNA ADM 116/1231B, pp. 1–3 Anglo-Japanese agreements 1902–1917, Vol. 1; TNA ADM 116/1231C Anglo-Japanese agreements 1902–1917, Vol. 2.
94. Evans and Peattie, *Kaigun*, p. 66.
95. TNA ADM 116/1231, unnumbered page.
96. Jane, *The Imperial Japanese Navy*, pp. 234–7.
97. Wilson, *Battleships in Action*, Vol. I, pp. 163–7.
98. Jane, *The Imperial Japanese Navy*, pp. 341–2.
99. Ibid., p. 346.
100. Evans and Peattie, *Kaigun*, pp. 98–100.
101. Wilson, *Battleships in Action*, Vol. I, pp. 193–227.
102. Richard Hough, *The Great Admirals* (London, 1977), p. 141.
103. Evans and Peattie, *Kaigun*, pp. 115–16.
104. Hough, *The Great Admirals*, p. 143.
105. Jane, *The Imperial Japanese Navy*, p. 413.
106. Wilson, *Battleships in Action*, pp. 260–1.
107. P.A. Towle, 'The effect of the Russo–Japanese War on British naval policy', *The Mariner's Mirror* 60/4 (November 1974), pp. 383–405, at p. 383.

4 Fisher and the Dreadnought

1. Ruddock F. Mackay, *Fisher of Kilverstone* (London, 1973), p. 311.
2. Arthur Marder (ed.), *Fear God and Dread Nought, The Correspondence of Admiral of the Fleet Lord Fisher of Kilverstone*, Vol. 1 (London, 1952), p. 305.
3. *Brassey's Naval Annual 1905*, pp. 455–6.
4. Ibid., pp. 458–9.
5. Mackay, *Fisher of Kilverstone*, p. 344.
6. Ruddock F. Mackay, 'The Admiralty, the German navy, and the redistribution of the British fleet 1904–1905', *The Mariner's Mirror* 56/3 (August 1970), pp. 341–6, at p. 341.

7. Ibid., p. 343.
8. Oscar Parkes, *British Battleships* (London, 1957), p. 426.
9. Mackay, 'The Admiralty, the German navy', pp. 345–6.
10. TNA ADM116/942 'The fighting characteristics of vessels of war', May 1904. See also Lord Fisher, *Records* (London, 1919), pp. 144–5.
11. *Brassey's Naval Annual 1905*, p. 456.
12. *Jane's Fighting Ships 1906–7*, p. 291.
13. TNA ADM1/7597 'Tactical value of speed, as compared with extra armour and guns'. See also John Roberts, *Battlecruisers* (London, 1997), pp. 16–17, 125. See also *Jane's Fighting Ships 1914*, pp. 173 (*Louisiana* and *Connecticut*), 179 (Washington class).
14. Parkes, *British Battleships*, pp. 436–9 and R.A. Burt, *British Battleships 1889–1904* (London, 1988), pp. 259–76.
15. *Brassey's Naval Annual 1905*, p. 456.
16. Richard Hill, *War at Sea in the Ironclad Era* (London, 2000), pp. 203–7 and David Brown, *Warrior to Dreadnought* (London, 1997), p. 175.
17. Eric Grove, 'The battleship is dead; long live the battleship. HMS *Dreadnought* and the limits of technological innovation', *The Mariner's Mirror* 93/4 (November 2007), pp. 415–27, at p. 416.
18. ADM1/7756 Director of Naval Ordnance Documents. DNO 13 January 1904. Report of battle firing for HMS *Vengeance* and HMS *Eclipse*.
19. Ibid.
20. Matthew S. Seligman, 'New weapons for new targets: Sir John Fisher, the threat from Germany, and the building of HMS *Dreadnought* and HMS *Invincible*, 1902–1907', *International History Review* 30/2 (June 2008), pp. 303–31, at pp. 309–12.
21. Ibid., p. 311.
22. Jon Tetsuro Sumida (ed.), *The Pollen Papers*, Navy Records Society, Vol. 124 (London, 1984), p. 366.
23. Brown, *Warrior to Dreadnought*, p. 181; Norman Friedman, *Naval Firepower, Battleship Guns and Gunnery in the Dreadnought Era* (London, 2008), pp. 29, 41; John Brooks, *Dreadnought Gunnery and the Question of Fire Control* (London, 2005), pp. 24–5.
24. Grove, 'The battleship is dead', p. 417.
25. Sir Reginal Bacon, *Lord Fisher of Kilverstone*, Vol. 1 (London, 1929), pp. 249–50. See also Marder, *Fear God and Dread Nought*, Vol. 1, p. 293.
26. Parkes, *British Battleships*, p. 468.
27. *Brassey's Naval Annual 1905*, p. 168.
28. Arthur Marder, *British Naval Policy, 1880–1905: The Anatomy of British Sea-Power* (London, 1940), pp. 527–8.
29. R.A. Burt, *British Battleships of World War One* (London, 1986), p. 20.
30. Parkes, *British Battleships*, p. 299.

31. *Brassey's Naval Annual 1906*, p. 3, reprinted from *Engineering*, 9 February 1906.
32. Peter McOwat, 'The *King Edward* and the development of the mercantile marine steam engine', *The Mariner's Mirror* 88/3 (August 2002), pp. 301–6.
33. *Brassey's Naval Annual 1903*, pp. 120–1.
34. *Brassey's Naval Annual 1904*, p. 135.
35. N.R.P. Bonsor, 'Story of the Allan line', *Sea Breezes* (January and February 1975).
36. TNA ADM1/7873 Private Secretary to First Lord of the Admiralty to Commander-in-Chief Portsmouth, 5 February 1906.
37. Grove, 'The battleship is dead', p. 415. See also Brown, *Warrior to Dreadnought*, p. 190.
38. Brown, *Warrior to Dreadnought*, p. 190. See also TNA ADM226/14 *Dreadnought* model experiments.
39. Grove, 'The battleship is dead', p. 415. Brown, *Warrior to Dreadnought*, pp. 190–1.
40. Norman Friedman, *Battleship Design and Development 1905–45* (London, 1978), p. 57.
41. Ibid., pp. 76–7.
42. Parkes, *British Battleships*, pp. 484–5.
43. Ibid., pp. 466–7.
44. D.K. Brown, *The Grand Fleet* (London, 1999), p. 42.
45. Grove, 'The battleship is dead', p. 419, see also Parkes, *British Battleships*, p. 469.
46. Fisher, *Records*, pp. 144–5.
47. *Jane's Fighting Ships 1914*, pp. 219–222.
48. Bacon, *Lord Fisher of Kilverstone*, Vol. 1, p. 255.
49. K.G.B. Dewar, *The Navy from Within* (London, 1939), p. 117; Roberts, *Battlecruisers*, p. 10, Roberts places both statements together.
50. Lawrence Burr, *British Battlecruisers 1914–1918* (London, 2008), pp. 4–5.
51. Jon Tetsuro Sumida, *In Defence of Naval Supremacy* (Boston, 1989), p. 58.
52. *Jane's Fighting Ships 1906–7*, p. 57.
53. Sumida, *In Defence of Naval Supremacy*, p. 59.
54. Ibid., p. 60 and Roberts *Battlecruisers*, p. 19.
55. TNA ADM116/1012 *Dreadnought* and *Invincible*. A direct comparison of the armour scheme for *Minotaur* is made. See also *Conway's All the World's Fighting Ships 1906–1922*, p. 24.
56. Friedman, *Battleship Design and Development*, pp. 168–9.
57. V.E. Tarrant, *Battlecruiser Invincible* (London, 1986), p. 21.
58. *Jane's Fighting Ships 1914*, pp. 129–33, 265–71.
59. TNA ADM182/2 Admiralty Weekly Order No. 351 24 November 1911.

60. C.J. Bartlett, *Great Britain and Sea Power 1815–1853* (London, 1963), pp. 235–6.
61. Terry Coleman, *The Liners* (London, 1976), pp. 41–5.
62. Seligman, 'New weapons for new targets', pp. 317–21.
63. Coleman, *The Liners*, pp. 46–50.
64. Seligman, 'New weapons for new targets', pp. 320–1.
65. Ibid., p. 326.
66. Rear-Admiral Samuel Long, 'On the position of cruisers in naval warfare', *Transactions of the Institute of Naval Architects* 34 (1893), pp. 1–18, at p. 12.
67. Mackay, *Fisher of Kilverstone*, pp. 288–93.
68. John Brooks, 'Dreadnought: blunder, or stroke of genius', *War in History* 14/2 (2007), pp. 157–78, at p. 157.
69. Brown, *Warrior to Dreadnought*, p. 180.
70. Brooks, 'Dreadnought', p. 178.
71. Arthur Marder, *From the Dreadnought to Scapa Flow*, Vol. I: *The Road to War 1904–1914* (Oxford, 1961). See also Holger Herwig, *Luxury Fleet* (London, 1980), p. 56.

5 The Imperial German Navy (Kaiserliche Marine)

1. E.L. Woodward, *Great Britain and the German Navy* (Oxford, 1935), p. 22.
2. *Conway's All the World's Fighting Ships 1860–1905*, pp. 244–5.
3. David H. Olivier, *German Naval Strategy 1856–1888* (London, 2004), pp. 84–5.
4. Lawrence Sondhaus, *Preparing for Weltpolitik: German Sea Power before the Tirpitz Era* (Annapolis, MD, 1997), pp. 106–8.
5. Richard Hough, *The Pursuit of Admiral Von Spee, A Study in Loneliness and Bravery* (London, 1969), p. 26.
6. Sondhaus, *Preparing for Weltpolitik*, p. 144.
7. Ibid., p. 145.
8. Ibid., pp. 125–7.
9. Ibid., p. 165.
10. Admiralty Library Pamphlets, Vol. 829 1886, FIC No. 121, December 1886, report by Captain Kane RN.
11. TNA ADM231/10 FIC No. 113 September 1886.
12. Olivier, *German Naval Strategy 1856–1888*, p. 174, see also *Conway's 1906–1922*, pp. 245–6.
13. *Conway's 1860–1905*, p. 247.
14. Gary E. Weir, *Building the Kaiser's Navy* (Annapolis, MD, 1992), pp. 9–10, 211.
15. Sondhaus, *Preparing for Weltpolitik*, pp. 192–9.
16. Woodward, *Great Britain and the German Navy*, p. 19.

NOTES TO PAGES 109–120

17. Robert K. Massie, *Dreadnought* (London, 1992), p. 223.
18. Emil Ludwig, *Kaiser Wilhelm II* (London, 1926), pp. 175–9.
19. Massie, *Dreadnought*, p. 226.
20. Ludwig, *Kaiser Wilhelm II*, p. 177, see also Weir, *Building the Kaiser's Navy*, p. 37.
21. Ibid., pp. 33–4 and 41.
22. Ibid., pp. 33–4.
23. Philip Magnus, *King Edward VII* (London, 1964), pp. 200–1.
24. Ludwig, *Kaiser Wilhelm II*, pp. 66–7.
25. Massie, *Dreadnought*, p. 90.
26. Ludwig, *Kaiser Wilhelm II*, pp. 105–7.
27. Ibid., p. 78.
28. Ibid., pp. 143–4.
29. Woodward, *Great Britain and the German Navy*, p. 259.
30. Holger Herwig, *Luxury Fleet* (London, 1980), p. 41.
31. Ibid., p. 40.
32. Jonathan Steinberg, *Tirpitz and the Birth of the German Battle Fleet* (London, 1965), pp. 209–11.
33. Ludwig, *Kaiser Wilhelm II*, p. 143.
34. Woodward, *Great Britain and the German Navy*, pp. 24, 32–9, 115–16, 151, 200, 408–31.
35. Sondhaus, *Preparing for Weltpolitik*, pp. 223–5.
36. Steinberg, *Tirpitz and the Birth of the German Battle Fleet*, p. 129.
37. *Conway's 1860–1905*, pp. 247–8 and *Jane's Fighting Ships 1906–7*, pp. 235–6. *Conway's* omits the Kaiser class battleship, *Kaiser Karl de Grosse*, built by Blohm & Voss 1898–1901.
38. Lawrence Sondhaus, *Navies in Modern World History* (London, 2004), p. 175.
39. Weir, *Building the Kaiser's Navy*, pp. 37–8, 211.
40. Steinberg, *Tirpitz and the Birth of the German Battle Fleet*, p. 53.
41. Lawrence Sondhaus, *Naval Warfare 1815–1914* (London, 2001), pp. 180–1.
42. Woodward, *Great Britain and the German Navy*, pp. 30–1.
43. Gary Staff and Paul Wright, *German Battleships 1914–18 (1)* (London, 2009), p. 6.
44. *Brassey's Naval Annual 1900*, p. 432.
45. Steinberg, *Tirpitz and the Birth of the German Battle Fleet*, p. 20.
46. *Jane's Fighting Ships 1914*, p. 120.
47. Herwig, *Luxury Fleet*, pp. 57–8.
48. Norman Friedman, *Battleship Design and Development 1905–1945* (London, 1978), p. 51.
49. Staff, and Wright, *German Battleships 1914–18 (1)*, pp. 20–1.
50. *Jane's Fighting Ships 1906–7*, p. 232.
51. *Brassey's Naval Annual 1908*, p. 26.

52. Richard Hough, *Dreadnought: A History of the Modern Battleship* (London, 1964), pp. 26–8.
53. Staff and Wright, *German Battleships 1914–18 (1)*, pp. 35, 38–9.
54. *Jane's Fighting Ships 1906–7*, p. 57.
55. *Brassey's Naval Annual 1908*, p. 27; *Brassey's Naval Annual 1909*, p. 23.
56. Friedman, *Battleship Design and Development*, p. 91fn.
57. Gary Staff and Tony Brian, *German Battlecruisers 1914–1918* (London, 2006), pp. 4–8.
58. Ruddock F. Mackay, *Fisher of Kilverstone* (London, 1973), p. 344.
59. Staff and Brian, *German Battlecruisers 1914–1918*, p. 7.
60. Friedman, *Battleship Design and Development*, pp. 168–9 (Britain), 172–3 (Germany).
61. John Roberts, *Battlecruisers* (London, 1997), pp. 72–3.
62. Filson Young, *With the Battlecruisers* (London, 1921), pp. 25–6.
63. *Jane's Fighting Ships 1914*, p. 123.
64. *Brassey's Naval Annual 1910*, pp. 107–8.
65. Woodward, *Great Britain and the German Navy*, pp. 55–6.
66. George D. Boyce (ed.), *The Crisis of British Power: The Imperial and Naval Papers of the Second Earl of Selborne, 1895–1910* (London, 1990), pp. 133–5.
67. Ibid., p. 136.
68. TNA ADM116/940B, pp. 1–3.
69. Ibid., p. 7 and *Jane's Fighting Ships 1906–7*, p. 225.
70. John Brooks, 'Dreadnought: blunder, or stroke of genius?', *War in History* 14/2 (2007), pp. 157–78, fn at p. 159.
71. TNA ADM116/940B, pp. 8–34.
72. Woodward, *Great Britain and the German Navy*, p. 84.
73. *Vanity Fair*, 3 November 1904.
74. Woodward, *Great Britain and the German Navy*, pp. 85–6.
75. G.P. Gooch and Harold Temperley, *British Documents on the Origins of the War 1898–1918*, Vol. II: *The Anglo-Japanese Alliance and the Franco-British Entente* (London, 1927), p. 312.
76. Mackay, *Fisher of Kilverstone*, pp. 327.
77. Ibid. p. 350.
78. A.P. Newton, *A Hundred Years of the British Empire* (London, 1940), p. 359.
79. TNA ADM116/940B, pp. 1–2.
80. G.P. Gooch and Harold Temperley, *British Documents on the Origins of the War 1898–1914*, Vol. III: *The Testing of the Entente 1904–6* (London, 1928), p. 400.
81. Ibid., p. 402.
82. Paul M. Kennedy, *The Rise and Fall of British Naval Mastery* (London, 1976), p. 242.
83. Paul M. Kennedy, *The Rise of the Anglo-German Antagonism 1860–1914* (London, 1980), p. 313.

84. Arthur Marder, *From the Dreadnought to Scapa Flow*, Vol. 1 (London, 1961), pp. 3–4.
85. J.A. Cramb, *Germany and England* (London, 1914), p. 16.
86. Kennedy, *The Rise of the Anglo-German Antagonism*, p. 312.
87. Ibid., p. 310.
88. Gooch and Temperley, *British Documents on the Origins of the War 1898–1914*, Vol. III, p. 405.
89. Jonathan Steinberg, *Tirpitz and the Birth of the German Battle Fleet*, p. 42.
90. Annika Mombauer and Wilhelm Deist (eds), *The Kaiser* (London, 2003), p. 1.

6 The Politics and Diplomacy of Naval Policy

1. Ruddock F. Mackay, *Fisher of Kilverstone* (Oxford, 1973), p. 341.
2. Ibid., pp. 342–3.
3. Oscar Parkes, *British Battleships* (London, 1957), p. 497.
4. Nicholas Lambert, *Sir John Fisher's Naval Revolution* (Columbia, SC, 1999), p. 143.
5. Mackay, *Fisher of Kilverstone*, p. 345.
6. Lambert, *Sir John Fisher's Naval Revolution*, pp. 130–1.
7. Arthur J. Marder (ed.), *Fear God and Dread Nought: The Correspondence of Admiral of the Fleet Lord Fisher of Kilverstone*, Vol. II: *Years of Power 1904–1914* (London, 1956), pp. 90–1.
8. Lambert, *Sir John Fisher's Naval Revolution*, p. 133.
9. Richard Hough, *First Sea Lord* (London, 1969), pp. 258–9.
10. Mackay, *Fisher of Kilverstone*, p. 384.
11. Hough, *First Sea Lord*, p. 259.
12. Parkes, *British Battleships*, p. 503.
13. Lambert, *Sir John Fisher's Naval Revolution*, pp. 139–42.
14. Hough, *First Sea Lord*, pp. 261–2.
15. E.L. Woodward, *Great Britain and the German Navy* (Oxford, 1935), p. 158.
16. Hough, *First Sea Lord*, p. 262.
17. Emil Ludwig, *Kaiser Wilhelm II* (London, 1926), pp. 338–40.
18. *Daily Telegraph*, 28 October 1908.
19. Woodward, *Great Britain and the German Navy*, pp. 196–7.
20. Robert K. Massie, *Dreadnought: Britain, Germany and the Coming of the Great War* (London, 1992), p. 685.
21. Woodward, *Great Britain and the German Navy*, p. 197.
22. G.P. Gooch and Harold Temperley, *British Documents on the Origins of the War 1898–1914*, Vol. VI: *Anglo-German Tension, Armaments and Negotiation 1907–12* (London, 1930), p. 211.
23. Ludwig, *Kaiser Wilhelm II*, pp. 372–3.

24. Matthew S. Seligman (ed.), *Naval Intelligence from Germany: The Reports of the British Naval Attachés in Berlin 1906–1914* (Aldershot, 2007), N.A. Reports 29/06, 32/06, 38/06, 45/06.46/06, 52/06, 59/07.
25. Ibid., Naval Attaché Report 52/06, German Shipbuilding Capacity.
26. Ibid., Naval Attaché Report 53/07, The Rumoured New Navy Bill to be Introduced in the Next Reichstag.
27. Ibid., Naval Attaché Report 47/08, General Review of Naval Questions.
28. Ibid., Naval Attaché Report 48/08, Contract for the New Ship and other Naval Matters.
29. The dates given are those for commissioning trials, the actual completion dates are usually given as some months later, when the new ship has completed its shakedown cruises.
30. Seligman, *Naval Intelligence from Germany*, Naval Attaché Report 8/09.
31. Woodward, *Great Britain and the German Navy*, p. 206.
32. Ibid., pp. 208–11.
33. Ibid., pp. 213, 484.
34. Hedley P. Willmott, 'The Navy Estimates 1906–09', MA dissertation, University of Liverpool (1970), p. 227. See also Gooch and Temperley, *British Documents on the Origins of the War*, Vol. VI, pp. 250–2.
35. Willmott, 'The Navy Estimates 1906–09', pp. 245–51.
36. Woodward, *Great Britain and the German Navy*, pp. 231–2.
37. Ibid., p. 211fn.
38. Mackay, *Fisher of Kilverstone*, pp. 350–422.
39. Arthur Marder, *From the Dreadnought to Scapa Flow*, Vol. 1 (London, 1961), p. 56.
40. Lambert, *Sir John Fisher's Naval Revolution*, p. 137.
41. Marder, *From the Dreadnought to Scapa Flow*, Vol. 1, p. 56.
42. Lambert, *Sir John Fisher's Naval Revolution*, pp. 158–9.
43. Geoffrey Penn, *Infighting Admirals: Fisher's Feud with Beresford and the Reactionaries* (London, 2000), p. 70.
44. Geoffrey Bennett, *Charlie B* (London, 1968), p. 268.
45. Mackay, *Fisher of Kilverstone*, p. 360.
46. Ibid., p. 362.
47. Ibid., p. 363.
48. Hough, *First Sea Lord*, pp. 213–14.
49. Penn, *Infighting Admirals*, p. 218.
50. Mackay, *Fisher of Kilverstone*, pp. 393–4.
51. Bennett, *Charlie B*, p. 290.
52. TNA ADM1/7992.
53. Ibid.
54. Mackay, *Fisher of Kilverstone*, pp. 412–13.
55. Ibid.

56. Hough, *First Sea Lord*, p. 233.
57. Shawn T. Grimes, *Strategy and War Planning in the British Navy, 1887–1918* (London, 2012), p. 155.
58. Mackay, *Fisher of Kilverstone*, pp. 412–14, and Bennett, *Charlie B*, pp. 302–4.
59. Bennett, *Charlie B*, p. 305fn.
60. Penn, *Infighting Admirals*, p. 221.
61. Lambert, *Sir John Fisher's Naval Revolution*, pp. 191–3.
62. Penn, *Infighting Admirals*, p. 222.
63. Hough, *First Sea Lord*, p. 293.
64. Ibid., pp. 368–9 (Appendix 3 summarises the report of the CID).
65. Bennett, *Charlie B*, pp. 305–6.
66. Hough, *First Sea Lord*, p. 295.
67. Lambert, *Sir John Fisher's Naval Revolution*, pp. 56–60.
68. Neil Summerton, 'The development of British military planning for a war against Germany 1904–1914', PhD thesis, Vol. I, University of London (1970), pp. 16–17.
69. Arthur Marder, *British Naval Policy 1880–1905* (London, 1940), p. 365.
70. Mackay, *Fisher of Kilverstone*, pp. 350–2.
71. Penn, *Infighting Admirals*, p. 160.
72. Lambert, *Sir John Fisher's Naval Revolution*, p. 135.
73. Mackay, *Fisher of Kilverstone*, pp. 396–7 and Penn, *Infighting Admirals*, p. 163.
74. Marder, *Fear God and Dread Nought*, Vol. II, p. 145, letter to Lord Esher, 7 October 1907 and p. 154, letter to Lord Esher, 13 December 1907.
75. Christopher Lloyd, 'The Royal Naval Colleges at Portsmouth and Greenwich', *The Mariner's Mirror* 52/2 (May 1966), pp. 145–56, at pp. 154–5.
76. TNA CAB17/8.
77. Lambert, *Sir John Fisher's Naval Revolution*, pp. 179–80.
78. Ibid., p. 181.
79. Marder, *British Naval Policy 1880–1905*, p. 368.
80. Lambert, *Sir John Fisher's Naval Revolution*, p. 168.
81. Mackay, *Fisher of Kilverstone*, pp. 330, 411, 430, and Lambert, *Sir John Fisher's Naval Revolution*, p. 204.
82. Lambert, *Sir John Fisher's Naval Revolution*, p. 169.
83. Mackay, *Fisher of Kilverstone*, p. 430.
84. Lambert, *Sir John Fisher's Naval Revolution*, p. 207.
85. Ibid., pp. 207–8.
86. Mackay, *Fisher of Kilverstone*, p. 367.
87. Matthew Allen, 'Rear Admiral Reginald Custance: Director of Naval Intelligence 1899–1902', *The Mariner's Mirror* 78/1 (February 1992), pp. 61–75, at p. 61.
88. Ibid., p. 65.
89. Ibid., p. 66.

90. Arthur J. Marder (ed.), *Fear God and Dread Nought: The Correspondence of Admiral of the Fleet Lord Fisher of Kilverstone*, Vol. I: *The Making of an Admiral 1854–1904* (London, 1952), p. 355.
91. Ibid., p. 205.
92. Mackay, *Fisher of Kilverstone*, pp. 256–8.
93. Ibid., p. 420.
94. Nicholas Black, *The British Naval Staff in the First World War* (London, 2009), pp. 56–62.
95. Paul M. Kennedy, *The War Plans of the Great Powers 1880–1914* (London, 1979), p. 129.

7 From Dreadnoughts to Super-Dreadnoughts

1. Oscar Parkes, *British Battleships* (London, 1956), pp. 503–5.
2. R.A. Burt, *British Battleships of World War One* (London, 1986), pp. 105–10. See also D.K. Brown, *The Grand Fleet, Warship Design and Development 1906–1922* (London, 1999), pp. 40–1.
3. Ibid., p. 57.
4. Norman Friedman, *Battleship Design and Development 1904–1945* (London, 1978), pp. 168–9.
5. Brown, *The Grand Fleet*, p. 57.
6. Parkes, *British Battleships*, p. 514, see also Brown, *The Grand Fleet*, pp. 57–8.
7. Ibid., p. 523.
8. Brown, *The Grand Fleet*, pp. 41–2.
9. Parkes, *British Battleships*, pp. 525–7, see also Burt, *British Battleships of World War One*, pp. 131–50.
10. Ibid., pp. 538–42; see also pp. 169–88.
11. John Roberts, *Battlecruisers* (London, 1997), pp. 29–30.
12. Parkes, *British Battleships*, p. 545, see also Admiral Mark Kerr, *The Navy in My Time* (London, 1933), pp. 48–9.
13. Brown, *The Grand Fleet*, pp. 42–5.
14. Roberts, *Battlecruisers*, pp. 37–8.
15. Alan Raven and John Roberts, *Queen Elizabeth Class Battleships* (London, 1975), pp. 1–4.
16. Jon Tetsuro Sumida (ed.), *The Pollen Papers*, Navy Records Society, Vol. 124 (London, 1984), pp. 4–7.
17. John Brooks, *Dreadnought Gunnery and the Battle of Jutland* (London, 2005), pp. 29–30.
18. Anthony Pollen, *The Great Gunnery Scandal* (London, 1980), p. 23 and pp. 35–6.
19. Norman Friedman, *Naval Firepower, Battleship Guns and Gunnery in the Dreadnought Era* (London, 2008), pp. 42–3.

20. Pollen, *The Great Gunnery Scandal*, pp. 54–63.
21. Sumida, *The Pollen Papers*, p. 131.
22. Ibid., 156–9.
23. Pollen, *The Great Gunnery Scandal*, pp. 68–9.
24. Sumida, *The Pollen Papers*, pp. 178–9.
25. Pollen, *The Great Gunnery Scandal*, pp. 75–81.
26. Sumida, *The Pollen Papers*, pp. 291–4.
27. Stephen Roskill, *Admiral of the Fleet Earl Beatty: The Last Naval Hero* (London, 1979), p. 62.
28. *Conway's All The World's Fighting Ships 1906–1921* (London, 1985), p. 147. See also, Siegfried Breyer, *Battleships and Battlecruisers 1905–1970* (London, 1973), pp. 273–6.
29. Friedman, *Battleship Design and Development 1904–1945*, pp. 168–9.
30. *Conway's 1906–1921*, pp. 147–8; Breyer, *Battleships and Battlecruisers 1905–1970*, pp. 274–6.
31. *Conway's 1906–1921*, pp. 149–50, Breyer, *Battleships and Battlecruisers 1905–1970*, pp. 274–7.
32. Gary Weir, *Building the Kaiser's Navy* (Annapolis, MD, 1992), pp. 49, 51, 71–2.
33. F. Ruge, *Warship Profile 14: SMS Seydlitz, Grosser Kreuzer 1913–1919* (Windsor, 1972), pp. 26–7. See also *Conway's 1906–1922*, pp. 152–3.
34. Ibid., pp. 154–5. See also Breyer, *Battleships and Battlecruisers 1905–1970*, pp. 277–80 and Friedman, *Battleship Design and Development 1904–1945*, pp. 172–3.
35. *Conway's 1906–1921*, pp. 155–6, Breyer, *Battleships and Battlecruisers 1905–1970*, pp. 282–5.
36. Ibid, p. 2.
37. *Jane's Fighting Ships 1914*, p. 68.
38. Ibid., pp. 64–7.
39. Ibid., pp. 135–6.
40. David K. Brown, *Warrior to Dreadnought* (London, 1997), pp. 137–9.
41. Edgar J. March, *British Destroyers 1892–1953* (London, 1966), pp. 71–5.
42. Ibid., pp. 84–5.
43. T.D. Manning, *The British Destroyer* (London, 1961), p. 51.
44. March, *British Destroyers*, pp. 96–9, 151–9.
45. Lawrence Sondhaus, *Naval Warfare 1815–1914* (London, 2001), p. 155.
46. Richard Compton-Hall, *Submarine Boats, The Beginning of Underwater Warfare* (London, 1983), p. 87.
47. Admiralty Library Pamphlets, Vol. 832 1889, NID No. 205, 16 March 1889. French Fleet and Dockyard. Report by Captain Sir W. Cecil H. Domville Bart. RN.
48. Compton-Hall, *Submarine Boats*, pp. 94–7.

49. Ibid., pp. 130–9.
50. Ibid., pp. 118–19.
51. R.F. Pocock and G.R.M. Garrat, *The Origins of Maritime Radio*, Science Museum Monograph (London, 1972), p. 3.
52. Ibid., pp. 5–7.
53. Ibid., pp. 7–11.
54. Ibid., pp. 26–8.
55. A.J.L. Blond 'Technology and tradition: wireless telegraphy and the Royal Navy 1895–1920', PhD thesis, Vol. I, University of Lancaster (1993), p. 107.
56. Ibid., pp. 113–14.
57. Nazli Choucri and Robert C. North, *Nations in Conflict: National Growth and International Violence* (San Francisco, 1975) quoted in Richard J. Stoll, 'Steaming in the dark? Rules, rivals, and the British Navy, 1860–1913', *The Journal of Conflict Resolution* 36/2 (June 1992), pp. 263–83, at p. 265.
58. E.L. Woodward, *Great Britain and the German Navy* (Oxford, 1935), p. 238.

8 The Worldwide Dreadnought Arms Race

1. David C. Evans and Mark R. Peattie, *Kaigun: Strategy, Tactics and Technology in the Imperial Japanese Navy 1887–1941* (Annapolis, MD, 1997), p. 133.
2. Ibid., p. 129.
3. Ibid., pp. 134–5.
4. Ibid., pp. 136–44.
5. Ibid., pp. 144–6.
6. *Conway's 1906–1922*, p. 233, describes these four ships as battlecruisers, while *Jane's Fighting Ships 1914*, p. 222, describes *Ibuki* and *Kurama* as armoured ships, in italics ('*Battle Cruisers*').
7. *Jane's Fighting Ships 1914*, p. 217.
8. David K. Brown, *The Grand Fleet* (London, 1999), p. 59 and fn.21.
9. *Conway's 1906–1922*, p. 234; see also *Jane's Fighting Ships 1919*, p. 256.
10. Ibid., pp. 229, 254.
11. Ibid., pp. 230, 253.
12. Harold and Margaret Sprout, *The Rise of American Naval Power 1776–1918* (Princeton, NJ, 1939), pp. 252–3.
13. George Baer, *One Hundred Years of Sea Power* (Stanford, CA, 1993), pp. 43–5.
14. Norman Friedman, *Battleship Design and Development 1904–1945* (London 1978), p. 134.
15. *Jane's Fighting Ships 1914*, pp. 166–9.
16. Friedman, *Battleship Design and Development 1904–1945*, pp. 74, 166–7.
17. *Jane's Fighting Ships 1919*, pp. 187–94.
18. Ibid., pp. 188–9.
19. Friedman, *Battleship Design and Development 1904–1945*, pp. 92–3.

20. *Conway's 1906–1922*, pp. 403–5.
21. R.A. Burt, *British Battleships of World War I* (London, 1986), p. 241.
22. Richard Hough, *Dreadnought: A History of the Modern Battleship* (London, 1964), p. 74.
23. *Conway's 1906–1922*, pp. 404–5.
24. Ibid., pp. 400–1.
25. *Jane's Fighting Ships 1914*, p. 441.
26. http://en.wikipedia.org/wiki/Italian_irredentism (accessed 6 November 2014).
27. *Conway's 1906–1921*, p. 328.
28. Lawrence Sondhaus, *The Naval Policy of Austria-Hungary 1867–1918* (West Lafayette, IN, 1994), pp. 153, 396.
29. *Conway's 1906–1921*, p. 328.
30. Ibid., p. 333.
31. Sondhaus, *The Naval Policy of Austria-Hungary*, p. 396.
32. *Conway's 1906–1921*, pp. 334–6.
33. *Brassey's Naval Annual 1911*, pp. 28–9.
34. *Conway's 1906–1921*, p. 335.
35. Sondhaus, *The Naval Policy of Austria-Hungary*, pp. 156–7.
36. *Brassey's Naval Annual 1908*, pp. 160–8.
37. *Conway's 1860–1906*, pp. 342–4.
38. Sondhaus, *The Naval Policy of Austria-Hungary*, p. 157.
39. Arthur Marder, *British Naval Policy 1880–1905* (London, 1940), p. 271.
40. *Conway's 1906–1921*, pp. 259–60.
41. E.W.R. Lumby (ed.), *Policy and Operations in the Mediterranean 1912–14* (London, 1970), pp. xi–xv.
42. H.I. Lee, 'Mediterranean strategy and Anglo-French relations 1908–1912', *The Mariner's Mirror* 57/3 (August 1971), pp. 267–85, at pp. 269–70.
43. Ibid., p. 271.
44. G.P. Gooch and Harold Temperley, *British Documents on the Origins of the War 1898–1914*, Vol. X Part II: *The Last Years of Peace 12* (London, 1936), ch. XCVI, Mediterranean Agreements, enclosure No. 386, Memorandum on the effect of a British Evacuation of the Mediterranean on Questions of Foreign Policy by Sir Eyre Crowe, 8 May 1912, pp. 585–9.
45. *Conway's 1906–1921*, p. 190.
46. H.W. Wilson, *Battleships in Action*, Vol. II (London 1927), pp. 300–6. See also *Brassey's Naval Annual 1912*, pp. 42–3, 329–32.
47. *Brassey's Naval Annual 1910*, pp. 14–19.
48. *Conway's 1906–1921*, pp. 196–8.
49. Lee, 'Mediterranean strategy and Anglo-French relations 1908–1912', p. 279. See also, Lumby, *Policy and Operations in the Mediterranean 1912–14*, p. 5.
50. Lee, 'Mediterranean strategy and Anglo-French relations 1908–1912', pp. 279–82.

51. *Brassey's Naval Annual 1914*, pp. 67–9; Oscar Parkes, *British Battleships* (London, 1957), pp. 496, 516.
52. Lee, 'Mediterranean strategy and Anglo-French relations 1908–1912', p. 275.
53. *Conway's 1906–1921*, p. 291.
54. Ibid., pp. 302–3.
55. Ibid., pp. 388–90.
56. Ibid., p. 384.
57. *The Times*, London, 22 July 1911.
58. E.L. Woodward, *Great Britain and the German Navy* (London, 1935), p. 269.
59. Ibid., pp. 286–7.
60. Ibid., pp. 329–37, 276.
61. Ibid., pp. 318–19.
62. Holger Herwig, *Luxury Fleet, The Imperial German Navy 1888–1918* (London, 1980), pp. 74–5.
63. Michael Epkenhans, 'Wilhelm II and "his" navy, 1888–1918', in Annika Mombauer and Wilhelm Deist (eds), *The Kaiser, New Research on Wilhelm's Role in Imperial Germany* (London, 2003), p. 17.
64. Ibid., pp. 26–7.
65. Holger Herwig, *Luxury Fleet* (London, 1980), p. 77.
66. Woodward, *Great Britain and the German Navy*, p. 372.
67. Ibid., pp. 472–3. See also ADM116/1605, which reviews the history of the two-power standard.
68. Woodward, *Great Britain and the German Navy*, pp. 398–403.
69. Annika Mombauer, 'Germany's last Kaiser – Wilhelm II and political decision-making in Imperial Germany', *New Perspective* 4/3 (March 1999), pp. 194–8.
70. Herwig, *Luxury Fleet*, p. 71. (To convert Goldmarks to sterling, £1 = 20.43 Goldmarks.)
71. Ibid., p. 61.
72. Woodward, *Great Britain and the German Navy*, p. 405.

9 World War I to Jutland

1. Donald Macintyre, *Jutland* (London, 1957), pp. 29–30.
2. Ibid., pp. 31–3.
3. Nicholas Black, *The British Naval Staff in the First World War* (Boydell Press 2009), pp. 60–71.
4. Arthur Marder, *From the Dreadnought to Scapa Flow*, Vol. 2 (London, 1964), pp. 3–5.
5. Frederic Dreyer, *The Sea Heritage* (London, 1955), pp. 83–4. Dreyer gives the full text of Jellicoe's letter.
6. Oscar Parkes, *British Battleships 1860–1957* (London, 1957), p. 625.
7. Marder, *From the Dreadnought to Scapa Flow*, Vol. 2, pp. 55–7.

8. Ibid., pp. 105–7.
9. Stephen Roskill, *Admiral of the Fleet Earl Beatty: The Last Naval Hero* (London, 1981), p. 100.
10. Macintyre, *Jutland*, p. 53.
11. John Campbell, *Jutland: An Analysis of the Fighting* (London, 1986), p. 374.
12. Ibid., p. 8.
13. Marder, *From the Dreadnought to Scapa Flow*, Vol. 2, pp. 192–3.
14. Richard Hough, *First Sea Lord* (London, 1969), pp. 330–1.
15. William James, *A Great Seaman. The Life of Admiral of the Fleet Sir Henry Oliver* (London, 1956), p. 138.
16. Ruddock F. Mackay, *Fisher of Kilverstone* (London, 1973), pp. 482–3.
17. Arthur Marder, *Fear God and Dread Nought, The Correspondence of Admiral of the Fleet Lord Fisher of Kilverstone*, Vol. 2: *Years of Power 1904–1914* (London, 1956), p. 84.
18. Richard Hough, *Former Naval Person: Churchill and the Wars at Sea* (London, 1985), pp. 91–2.
19. Mackay, *Fisher of Kilverstone*, p. 492.
20. Stephen Roskill, *Churchill and the Admirals* (London, 1977), p. 51.
21. Richard Hough, *The Great War at Sea 1914–1918* (London, 1983), pp. 169–71.
22. Marder, *From the Dreadnought to Scapa Flow*, Vol. 2, pp. 342–3.
23. http://en.wikipedia.org/wiki/Contraband (accessed 7 October 2014).
24. Elmer Belmont Potter, Roger Fredland and Henry Hitch Adams, *Sea Power: A Naval History* (Annapolis, MD, 1981), p. 223.
25. Ernest C. Fayle, *Seaborn Trade*, Vol. 3 (London, 1924), p. 465, Table I [a].
26. Patrick Beesley, *Room 40: British Naval Intelligence 1914–18* (London, 1982), p. 96.
27. Terry Coleman, *The Liners* (London, 1976), p. 100.
28. Beesley, *Room 40*, p. 84.
29. http://en.Wikipedia.org/wiki/U-boat_Campaign_(World_War I) (accessed 7 October 2014).
30. Black, *The British Naval Staff in the First World War*, p. 202.
31. http://en.wikipedia.org/wiki/Sussex_pledge (accessed 7 October 2014).
32. Roskill, *Beatty*, pp. 152–3.
33. Macintyre, *Jutland*, p. 88.
34. H.W. Wilson, *Battleships in Action*, Vol. II (London, 1924), p. 132.
35. Macintyre, *Jutland*, p. 92.
36. Campbell, *Jutland*, pp. 31–2.
37. Macintyre, *Jutland*, p. 95.
38. Roskill, *Beatty*, p. 161.
39. J.E.T. Harper, *The Truth about Jutland* (London, 1927), pp. 69–70.

40. TNA ADM116/1485 From Commander-in-Chief to Secretary of the Admiralty, 20 June 1916.
41. Andrew Gordon, *The Rules of the Game: Jutland and British Naval Command* (London, 1996), pp. 403–6 (contradicts Campbell, *Jutland*, p. 102).
42. Macintyre, *Jutland*, pp. 122–3, and Campbell, *Jutland*, p. 120.
43. Geoffrey Bennett, *The Battle of Jutland* (London, 1964), p. 105.
44. Macintyre, *Jutland*, p. 120.
45. Campbell, *Jutland*, pp. 159–60.
46. Julian Corbett, *Naval Operations* Vol. III (London, 1923), p. 369.
47. Macintyre, *Jutland*, p. 140.
48. Ibid., p. 143.
49. Charles London, *Jutland 1916: Clash of the Dreadnoughts* (London, 2000), p. 65.
50. Roskill, *Beatty*, p. 177.
51. Campbell, *Jutland*, p. 211.
52. Macintyre, *Jutland*, p. 146.
53. Roskill, *Beatty*, p. 177.
54. Macintyre, *Jutland*, pp. 144–6.
55. Roskill, *Beatty*, pp. 179–80.
56. Campbell, *Jutland*, p. 282.
57. Roskill, *Beatty*, p. 182.
58. Campbell, *Jutland*, pp. 295–6.
59. Ibid., pp. 309–14.
60. Corbett, *Naval Operations*, Vol. III, p. 424.
61. A.A. Hoehling, *The Great War at Sea* (London, 1965), p. 148.
62. Macintyre, *Jutland*, p. 196.
63. Hoehling, *The Great War at Sea*, p. 148.
64. Wilson, *Battleships in Action*, Vol. II, pp. 185–9.
65. Campbell, *Jutland*, p. 338.
66. Georg von Hase, *Keil and Jutland* (London, 1921), pp. 64–5.
67. Geoffrey Bennett, *Naval Battles of the First World War* (London, 1968), p. 246.
68. Carlyon Bellairs, *The Battle of Jutland: The Sowing and Reaping* (London, 1920), pp. 158–75.
69. Admiral Sir Reginald Bacon, *The Jutland Scandal* (London, 1925) and Harper, *The Truth about Jutland*.
70. See Roskill, *Beatty* and various others.
71. Wilson, *Battleships in Action*, Vol. II, p. 173.
72. Campbell, *Jutland*, pp. 354–5.
73. Macintyre, *Jutland*, pp. 35–8.
74. Campbell, *Jutland*, p. 3.
75. Arthur Marder, *From the Dreadnought to Scapa Flow*, Vol. 3: *Jutland and After* (London, 1965), p. 181.

10 From Jutland to Washington

1. Reinhard Scheer, *Germany's High Seas Fleet in the Great War* (London, 1920), p. 169.
2. H.W. Wilson, *Battleships in Action*, Vol. II (London, 1924), p. 222.
3. Arthur Marder, *From the Dreadnought to Scapa Flow*, Vol. 4: *1917 Year of Crisis* (London, 1969), p. 150.
4. Stephen Roskill, *Admiral of the Fleet Earl Beatty: The last Naval Hero* (London, 1979), p. 266.
5. Ibid., p. 267.
6. Wilson, *Battleships in Action*, pp. 232–3.
7. Willem Hackmann, *Seek and Strike, Sonar, Anti-submarine Warfare and the Royal Navy 1914–1954* (London, 1984), p. 68.
8. John Grainger (ed.), *The Maritime Blockade of Germany in the Great War: The Northern Patrol 1914–1918* (Leicester, 2003), pp. 1–10.
9. Ibid., pp. 11–16.
10. Ibid., p. 503.
11. Ibid., p. 723.
12. Paul M. Kennedy, *The Rise and Fall of British Naval Mastery* (London, 1976), pp. 262–3.
13. Ibid.
14. Ibid., p. 254.
15. Ibid., p. 259.

Bibliography

The National Archives (TNA)

Admiralty Records

ADM1/7597 'Tactical Value of Speed, as compared with Extra Armour and Guns'.

ADM1/7756 Director of Naval Ordnance Documents. 13 January 1904. Report of battle firing for HMS *Vengeance* and HMS *Eclipse*.

ADM1/7873 Private Secretary to First Lord of the Admiralty to Commander-in-Chief Portsmouth, 5 February 1906.

ADM1/7992

ADM182/2 Admiralty Weekly Order No. 351 24 November 1911.

ADM226/14 *Dreadnought* model experiments.

ADM231/5 Remarks on a Naval Campaign, 24 September 1884.

ADM231/6 General Outline of Possible Naval Operations against Russia, 14 March 1885.

ADM231/10 FIC No. 113 September 1886.

ADM231/24 NID No. 381 US Navy, Ship Construction etc. Report by Captain Custance RN Naval Attaché.

ADM231/24 NID No. 381 United States, Navy, Ship Construction etc. 1894.

ADM231/21 NID No. 297 February 1892.

ADM231/22 NID No. 351 United States Navy, Dockyards, Materials etc.

ADM116/31 Royal Corps of Naval Constructors. The order in council establishing the Royal Corps.

ADM116/267 Naval Armaments: November 1886. Question of transfer of responsibility for provision from Army to Navy votes 23 August 1883.

ADM116/446 *Cressy* class twin-screw armoured cruisers and Cruiser Policy.

ADM116/878 Shipbuilding Papers 1893–1899.

ADM116/940B
ADM116/942 'The fighting Characteristics of Vessels of War', May 1904.
ADM116/3089 Mediterranean Station, Naval Strategy and Policy 1887–94.
ADM116/1231B Anglo-Japanese agreements 1902–1917 Vol. One.
ADM116/1231C Anglo-Japanese agreements 1902–1917 Vol. Two.
ADM116/1012 *Dreadnought* and *Invincible*.
ADM116/1605, Reviews the history of the two-power standard.
ADM116/1485 From Commander-in-Chief to Secretary of the Admiralty, 20 June 1916.

Cabinet Office Papers

CAB37/22 No. 36, 14 November 1888, No. 28 1888 and No. 40 December 1888.
CAB Vol. 35, 37/55, December 1893, Requirements in Modern Cruisers.
CAB17/8

Primary Sources

Admiralty Library: Pamphlets Vols 825 for 1881, Reports of Naval Attachés: Report by Captain William Arthur CB dated 6 August 1881, pp. 3–4
_____ FIC No. 9 Vol. 842 (1883)
_____ FIC No. 121, December 1886, report by Captain Kane RN
_____ Vol. 832 1889, NID No. 205, 16 March 1889. French Fleet and Dockyard. Report by Captain Sir W. Cecil H. Domville Bart. RN
Daily Telegraph, 28 October 1908
Ellis, C.E., 'Recent experiments in armour', *Transactions of the Institute of Naval Architects* XXXV/215–41 (1894)
Flannery, Fortescue, 'On water-tube boilers', *Transactions of the Institute of Naval Architects* XVII (1876), pp. 259–82
Laughton, J.K., 'On the several European systems of naval education', *Journal of the Royal United Services Institution* XXIV (1880–81), pp. 849–69
Long, Samuel, 'On the position of cruisers in naval warfare', *Transactions of the Institute of Naval Architects* 34 (1893), pp. 1–18
Parker, William, 'On the progress and development of marine engineering', *Transactions of the Institute of Naval Architects* XVII (1886)
Samuda J. d'A., 'The Riachuelo, Brazilian armour-clad turret-ship; its construction and performances', *Transactions of the Institute of Naval Architects* 25 (1884), pp. 1–16

Soliani, Nabor, 'Steam trials of the Royal Italian ironclad *Lepanto*', *Transactions of the Institute of Naval Architects* 33 (1889)

The Times, 22 January 1877, 19 May 1877, 11, 13, 14, 17, 25, 28, 31 October 1893, 8, 10, 13, 14, 15, 17, 20, 21 November 1893, 4, 13, 22, 23 December 1893, 22 July 1911.

National Maritime Museum (NMM) MLN163/10,11,12 First, Second and Third Carnarvon Commission reports 1880

Vanity Fair, 3 November 1904

White, W.H., 'On the Designs for the New Battleships', *Transactions of the Institute of Naval Architects* XXX (1889)

Parliamentary Session Papers and Hansard Debates

House of Commons Parliamentary Papers C.5632
Hansard 3rd Ser. CCCXXIII, 1171: 7 March 1889

Secondary Sources

Allen, Matthew, 'Rear Admiral Reginald Custance: Director of Naval Intelligence 1899–1902', *The Mariner's Mirror* 78/1 (February 1992), pp. 61–75

Bacon, Sir Reginald, *The Jutland Scandal* (London, 1925)

——— *The Life of Lord Fisher of Kilverstone*, Vols 1 and 2 (London, 1929)

Baer, George, *One Hundred Years of American Sea-power* (Stanford, 1993)

Ballard, G.A., 'British frigates of 1875, the *Inconstant* and *Raleigh*', *The Mariner's Mirror* 22/1 (February 1936), pp. 42–53

——— 'British frigates of 1875, the *Shah*', *The Mariner's Mirror* 22/3 (August 1936), pp. 305–15

——— 'British corvettes of 1875, the *Volage*, *Active* and *Rover*', *The Mariner's Mirror* 23/1 (February 1937), pp. 53–67

Barnaby, Nathaniel, *Naval Developments of the Century* (London, 1904)

Bartlett, C.J., *Great Britain and Sea Power 1815–1853* (London, 1963)

Beesley, Patrick, *Room 40: British Naval Intelligence 1914–18* (London, 1982)

Bellairs, Carlyon, *The Battle of Jutland: The Sowing and Reaping* (London, 1920)

Bennett, Geoffrey, *The Battle of Jutland* (London, 1964)

——— *Charlie B* (London, 1968)

——— *Naval Battles of the First World War* (London, 1968)

Berry, Warren, *The Pre-Dreadnought Revolution* (London, 2013)

Black, Nicholas, *The British Naval Staff in the First World War* (London, 2009)

Blake, Robert, *The Conservative Party from Peel to Churchill* (London, 1970)

Blond A.J.L., 'Technology and tradition: wireless telegraphy and the Royal Navy 1895–1920', PhD thesis, University of Lancaster (1993)

Bonsor, N.R.P., 'Story of the Allan line', *Sea Breezes* (January and February 1975)

Boyce, George D. (ed.), *The Crisis of British Power: The Imperial and Naval Papers of the Second Earl of Selborne, 1895–1910* (London, 1990)

Breyer, Siegfried, *Battleships and Battlecruisers 1905–1970* (London, 1973)

Brice, Martin H., *The Royal Navy and the Sino-Japanese Incident 1937–41* (London, 1973)

Brock, P.W. and Basil Greenhill, *Sail and Steam in Britain and North America* (London, 1973)

Brogan, Hugh, *The Penguin History of the United States of America* (London, 1985)

Brooks, John, *Dreadnought Gunnery and the Battle of Jutland, The Question of Fire Control* (London, 2005)

―――― 'Dreadnought: blunder, or stroke of genius', *War in History* 14/2 (2007), pp. 157–78

Brown, David K., 'Marine engineering in the RN 1860–1905 Part II. The ship is a steam being', *Journal of Naval Engineering* 34/3 (1993)

―――― *Warrior to Dreadnought* (London, 1997)

―――― *The Grand Fleet* (London, 1999)

Burr, Lawrence, *British Battlecruisers 1914–1918* (London, 2008)

Burt, R.A., *British Battleships of World War One* (London, 1986)

―――― *British Battleships 1889–1904* (London, 1988)

Buxton, Ian, *Big Gun Monitors* (London, 1978)

Campbell, N.J.M., *Jutland: An Analysis of the Fighting* (London, 1986)

―――― 'The development of naval guns 1850–1900', in Robert D. Smith (ed.), *British Naval Armaments*, Royal Armouries Conference Proceedings (London, 1989)

Choucri, Nazli and Robert C. North, *Nations in Conflict: National Growth and International Violence* (San Francisco, CA, 1975)

Clarke, George and James Thursfield, *The Navy and the Nation* (London, 1897)

Coleman, Terry, *The Liners* (London, 1976)

Colomb, P.H., *Some Memoirs of Sir Astley Cooper-Key* (London, 1898)

Compton-Hall, Richard, *Submarine Boats, The Beginning of Underwater Warfare* (London, 1983)

Corbett, Julian, *Naval Operations*, Vol. III (London, 1923)

Cramb, J.A., *Germany and England* (London, 1914)
Dewar, K.G.B., *The Navy from Within* (London, 1939)
Dreyer, Frederic, *The Sea Heritage* (London, 1955)
Eardley-Wilmot, Sydney, *The Development of Navies* (London, 1892)
―――― *Our Fleet Today* (London, 1902)
Edwards, Bernard, *Classic Naval Gun Actions* (London, 1999)
Epkenhans, Michael, 'Wilhelm II and "his" navy, 1888–1918', in Annika Mombauer and Wilhelm Deist (eds), *The Kaiser, New Research on Wilhelm's Role in Imperial Germany* (London, 2003)
Evans, David C. and Mark R. Peattie, *Kaigun, Strategy, Tactics and Technology in the Imperial Japanese Navy 1887–1941* (Annapolis, MD, 1997)
Fayle, Ernest C., *Seaborn Trade*, Vol. 3 (London, 1924)
Fisher, Lord, *Records* (London, 1919)
Friedman, Norman, *Battleship Design and Development 1905–1945* (London, 1978)
―――― *Naval Firepower, Battleship Guns and Gunnery in the Dreadnought Era* (London, 2008)
Gardiner, Robert, *Steam Steel and Shellfire: The Steam Warship 1815–1905* (London, 1992)
Gooch, G.P. and Harold Temperley, *British Documents on the Origins of the War 1898–1918*, Vol. II: *The Anglo-Japanese Alliance and the Franco-British Entente* (London, 1927)
―――― *British Documents on the Origins of the War 1898–1914*, Vol. III: *The Testing of the Entente 1904–6* (London, 1928)
―――― *British Documents on the Origins of the War 1898–1914*, Vol. VI: *Anglo-German Tension, Armaments and Negotiation 1907–12* (London, 1930)
―――― *British Documents on the Origins of the War 1898–1914*, Vol. X Part II: *The Last Years of Peace 12* (London, 1936)
Gordon, Andrew, *The Rules of the Game: Jutland and British Naval Command* (London, 1996)
Gordon, Peter, *The Red Earl, The Papers of the Fifth Earl Spencer 1835–1900*, Vol. II: *1885–1910* (London, 1986)
Grainger, John (ed.), *The Maritime Blockade of Germany in the Great War: The Northern Patrol 1914–1918* (Leicester, 2003)
Grenville, J.A.S., 'Goluchowski, Salisbury, and the Mediterranean agreements, 1895–1897', *The Slavonic and East European Revue* 36 (1957–8), pp. 340–69
Grimes, Shawn T., *Strategy and War Planning in the British Navy, 1887–1918* (London, 2012)

Grove, Eric J., *The Royal Navy since 1815: A New Short History* (London, 2005)
—— 'The battleship is dead; long live the battleship. HMS *Dreadnought* and the limits of technological innovation', *The Mariner's Mirror* 93/4 (November 2007), pp. 415–27
—— 'The battleship *Dreadnought*: technological, economic and strategic contexts', in Robert J. Blyth, Andrew Lambert and Jan Rüger (eds), *The Dreadnought and the Edwardian Age* (London, 2011)
Haas, J.M., *A Management Odyssey: Royal Dockyards 1714–1914* (Lanham, MD, 1994)
Hackmann, Willem, *Seek and Strike, Sonar, Anti-submarine Warfare and the Royal Navy 1914–1954* (London, 1984)
Hase, Georg von, *Keil and Jutland* (London, 1921)
Harper, J.E.T., *The Truth about Jutland* (London, 1927)
Hattendorf, John B., R.J.B. Knight, A.W.H. Pearsall, N.A.M. Rodger and Geoffrey Till (eds), *British Naval Documents 1204–1960* (Leicester, 1993)
Herwig, Holger, *Luxury Fleet* (London, 1980)
Hill, Richard, *War at Sea in the Ironclad Age* (London, 2000)
Hoehling, A.A., *The Great War at Sea* (London, 1965)
Hough, Richard, *Admirals in Collision* (London, 1959)
—— *Dreadnought: A History of the Modern Battleship* (London, 1964)
—— *First Sea Lord* (London, 1969)
—— *The Pursuit of Admiral Von Spee, A Study in Loneliness and Bravery* (London, 1969)
—— *The Great Admirals* (London, 1977)
—— *The Great War at Sea 1914–1918* (London, 1983)
—— *Former Naval Person: Churchill and the Wars at Sea* (London, 1985)
Hovgaard, William, *Modern History of Warships* (London, 1978)
James, William, *A Great Seaman. The Life of Admiral of the Fleet Sir Henry Oliver* (London, 1956)
Jane, Fred T., *The Imperial Japanese Navy* (London, 1904)
—— *The British Battle Fleet*, Vol. 2 (London, 1915)
Kennedy, Paul M., *The Rise and Fall of British Naval Mastery* (London, 1976)
—— *The Rise of the Anglo-German Antagonism 1860–1914* (London, 1980)
Kerr, Mark, *The Navy in My Time* (London, 1933)
Lambert, Andrew, 'Preparing for the long peace: the reconstruction of the Royal Navy 1815–1830', *The Mariners Mirror* 82/1 (February 1996)
Lambert, Nicholas, *Sir John Fisher's Naval Revolution* (Columbia, SC, 1999)
Lee, H.I., 'Mediterranean strategy and Anglo-French relations 1908–1912', *The Mariner's Mirror* 57/3 (August 1971), pp. 267–85

Lloyd, Christopher, 'The Royal Naval Colleges at Portsmouth and Greenwich', *The Mariner's Mirror* 52/2 (May 1966), pp. 145–56
London, Charles, *Jutland 1916: Clash of the Dreadnoughts* (London, 2000)
Ludwig, Emil, *Kaiser Wilhelm II* (London, 1926)
Lumby E.W.R. (ed.), *Policy and Operations in the Mediterranean 1912–14* (London, 1970)
Macintyre, Donald, *Jutland* (London, 1957)
Mackay, Ruddock F., *Fisher of Kilverstone* (London, 1973)
―――― 'The Admiralty, the German Navy, and the redistribution of the British fleet 1904–1905', *The Mariner's Mirror* 56/3 (August 1970), pp. 341–6
Magnus, Philip, *King Edward VII* (London, 1964)
Mahan, Alfred T., *The Influence of Sea Power upon History 1660–1783* (London, 1890)
―――― 'Retrospect and Prospect', The World's Work (February 1902)
Manning, Frederic, *The Life of Sir William White* (London, 1923)
Manning, T.D., *The British Destroyer* (London, 1961)
March, Edgar J., *British Destroyers 1892–1953* (London, 1966)
Marder, Arthur, *British Naval Policy, 1880–1905: The Anatomy of British Sea-Power* (London, 1940)
―――― *Fear God and Dread Nought, The Correspondence of Admiral of the Fleet Lord Fisher of Kilverstone*, Vol. I: *The Making of an Admiral 1854–1904* (London, 1952)
―――― (ed.), *Fear God and Dread Nought: The Correspondence of Admiral of the Fleet Lord Fisher of Kilverstone*, Vol. II: *Years of Power 1904–1914* (London, 1956)
―――― *From the Dreadnought to Scapa Flow*, Vol. 1: *The Road to War 1904–1914* (Oxford, 1961)
―――― *From the Dreadnought to Scapa Flow*, Vol. 2: *To the Eve of Jutland* (London, 1964)
―――― *From the Dreadnought to Scapa Flow*, Vol. 3: *Jutland and After* (London, 1965)
―――― *From the Dreadnought to Scapa Flow*, Vol. 4: *1917 Year of Crisis* (London, 1969)
Massie, Robert K., *Dreadnought: Britain, Germany and the Coming of the Great War* (London, 1992)
McBride, Keith, 'Queen Victoria's battlecruisers: the *Canopus* and *Duncan* class battleships', *The Mariner's Mirror* 80/4 (November 1994), pp. 431–49
McOwat, Peter, 'The *King Edward* and the development of the mercantile marine steam engine', *The Mariner's Mirror* 88/3 (August 2002), pp. 301–6

Mills, J. Saxon, *The Panama Canal* (London, 1913)
Mitchell, Donald, *History of the Modern American Navy* (London, 1947)
Mombauer, Annika, 'Germany's last Kaiser – Wilhelm II and political decision-making in Imperial Germany', *New Perspective* 4/3 (March 1999), pp. 194–8
———— and Wilhelm Deist (eds), *The Kaiser* (London, 2003)
Newton, A.P., *A Hundred Year of the British Empire* (London, 1940)
Nichol, Rupert and Alan York, *RNEC 1880–1980* (Plymouth, 1980)
Nish, I.H., 'The Royal Navy and the taking of Weihaiwei 1898–1905', *The Mariner's Mirror* 54/1 (February 1968), pp. 39–54
Olivier, David H., *German Naval Strategy 1856–1888* (London, 2004)
Parkes, Oscar, *British Battleships* (London, 1957)
Penn, Geoffrey, *Infighting Admirals: Fisher's Feud with Beresford and the Reactionaries* (London, 2000)
Pocock, R.F. and G.R.M. Garrat, *The Origins of Maritime Radio*, Science Museum Monograph (London, 1972)
Pollen, Anthony, *The Great Gunnery Scandal* (London, 1980)
Potter, Elmer Belmont, Roger Fredland and Henry Hitch Adams, *Sea Power: A Naval History* (Annapolis, MD, 1981)
Preston, Antony, 'The end of the Victorian Navy', *The Mariner's Mirror* 60/4 (November 1974), pp. 363–81
———— 'Corps of Constructors', *Navy International* (August 1980)
Raven, Alan and John Roberts, *Queen Elizabeth Class Battleships* (London, 1975)
Rippon, P.M., *Evolution of Engineering in the Royal Navy*, Vol. 1: *1827–1939* (London, 1988)
Reading, Brian, *Japan the Coming Collapse* (London, 1992)
Roberts, Andrew, *Salisbury: Victorian Titan* (London, 1999)
Roberts, John, *Battlecruisers* (London, 1997)
Rodger, N.A.M., 'The design of the *Inconstant*', *The Mariner's Mirror* 61/1 (February 1975)
———— 'The dark ages of the Admiralty, 1869–85, Part III: Peace, retrenchment and reform', *The Mariner's Mirror* 6/2 (May 1976), pp. 121–8
———— 'British belted cruisers', *The Mariner's Mirror* 64/1 (February 1978), pp. 23–36
Ropp, Theodore, *The Development of a Modern Navy* (Annapolis, MD, 1987)
Roskill, Stephen, *Churchill and the Admirals* (London, 1977)
———— *Admiral of the Fleet Earl Beatty: The Last Naval Hero* (London, 1979)
Ruge, F., *Warship Profile 14: SMS Seydlitz, Grosser Kreuzer 1913–1919* (Windsor, 1972)

Ruger, Jan, *The Great Naval Game* (London, 2007)

Scheer, Reinhard, *Germany's High Seas Fleet in the Great War* (London, 1920)

Schurman, Donald M., *The Education of a Navy* (London, 1965)

_____ *Imperial Defence 1868–1887* (London, 2000)

Seligman, Matthew S., 'New weapons for new targets: Sir John Fisher, the threat from Germany, and the building of HMS *Dreadnought* and HMS *Invincible*, 1902–1907', *International History Review* 30/2 (June 2008), pp. 303–31

_____ *Naval Intelligence from Germany: The Reports of the British Naval Attachés in Berlin 1906–1914* (Aldershot, 2007)

_____ *The Royal Navy and the German Threat* (London, 2012)

Simmons, W.H., 'A short history of the royal gunpowder factory at Waltham Abbey', monograph produced by the Controllerate of Royal Ordnance Factories (1963)

Sondhaus, Lawrence, *The Naval Policy of Austria-Hungary 1867–1918* (West Lafayette, IN, 1994)

_____ *Preparing for Weltpolitik: German Sea Power before the Tirpitz Era* (Annapolis, MD, 1997)

_____ *Naval Warfare 1815–1914* (London, 2001)

_____ *Navies in Modern World History* (London, 2004)

Sprout, Harold and Margaret Sprout, *The Rise of American Naval Power 1776–1918* (Princeton, NJ, 1939)

Staff, Gary and Tony Brian, *German Battlecruisers 1914–1918* (London, 2006)

_____ and Paul Wright, *German Battleships 1914–18 (1)* (London, 2009)

Steele, David, *Lord Salisbury: A Political Biography* (London, 1999)

Steinberg, Jonathan, *Tirpitz and the Birth of the German Battlefleet* (London, 1965)

Stoll, Richard J., 'Steaming in the dark? Rules, rivals, and the British Navy, 1860–1913', *The Journal of Conflict Resolution* 36/2 (June 1992), pp. 263–83

Sumida, Jon Tetsuro, *The Pollen Papers*, Navy Records Society, Vol. 124 (London, 1984)

_____ *In Defence of Naval Supremacy* (Boston, 1989)

_____ *Inventing Grand Strategy and Teaching Command: The Classic Works of Alfred Thayer Mahan Reconsidered* (Annapolis, MD, 1997)

_____ 'Geography, technology, and British naval strategy in the *Dreadnought* era', *Naval War College Review* 59/3 (Summer 2006), pp, 89–102

Summerton, Neil, 'The development of British military planning for a war against Germany 1904–1914', PhD thesis, Vol. I, University of London (1970)

Tarrant, V.E., *Battlecruiser Invincible* (London, 1986)

Taylor, A.J.P., *The Struggle for Mastery in Europe, 1848–1918* (Oxford, 1960)

Thiesen, William, 'Construction of America's "new navy" and the transfer of British naval technology to the United States 1870–1900', *The Mariner's Mirror* 85/4 (November 1999), pp. 428–45

Towle, P.A., 'The effect of the Russo–Japanese War on British naval policy', *The Mariner's Mirror* 60/4 (November 1974), pp. 383–405

Tylcote, Andrew, *The Long Wave in the World Economy* (London, 1992)

Weir, Gary E., *Building the Kaiser's Navy* (Annapolis, MD, 1992)

White, William H., *A Manual of Naval Architecture* (London, 1877)

────── 'On the designs for the new battleships', *Transactions of the Institute of Naval Architects* XXX (1889), pp. 150–80

Willmott, H.P., 'The Navy Estimates 1906–09', MA dissertation, University of Liverpool (1970)

────── *Battleship* (London, 2002)

Wilson, H.W., *Battleships in Action*, Vols I and II (London, 1927)

Woodward, E.L., *Great Britain and the German Navy* (Oxford, 1935)

Young, Filson, *With the Battlecruisers* (London, 1921)

Reference Works

Brassey's Naval Annuals 1887–1915
Chambers Encyclopaedia 1927
Conway's All The Worlds Fighting Ships 1860–1905 (London, 1979)
Encyclopaedia Britannica 1960
Jane's Fighting Ships 1906–7, 1914, 1919
Parry, Clive (ed.), *The Consolidated Treaty Series*, Vol. 169 [1887] (Dobbs Ferry, NY, 1978)

Index

Aberdeen, Hong Kong, 66, 67
Aboukir, HMS, 219
Active, HMS, 19, 178
Admiralstab, (Admiralty staff), 115
Admiralty, the, also Board, 2, 3, 6, 7, 16, 17, 23, 25, 26, 28, 34, 38, 40, 43, 45, 49, 74, 79, 81, 84, 88, 95, 97–9, 102, 120, 137, 138, 141–4, 146, 148, 150–2, 154, 157, 158, 161, 172, 173, 181, 202, 211, 216, 218, 224, 233, 234, 235, 241
Admiral class battleships, 18, 19, 22, 27, 42
Adriatic, 12, 27
Adventure, HMS, 178
Adzuma, 67
AEG Curtis, 174, 177
AEG Vulkan, 175, 177
Aegean, 12
Afghanistan, 5
Agadir, 156, 202, 207
Agamemnon, HMS, 18, 39, 83, 89, 91
Agincourt, HMS, 196
Ägir, 174
Aigun, Treaty of, 71
Ajax, HMS, 18, 166
Akagi, 70
Aki, 93, 94, 190, 191
Akitsushima, 69
Alabama, 4, 19, 23, 54, 59, 61, 64
Alaska, 62
Alexandria, 5, 7, 41, 45, 147
Algeria, 129
Allan Line, 88
Almirante Cochrane, 196, 197
Almirante Latorre, 196, 197
America, see United States
American Navy, see United States Navy
Amethyst, HMS, 89
Ammiraglio Di Saint Bon, 201
Amphion, HMS, 178
Andrea Doria, 202
Anglo-Japanese alliance, 73, 93, 100, 103
Ansaldo, 200, 201

Anson, HMS, 18
Apia, 60
Apollo class, 21
Aquidaban, 57, 58, 59
Arabic, 226
Arethusa, HMS, 178
Argentina, xv, 161, 187, 195, 196, 200
Argo, 170, 172, 173
Ariadne, HMS, 171, 172
Ariadne, 218
Arizona, 62
Arizona, 194
Arkansas, 193
Armstrong (Shipbuilder), 14, 17, 18, 28, 46, 72, 87, 164, 195, 196, 197, 200, 201, 207
Arnold-Foster, Hugh, 127, 128, 130
Asahi, 72
Asama, 73
Asan, Gulf of, 69
Ascension, 80
ASDIC (Admiralty Submarine Detection Investigation Committee), 241
Asquith, Herbert, 102, 136, 138, 144, 147, 151, 152, 156, 162, 216, 223
Atlanta, 54
Atlantic Fleet, 80, 81, 147, 154
Attentive, HMS, 178
Aube, Hyacinthe-Laurent-Théophile, 9, 180
Audacious, HMS, 166, 217
Ausfallflotte (sallying fleet), 114
Australia, 80, 205
Australia, 166
Austria, 12, 13, 31, 111, 112, 130, 197, 202, 211, 216
Austria-Hungary, xiii, xv, 12, 13, 26, 101, 105, 111, 130, 143, 145, 187, 197, 198–202, 204
Azuma, 73

Babcock, 43, 124
Bacon, Reginald, 50, 94, 171, 172, 173, 181, 236
Baden, 118, 175, 177

297

Balfour, Arthur, 101, 102, 129, 135, 136, 151, 153, 154
Ballard, George, 155, 159, 217
Ballin, Albert, 208, 209
Ballistite, 15
Baltic, 2, 3, 33, 39, 76, 105, 107, 108, 115, 120, 130, 140, 146, 148, 154–6, 200, 205, 215, 220, 222, 224
Baltimore, 54
Barham, HMS, 167, 169
Barnaby, Nathaniel, 13
Barr (and Stroud), rangefinders, 85, 172, 173
Barraca, 46
Barrow, John, 58
Battenberg, Prince Louis, 81, 98, 99, 149, 158, 159, 219
Battlecruisers, 35, 92, 93, 94, 95, 96, 103, 104, 122, 124, 125, 138, 141, 143, 164–7, 177, 178, 185, 189, 201, 204, 206, 207, 211, 212, 220, 221, 228, 229, 230, 232, 239, 245
Bayern, 118, 175, 177
Beardmore (Shipbuilder), 164
Beatty, David, 210, 218, 221, 227, 228, 229, 230, 231, 234, 236, 237, 238, 244
Belgium, 130, 154
Belle Époque, 1
Bellerophon, HMS, 40, 41, 92, 137, 161, 212
Belleville boilers, 33, 43
Bellona, HMS, 178
Benbow, HMS, 18, 166, 168
Benedetto Brin, 201
Beowulf, 121
Berehaven, 10
Beresford, Lord Charles, 7, 45, 46, 48, 138, 147, 148, 149, 150–152, 154, 156–60
Bergmann, 175, 177
Bering Sea, 62
Berlin, xv, 61, 129, 137, 139, 208, 209, 218, 221
Bessemer Steel, 13
Bethell, Sir Alexander, 151, 152
Bethmann-Hollweg, Theobald von, 140, 209, 211, 240
Bighi Bay, 46
Bismarck, Otto, 106, 111, 112, 130
Black Prince, 205, 231, 234
Black Sea, 2, 12, 32, 39, 205
Blanche, HMS, 178
Blohm and Voss, 142
Blonde, HMS, 178
Blücher, 121–4, 127, 178, 220, 221
Blue Funnel Line, 4
Boadicea, HMS, 178
Boer War, 24, 50, 63, 101, 102, 116, 127, 132, 140, 153
Borkum, 130
Boston, 54
Bramah press, 14
Brandenburg, 108, 141, 175, 206
Brassey, Lord, 91, 98

Brassey's Naval Annual, 33, 35, 36, 38, 86, 87, 88, 117, 120, 122
Braunschweig, 116
Brazil, xv, 57, 161, 187, 195, 196, 206
Brennus, 25, 43
Breslau, 218
Brest, 9
Bretagne, 204
Bridge, Cyprian, 86
Bridgeman, Francis, 148, 149, 151, 159
Brin, Bernadetto, 17
Bristol, HMS, 178
Britain, xv, xvi, 3, 9, 12, 15, 31, 52, 57, 60–2, 64–7, 69, 73, 74, 78, 79, 83, 100, 105, 111, 114, 116–18, 127–31, 140, 141, 143–5, 185, 189, 197, 199, 202–7, 210–13, 215, 216, 218, 224, 225, 226, 227, 239–43, 245, 246, 248
Britannia, HMS, 47
Budapest, 26
Bulgaria, 5, 222
Bülow, Bernard, Prince Von, xiii, 100, 105, 128, 129, 139, 140, 185
Bulwer, Sir Henry, 62
Bulwer-Clayton Treaty, 62, 63
Bundesrath, 110

Caesar, HMS, 28
Calcutta, HMS, 39
California, 62
Calliope, HMS, 61
Cambon, Paul, 100, 204
Cambridge, 8
Campbell-Bannerman, Sir Henry, 102, 135, 138, 147
Camperdown, HMS, 18
Canada, 60, 61, 62, 65
Canada, HMS, 197
Canopus, HMS, 219
Canopus class, 28, 29, 43, 44
Cape of Good Hope, 3, 80, 205
Cape Horn, 59, 192
Caprivi, Leo Von, 107, 108
Caracciolo, 202
Caribbean, 65, 192
Carmania, 89
Carnegie, Andrew, 98
Carnarvon, Lord, 3
Carnarvon Commission, 4, 5, 6, 7, 23, 52
Cassal, Sir Ernest, 208, 209
Castlereagh, Lord, 2, 11
Cawdor, Earl of, 135
Centurion, HMS, 166
Ceylon, 38
Channel Fleet, 80, 148, 149, 150, 151, 152, 154
Chamberlain, Joseph, 100
Charlestown, 54
Charmes, Gabriel, 9
Chatham, 148

INDEX

Chemulpo Convention, 69
Chen Yuen, 68, 70, 71, 106
Cherbourg, 9
Chicago, 54
Chile, xv, 83, 187, 195, 196
China, 28, 66, 67, 68, 69, 72, 74, 80
Chiyoda, 70
Chiyodogata, 67
Chi Yuen, 70
Churchill, Winston, 150, 159, 164, 167, 202, 210, 212, 313, 219, 222, 223, 224
Clarke, Sir George, 101, 154
Clayton, John M., 62
Clemenceau, 9
Cleveland, Grover, 61, 62
Clydebank, 68, 72, 103
Cobra, HMS, 179
Coerper, Carl, 128
Collingwood, HMS, 17, 18 22, 29, 87, 137
Colomb, John, 7, 8, 188
Colomb, Philip, 8, 188
Colorado, 246
Colossus, HMS, 14, 18, 162, 174
Committee for Imperial Defence, 101, 102, 151, 153, 203
Comus class, 4, 19
Condor, HMS, 7, 45, 147, 148
Condorcet, 203
Congress of Berlin, 3, 12
Connecticut, 83
Conqueror, HMS, 164
Constantinople, 3, 32, 41, 203, 218, 222
Constellation, 245
Constitution, 83
Conte Di Cavour, 202
Convoy, 4, 6, 7, 10, 23, 57, 217, 240, 241, 243
Cooper-Key, Sir Astley, 39, 40, 41
Cordite, 15
Coromandel, HMS, 39
Corradino Heights, 45, 147
Corvettes, 2
Courbet, 204
Cressy (class), 36, 219
Crimean War, 4, 12, 23, 39, 42, 216, 224
Crowe, Sir Eyre, 131, 132, 203
Cuba, 59, 60, 192
Cunard Line, 4, 88, 97, 98, 99
Cuniberti, Vittorio, 92
Curtis Turbines, 94, 194
Custance, Sir Reginald, 91, 98, 151, 157, 158, 159

Daily Mail, 128, 138, 157, 221
Daily Telegraph, 139, 140, 149, 208, 210
Daimyo, 65
Dandalo, 17
Dante Alighieri, 201, 204
Danton, 203
Dardanelles, 3, 5, 12, 32, 33, 39, 222, 223, 224, 227

Dartmouth, 48
De Bange, 15
Declaration (Treaty) of Paris, 4
Defence, HMS, 205, 231, 234
Defiance, HMS, 182, 183
Delagoa Bay, 110
Delaware, 161, 193, 194
De Lesseps, Ferdinand, 63
Démocratie, 203
Derfflinger, 177, 212, 220, 221, 229, 231, 232, 239
Deutschland, 97, 115, 116, 117, 120
Devastation, HMS, 95
Devonport, 165, 182
Dewar, Kenneth, 95
Dewey, George, 59, 60
Diadem class, 36
Diderot, 203
Disraeli, Benjamin, 3, 5
Dogger Bank, 76, 167, 220, 221, 238
Dolphin, 54
Dover, 148, 153, 159, 203, 217
Drake class, 36
Dreadnought (and dreadnoughts), xiii, xiv, xv, 38, 81, 86, 87–9, 91, 92–5, 96, 99, 101–4, 110, 116, 118, 120, 124, 136, 137, 147, 150, 160, 161, 170, 175, 185, 187, 189, 191, 193–6, 199, 203, 204, 206, 211–13, 215, 237, 243–5, 248
Dreadnoughtschweinerei, xiii, 185
Dreikaiserbund, 111, 112
Dresden, 179
Dreyer, Frederic, 171, 172, 173
Duilio, 17, 202
Duke of Edinburgh, 205
Dumaresq, John Saumarez, 85, 170, 172
Dumas, Philip, 142
Duncan class, 29
Dunkirk, 130
Dupuy De Lôme, 35, 180
Du Temple, 43

Eagle, HMS, 197
Earle shipbuilding yard, 22
East Indies, 80
Eclipse, HMS, 84
Eden, HMS, 179
Edgar class, 241
Edinburgh, HMS, 14, 18
Edison, 14
Edward VII, 1, 50, 101, 110, 128, 139, 144
Egerton, George, 153
Egypt, 100, 203, 205
Ekaterina II, 25
Elbing, 228, 235
Elgar, Francis, 22
Elgin Commission, 101
Elsass, 116
Elswick, 72, 79, 103, 195, 197
Emanuele Filiberto, 201

Emden, 179
Emperor of India, HMS, 166, 168
Ems River, 130
En echelon, 17, 18, 32, 41, 57, 58, 68, 70, 95, 122, 161–3, 174, 195
Engine Room Artificers (ERA's), 48, 49
England, 8, 10, 11, 55, 64, 65, 109, 110, 113–15, 132, 138, 139, 140, 141, 145, 203, 239
Entente Cordiale, 100, 129–31, 135, 136, 208, 218
Erin, HMS, 191
Ersatz (Replacement), 114, 116, 118, 121, 127, 141, 142, 145, 174, 175, 178
Erzherzog Franz Ferdinand, 198
Esher, Lord, 101, 132, 138, 151, 155
Esquimalt, 80
Europa, HMS, 184
Excellent, HMS, xiv, 39, 40, 41, 42, 44, 52

Fairfield, 87, 103
Falaba, 225
Faraday, Michael, 14
Fashoda, 52
Fatshan Creek, 39
Fawkes, Wilmot, 157, 158
Fearless, HMS, 178
Fisher, John Arbuthnot, Admiral of the Fleet, xiii, xiv, 6, 34, 38–50, 52, 79, 81–4, 86, 87, 89, 91, 92–6, 100–3, 110, 120–2, 125, 129, 135–8, 146–61, 166, 170, 172, 178, 179, 189, 194, 198, 202, 219, 222, 223, 224
Fisher-Selborne scheme, 47, 48
Florida, 61, 193
Flotten-proffessoren (Fleet professors), 113
Foochow, 69
Foreign Intelligence Committee, 6, 8, 157
Foreign Office, 74, 139, 141, 142, 143, 203, 218
Forge et Chantiers, Le Havre, 68
Formidable class, 28, 29
France, xiii, xv, 2, 6, 9, 10, 12, 15, 25, 26, 31, 33–5, 51, 53, 64, 68, 73, 74, 78, 79, 96, 100, 114, 116, 129–32, 135, 140, 143, 144, 158, 187, 199, 200, 202–4, 207, 208, 211, 213, 218, 227, 240, 245, 246, 248
France, 204
Franco-Prussian War, 17, 105, 122
Francis-Joseph, Emperor of Austria, 130
Frauenlob, 235
Freya, 178
Friedrich der Grosse, 144, 174, 176
Friedrich Karl, 115, 178
Frisian Islands, 130, 156, 217
Frithjof, 121
Fuji, 72
Fürst Bismarck, 115, 178
Fuso, 67, 70, 191

Galatea, HMS, 147, 228
Gallipoli, 222, 223
Gangut, 205
Gard, W.H., 87
Garvin, J.L., 149
Gefechtskehrtwendung, 231, 232
Geneva, 61
Germany, xv, 12, 17, 31, 51, 53, 60, 64, 68, 69, 72, 94, 96, 100, 103, 105, 106, 108, 111, 112, 113, 114, 116–18, 120, 127–32, 135, 140, 143–6, 152, 154, 155, 158, 167, 175, 179, 185, 199, 202, 205–12, 216, 218, 224, 225, 227, 235, 240, 243
Gervais, Admiral, 25, 26
Gibraltar, 11, 81, 116, 153, 193, 241
Giulio Cesare, 202
Gladstone, William, 5, 6, 7, 23, 26
Glasgow University, 22
Glitra, 224
Gneisenau, 121, 178, 219
Goeben, 125, 126, 165, 174, 177, 218, 219
Goltz, Colmar Von der, 108
Good Hope, HMS, 150, 219
Goodrich, Caspar F., 55
Gracie, Alexander, 87
Graf Spee, 178
Gramme, 14
Grand Fleet, 164, 216, 217, 219, 220, 221, 222, 227, 228, 230–3, 236, 239, 243–5
Grey, Sir Edward, 129, 140, 144, 145, 151, 204, 208, 210, 211
Grierson, Sir James, 129, 154
Grosser Kurfurst, 106, 107, 175, 176, 232
Guerre de course, 54, 55, 107, 239, 242
Gulf of Mexico, 59, 65
Gulf of Pecheli, 72, 74
Gunboats, 2
Guncotton, 15
Gun vessels, 2
Gymnote, 180

Hagen, 174
Hague Conference, 44, 45, 136, 137
Hakodate, 65
Haldane, Lord, 151, 209, 210
Halifax, 80
Hall, Sir Reginald, 6, 120
Hall, W.H., 6, 7, 9, 120
Hamburg-America, 97, 208
Hamilton, Lord George, 11, 22
Hankey, Maurice, 102
Hannover, 116
Harcourt, Sir William, 26
Harding, Edward, 84
Haruna, 191
Harvey armour, 27, 28, 36, 44
Hashidate, 68, 70
Hatsuse, 72, 76
Havana, 58, 59
Havock, HMS, 42

Hawaiian Islands, 60, 192
Hay, Lord John, 7
Hay, John, 63
Hay-Pauncefote Treaty, 63
Heath, Herbert, 142, 143
Heeringen, August Von, 122
Heimdall, 174
Heireddin Barbarossa, 206
Helgoland, 119, 121, 146, 212
Heligoland, 113, 155, 156, 217, 218, 222
Herbert, Mr, 55
Hercules, HMS, 41, 162
Hertha class, 115
Hertz, Albert, 40
Hessen, 116
He-yei, 67, 70
Hicks-Beech, Sir Michael, 50
Hiei, 70, 191
Highflyer, HMS, 39
High Seas Fleet, 206, 215, 218, 220, 228, 230, 231, 233, 234, 243
Hildebrand, 174
Hindenburg, 177
Hindustan, HMS, 47
Hipper, Franz Von, 221, 229, 230, 232, 236, 237, 238
Hiuga, 191
Hogue, 219
Hohenzollern, 112, 215
Holland, 130
Holland boats, 50, 181
Hollman, Friedrich, 108, 115
Holstein, Baron Friedrich von, 100, 129
Holt, Alfred, 4
Home Fleet, 80, 147, 150, 151, 152
Hong Kong, 59, 66, 153
Hood, Sir Arthur, 7, 33
Hood, HMS, 19, 33, 243, 245
Hope dry-dock, 66
Hornet, HMS, 42
Howaldt, 69
Howe, HMS, 18

Iata, 58
Ibuki, 94, 189, 190, 191
Idaho, 194, 206
Iéna, 204
Ikoma, 94, 189, 191
Illinois, 59
Illustrious, HMS, 28
Imperatritsa Ekaterina Velikaya, 205
Imperatritsa Mariya, 205
Imperieuse, HMS, 22
Implacable, HMS, 158
Inconstant, HMS, 19
Indefatigable, HMS, 162, 164, 204, 205, 229, 231, 234
Indiana, 58, 59, 245
Indomitable, HMS, 96, 97, 103, 121, 205

Indo-China (Viet-Nam), 71
Inflexible, HMS, 14, 17, 18, 41, 57, 95, 96, 97, 103, 121, 205, 219, 231
Ingles, John, 68
International Mercantile Marine (IMM), 98
Invincible, HMS, 88, 92, 94, 95, 96, 97, 99, 100, 103, 121, 122, 124, 125, 136, 137, 162, 165, 185, 189, 204, 205, 207, 212, 219, 231, 234, 235
Iowa, 59
Iron Duke, HMS, 124, 166, 167, 168, 175, 191, 194, 197, 204
Iris, HMS, 14, 19
Ironclad, 15, 17, 19, 39, 51, 105
Ise, 191
Ismay, Thomas, 4
Italia, 18, 26
Italy, xiii, xv, 9, 12, 13, 26, 31, 32, 105, 111, 127, 130, 183, 187, 197 198, 201, 202, 203, 204, 245, 246
Ito, Yoko, 70, 71
Itsukushima, 68
Iwate, 73
Izumo, 73

Jackson, Sir Henry, 171, 182, 183, 184, 224
Jamaica, 80
Jameson Raid, 109, 110
Jane's Fighting Ships, 92, 94, 95, 120, 121
Japan, xiii, xv, 28, 51, 53, 65–9, 71–7, 83, 87, 93, 94, 100, 102, 103, 127, 131, 132, 140, 167, 187, 188, 189, 191–4, 205, 245, 246
Jean Bart, 204
Jeanne d'Arc, 36
Jellicoe, John, 92, 164, 217, 218, 220, 228, 229, 230, 231, 233–40, 244
Jeune École, 7, 9, 23, 25, 26, 35, 68, 107, 108, 180
Juno, HMS, 184
Justice, 203
Jutland, xv, 177, 221, 227, 229, 230, 232, 234–40, 245, 247

Kaga, 245
Kagoshima, 66, 67
Kaiser, 106, 115, 174, 175, 176, 177, 212
Kaiserin, 174, 176
Kaiserin Augusta, 115
Kaiser Friedrich III, 175
Kaiserliche Marine, 105
Kaiser Wilhelm, xiii, 105, 108, 109, 110–13, 115, 116, 118, 122, 128, 129, 130, 137–41, 143, 149, 185, 196, 208, 209, 210, 211, 218, 221, 239, 240
Kaiser Wilhelm II, 97, 175
Kaiser Wilhelm de Grosse, 97
Kashima, 72, 74
Katori, 72, 74
Kawachi, 189, 191

Kawasaki, 191
Kearsage, 59
Kellet, Sir Henry, 40
Kentucky, 59
Kerr, Lord Walter, 46, 49, 157, 158
Keyham, 47
Kiel (harbour and canal), 107, 117, 120, 121, 128, 142
Kilkis, 206
King Edward, 88
King Edward class, 72, 81
King George V, HMS, 166, 175, 191, 247
King Yuen, 69, 70
Kirishima, 191
Klondyke, 62
Koln, 218
Kongo, 67, 189, 191
König, 167, 175, 176, 177, 232
König Albert, 174, 176
König Wilhelm, 106, 115
Königsberg, 179
Korea, 69, 71, 73
Korietz, 75
Kowshing, 69
Kronprinz, 175, 176
Kronprinz Wilhelm, 97
Kronsprinzessin Cecilie, 97
Kruger, Paul, 109, 110
Krupp (Essen and building yard), 121, 142, 143, 146, 177
Krupp cemented armour, 29, 36, 44, 83
Krupp guns, 68
Kurama, 94, 189, 190, 191
Kurfurst Friedrich Wilhelm, 108, 175, 206
Kure, 74, 93, 189
Kwang Yi (Kuang Yi), 69

Laird shipyard, 61
LaiYuan, 69, 70
Landore steelworks, 14
Lansdowne, Lord, 100, 129
Laubeuf, Maxime, 51
Laughton, John Knox, 8, 9, 188
Leander class, 21
Leonardo da Vinci, 202
Lepanto, 18, 26
Leyland Line, 98
Liaotung Peninsular, 71, 76, 187
Libertad, 83
Liberté, 203, 204
Lightfoot class, 180
Limnos, 206
Lion, HMS, 164, 165, 166, 167, 191, 212, 229, 234, 236, 237
Lloyd-George, David, 147, 150, 207
Lloyd Register of Shipping, 13, 22
London, 1, 10, 12, 98, 112, 196, 211
London class, 28
Long, Samuel, 35, 36, 38, 93, 94, 100

Lord Nelson, HMS, 83, 89, 91, 136, 189, 203
Lorraine, 204
Lothringen, 116
Louisiana, 83
Lowry, L.S., 46
Luce, Stephen B., 55
Lusitania, 99, 225, 226
Lützow, 125, 177, 229, 231, 232, 235, 239

Maciver, Charles, 4
Mackay, Ruddock, 81
Mackensen, 178
Maddelena Island, 12
Magdeburg, 220
Mahan, Alfred Thayer, 54, 55, 57, 65, 91, 109, 113, 131, 188, 192, 244
Maiji dynasty, 66
Maine, 58, 59
Mainz, 218
Majestic class, 27, 28, 32, 44
Makarov, Stepan, 75
Malta, 32, 45, 81, 147, 153, 171, 203, 204
Malaya, HMS, 167, 169, 170
Managua, 63
Manchester Guardian (Newspaper), 147
Manchuria, 75, 187
Manila, 77
Manila Bay, 59, 192
Marconi, Guglielmo, 183, 184
Marder, Arthur, xiv, 1, 2, 81, 132, 237
Marine Français, 36, 203
Marinekabinnette, 108
Marine-Rundschau (journal), 113
Markgraf, 175, 176, 232
Marlborough, HMS, 166, 168
Maryland, 246
Massachusetts, 58
Matsushima, 68, 70
Mauretania, 99, 100
May, H.J., 155
McKenna, Reginald, 139, 143, 144, 150–2, 159, 172, 202
Mediterranean, 2, 3, 10, 11, 12, 26, 31, 32, 41, 45, 46, 51, 65, 80–4, 109, 112, 115, 147–9, 150, 157–9, 187, 199, 200, 202, 203, 204, 205, 206, 227
Mehemet Ali, 12
Mercury, HMS, 14, 19
Mersey class, 21
Miantonomoh class, 53
Miantonomoh, 54
Michigan, 92, 193
Mikasa, 72
Milne, Sir Alexander, 3
Minas Gerais, 195, 196
Minotaur class, 96
Mirabeau, 203
Mississippi, 194, 206
Mogador, 129

INDEX

Moltke, 125, 126, 165, 174, 177, 220, 229, 232
Moltke, Helmuth, 105, 211
Monadnock, 54
Monarch, 26, 164
Monmouth, 219
Monroe Doctrine, 61, 62
Montana, 83
Montecuccoli, Rudolf, 198, 199, 201
Monts, Alexander, 108
Moore, Archibald, 173
Moreno, 196
Morgan, J.P., 98, 99
Morning Post (Newspaper), 109
Morocco, xv, 100, 103, 129, 130, 135, 200, 207, 208, 218
Mumford, 43
Mutsu, 245, 246

Nagasaki, 66, 191
Nagato, 245, 246
Naniwa, 69
Napoli, 201
Nassau, 117, 118, 119, 120, 121, 122, 124, 137, 146, 189, 212
Natal, HMS, 172, 173
Nauticus (naval annual), 113
Naval Defence Act, xiv, 3, 6, 7, 10, 11, 14, 17, 21–3, 25, 26, 28, 31–4, 51, 52, 102, 114, 116, 117, 127, 180, 241
Naval Intelligence Division, 6, 10, 152, 156, 157, 160
Naval Staff, 152, 157, 158, 159, 160, 217, 223, 224
Naval War College, 55
Navarino, 12
Navy laws (1898 and 1900), 113, 114, 116, 117, 141
Nelson, 247
Nelson, Lord, 12
Neptune, HMS, 125, 161, 162, 163, 174
Nevada, 62
Nevada, 194
Newark, 54
New Granada (Columbia), 62
New Mexico, 62
New Mexico, 194
New York, 3, 192, 226, 235
New York, 194
New Zealand, 166, 205, 229
Nicaragua, 63
Nicholson, Sir William, 155, 156
Niclausse, 43
Nile, HMS, 19
Nitroglycerine, 15
Noble, Sir Andrew, 79
Noel, Gerard, 46
Northampton, HMS, 41
Northbrook, Lord, 6
Northbrook programme, 14, 18, 27
North Carolina, 83

North Dakota, 161, 193, 194
North German Lloyd, 97, 177
North Sea, 81, 103, 105, 107, 114, 115, 118, 131, 140, 148, 150, 152, 155, 166, 213, 215, 217, 218, 220, 221, 222, 223, 225, 235, 242
Novelle, (Modification to Navy Law), 126, 141, 142, 145, 210, 212
Nürnberg, 179

Oberkommando der Marine, 108
Observer (Newspaper), 149
Obturation, 15
Ocean, HMS, 40, 41
Oceanic, 98
Odin, 174
Oklahoma, 194
Oldenburg, 107, 115, 119, 121, 141, 144, 146
Ordnance Committee, 17
Oregon, 58, 59
Orion, HMS, 163, 164, 166, 173, 175, 247
Orkneys, 216
Orlando class, 14
Osborne, 47, 48, 104
Osliabia, 29
Ostfriesland, 119, 121, 233
Ottley, Charles, 154
Ottoman Empire, 12, 13, 197, 206

Pacific Ocean, 63
Pallada, 75
Pallas, HMS, 40, 41
Pall Mall Gazette, 5, 6, 52
Palmers (Shipyard), 162
Panama Canal, 59, 63
Panther, 207
Paris, 63, 132
Paris, 204
Parkes, Oscar, 18, 87, 121
Parsons steam turbines, 88, 121, 124, 125, 163, 174, 175, 177, 179, 194, 199, 202, 238
Particular Service Squadron, 2, 3, 5, 33, 41
Patrie, 203
Pauncefote, Sir Julian, later Lord, 45, 63
Pax Britannica, xiv, xvi
Pearl Harbor, 192
Peiho forts, 39
Pembroke, 14
Pennsylvania, 194
Peresviet, 29
Perry, Matthew Calbraith, 65, 66, 67
Petropavlovsk, 75, 205
Phaeton, HMS, 228
Philippines, 59, 60
Phung-Do, 69
Pinafore, HMS, 2
Ping Yuen, 70
Plunger, 181
Plymouth, 153
Pobieda, 29
Pollen, Arthur, 170, 171, 172, 173, 174

Poltava, 205
Pommern, 116, 235
Port Arthur, 71, 72, 73, 75, 77, 187
Portsmouth, 49, 50, 79, 87, 89, 103, 130, 136, 153, 155, 163, 234
Posen, 118, 120
Powerful, 34, 35, 36, 43, 44, 52
Pre-dreadnought, xiv, 13, 17, 19, 18, 29, 32, 33, 44, 51, 63, 83, 117, 118, 120, 124, 163, 167, 201, 206, 212, 213, 215, 222, 224, 231
Preussen, 106, 116
Prince Eitel Friedrich, 178
Princess Royal, HMS, 164, 165, 166, 219, 229
Prinz Adalbert, 115
Prinz Eugen, 198
Prinz Heinrich, 115
Prinzregent Luitpold, 174, 176
Prismatic brown powder (PBC), 15
Provence, 204
Prussia, 12
Puritan, 53
Puerto Rica, 60

Queen Elizabeth, HMS, 167, 169, 170, 175, 177, 191, 194, 210, 228
Queen Mary, HMS, 165, 166, 205, 229, 230, 231, 234, 235

Radetzky, 198
Ramilles, HMS, 169
Red Star Line, 98
Regina Elena, 201
Regina Margherita, 201
Reichmarineamt (RMA), 108, 113, 115, 143, 177
Reichstag, 108, 114, 116, 125, 142, 146, 212
Renown, HMS, 44, 45, 75, 82, 245
Repington, Charles, 154
République class and ship, 81, 203
Repulse, HMS, 245
Reshadieh, 191, 206
Resolution, HMS, 169
Retvisan, 75
Revenge, HMS, 169
Re Umberto, 201
Riachuelo, 57, 58, 59
Rio de Janeiro, 196, 206
Rivadavia, 196
Rheinland, 118, 119
Richards, Sir Frederick, 26, 32
Richardson, Charles, 66
Rifled large grain powder (RLG), 15
Risikogedanken (Risk theory), 114, 117, 213
River class, 179
Roberts, John, 95
Rodjestvenski, Zinovi, 76
Rodney, HMS, 18, 247
Roma, 201
Roosevelt, Theodore, 192, 193, 243
Rosebery, Lord, 26

Rossiya, 34, 43
Rostock, 235
Rosyth, 217, 220, 227
Royal Corps of Naval Constructors, 22, 23
Royal Naval College Greenwich, 8, 21
Royal Naval College Portsmouth, 8
Royal Naval Engineering College, 47
Royal Navy, xv, 2, 5, 8, 12, 15, 23, 27, 33, 57, 81, 83, 84, 118, 128, 130, 160, 166, 174, 178, 179, 181, 184, 191, 196, 197, 202, 206, 215, 217, 218, 248
Royal Oak, HMS, 168
Royal Sovereign, HMS, 42, 191
Royal Sovereign class, 11, 19, 27, 29, 32, 33, 169
Royal United Service Institution (RUSI), 8, 43, 47
St Lucia, 80
St Vincent, 137, 161, 212
Rurik, 24, 43
Russia, xiii, xv, 2, 6, 10, 12, 25, 26, 31–4, 51, 53, 62, 65, 71–4, 78, 83, 87, 96, 100, 103, 111, 112, 117, 127, 130, 140, 143, 158, 187, 200, 205, 207, 211, 213, 216
Russian Siberia, 66
Russo-Japanese War, 75, 86, 94

Sachen class, 115
Sachen, 118, 175
Salamis, 206
Salisbury, Lord, 3, 7, 10, 11, 13, 23, 32, 61, 63, 72, 73, 127, 147
Samoa, 60, 106
Sampson, William T., 55
Samuda, 57
Samurai, 66
San Francisco, 58, 59, 192, 193
San Francisco, 54
San Juan de Nicaragua, 62
Sans Pareil, HMS, 14, 18
San Stephano, 3
Sao Paulo, 195, 196
Sardegna class, 32
Sardegna, 201
Sassebo, 74
Satsuma, 93, 94, 189, 190, 191
Scapa Flow, 216, 217, 227, 243
Scharnhorst, 121, 178, 219
Scheer, Reinhard, 227, 228, 230, 231, 232, 233, 235, 237, 238–40
Schichau, 142, 144, 146, 174, 177
Schlesien, 116
Schleswig-Holstein, 116,
Schleswig-Holstein, 154, 155
Schneider of Creusot, 17, 35
Schnelladenkanonen (Quick-firing), 116, 118
Schulz-Thorneycroft, 124, 175, 177, 238
Scott, Sir Percy, 45, 85, 149, 150
Scotts (Shipyard), 162
Scribner's Magazine, 64
Sea of Marmora, 3, 32

INDEX

Selborne, Lord, 46, 50, 52, 73, 79, 80, 81, 83, 127, 128, 135, 152, 157, 158, 159
Settsu, 189, 191
Sevastopol, 205
Seydlitz, 126, 167, 177, 220, 221, 229, 232, 239
Shenandoah, 61
Shikishima, 72
Shimoda, 65
Shimonoseki, Treaty of, 71
Shoeburyness, 28
Shogun, 66
Sicilia, 201
Siegfried class, 107, 116, 145
Siegfried, 121, 141, 174
Siemens-Martin Steel, 13, 14, 18
Siemens-Schuckert, 177
Sims, William, 91
Singapore, 66, 68
Sino-Japanese War, 68, 71, 74
Skoda works, 198
Slade, Edward, 130, 154, 155
Sloops, 2
Slow burning cocoa powder (SBC), 15
Soley, Russell, 64
South Africa, 101, 135, 159
South Carolina, 92, 193
Southampton, HMS, 230
Spain, 60, 63, 129, 187, 192, 203, 206, 207
Spanish-American War, 58, 59, 188, 206
Spencer, Lord and programme, 26, 27, 51, 52
Stabilimento Tecnico Triestino (STT), 198
Standard (newspaper), 10
Stead, W.T., 7
Stettin, 179
Stoch, Von, 105, 106, 107
Stuart-Wortley, Edward J.M., 139
Stuggart, 179
Sublime Porte, 12, 32
Sudan, 52, 100, 129
Suez Canal, 12, 28, 29, 32, 63
Sultan Osman I, 196, 206
Superb, HMS, 92, 137
Superdreadnought, 161, 163, 166–9, 173, 174, 197, 204, 213, 215
Sussex, 227
Swan, 14
Swift, HMS, 179
Swiftsure, HMS, 83
Szent Istvan, 198, 199

Taku, 69
Talien Bay (Darien), 70
Tangiers, 129, 148
Tche Yuen (Chi Yuen), 69
Tegetthoff, 198
Temeraire, HMS, 92, 137
Tennessee, 83
Terrible, HMS, 34, 35, 43, 44, 52
Terrible (French), 18
Terror, 54

Texas, 58, 194
Thames, 113, 164
Thames Ironworks, 72, 164
Thunderer, HMS, 164
Thüringen, 119, 121
Tiger, HMS, 167, 168, 191, 229
Ting, Ju-ch'ang, 70, 71
Ting Yuen, 68, 70, 71, 106
Times, The (newspaper), 32, 110, 138, 139, 149, 154
Tirpitz, Alfred, 105, 107, 108, 109, 110, 113, 114, 115, 117, 118, 120, 121, 132, 140–3, 177, 198, 209, 211–3
Togo, Heihachiro, 69, 75, 77
Tokiwa, 73
Tokyo, 67, 74
Torgud Reis, 206
Tosa, 245
Toulon, 9, 10, 12, 31, 32, 46, 200
Tracy, Benjamin, 54
Trafalgar, HMS, 19
Treaty of Paris, 12, 23
Trenton, 54
Tressider, Captain, 27, 28
Tribal class, 179
Trieste, 197, 200
Triplice (Triple Alliance), 12, 31, 111, 112, 127, 197, 199, 200, 202, 203, 204, 208
Triple entente, 207, 298
Triumph, HMS, 83
Tryon, Sir George, 10
Tsarevitch, 75, 76
Tsingtau, 72
Tsi Yuen, 70
Tsukuba, 94, 189, 191
Tsushima, 76, 77, 91, 93, 100, 187, 189
Tunis, 12
Turkey, 13, 187, 191, 196, 203, 206, 218
Tweedmouth, Lord, 136, 137, 138, 139, 144, 148, 208, 223
Two-power standard, 2, 53, 136, 210, 211

Undaunted, HMS, 147
Unebi, 68
United Kingdom, 8
United States, xii, xiii, xv, xvi, 2, 15, 51, 53, 55, 58, 60–5, 78, 83, 102, 117, 127, 167, 181, 188, 192, 193, 196, 211, 225, 226, 241–3, 245, 246
United States Navy, 48, 65, 91, 184, 188, 194
Untakeable, HMS, 86
Utah, 193

Valiant, HMS, 167, 169
Valorous, HMS, 41
Vanguard, HMS, 137, 161
Vanity Fair (Periodical), 128
Variag, 75
Vasilefs Konstantinos, 206
Velox, HMS, 179

Venezuela, 61, 62
Vengeance, HMS, 28, 84, 172
Vergniaud, 203
Verité, 204
Vernon, HMS, 40, 182, 184
Versailles Treaty, 197
Vickers, 28, 50, 72, 85, 161, 165, 170, 172, 181, 189, 191, 195, 206
Victoria Cross, 127
Victoria, HMS, 14, 18
Victoria and Albert, 216
Victoria Louise, 178
Victoria, Queen, 5, 51, 110, 127
Victorian, 88, 89
Vienna, 112, 211
Viper, HMS, 179
Virginian, 88, 89
Viribus Unitis, 198, 199, 204
Vitgeft V.K., 76
Vitorio Emanuele class, 83, 201
Vladivostok, 71, 75, 76, 77
Volage, HMS, 19
Voltaire, 203
Volya, 205
Von der Tann, 121–5, 127, 212, 220, 229, 232
Vulkan, 68, 69, 142, 144, 206

Wake Island, 60, 192
Warrior, HMS, 39, 41, 205, 231, 234
War Office, 17, 101, 146, 153, 154, 203
Warspite, HMS, 22, 167, 169, 170
Washington, xvi, 54, 61, 62, 63, 132, 226, 239, 240, 247, 248
Washington, 83, 246
Waterloo, 53
Wei-hai-wei, 69, 71, 74
Wein, 26
Weisbaden, 235
Weissenburg, 108, 175, 206
Weltpolitik, 105, 113
Weser, 142
Westfalen, 118, 119, 231
West Indies, 40, 59, 61, 65, 82

West Virginia, 246
White, Arnold, 79
White Star Line, 4
White, Sir William, 19, 22, 26, 28, 91
Whitehead, Robert, 50
Whitehead torpedoes, 40
White Star Line, 98, 226
Widenmann, Wilhelm, 143, 144
Wilhelm, See Kaiser Wilhelm
Wilhelmshaven, 127, 128
Willan, L.P., 68
Wilson, Sir Arthur, 148, 149, 151, 156, 159, 160, 171–3, 202, 203, 222
Wisconsin, 59
Witkowitz, 198
Wittlesbach, 115, 128
Wolff-Metternich, Paul Z. Gracht, 140, 144, 208, 209
Woolwich Arsenal, 16, 17, 28
Workman, Clark and Co., 88
World War I, xiii, xiv, xv, 1, 6, 23, 45, 91, 99, 120, 125, 153, 156, 163, 187, 197, 199, 206, 218, 224, 242, 243, 244, 246, 248
Wörth, 108, 175
Württemburg, 118, 175
Wyoming, 193

Yakumo, 73
Yalu naval battle and river, 28, 70
Yamamoto, Gombei, 72
Yamashiro, 191
Yarrow, 42, 124
Yashima, 72, 76
Yellow Sea, 75
Yokohama, 66, 192, 193
Yokosuka, 74, 93, 191
Yorck, 178
Yoshino, 69

Zédé, Gustave, 180
Zeiss, 175
Zoelly Turbines, 177
Zrinyi, 198